DEVELOPING
TEXTBOOK
THINKING
Strategies for Success in College

FOURTH EDITION

Sherrie L. Nist
University of Georgia, Athens

William Diehl
The Corporation for Business, Work, and Learning

As part of Houghton Mifflin's ongoing commitment to the environment, this text has been printed on recycled paper.

Houghton Mifflin Company
Boston   New York

Senior Sponsoring Editor: Mary Jo Southern
Senior Associate Editor: Ellen Darion
Assistant Editor: Jennifer Roderick
Associate Project Editors: Gabrielle Stone/Rachel D'Angelo Wimberly
Senior Production/Design Coordinator: Sarah Ambrose
Manufacturing Manager: Florence Cadran

Cover Design: Diana Coe

Cover Image: © Stock Illustration Source

Printed in the United States of America.

Library of Congress Catalog Card Number: 97-72524

International Standard Book Number: 0-395-86838-6

123456789-DH   01   00   99   98   97

Preface

In this fourth edition of *Developing Textbook Thinking (DTT),* intended for college reading courses, we have maintained our basic philosophy that to be successful in college, students need a variety of learning and study strategies. Students can modify these strategies as a way of "owning" them. As with the first three editions, we assume that students who use this text have learned to read; *DTT* will teach them how to read to learn. To achieve this goal, *DTT* takes students through a progression of strategies, each building on another. The underlying premise of *DTT* is that what students do before and after reading is as important as the reading itself. Not only does the overall study system presented here encompass this three-pronged philosophy, but most of the strategies progress in stages that build upon one another. Another important aspect of the strategies presented in the fourth edition is the strong emphasis placed on modification, reflection, rehearsal, and monitoring. Every strategy is formatted to enable students to test themselves on important information, thus improving metacognitive abilities.

Although the basic philosophy has remained intact, there have been some changes to the content of the text. These changes were prompted by feedback received from several different sources. First, students who used the previous editions of *DTT* provided valuable comments about the strategies they found most helpful. Second, the reviewers—instructors who work with students across the country in a variety of college settings—suggested changes to meet the needs of diversified populations. Third, current learning theory and research on study strategies enabled us to make the ideas in this text the most current in the college reading market. The text is based on solid research and theory, transformed into a practical and systematic learning system.

Finally, those of you who have used previous editions of this text will quickly discover that the biggest change is in the chapter selections in the appendix. We have attempted to provide text selections that focus on more interesting and relevant topics, while still providing students practice applying strategies to a variety of disciplines.

Part I, "Understanding College Reading and Study Demands," has one major change. The chapter on notetaking, which used to be in Part III, has been moved to Part I. A majority of both students and instructors who use the text thought notetaking was a skill that students needed right from the beginning. We agreed; the earlier students could be taught how to take organized notes and study from them, the better off they would be. Another major change in Part I is the addition of a section called "A Scenario to Write About and Discuss," which is now in each chapter of Part I. Each scenario depicts a student who has some sort of studying problem. Students are asked to apply strategies and ideas that they learned in that chapter (and in previous chapters) to help the student in the scenario "solve" his or her problem. We believe these types of application exercises will help students solve problems that they themselves will most likely encounter at some point in their college career. Finally, in Part I we have included some new readings that students may find more interesting and current.

In Part II, "Developing the BCA's of College Reading and Study Strategies," we have maintained the **BCA**'s as the moniker for the study system we use in the fourth edition. We introduce this idea in Part I, and it is followed through in the second part of *DTT*. We have modified the application exercises to go along with the new text chapters in the appendix. In addition, those of you who have used previous editions of *DTT* will notice that we have incorporated what used to be Part III, "Expanding College Reading and Study Strategies," into other parts of the book. The chapter on notetaking is now in Part I (Chapter 5), and "Pulling Everything Together: Preparing for Examinations" is now the last chapter in Part II (Chapter 12).

As mentioned earlier, however, the biggest difference between the third and fourth editions is the selections in the appendix. We have kept the "Psychology of Memory" selection because students and instructors see connections between the content of this selection and the strategies presented in *DTT*. But all of the other selections are new. We have tried to select text pieces that are interesting and reflect content that is being emphasized on college campuses nationwide, particularly focusing on diversity and multiculturalism and the continuing growth of computer applications. In addition, although users of previous editions liked the 1960s as a topic, many felt that the earlier selection on this topic was not reader friendly. Thus we replaced "The Stormy Sixties" with a much more reader friendly selection entitled "Great Promises, Bitter Disappointments, 1960–1968," which covers similar topics. Two science excerpts focus on genetics and weather forecasting, so students can be exposed to both the natural and physical sciences. As in the last edition, vocabulary and application exercises follow each appendix selection. We believe that the fourth edition of *DTT* strikes a good balance between new and old information. Although it contains primarily all new appendix chapters, the philosophy and strategies presented should still feel familiar to those of you who have used the previous editions. We think that such revisions keep *DTT* on the cutting edge of synthesizing current research findings and applying them in practical settings.

Acknowledgments

Numerous individuals deserve a grateful thank you for assisting with the revisions for the fourth edition of *Developing Textbook Thinking*. As with the first three editions, we continue to draw some of our most constructive criticism from our students. Just when we think we have honed a particular strategy or selected an outstanding reading, students make suggestions that we hadn't even thought about! In addition, they are the ones who keep us on our toes and keep us in touch with what it takes to be successful in college. Students tell us more quickly and honestly than anyone else which strategies and ideas are useful and which ones are not. We are also especially grateful to our colleagues at the University of Georgia and around the country who use the text and provide honest feedback about how their students respond to *DTT* and how they modify their use of the text depending on their particular situation.

For their helpful reviews of the third edition, we would like to thank Mary Lee Bass, Monmouth University (NJ); Donna Clack, Schoolcraft College (MI); Rosann Cook, Purdue University, Calumet; Ronnie Love, Kent State University; Mitye Jo Richey, Community College of Allegheny (PA); and Mary Thompson, North Hennepin Community College (MN).

We would like to acknowledge Mary Jo Southern, Jennifer Roderick, and Gabrielle Stone for their work on this edition and for helping us make the transition from D. C. Heath to Houghton Mifflin.

Last, but certainly not least, we owe special thanks to our respective families for their continued love, support, and encouragement. So to Steve, Kama (who lives in California now!), and Mollie Doone (my lapdog writing companion) and to Jeanne and David and Amy (both of whom are now university students), we appreciate all you do.

S. L. N.
W. D.

Contents

Chapter 5   Taking Notes from Lectures   72

Chapter 6   Vocabulary Development   82

Chapter 7   Flexibility and Efficiency in Studying 115

Chapter 10   After You Read: Studying   194

Chapter 11   After You Study: Reviewing   219

Chapter 12   Pulling Everything Together: Preparing for Examinations   243

Appendix: Selections from a Variety of Texts   271

Index   423

To the Student

High school students often think that the most difficult thing about college is getting in. We feel, on the contrary, that the most difficult aspect of college is staying in. Many of you probably know fellow students who were accepted into college but for a variety of reasons were unable to continue. Some students are unsuccessful in college because they do not possess the study strategies needed to make good grades, others because they lack motivation. Students who know a variety of study strategies and are self-motivated are much more likely to be successful. In fact, research bears this out; those who use proper study strategies tend to outperform those who use incorrect or inadequate strategies. Also, highly motivated students outperform those with low motivation across all ability levels.

The purpose of the fourth edition of *Developing Textbook Thinking (DTT)* is to expose you to strategies that, if properly applied, will increase your understanding of course material and subsequently your performance on exams. *DTT* not only outlines a complete study method but also gives you practice in applying this method to complete text chapters from a variety of disciplines. By using complete chapters, you can learn to think like a biologist or a historian. Thus this book can supply the strategies and techniques, and your instructor can supply the guidance for improving your study skills. However, you must provide the motivation to learn, apply, and modify these strategies.

As you proceed through this book, you will find that studying and learning are hard work. Few people can read something once, do nothing else with the information, and score high on classroom examinations. Learning and remembering take determination and hard work, but if you use the strategies in this text, you will be able to study more efficiently and effectively. This book presents a variety of methods so that you can try each of them, discover which ones work best for you, and make them part of your regular reading and studying habits.

Developing Textbook Thinking, Fourth Edition, is divided into two parts. Part I, "Understanding College Reading and Studying Demands," presents three diagnostic tests to make you more aware of your strengths and weaknesses in the areas of reading and studying; suggests ways you can develop and maintain motivation; introduces basic time-management strategies; gives you some hints for getting started; presents how to take lecture notes; discusses how to improve your vocabulary; explores how texts from the humanities, social sciences, and physical sciences differ; and presents techniques for developing reading-rate flexibility.

Part II, "Developing the **BCA**'s of College Reading and Studying Strategies," focuses on an approach called the **BCA**'s of studying—what you do **Be**fore you read, staying **C**onnected during reading, what you do **A**fter you read, and what you do **A**fter you study. You can become an efficient and effective learner using this method because you are engaged in learning and monitoring activities before, during, and after reading. We believe that this type of active interaction is necessary in order for maximum learning to occur. We have introduced the **PLAE** (**P**replan, **L**ist, **A**ctivate, and **E**valuate) procedure to help you become more goal directed in your test preparation. Finally, this portion of *DTT* gives you helpful hints for preparing for both objective and essay exams.

Application Exercises follow each chapter and sample reading in *DTT*. There are two types of Application Exercises: exercises that focus on the strategies and content from *DTT* and exercises that can be applied to your own textbooks. Both types of exercises will give you practice with the techniques presented. You will also be able to apply the strategies discussed in this text to the sample chapters in the appendix. In addition, most chapters contain at least one scenario, concerning a college student, that you can think and write about at length.

As in previous editions, the changes that we have made in this fourth edition are a direct result of what we have heard from our own students and from college reading instructors from all over the United States. We initially discovered the need for such a text through working with our students, and over time we have revised it to add information that they have found useful. This edition contains changes made in response to both praise and criticism of the previous editions, and in light of recent research in the area of college reading and self-regulated learning. We believe all of these considerations make this an even better book. We are particularly proud of the breadth of the new chapters included in the appendix; students provided considerable input concerning the interest level of these selections. We feel that they will give you a flavor for many of the courses that colleges and universities require. We cover issues such as multiculturalism and computer use, which are widespread on virtually all campuses.

We encourage you to keep an open mind as you work through *Developing Textbook Thinking,* Fourth Edition. Try out the new strategies and see which ones work best for you. Discover which techniques make you a more efficient and effective learner. Discuss your studying problems and the scenarios with your instructor and your classmates. Through your reading journal, keep track of your reading and studying progress. Remember, the strategies you learn from this text will help you not only today but also as you progress through your entire college program and beyond. We want to help every student become a life-long learner.

S. L. N.
W. D.

Understanding College Reading and Studying Demands

I will prepare and someday my chance will come.

Abraham Lincoln

*C*ollege study demands differ considerably from those of high school. High school often stresses memorizing facts and details, and testing occurs more frequently and covers smaller amounts of course material. College stresses higher-level and critical-thinking skills. Testing occurs less frequently (perhaps only two or three times a term), and students must learn and remember large amounts of new information. Therefore, college students who continue to use the same reading and studying strategies that they used in high school may learn inefficiently and ineffectively.

Many of you may not have any idea of what your reading and studying habits are. Because self-awareness is the key to improvement, whether in reading or anything else, the first step in developing effective strategies for college learning is to become aware of your own strengths and weaknesses. The three assessment tools in Chapter 1 can give you valuable information and help you to assess your knowledge of what college studying entails. The first chapter also discusses the reading journal, another tool for evaluating your awareness of what happens as you read as well as your level of comprehension. Remember, only self-evaluation, followed by motivation, will help you to develop reading and studying strategies that will contribute significantly to your success at the college level.

Chapter 2 will give you a jump start in becoming a more efficient and effective learner. This chapter not only provides valuable suggestions that should become an important part of studying for every class but also gives you an overview of the principles that guide effective studying. In addition, this chapter introduces you to the **BCA**'s of studying—what you do **B**efore reading;

how you stay **C**onnected during reading; and what you do **A**fter reading and studying. These ideas will be discussed in greater detail later in the text.

Chapter 3 addresses the issue of motivation in detail. Perhaps more than any other factor, motivation can determine how successful you will be in college. This chapter focuses on reasons why students may not be motivated and provides some suggestions for improving motivation. As you read Chapter 3, keep in mind that a high degree of motivation makes up for academic weaknesses; the opposite, however, is usually not true. All of us have known people who were very smart, but not motivated. Students who fall into this category tend to drive teachers crazy!

Time management, another crucial aspect of being a successful student, is discussed in Chapter 4. Students are busy people and as such need a certain degree of structure to their daily lives, whether they want it or not. Those who plan a term schedule, in addition to more task-specific weekly schedules and daily "To Do" lists, tend to accomplish more in shorter periods of time. Such students have more, rather than less, time for fun activities. In Chapter 4, you will learn how to budget your time more effectively so that you have enough time each day to accomplish all your goals.

Chapter 5 presents efficient and effective ways to take lecture notes based on the **BCA** model for studying. Since many students who use this book are taking other courses, including classes with lectures, we include this note-taking chapter in the first section. In this chapter, we present ideas and strategies to help you to get the most out of lectures. Just as in reading, there are tasks you must do **b**efore the lecture, during the lecture (so you stay **c**onnected), and **a**fter the lecture, if you are going to learn and remember the information effectively.

Chapter 6 focuses on vocabulary development. College students often are confronted with many new words in their texts and lectures, a challenge that professors expect students to handle primarily on their own. This chapter discusses three key methods you can use to unlock the meanings of new words as well as a variety of generative vocabulary strategies that can help you to remember them.

Finally, Chapter 7 provides strategies to help you to become more flexible and efficient in your studying. It presents ideas for assessing your own background knowledge and the learning tasks posed by your courses and textbooks, along with suggestions for adjusting your study strategies and reading rates. Lastly, the chapter provides methods for increasing your reading efficiency.

By the time you complete Part I of *Developing Textbook Thinking,* you should have a good idea of what kind of reader you are and what you need to do to become a more efficient and effective student. Right from the start, develop the motivation to want to develop your skills. This text can provide the awareness of what you need to do, and the techniques for doing it; *you* must provide the motivation.

Chapter 1

What You Have to Do

Measure your mind's height by the shade it casts!

Elizabeth Barrett Browning

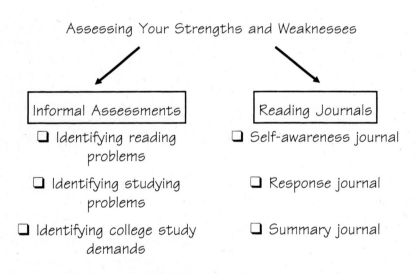

Assessing Your Strengths and Weaknesses

Informal Assessments
- ❏ Identifying reading problems
- ❏ Identifying studying problems
- ❏ Identifying college study demands

Reading Journals
- ❏ Self-awareness journal
- ❏ Response journal
- ❏ Summary journal

This text is designed to help you to evaluate your reading, critical-thinking, and learning abilities and expand those abilities, build upon them, and use them to learn how to study and to think effectively in college-level courses. By using the strategies outlined here, you can better draw from your own prior knowledge and experiences to make learning easier. You will also learn how to monitor your learning progress to make test preparation and studying more effective. *Developing Textbook Thinking* exposes you to principles, techniques, and exercises that show you how to use your abilities to meet a variety of college study demands.

But merely reading this text will not be enough. You must practice applying the techniques again and again and learn to reflect upon your learning, because, in most cases, the reading and studying demands in college are very different from those in high school. Not only is there more material to read and study in college, but expectations about what you should gain from your studying differ, as well. High school stresses facts; college courses stress concepts, theories, critical-thinking, and comprehension. You are responsible for taking a wide range of information, analyzing it, criticizing it, applying it to new situations, and then putting it into a meaningful form. In short, in college there is a close relationship between reading, studying, reflecting, and thinking. Thus reading and studying without reflecting and thinking, or reading, reflecting, and thinking without studying, will not help you to reach your full academic potential. However, the right combination of all four will contribute significantly to your academic success.

In order for you to absorb as much knowledge as possible in college, it is imperative that you become responsible for your own learning. College instructors are not responsible for your learning. Their function is to present the material in a clear, organized fashion, to stimulate original thought, and to guide you through new information. They expect you to know what to do with the course material; that is, you must listen attentively in class, read your assignments, think about and analyze what you read, and develop rehearsal and reviewing strategies to avoid cramming. The suggestions you will find in this text will help you to become an active self-regulated learner who is responsible for his or her actions and can monitor his or her personal learning. As you read and work through the application exercises in *Developing Textbook Thinking* and as you ask questions and make connections between information and ideas, you should realize quickly that reading to learn and learning how to learn are not easy tasks. They are hard work, especially if you want to learn for the sake of learning as well as for receiving good grades.

Assessing Your Strengths and Weaknesses

Before beginning a program that will help you to become a reflective, independent learner and critical thinker, it is important that you have a more structured idea of your reading and studying strengths and weaknesses. Although you may already realize some of your traits, this realization may be too generalized to enable you to target any specific problem areas. There are three main purposes in assessing where you are before you begin to learn the strategies in *Developing Textbook Thinking:* First, once you know your strengths, you can learn to capitalize on them. Capitalizing on strengths helps reduce weaknesses. Second, once you find your weak areas, you can learn strategies that are specifically targeted to improve them. Third, knowing both strengths and weaknesses enables you to adapt and modify strategies as a way of keeping your weaknesses in tow.

Standardized Assessments

One way to discover more about yourself as a reader and studier is through taking one of a variety of standardized tests. These tests provide information about where you stand in relation to other groups of students like yourself. In your precollege education you probably took numerous tests such as these in reading, English, and mathematics. The results of such tests were generally sent home to your parents, but rarely were results shared with you, the student, as a way of helping you to improve.

Drawing by Brian Savage © 1972 The New Yorker Magazine, Inc. All rights reserved.

In college, however, you are considered an adult, even though you may be under twenty-one years of age, so the results of standardized tests are shared with you rather than with your parents. Therefore, if your instructor gives you a standardized test, most likely he or she will talk with you about your test results as part of the assessment process.

If you are enrolled in a course to improve your reading, you probably will have to take at least one traditional standardized reading test. The test will probably consist of several rather brief passages, each followed by a series of multiple-choice questions. Sometimes these tests have separate vocabulary and rate sections; at other times, vocabulary and rate are part of the regular reading passages. The *Nelson-Denny,* the *Nelson,* and some reading tests that are required within individual states are structured in this way. We feel that such tests provide little information for either instructors or college students; providing a score fails to give information about students' strengths and weaknesses, the first step in assessment.

However, there are some study-strategy inventories (also standardized, because your answers on these inventories are compared with those of a normative group) that can give you much information if you answer them honestly. Honesty is the key, however. Although most reading courses do not give these inventories as placement devices because they are self-report instruments, they are often given as a self-diagnosis tool once students are enrolled in a reading or studying course. Our favorite of these standardized tests is the *Learning and Study Strategies Inventory,* or the LASSI (Weinstein and Palmer, 1987). The LASSI is available in both paper-and-pencil and computerized versions. However, if you do not have access to a standardized test, informal measures are often sufficient. Because the LASSI measures a variety of reading and studying characteristics, it can provide students with a good profile of themselves as learners.

Informal Assessments

Even if you have taken tests similar to one discussed earlier, the information you have learned about yourself is probably still insufficient. Therefore, we have included three informal assessments to help you to further pinpoint your strengths and weaknesses. The first one assesses your reading strengths and weaknesses. The second looks at what you know about studying. The third instrument has two parts. Part I examines your knowledge of the demands placed on college students, and Part II provides information about a specific situation that a college student might encounter and asks you to explain what you would do. Be honest when taking these assessment devices, and be reflective as you examine your results. Your reading and studying abilities can only begin to improve through self-awareness.

Answers or scoring procedures follow each assessment.

Assessment I: Locating Your Reading Problems

The American Heritage Dictionary defines *habit* as "a constant, often unconscious inclination to perform some act, acquired through its frequent repetition." Not all habits are bad, of course. Reading habits can be helpful or distracting. But even bad reading habits can be changed. What enables one person, but not another, to break or modify a bad habit? The answer has two parts: awareness and motivation. First, people must become aware of their bad habits. Second, they must make a conscious effort to change. Notice that although habits occur unconsciously, it takes a conscious effort to alter them.

Consider the following questions about your reading habits in terms of how frequently you engage in each. In order for this assessment to be of any value, you must answer each item honestly. The chapter in *Developing Textbook Thinking* that addresses each question is indicated in parentheses.

Directions: Respond to the questions below by indicating the frequency of each of the behaviors. *Rarely* indicates that you do not engage in this behavior very often; *occasionally* indicates that you engage in this behavior about half of the time; and *almost always* indicates that you engage in this behavior as a general rule.

	Rarely (1)	Occasionally (2)	Almost Always (3)
1. How often do you pick up a book, magazine, or newspaper and begin to read immediately, without considering your purpose? (Chapter 8)			X
2. How often does every statement seem equally important? (Chapter 9)			X
3. How often do you go back to reread a phrase or sentence you have already read? (Chapter 7)		X	
4. How often do you skip unfamiliar words in your reading? (Chapter 6)		X	
5. How often do you have difficulty defining the main idea in a passage? (Chapter 9)		X	
6. How often do you have difficulty remembering telephone numbers that you have just looked up? (Chapter 10)		X	
7. How often do you discover that you remember no details of a magazine article you read last week? (Chapter 10)		X	

	Rarely (1)	Occasionally (2)	Almost Always (3)
8. How often do you read everything at the same rate? (Chapter 7)			X
9. How often do you refer to your dictionary? (Chapter 6)	X		
10. How often can you rapidly locate the main thought in a long, involved sentence? (Chapter 9)		X	
11. How often can you follow and summarize the train of thought as you read a long selection? (Chapter 9)	X		
12. How often do you mark your textbook as you read? (Chapter 9)	X		
13. How often do headings and subheadings seem significant to you when you are reading? (Chapter 8)	X		
14. How often do you notice a lack of logic in the articles or texts you read? (Chapter 9)		X	
15. How often can you distinguish between fact and opinion? (Chapter 9)			X
16. How often can you explain exactly why you liked or disliked a story or novel you read recently? (Chapter 7)	X		

Answers and Discussion

In order to assess your reading habits, count the number of times you answered *rarely* in questions 1–8. Each *rarely* indicates a good reading habit that you want to work hard to keep. If you answered *occasionally* to many of these questions, you will need to work on refining this habit.

Now look at your responses for questions 9–16. For this group, each *rarely* response indicates a poor habit, one that you will consciously need to work on as you do the activities in *Developing Textbook Thinking*. Again, if you answered *occasionally* to many of the questions, you are on the right track but you will need to make a more concerted effort to maintain positive reading habits.

Note which chapters in *Developing Textbook Thinking* address your weaknesses. You can use the ideas presented in these specific chapters to improve your personal reading habits. In addition, as you read this text and learn more about how to read and study efficiently, periodically reassess your reading habits. Then go back and review the chapters noted in the parentheses if necessary.

Assessment 2:
Study-Strategies Inventory

	Rarely (1)	Occa-sionally (2)	Almost Always (3)
1. I look through a chapter before reading it. (Chapter 8)	X		
2. I mark my text while I am reading. (Chapter 9)		X	
3. I have a difficult time maintaining concentration for a period of time. (Chapter 7)			X
4. I tend to cram for major tests. (Chapter 12)		X	
5. I understand my notes weeks after I have taken them. (Chapter 5)		X	
6. I plan study sessions well in advance of a major exam. (Chapter 12)	X		
7. I use a variety of study techniques. (Chapter 10)	X		
8. I can use the proper strategies for specific content areas. (Chapter 10)	X		
9. I read an entire chapter before stopping to think about it. (Chapter 7)			X
10. To prepare for a test, I try to memorize lots of facts. (Chapter 12)			X
11. I have very little trouble with content-specific vocabulary. (Chapter 6)	X		
12. I try to predict items that an instructor might ask on a test. (Chapter 12)			X
13. I do well only in subjects that interest me. (Chapter 7)			X
14. I get extremely anxious during tests. (Chapter 12)			X
15. I have a systematic method for taking lecture notes. (Chapter 5)	X		
16. I take detailed notes from my text while I am reading. (Chapter 9)	X		
17. I spread my studying over several days. (Chapter 11)	X		
18. I give daily attention to each of my classes. (Chapter 11)	X		
19. I test myself or get someone to test me on key information. (Chapter 11)	X		
20. I skip class. (Chapter 2)	X		

	Rarely (1)	Occa- sionally (2)	Almost Always (3)
21. I study in a place that is quiet and free from distractions. (Chapter 2)	____	X	____
22. I try to find interesting information in my classes. (Chapter 8)	____	X	____
23. I use what I already know to help me learn new information. (Chapter 8)	____	____	X

Answers and Discussion

For numbers 1, 5, 6, 7, 8, 11, 12, 15, 17, 18, 19, 21, 22, and 23, you should have answered *almost always,* because each represents a valuable study strategy. You should have answered *rarely* to numbers 2, 3, 4, 9, 10, 13, 14, 16, and 20. These items describe inefficient or ineffective strategies that you should try to change.

If you answered *occasionally* to a number of items, you are probably inconsistent in your use of study strategies. You may be somewhat aware of what you should do, but you may often choose not to apply your knowledge.

As with Assessment 1, pay particular attention to the chapters indicated following each item. Reassess your study behaviors at midterm, as well as at the end of the term, to see how much you have improved.

Assessment 3, Part I: College Study Demands

In the space provided, place a **T** if the statement is true and an **F** if the statement is false.

____ 1. The two factors that best differentiate between good and poor students are: (1) good study habits and (2) interest.

____ 2. Studying can make you tired.

____ 3. Students taking three core courses (courses all students are required to take regardless of their major) in a term average about 100 pages of reading a week.

____ 4. The more details you can memorize from the textbook, the better you will do on exams.

____ 5. Reviewing material more than triples your memory of it.

____ F 6. If you know the material in the textbook, you do not have to be as attentive during lectures.

____ 7. Given enough study time, almost any student can perform at the top of the class.

____ 8. On average, students have about ten hours per day of free time (time not spent in class, studying, eating, or sleeping).

___ 9. You should read most materials (such as newspapers, novels, and textbooks) at about the same rate of speed.

___ 10. Monitoring your learning during studying—knowing what you know and what you don't know—influences your test performance.

___ 11. Basically, you should study the same way for multiple-choice and essay exams.

___ 12. If you know good study strategies, it is less important for you to attend class regularly.

___ 13. In Figure 1.1, try to connect the nine dots by drawing four straight lines without taking the pencil from the paper.

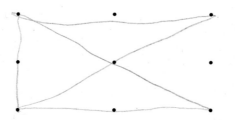

Figure 1.1 Creativity Exercise

Answers and Discussion

1. True. Research shows that good study habits and interest in the subject most clearly differentiate between students who do well and those who do poorly in class.[1] This text will show you ways to develop good study habits and to develop interest—even in a boring subject.

2. False. Actually, lack of interest is usually what tires you. One key to effective study is to make boring material more interesting; this text will examine ways of doing so.

3. False. Various surveys of courses at colleges across the United States show that if you took three core courses, you would have about 250 pages of reading per week, for an average of 83 pages per week per course. Reading matter includes textbooks, lab materials, novels, and supplementary materials.

4. False. This statement is false for two reasons. First, many survey courses stress the general principles, theories, and concepts in the field. If you memorize details, you might easily miss these broader areas on which you are tested. Second, with so many pages to read per week, it is difficult, if not impossible, to memorize all the details.

You must select what the author and the instructor stress. This text stresses the principle of selecting.

5. True. Research shows that if you do not review material, you will remember about 33 percent of it after a week and about 14 percent after a quarter. If you do review, you should be able to remember 87 percent of it after a week and 70 percent at the end of the term.[2] There is a huge payoff in reviewing!

6. False. Many lectures cover information not in the textbook. Professors also use lectures to explain and stress the topics that they feel are the most important. You can bet that these topics will be covered on exams. Lectures help you to review, understand, and gain information and to study selectively.

7. True. We know that most students can perform in the top 20 percent of a class if they study the material to mastery.[3] Some students can master a chapter with one reading and a review. Others need to read, reread, make notes, summarize, and review several times. This text will discuss ways to use your study time effectively. You can perform at the top of most classes, but you will probably have to work hard at it.

8. True. According to studies done by Arthur Dole,[4] average students spend their time each week in roughly the following ways:

Sleep	49.3 hours
Study	19.8 hours
Classes	18.7 hours
Meals	10.7 hours
Total	98.5 hours

This schedule leaves 69.5 hours per week free for recreation, social events, free reading, and the like. Students may have ten hours free a day to devote to additional studying and recreation.

9. False. To make efficient use of your time, you need to read different materials at speeds that vary with your purpose and background knowledge. This text will show you ways to vary your reading speed.

10. True. Research indicates that self-monitoring influences test performance more than any other study practice.[5] This is because students who monitor their performance know what they need to spend more time on, thus influencing their plan of study.

11. False. Because objective tests (multiple-choice, true/false, matching) are recognition tasks and essay tests are recall tasks, you should study for each kind of test differently. Students should always be aware of the task (what the professor expects) and adjust their studying accordingly.[6]

12. False. Although knowing good strategies is important and will certainly help your performance, class attendance is crucial. Simpson and Nist found that there was a direct positive relationship between attending class regularly and level of grade received.[7]

13. This problem can be solved only by looking beyond a limited view of the solution and seeing that one does not have to stay within the dots, as shown in Figure 1.2.

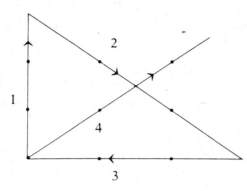

Figure 1.2 Solution to Creativity Exercise

In short, your study and reading habits from high school are not completely appropriate for college. You need to expand your limits and risk new ways of reading and studying in order to better prepare yourself. *Developing Textbook Thinking* challenges you to try new techniques that will increase your ability to meet the demands of college courses.

Assessment 3, Part II: A Scenario to Write About and Discuss

Directions: Read the following scenario and then write a response. Try not to think about the "correct" way to go about this task; rather, explain what you would really do. Be specific and explain *why* you would follow your course of action.

Scenario

You are a journalism major enrolled in a survey biology course partially to fulfill your undergraduate science requirements. You are getting ready for your first of three exams which will cover six text chapters and four weeks of lecture notes. (You will have a separate lab exam.) The test will consist of 50 multiple-choice items and 30 true/false items, each worth 1 point. There will also be 10 identification questions, each worth 2 points. Old copies of the test show that past exams have been quite difficult because about 75 percent of the items ask questions that require critical thinking about facts you have studied. How would you prepare for this test?

*review all notes taken
& test myself to be sure
I can answer
them, then I would feel
secure that I have the knowledge needed.*

Get in groups of three or four to discuss what you wrote. What are some of the common elements? Where is there agreement and disagreement? How might you prepare differently from the way you did in high school?

After you have had an opportunity to discuss your writing, your instructor may add some comments. It might be a good idea to save your answer and, as you learn new strategies in *Developing Textbook Thinking,* think about how your response might change. Finally, repeat this exercise after you have finished the text and the course in which it is being used to see how your perceptions of how to carry out this task have changed.

The Reading Journal: Becoming More Aware

You thus begin this book armed with three pieces of valuable information: the demands of college reading and studying, an awareness of your reading habits, and your own assessment of your use of study strategies. You also now have some indication of how you and your classmates would approach a specific learning task. It is important to go a step further and examine more closely what happens when you read specific kinds of material (for example, magazines versus novels versus textbooks). There are three types of reading journals you can keep as a valuable means to this end. Although your instructor may want to evaluate your journal regularly, remember that the journal is primarily for your benefit. If you write good entries and consciously think about what happens when you read, your journal will be valuable in helping you not only to discover exactly what happens when you read certain kinds of material, but also to determine why you may have problems.

Self-Awareness Journal

Few students actually evaluate what happens when they read. If you asked fellow students to tell you what happens as they read a text, newspaper, or magazine, they probably would respond with "I don't know" and give you a strange look.

Because self-awareness is vital in improving reading habits and abilities, thinking and then writing about what happens as you read can be a powerful self-assessment tool. After you have read an article, chapter, or the like, use the following questions to guide your writing:

1. How interesting was the article? Did it hold your interest the whole way through? Why or why not?

2. Could you concentrate? If not, why do you think concentration was a problem? Where were you reading? At what time? Did you have other things on your mind?

3. Was the reading easy to understand? What made it easy or difficult? How was the article organized?

4. How difficult was the vocabulary? About how many words were unfamiliar to you? Did the difficulty of the vocabulary affect your comprehension?

5. What do you think your rate was? very slow? slow? very fast? Why do you think you had that rate?

6. How much did the length of the article affect your reading? Do you think the article was too long? too short?

7. What kinds of information do you remember? major concepts? details?

8. How does the article personally affect you?

9. What did you know about this topic before you began your reading? Would you like to know more? Why?

After answering these questions honestly and recording your responses over a period of time, you will see patterns emerging. Use these patterns to improve your reading skills and habits. For example, you may discover that as your interest declines, your rate, comprehension, and concentration decline as well. You may realize that you get bogged down in details. Realizations such as these are valuable because they point to problems that can be remedied by a combination of your motivation and your instructor's guidance.

To avoid certain pitfalls when you write your entries, read the following two examples. Then decide which entry is the better of the two. Explain your choice.

Example 1:

The article was on Social Security. It gave a history of the Social Security system and talked about what might happen if the Social Security system continues the way it is now. I thought it was boring, and I don't like to read stuff about the government.

Example 2:

The article, "The Social Security Crisis," was not very interesting to me. There were so many statistics that I got lost. While I was reading, I thought I understood the main ideas, but when I finished, I realized that I could remember only a few unimportant details, such as the number of people who are on Social Security. Because the article was so long, I could feel my rate getting slower and slower. The more slowly I read, the poorer my concentration became. I even nodded off two or three times. It was hard to maintain interest in something that is not going to affect me for 45 years! Besides, the vocabulary was really hard. I underlined 12 words that I did not know the meaning of. I think it's terrible that people who have to pay Social Security all their lives may not get any money when they retire. How unfair!

Which example was better? _#2_____

Why? _Because it gave more information about the entry covered all the questions in the Self Awareness Journal_____

Example 2 is the better entry, because the student included information about the following:

1. Interest level
2. Ability to concentrate
3. Understandability of the article
4. Vocabulary level of the article
5. Reading-rating awareness
6. Length factor in the article
7. Types of information remembered
8. A personal reaction

Notice that this type of journal entry is not a summary. The purpose of this entry is to make you aware of what happens when you read and why it happens. Summaries serve different purposes.

Response Journal

Sometimes you may be asked to write a response to what you have read, especially if the article is of a controversial nature. Such a response forces you to clarify your thinking on a topic and to back up your reactions with information from your reading. The important aspect of a response is to support your viewpoint with facts. Doing so shows you whether you understand the issue well enough to support your stand.

For example, suppose you are asked to write a response to an article about an individual who was charged with murder, convicted, and sentenced to death.

Support your view with facts

Following the electrocution, evidence emerged that proved the person actually had been innocent of murder. Your response is to state whether you believe in capital punishment and to use evidence from the article to support your stand. You probably would want to include the information about electrocuting an innocent individual. Simply stating that you do not believe in capital punishment because it is immoral to kill a person under any circumstances will not suffice.

What follows is an example of a good response-journal entry. Notice that this student took a stand on the issue and then supported that stand with both examples and opinions. Since this is not a summary journal, it is fine to express your opinion; in fact, in a response journal, an opinion is expected. Remember that it is not important what stand you take. Instead, how you support your stand is the key issue.

> Even though John Doe was executed for a crime that it *appears* that he did not commit, I remain in favor of the death penalty. In this particular instance, the article did not do a very good job of convincing me that John Doe was actually innocent. Just because another person comes forward and confesses to the crime does not mean that he is telling the truth. In fact, the confessor had admitted guilt to two other crimes that he could not have possibly committed. Doe, however, had a history of prior crimes similar to the one for which he was given the chair. In addition, he had a retrial as well as numerous appeals to try to prove his innocence. Both failed to produce convincing evidence.
>
> Crimes such as the one committed by John Doe are awful and should be punished to the full extent of the law. John Doe violently assaulted and then killed a six-year-old child. He showed no remorse for what he did. People like this serve no purpose in society except to make it more violent and less moral. Why should tax-paying citizens have to pay to feed and clothe individuals like John Doe? Take the money that would be spent keeping someone like Doe alive and give it to the families of their victims. That's where the support should go.

Summary Journal

Another way to write a journal entry is to summarize your reading. Summarizing an article or a portion of a text chapter is one way to determine whether you understand the author's message. Summaries also can be used as a secondary rehearsal strategy (see Chapter 10).

Writing a good summary takes considerable practice. You will be well on your way if you keep in mind the following suggestions:

1. Read the entire article first. As you read, underline key points and make brief notes in the margin.
2. After reading and marking, stop and ask yourself what important ideas are presented. Determine which details you should include in your summary. Make a skeletal map.

3. Organize your thoughts before beginning to write. A summary does not have to be organized in exactly the same manner as the article.

4. Do not write as you read. Writing as you read often causes you to include unnecessary details. It also tires you before you complete your reading, so your summary will not be comprehensive.

5. Putting information in your own words indicates that you really understand what you have read. Often students think they are summarizing when actually they have merely copied random sentences from the reading.

6. When you have finished, read the entire summary. Check to see if it is well organized and captures the author's thrust. Could someone else read your summary and make sense of it?

Read the selection entitled "Blood and Money" at the end of this chapter. Then, using the skeletal map in Figure 1.3 to guide you, fill in the map with the important supporting details and write your summary using the six guidelines for writing good summaries.

Share Your Entries

When classmates share journal entries, they gain insight into the thinking processes and ideas of others. Shared responses to reading are particularly helpful. Make your writing someone else's reading.

Use what you learned about your own reading and studying habits from the assessments at the beginning of the chapter to guide your reading and journal writing. Then compare your results with those of your classmates. It is

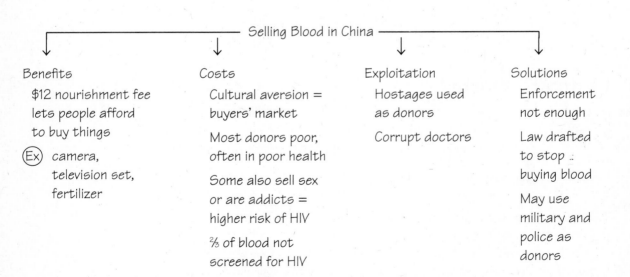

Figure 1.3 Skeletal Map for "Blood and Money"

likely that others have some of the same weaknesses. It often makes people feel better when they know that others share their problems. If you know that your reading rate is a problem, you can strengthen that area as you read. Discussing with others how you attempt to solve your problems will also help you to strengthen those areas. After sharing and discussing, write about your experiences in your journal. Keep in mind that as you do journal entries for different types of materials—magazines, novels, and texts—you will be better able to define your strengths and work on your weaknesses. Be careful about becoming too blasé about your entries. Students often get into the rut of saying almost the same thing in every journal. This occurs most often in the self-awareness journals. If you seriously reflect on your reading, however, your journals will indicate your growth toward self-regulated learning.

Key Ideas

1. The demands of college differ considerably from those of high school. Therefore, study demands must also be different.

2. Assessing your reading and studying strengths and weaknesses is an important step in becoming a more efficient learner.

3. Reading journals are tools to make you aware of your reading habits and your level of comprehension. The three types of journals serve different purposes.

4. Sharing your journals with classmates is a good way to reflect.

Application Exercises (DTT*)

1. At the end of this chapter are two articles, "Blood and Money" and "Prisoners of Pain." Read both articles, and then write three different journal entries on each one.

   - a self-awareness journal

   - a response journal

   - a summary journal

   Use what you have learned in the chapter to guide your writing. Refer to the questions on page 15 when you write the journal.

2. Now read the first sections of "The Psychology of Memory" from the appendix (pages 273–295). Write what happened as you read this selection, and compare it to what happened when you read "Blood and Money" and "Prisoners of Pain."

   *DTT (Developing Textbook Thinking) exercises use material found in this textbook and give you practice on typical college material.

3. As you read this text, continue to keep writing your journal entries. Your entries will be particularly helpful when you begin reading the complete text chapters in the appendix. Think carefully about what happens as you read and write about it. These entries can help you to determine what you need to change in your reading habits.

Application Exercises (Your Texts*)

1. As you read a chapter in one of your own texts, think about what happens as you read. Then write a self-awareness-journal entry to indicate what you observe.

2. Compare and contrast what happens when you read something from a newspaper to what happens when you read something from your text. How does interest affect what happens?

3. Write a summary-journal entry for one section of the text chapter that you read. Use the guidelines discussed earlier in this chapter for writing your summary. Make sure to sketch out a skeletal map prior to writing your summary.

Selection from a Magazine

Blood and Money

George Wehrfritz

They come for the money. And the $12 "nourishment fee" Chinese blood donors typically get for filling up the equivalent of a pint bag can make a big difference. Zhang Yimou, a top film director, sold blood to buy his first camera. The peasant heroine of a 1994 hit film, "Ermo," sells blood to buy a television. At a Beijing clinic recently a pale girl in a yellow blouse sold her blood for the first time to buy fertilizer for the family farm. Then there are career donors such as old Mr. Sun, a Beijing fruit peddler who has sold blood 22 times since 1984. Working through a blood broker, or "bloodhead," he stands in illegally for people drafted as donors by their work units—and makes $50 a visit. He has bought a fancy new cart and moved his family to the outskirts of the capital. "Today's happiness is due to Dad's blood," his wife tells their children.

But the blood business costs China dearly. A cultural aversion to giving blood has fostered a seller's market that all but guarantees disaster. Most donors are poor migrants struggling to make ends meet. Some sell sex as well as blood, and some are drug addicts. Even government clinics reuse the needles

Your Texts exercises are designed to give you practice in applying study techniques to textbooks you are using in your other classes.

used to draw blood. And only a third of the nation's blood supply is screened for HIV contamination. Now, finally, officials have begun acknowledging the crisis. Last month Beijing recalled a popular blood serum after discovering samples contaminated with HIV antibodies. The manufacturer: an unregulated military factory. The Health Ministry also disclosed 4,305 cases of HIV infection; privately, experts say the real number exceeds 100,000.

Blood profiteers have taken exploitation to the limit. Court officials in rural Hejian told *Newsweek* that police recently broke up a ring of a dozen bloodheads who were holding 74 people hostage as blood producers. Authorities also closed the local blood station and arrested its two directors. One of those rescued was ill with tetanus when kidnapped by gang members posing as work contractors. Bloodheads had to carry him to the clinic; in four days they drained 2½ pints of his blood. He died six days after the rescue. In other raids, police have arrested corrupt health workers and factory managers who contract illicit donors.

Better enforcement may not be enough. Western public-health experts long ago concluded that paying donors invariably corrupts blood stocks because it creates incentives to lie and cheat. "Blood will bring disease and danger so long as it remains a commodity," says Sun Baiqiu, vice president of China's Red Cross. A draft law circulating among senior health officials would outlaw the buying and selling of blood for clinical use. The model may be Hong Kong, which in 40 years changed attitudes through humanitarian appeals. "Reach out, spread some love today," sings pop star Jackie Cheung in the current Red Cross theme song. But Beijing can't expect quick results, and bringing its clinics into the AIDS age is dauntingly expensive. Officials could fall back on coercion—imposing donation on the army, police, and state unions. But that won't necessarily stop China's fledgling capitalists from trying to turn a buck on blood.

Source: George Wehrfritz, "Blood and Money." From *Newsweek,* November 11, 1996, p. 50. Copyright © 1996 by Newsweek, Inc. All rights reserved. Reprinted by permission.

Selection from a Magazine

Prisoners of Pain

Fear and numbing may keep victims in place

How could he be such a monster? Why didn't she leave him? Why didn't she protect her child?

The trial of Joel Steinberg, with the continuing, appalling testimony of his brutalized wife, Hedda Nussbaum, is the sort of public scandal that creates instant judges and juries around the dinner table. But behavioral experts caution against judging too quickly. The relationship between a battered woman and the man who batters her is a complicated one. It is not usually the lurid, sadomasochistic dance imagined by sidewalk psychiatrists, but something even more insidious, because it happens so often within the charmed circle of the family. "Daddy had a hard day at the office today," says the mother, hurriedly making excuses to shield the child who has just witnessed her beating—and to deny that her marriage is in trouble.

It starts with a slap, or a shove, a domestic squabble that gets out of hand, though not shockingly. It escalates only slowly, to a punch, a kick, a pummeling. Before long, the victim has grown "familiar" with violence—the beginnings of becoming a prisoner of it. "We all say we would leave if we were beaten once," says Dr. Penelope Grace, a specialist in family violence at Children's Hospital in Boston. "But we can all think of a situation that wasn't good with us, and that we stayed with long after. It's rare for a person to extricate himself at exactly the [right] moment."

And what are a woman's alternatives to staying? She may be terrified that even worse will happen if she leaves—that a battering husband will carry out his frequent threats to maim or murder her. There are few accurate statistics on battered women, but data suggest the "highest risk" period for homicide is during separation. "Over 50 percent of all women killed are killed by former or present partners," says Dr. Lenore Walker, author of *The Battered Woman*.

The relationship between abuser and victim can begin quite conventionally. The man may be a loving, charismatic figure, successful at work, someone who never loses control at the office or in front of witnesses. "Joel Steinberg, for example, is always in control," notes psychotherapist Janis Altman, director of training for the New York–based Victim Services. "I've watched him at his trial, joking and laughing with his lawyers." But at home, jagged cracks appear. The man grows jealous and increasingly possessive of the woman. He seems determined to "control" her. Sometimes there is no violence until she becomes pregnant. Then it begins as verbal abuse—"You're really stupid . . . What kind of mother are you?"—before the blows begin falling. Says Grace: "It's an eroding of self-worth. The batterer attacks every part of you, physical and emotional."

Why, then, *do* women stay on? Psychologists say many think they can weather the beatings. In the "cycle" of violence, as described by Walker in her book, there are periods of abatement that encourage the woman to believe she can soothe her husband and outlast his rages. That is seldom the case, but a woman may feel compelled to try. By the time she realizes his violence is beyond her control, it is too late. "They're so beaten down, they can't leave," says psychotherapist Daniel Sonkin, author of the forthcoming book *Wounded Men*.

That may happen, as it allegedly did with Hedda Nussbaum, even where a child is sharing the brunt of the beatings. Mental-health professionals who treat battered women compare them to Vietnam veterans suffering from the "psychic numbing" of posttraumatic stress disorder. "It's easy for the general public to lose sympathy for a mother who lets her child be killed," says Walker, who conducted a major research program on battered women funded by the National Institute of Mental Health. "[But] these are the kinds of distortions that happen to these women. They lose the ability to think carefully, to feel. You cannot walk around in the middle of a firing range all the time without growing numb."

The men, meanwhile, wrestle with their own demons. They are likely to be products of violent families, where they were abused themselves. Research indicates that more often they witnessed abuse. Turning it against their wives or children may represent a perverse attempt at "mastery" over their trauma. The issue of control is vital to them, but they have usually never learned to deal with stress except through violence.

Shelter and Support: For women who escape, an abundance of support is available. The prevalence of the problem has spawned a network of shelters, as many as 1,000 nationwide, offering services from counseling to legal advocacy to children's programs. "A lot of times, therapy comes in the form of giving information about rights and services," says Sonkin. "Some women don't know that you can get a temporary restraining order; they don't know battering is against the law."

Therapy itself can be painfully slow, as it moves victims through stages of denial, coming to terms, then learning to cope. Although Nussbaum is under the care of a male psychiatrist, many of the therapists are women who treat patients from a feminist perspective. "The goal is to reempower the woman, to help her regain control of her life," says Walker. Yet some therapists see the culture itself as the greatest obstacle to recovery—a culture that manages to glorify the wholesome values of the family at the same time that it seems to tolerate and occasionally even exalt violence.

Source: D. Gelman and R. Elam, "Prisoners of Pain." From *Newsweek,* December 12, 1988, p. 65. Copyright © 1988 by Newsweek, Inc. All rights reserved. Reprinted by permission.

Notes

1. H. C. Lindgren, *The Psychology of College Success* (New York: John Wiley and Sons, 1969).

2. H. F. Spitzer, "Studies in Retention," *Journal of Educational Psychology,* Vol. 30, pp. 641–56.

3. J. Block, ed., *Mastery Learning: Theory into Practice* (New York: Holt, Rinehart and Winston, 1983).

4. A. A. Dole, "College Students Report on the Use of Time," *The Personnel and Guidance Journal,* Vol. 37, pp. 635–38.

5. S. L. Nist, M. L. Simpson, S. Olejnik, and D. Mealey, "The Relation Between Self-Selected Study Processes and Test Performance," *American Educational Research Journal,* Vol. 28, pp. 849–74.

6. M. L. Simpson and S. L. Nist, "A Case Study of Academic Literacy Tasks and Their Negotiation in a University History Course," in D. J. Leu and C. K. Kinzer, eds., *Forty-first Yearbook of the National Reading Conference* (Chicago: National Reading Conference, 1992).

7. Ibid.

Chapter 2

Getting Started: The **BCA**'s of Successful Study

Always bear in mind that your own resolution to succeed
is more important than any other one thing.

Abraham Lincoln

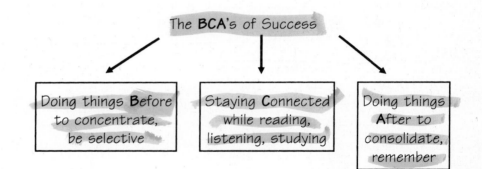

The **BCA**'s of Success

Doing things **B**efore
to concentrate,
be selective

Staying **C**onnected
while reading,
listening, studying

Doing things
After to
consolidate,
remember

Most students who use this book are enrolled in a college course on improving reading and study strategies. Many are, at the same time, enrolled in other courses that require textbook reading, note taking, studying, and preparing for exams. If you are one of these students, you may feel frustrated and anxious to get to the parts of *Developing Textbook Thinking* that will help you most in your other courses. From years of helping students develop reading and study strategies, we share your frustration. We wish we could give you all the strategies and tools you need on the first day so you can use them in your other courses.

It is not possible to give detailed strategies and tools immediately. However, a chapter that gives you some tips for getting on the right track will help you in all your courses. We will cover these strategies in detail later in the book, and we will talk about and give you practice in other strategies as well.

Notice that we are giving you "tips" in this chapter to get you started, and "strategies" later on in the book. These tips are like road signs: They will get you going in the right direction. But to be successful you will need a full map, and you will need to "go the distance" and really work at your studies.

Introduction—The BCA's

In the first chapter, we challenged you to move outside your usual ways of thinking about reading and studying, in other words, we encouraged you to think critically. Most importantly, successful reading does not occur only by moving your eyes across a page, just as successful note taking does not happen only when your pen is moving. Of course, moving your eyes and your pen is necessary; they are the "ABC's" of reading and writing.

But your challenge is to move beyond the ABC's, to think of reading and studying as involving three critical elements:

- Doing things **B**efore you read, listen, and study.
- Staying **C**onnected while you read, listen, and study.
- Doing things **A**fter you read, listen, and study.

What 3 critical elements are needed for reading and studying? (BCA's)

You will find that we discuss these "**BCA**'s" of successful studying throughout the book. Whether you are reading, listening to a lecture, preparing for a discussion, taking notes, learning new concepts and terms, studying for a test, or writing a paper, the things you do **B**efore and **A**fter your eyes or your pen perform the actual task are as important as the task itself. And, of course, it is critical to stay **C**onnected to the task while doing it.

The **BCA**'s are based on key principles of learning. In this text, we will talk about these principles in some detail. It is important you know *why* a strategy will help you; it gives you the opportunity to adapt the strategy to your own needs. Following is a brief description of these three stages of studying and the learning principles on which they are based.

Before You Read, Listen, Take Notes, and Study

 '**B**'

What are 2 Factors to think about before you Begin to study?

There are two factors to think about before you begin to study. The first is to *create the best conditions for yourself to succeed*. The second is to *use strategies to help you be most effective* with the studying task itself.

Have you ever sat down and started studying and found you were moving your eyes across the text for a long time before you realized you hadn't actually read or understood anything? Or have you ever sat in a lecture and realized you were thinking about what you did last night instead—even though you were moving your pen? Successful students tend to pay attention to a number of elements that can contribute to successful studying.

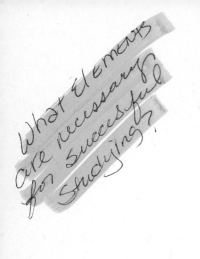

What Elements are necessary for Successful studying?

Developing Self-Discipline

Self-discipline is a critical element. This means disciplining yourself so that you study regularly, keep up with assignments, and continue working toward your long-range goals—to be successful in college. Chapters 3 and 4 discuss this in some detail, but to get you started, here are some tips:

- Write out your goals for each course you are taking. Include your personal goals, for example, What do I want to get out of the course? Include any scheduled tests and assignments, along with their due dates. You now have a framework for deciding how you have to discipline yourself.

- Think about when and how you concentrate best. Do you concentrate best in the morning, afternoon, or night? How long can you read and concentrate at a time? Does background music help you or hinder you?

- Make a weekly schedule for your courses. How much study time per week do you estimate you will need to meet your goals? When will you do your studying? Base your study times on when, and for how long, you think you can concentrate best. Block out the time you need. Block out school-related time before scheduling time for fun and relaxation. Most importantly, make a commitment to yourself that you will make this a priority, that you will not let other distractions interfere with that study time.

Learning Flexibility

Flexibility is critical. You will have too large a workload if you are not efficient in studying and doing the work. The key to efficiency is flexibility. Chapters 8 through 12 discuss this in some detail, but here are some tips:

- Think about your background knowledge and interest: If you already know a lot about the topic, you will not need to spend as much time as you would on a topic that is unfamiliar. Then, before you begin to study, decide how much time you should invest.

- Learn and try different strategies. If you find you are not successful in studying something, try a different approach; a number of strategies are presented throughout this book to help you.

- Make strategies your own. That is, modify strategies to meet the needs of the courses you are taking and your own studying preferences.

Finding the Place

No matter where you are living—at home, in a dormitory, or in an apartment—one of your first priorities should be to find a place to study that is quiet and free from distractions. You cannot study efficiently with a radio or television playing because your attention will be divided. Part of you will be studying; the other part of you will be listening to music or watching television. Stay away from entertainment during study time.

Your study place should not only be free from distractions but also have everything you need. Paper, pens, dictionary, books, notes, and the like should be at hand, so that you do not have to get up constantly to find what you need. Try to study in the same place as often as possible. Once you have established a special study place, you can slip easily into a studying mindset. Your mind will know that once you are in your study place, it is study time, not time for socializing or daydreaming.

Make sure that you have proper lighting and that you sit in a straight-backed chair. You should not be too comfortable! The worst place you can choose for studying is your bed. Go to bed when you are tired, but do not go to bed to study.

Utilizing Resources

Using all the resources available to you is important. College campuses have many resources to help students to succeed in their classes. Unfortunately, often these resources go unnoticed, or students fail to take advantage of them. Some resources are more obvious. The library, of course, is a must when it comes time to write papers or do outside research. But on many campuses, there is a wealth of additional information nestled in the library. Many libraries keep test files in which instructors can place retired test copies. Such tests, though not the exact test you would take in that class, indicate the kinds of items that the professor might stress, how long the test might be, and the ratio of text to lecture items. Armed with this kind of information, you can carry out test preparation more effectively and efficiently.

Another way to find more information about courses and professors is to ask other students who have taken a particular course or studied under a professor. Word travels fast on both large and small campuses about instructors who tend to be either very good or very poor. Although sometimes you may not have extensive choices about the course or the instructor, when you do, make it a policy to check around. But also remember, the "easiest" professor isn't necessarily the best choice. Weigh all the reasons for taking the course before deciding.

Yet another resource that is rapidly becoming available on many campuses is the use of technology. College instructors or courses now have their own web sites that students can access using computers on campus. These web sites can remind you of assignments or even provide you with the lecture that you may have missed (due to illness, of course!). In addition, many campus libraries are easily accessible via computer through the Internet. E-mail correspondence with other students as well as professors certainly broadens learning connections. Such advances in technology are becoming increasingly popular, and you should be sure to make use of these resources if they are available to you.

Forming Study Groups

Some of you may remember the now-defunct television show called "The Paper Chase," which purported to give a fairly accurate picture of the trials and tribulations of law students. Others may personally know law students and can better understand the academic rigors they face, particularly during their first year. One of the ways law students manage to meet their study demands is by forming study groups. If it works for them, it might work for you, also.

Study groups are an efficient way to learn in a variety of situations. Most students think of forming a study group only in classes where the reading/learning demands are too heavy for them to handle effectively on their own. They organize by forming a study group of two or more students who all want to do well in the course. The tasks are equally divided among group members. For example, if you were in a political science class in which the instructor assigned 150 pages of reading weekly, you might form a study group consisting of three students and divide the load. Although each person would be responsible for reading all 150 pages, each would be responsible for thoroughly knowing only 50 pages to the point where he or she could "teach" it to the other members of the group. In addition, members of this type of study group would usually be responsible for summarizing the information on paper in some way, in the form of a map, an outline, or a more traditional paragraph summary.

But study groups can be formed for other reasons. Students enrolled in courses where the reading load is light or moderate can also use the idea. These groups are generally smaller, often consisting of only two individuals who meet on a regular basis to "talk through" key ideas presented in lectures, texts, and/or outside readings.

No matter which type of group you might form, there are several points that you should keep in mind in order for all members of your group to be successful:

- Invite individuals who are serious about learning and who will do their fair share of the workload to participate. Nothing makes group members angrier than one member consistently showing up without having his or her task completed. Remember, if one member of the group fails to carry out his or her obligation, the rest of the group suffers.

- Devise consequences for those who fail to meet their obligations. For example, individuals who come unprepared might be banned from attending one or two subsequent sessions. Other group members can pick up their share of the work during their absence.

- Set up a regular time to meet, as well as a specified meeting place. When you set up a regular time, you can include it on your weekly schedule and on your daily "To Do" list. Just as with other meetings, once you become accustomed to attending, you will feel guilty if you don't.

4. • Study groups should be ~~serious studying/learning situations,~~ not social events. If you want to socialize with members of your group, do it at another time.

5. • ~~Study groups do not take the place of individual preparation and studying.~~ They are supplements to, not exclusive of, individual study time. As suggested earlier, in a study group in which you are responsible for teaching one-fourth of the material to the group, you must still read the other three-quarters. Your study partners may supply you with detailed strategies that outline the important points of the material, but you should be at least familiar with all of the information when you attend the meeting. Likewise, if your group or partner meets to talk through course information, don't show up totally unprepared and expect others to spoonfeed you the materials.

Forming a study group is rather simple. Find two or more people who are interested in doing well in the course. In a sense, it works better if you are not friends with the other members. The most successful groups often consist of people who do little together socially. That way, when you get together, you tend to study and learn rather than to socialize. Next, find a quiet place to meet, as well as a time that suits all members. Some study groups meet once a week; others find that they need two to three sessions per week to complete all of the work. Finally, divide the workload and decide on a format for the strategies that each member will devise or for the way in which "teaching" sessions will be carried out. Keep focused on the task, and begin and end on time as much as possible.

If formed and used properly, study groups or study partnerships are effective tools. You have a chance to hear someone else's interpretation of the material, as well as a chance to have the information filter into your memory by ways other than just reading it. In addition, such groups help clarify fuzzy information. Many times students respond to a peer's explanation better than they responded to the way the text or the instructor presented the information. It is a reciprocal method of learning: You teach your partner, and your partner teaches you. And both gain something positive from the arrangement.

Getting Assistance

Once you learn and use the strategies outlined in *Developing Textbook Thinking,* you should see a marked improvement in your test grades. However, sometimes, in spite of all of the strategies you might try, your grades might not be as good as you would like. In such cases, ~~seek help early.~~ Students who do poorly on the first test and who procrastinate about asking for assistance often find themselves in situations where it is difficult to regroup. For example, individuals who have failed the first two of only four course tests are in academic deep water that is difficult to tread.

If you are working hard to understand the course material—that is, you are

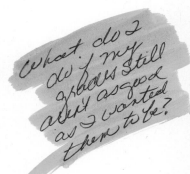

What do I do if my grades still aren't as good as I wanted them to be?

keeping up with the reading, doing the assignments, using good study strategies, and budgeting your time adequately—without a positive effect on your grade, don't be afraid to ask for assistance.

The first place to start is with your instructor. See him or her either before or after class to set up an appointment; do not go into any detail as to the nature of your problem at that time. Simply ask when it would be convenient for you to meet. Before you go to your instructor's office, make sure you have thought about what you want to say. Comments such as, "You expect too much from us" or "The reading load in this course is just too heavy" usually receive unsympathetic responses. Rather, explain to the professor why you are concerned and what you have been doing in an attempt to help yourself. Chances are that he or she will either personally give you some help or steer you in the direction of another person who can. Most instructors stand ready to assist students who are trying hard. But don't expect sympathy if you are not attending class and making a valiant effort at trying to understand the material on your own.

In addition to the course instructor, you might seek out the college's learning assistance center. Most campuses offer some degree of learning help in the form of tutors for traditionally difficult courses. Help on how to study, as well as counseling services, are also offered in traditional learning assistance centers. Additionally, sometimes assistance is available from a web site for a particular course. Your adviser or your instructor should be able to point you toward the services available on your campus. Usually, these services are free of charge.

Drawing by Bruce Eric Kaplan © 1992 The New Yorker Magazine, Inc. All rights reserved.

Using Your Course Syllabus

The last tip to use before you read, listen, and study has to do with using and understanding course syllabi (*syllabi* is the plural of *syllabus*). In high school, most teachers do not distribute a course syllabus, so many first-year college students are not familiar with the nature and purpose of a syllabus. In a sense, the course syllabus is a contract between you and your instructor. It generally outlines what the professor expects of you both in and out of the classroom. Most syllabi indicate what you should be responsible for in terms of reading the text, when tests will be given, how grades will be determined, and any specific policies that instructors might have in terms of absences, test retakes, and academic dishonesty.

Many professors feel that once they have given the syllabus to you it becomes your job to keep abreast of the requirements. For example, few professors will remind you of weekly reading assignments once they have distributed the syllabus. Most will still remind you of test dates, study sessions, and when major requirements such as term papers are due. However, some do not. The final warning here is to read the syllabus carefully and make sure that you understand the expectations. Ignorance of the law is no excuse!

What is the course of syllabus?

Following Effective Strategies

Before You Read

The study techniques in this book include strategies to use *before* you read the text, listen to the lecture, or prepare for the test. These strategies are based on four principles of learning (discussed in more detail in Chapter 8). To be most efficient and effective, use the following principles:

Principle 1: Psyche yourself up.
Principle 2: Use what you already know about the topic to help you.
Principle 3: Purposely intend to remember what you read or hear.
Principle 4: Anticipate test questions as a way to decide when and how to take notes, or what to concentrate on most.

Such strategies are part of the techniques taught throughout this textbook. To get you started, here are some tips for *before* you do any studying:

- *Preview* what you are going to study. In a textbook, look over the headings and subheadings and read any introductions or conclusions. For a lecture, look over the assigned textbook material or your last set of lecture notes. For a discussion, look over any questions or assignments that went with the discussion session.

- In your preview, try to get a good sense of what will be covered in the textbook, lecture, or discussion, and how it will be organized. When you have

What is Activating your prior knowledge?

this sense, *reflect on what you already know* about what will be covered. This is called activating your prior knowledge.

- *Think about questions* that will be answered in the study material. Devise these questions to help you pick up information you don't already know. Try to make the questions similar to those you might expect on a test. Questions help you to concentrate, determine what information is most important, and prepare for tests. Self-questioning is used in many of the techniques in this book. Studying to answer questions, if they are good questions, is one of the easiest and most powerful things you can do from the first day of any class.

Stay Connected As You Read, Listen, Take Notes, and Study

It is important that you stay *connected*. By connected we mean that you are concentrating and comprehending whatever it is you are reading. Your concentration, your success in understanding and remembering information, and your ability to integrate new information with what you already know all depend on your ability to stay *connected* with the reading, listening, or writing task.

The study techniques in this book for helping you to stay *connected* are based on the following two principles of learning (discussed in more detail in Chapter 9):

Principle 5: Be selective for key information and isolate it for later study.
Principle 6: Create meaningful organization of what you are studying.

Strategies to help you are part of the techniques taught throughout this textbook. To get you started, here are some tips for staying connected while studying:

- *Be active* as you study. Don't just read or listen to the lecture. Take notes, write answers to your questions, and discuss what you read or heard with other classmates. This doesn't mean you should copy material or try to write down the lecturer's exact words. It *does* mean that you should read or listen, reflect for a moment, and then use your own words to express the major points. The more you can actively do something with information, the more the material will belong to you so that you will understand and remember it.

- *Think critically.* As you are reading or listening to lectures, think about what the author or lecturer is saying. Think *ideas* not just words! Ask yourself, What point am I supposed to glean from what I am reading or listening to? Why is this important? Students who can think critically during the reading or listening process are already well on their way to learning new information and integrating it with what they already know.

- *Make decisions* continuously while you study. Ask yourself, What should I pay attention to? What information, out of hundreds of pages of information, is most important to understand and remember? What can I do to improve my understanding and to ensure that I will remember? The questions you ask before you study will help you make these decisions.

- *Use cues.* In textbooks and other printed material that you may study, headings and subheadings, pictures, graphs, and questions are included, not just as "extras" but as cues to what the author thinks is important. In lectures, observe when the instructor raises his or her voice, writes something on the board, or uses nonverbal cues to indicate that something is important. Pay attention to what is repeated in the lecture or text; good speakers or writers repeat those things they believe to be most important.

- *Monitor yourself.* If you start to lose your concentration or if you cannot understand the material, you cannot connect with your textbook. Become aware of these problems as soon as they start, and take action to reengage. If you need to take a break from reading in order to refocus, then take a short break. If you don't understand a key idea, find someone to ask or reread the text.

After You Read, Listen, Take Notes, and Study

No matter how well you read or take notes, if you do not do something with the information later you will forget over two-thirds of the material within a week. The study techniques in this book for you to do after your actual reading or listening are critical to learning and success in college. These techniques are based on two principles of learning (discussed in more detail in Chapters 10 and 11):

> Principle 7: Put the ideas into your own words.
> Principle 8: Organize and reduce the information each time you review.

Later in this textbook, you will learn strategies that will help you to remember and retrieve information during study and review. To get you started, here are some tips:

- After you read or listen to a lecture, *write down* information you think you will need to learn for a test.

- *Say this information out loud* (it aids your memory). Think about what you are saying.

- In your writing, *organize the information* in ways that will be meaningful to you; this will help you to understand and remember. You might outline, for instance, if that is a technique you know. This book shows you other ways to organize—for example, mapping or using concept cards. Or pose questions to yourself before the reading and then, after reading, write out your answers.

- *Review* what you wrote down the day after you first studied the material. Review it again a few days later and again before the exam. You will have to spend less time reviewing each time because you will have remembered more.

- In these reviews, once again *rehearse* the material. *Write down and organize* the material you still need to learn. *Say* it out loud. As you review, consolidate and reduce what you have to study. Not only will this make your test preparation easier, but you will also learn and remember much more.

- As you are reviewing and rehearsing, *continue to monitor.* Think about what you know and what you do not know. By monitoring, you can tell which concepts you need to spend more time on and which concepts you know well.

The Basic Strategies

You will learn a variety of strategies from this textbook. This chapter presents just the basics for the two major ways college students learn—from textbooks and from lectures. As you will see, these basic strategies are built on the **BCA** principles.

The BCA's for Textbook Reading

The basic strategy for learning from textbooks involves doing specific tasks *before* you read, *while* you read (so that you can stay connected), and *after* you read (so that you can study and review). Underlying these three phases of learning is the ability to think critically. The **BCA**'s of text reading are described in detail in the second section of this book. To get you started, though, here is an outline of the basic parts:

Before You Read

Activate prior knowledge as you get an idea of the chapter's focus.

- Read the title of the chapter and reflect on what you already know about the topic.

- Read the headings and subheadings and the chapter outline or chapter summary if they are included. Develop an organizational scheme for the entire chapter. Reflect on your background knowledge as you do this.

- Set learning and studying goals for yourself.

- Formulate questions about key concepts that you think you will need to learn.

- Reflect on your survey. Before you read, monitor by asking yourself, Do I have a clear idea of what this chapter is about?

Connect While You Read

Read and annotate the chapter, one section at a time.

- Set a goal for yourself in terms of how much you will complete.

- Read and annotate the text one section at a time. Write in the text margins or use outlines, word maps, or any other technique to isolate key concepts and supporting ideas.
- Reflect as you read. Think critically about ideas, not just words.
- Continue to formulate questions and read actively to answer your questions and remember key information.
- Reflect on your reading. As you read, monitor by asking yourself, Am I understanding the information in this chapter?

After You Read, Study

Write down material that you will need to learn for a test and say it out loud as a "talk-through."

- Isolate and write down the important information. Use maps, charts, concept cards, or other rehearsal strategies.
- Reread any material that is unclear. Do not reread entire chapters.
- Formulate and write down more specific test questions.
- Talk through the important information by covering up the answers to your test questions. Check your rehearsal strategies to make sure you are right.
- Reflect as you do these steps. After you study, monitor by asking yourself, Do I know this information thoroughly enough to do well on the test?

After You Read, Review

Say out loud the information that you have already learned. Practice over several days.

- Reduce your notes or other rehearsal strategies each time you review.
- Make sure that you can talk through supporting details and examples about your main points and concepts.
- Distribute your practice over several days. Do not cram.
- Try to predict more accurate test questions.
- Reflect as you do this. After you review, monitor by asking yourself, Specifically, what information do I know very well? What information do I need to review more?

The BCA's for Lecture Note Taking

The basic strategy recommended for lecture note taking is discussed in detail in Chapter 5. Here are the **BCA**'s of lecture note taking:

Before the Lecture

- Read the textbook material that goes with the lecture.
- Review your notes from previous lectures.
- From the text material and previous notes, think of questions that might be answered in the lecture.
- Arrive before the lecture starts and sit where you will be able to stay connected to the lecture.
- Take your notes in a loose-leaf notebook (so you have more flexibility when studying). Date and number your notes.
- Divide your paper so you have a two-inch margin on the left (you will use this *after* the lecture).

Staying Connected During the Lecture

- Listen for key points. Pay attention to cues (such as when the instructor repeats something or writes something on the board) that flag what the instructor thinks are key points.
- As you listen, *first* think about what is being said and *then* take notes. Try to stress general ideas and put things in your own words (unless the instructor is giving a specific definition or tells you to write something down word for word). Thinking critically during the lecture helps you later on.
- Ask yourself questions to guide your listening and note taking. If something is not clear, ask the instructor.

After the Lecture

- As soon after the lecture as possible, review your notes. Fill in any blanks in your notes while the lecture is still fresh in your mind.
- In the left-hand margin of your paper, annotate or write questions. These might be summary statements about the lecture or information that you know you will need to remember or questions to ask yourself later as you study.
- Review these notes before the next lecture and again in a few days and again before a test. When you review, use the reduced information (in the left margin) to self-test; refer to the rest of the notes only when you don't remember. As you review, say the material out loud.

Key Ideas

1. Effective studying requires more than reading or taking notes.

2. Doing things **B**efore, doing things to stay **C**onnected, and doing things **A**fter reading or taking notes is the key to effective study.

3. There are tips and techniques you can use from the first day of class to help you with the **BCA**'s of successful study.

A Scenario to Write About and Discuss

This is your first term in college, and you really want to do well. You are taking a full load of coursework this term and even though this is only the end of the first week, you can tell that there are many differences between what was expected of you in high school and what will be expected of you as a college student. You used to "study" by looking over your notes before class or going over the study guide that your teacher gave to you. You realize that being successful in college involves more than that. You have tried to change the way you study by rereading the assignments, but you also realize that it will not be realistic to reread everything. What tips did you get from this chapter that might help you get off on the right foot? Which suggestions seem like they would be helpful for the specific courses you are currently taking?

Application Exercises (DTT)

1. If you are in a course where you are using this textbook, it is probably safe to assume that you believe going to college is important to your future in some way. But not everyone believes that a college education is the key to success, or that you even learn things in college that will prepare you for life. Read the two following articles, "I Hate School" by a student, John Hingeley, and "Hire Education" by Marc Levinson (note the play on words: "hire" education not "higher" education). These articles focus on views of college that may be different from your own. Then write a journal entry that addresses your reasons for attending college. Compare and contrast your views with those of the authors of these articles.

2. How might you go about forming a study group? What would be most important to you in forming such a group?

3. What resources are available on your campus that will provide additional academic assistance to those who need it? Share this information with your classmates.

Application Exercises (Your Courses)

1. Examine the course syllabus from a class you are currently taking. What information is included on the syllabus? What information is missing? From reading the syllabus, do you know:

   - weekly reading assignments?
   - when tests are given?
   - how your grade is determined?
   - your instructor's office hours?
   - course policies?

2. For which of your present courses would you consider forming a study group? How would you form it? What factors would be most important to you when forming this group?

3. What resources are available on your campus to provide you with additional academic assistance, should you need it?

4. Interview one of your current instructors. Make an appointment in advance to discuss in more detail the types of tests you will have. Also ask your professor for any studying tips that might help you to be successful in the course. Compare and contrast the tips he or she gave you with those given in this chapter. Report back to the class about how your interview went.

Selections from a Magazine

Hire Education
Marc Levinson

Do you need college to get a good job?

Everybody's heard the news: more than ever before, if you want to make a buck you've gotta have the skills. The payoff to education has increased enormously in the 1990s, and the consequences are reverberating through schools everywhere. Just listen to parents demanding more computers in their third grader's classroom, or to teens who've figured out that dropping out of school means low wages forever. But while everyone talks about preparing today's kids for tomorrow's job market, one obstacle blocks the way. By and large, educators, parents, and students themselves don't have a clue as to what the job market demands.

That's what makes *Teaching the New Basic Skills,* by economists Richard Murnane and Frank Levy, such an important book. Murnane, who teaches at Harvard's Graduate School of Education, and Levy, who's at MIT, are best known for carefully dissecting the causes of America's slow income growth and rising inequality. Remember all those stories about the wage gap? That's Murnane and Levy. But instead of bewailing the problem, Murnane and Levy have turned their research into a practical guide for citizens who are mystified by the information economy. If you worry whether your local schools are preparing kids for good jobs at good wages, this is the book to read.

The underlying story is familiar enough. Workers whose education ended with high school are suffering sharp drops in real wages. That fact, Murnane and Levy say, has led millions of kids to make the hugely expensive mistake of going to college. Yes, college grads earn more, but almost all of that earnings increase can be predicted from a person's math test scores as a high-school senior. They overstate the case a bit; you can't become a big-ticket biochemist without a B.A. But Murnane and Levy assert that there are plenty of middle-class jobs available to high-school grads who skip college—if they've learned the right stuff.

Like what? For Murnane and Levy, "basic skills" mean far more than literacy, numeracy, and knowledge of Western culture's one hundred greatest hits. After studying how a host of companies do their hiring, they conclude that memorizing spelling lists and math tables doesn't make a young person employable. Workers need to be able to apply English and math to solve practical problems. And when it comes to succeeding on the job, initiative, flexibility, and teamwork belong right up there with reading, writing, and math. By pushing "hard" skills alone, they say, "Many of today's schools continue to educate children for an economy that no longer exists."

Murnane and Levy don't refight the old battles over school choice and statewide performance standards. Instead, they offer a startlingly simple suggestion. Each school should evaluate itself as a business might—not with internal measures such as test scores but by looking at how its products fare in the marketplace. The key question: Where are the children who graduated from this school two years ago? If they're not succeeding in their current setting, something is seriously wrong. Drawing on examples like ProTech, a Boston program that combines apprenticeships with a tough curriculum, they show how schools can analyze their own shortcomings and use that information to enlist teachers and parents in a process of change. Schools, unlike businesses, almost never look at how customers value their products. Unless they do, Murnane and Levy argue convincingly, advocates of school reform are just shooting in the dark.

Source: Marc Levinson, "Hire Education." From *Newsweek,* September 30, 1996, p. 52. Copyright © 1996 by Newsweek, Inc. All rights reserved. Reprinted by permission.

I Hate School

John Hingeley
Piedmont Virginia CC,
Charlottesville, Va.

I am a senior enrolled in a medium-size high school in the relatively affluent college town of Charlottesville, Va. Like most seventeen-year-old seniors, I am looking forward to graduating this spring. But unlike the majority of my classmates who are busy applying to colleges and eagerly anticipating the next academic year at a new school, I have applied nowhere. I want no part of college. After twelve excruciating years in America's public schools, the thing I am most looking forward to is a fall and a future free from an educational system that has wholly and without exception alienated me.

Am I a whining, immature, tuned-out malcontent who doesn't like much of anything, including school? No, I am intellectually curious, and I am eager to learn. I have grown up in a family that values education and intellectual accomplishment. My father is a lawyer, and my mother is a college professor. Both of them have a graduate degree, and they have even continued their education after establishing their professions. Throughout my childhood they tried to instill in me and my two brothers a love of learning and a joy in academic achievement, and they have succeeded. So how could someone in my situation end up a senior who hopes never to see the inside of a classroom again?

I ended up in 12th grade hoping never to see the inside of a classroom again precisely *because* I have been in school for twelve years. What have those years been like? Elementary school was reasonably harmless. I learned what I was supposed to learn. I washed my hands before lunch; I didn't run with scissors; and I happily agreed to take turns. I learned to read and write and do basic math, and I absorbed a little information about clouds, inventions, explorers, computers, and so on.

Then came middle school, which in my community begins at fifth grade. From the little close-knit community of my neighborhood school, I was thrust into a huge upper-elementary fifth and sixth grade of 450 students. Here the road to enlightenment began to get rocky. Added to the three R's were band, organized physical education, and even some highly competitive team sports, and classes in health, life issues, and drug-use prevention education. Every one of these supplements to the basic curriculum might sound valuable by itself, but in reality each one was nothing more than a distraction from the real business of learning and amounted to nothing more than time-consuming hoops to jump through to meet some federal or local requirement, often a fad of the times. As a result, in fifth grade my interest in school began to wane.

In seventh and eighth grade began the "accelerated" or advanced classes designed to keep students like me interested and challenged. These Quest classes, forerunners of advanced-placement (AP) courses in high school, were supposedly extremely demanding, difficult to get into, and, therefore, prestigious.

Once I had gained admission to the Quest program, however, I quickly discovered that my hardest work was done—getting into the program. The teachers usually assumed that our being in the program automatically meant that the students were smart and, therefore, didn't need much instruction or guidance. Creativity was encouraged and rewarded, and as in so many other similar situations, bizarre and unconventional ideas and projects without much intellectual merit passed for creative. The result was a different kind of class, but not at all an educational or thought-provoking experience.

All of us eighth graders looked forward to high school. We picked our courses in the late summer and talked about how the exciting and stimulating classes for which we had signed up would be a relief after the drudgery we had just endured. But instead of the academic Eden I had envisioned, I found only more of the same. There were a few interesting courses, to be sure, but they were greatly outnumbered by the useless subjects in the curriculum, making the whole experience frustrating and eventually numbing. In high school we faced for the first time Channel One, a marketing scam under the guise of TV news programs that we students were required to watch. To make matters worse, for the fifth straight year I was enrolled in classes designed solely to teach me to "say no to drugs." I found to my dismay that the AP courses in history, biology, and English were merely prep courses for a standardized test, and the teachers had so much information to cover and were required to move through the material so quickly that no discussion or true understanding was possible. Many of us did well on the tests; not many of us can remember much history or biology. We didn't learn the material; we learned to pass the test.

Contrasted with my actual school experience, what should it have been? I believe that schools and students enter into a contract, an unspoken contract, but a contract nonetheless. The school agrees to educate the students, and the students agree to obey rules, to work hard, and to learn to the best of their ability. Based on my experience and in view of the dropout rate across the country, I believe that public schools are failing to uphold their end of the bargain. Schools fail to live up to their contractual commitment to educate students to be productive members of society and responsible citizens capable of making informed decisions about themselves, their communities, and their nation. Instead schools are social-welfare centers, arenas for political ideologues, and sometimes even farm leagues for college athletic programs. Public schools have let the students down, and consequently, they have let the country down.

My experience could be unique, but I doubt that is so. I suspect that my classmates who will trot off to college like sheep next fall will go, not because their years of primary, middle, and secondary schooling have instilled in them intellectual curiosity or love of learning, but rather simply because freshman year in college is what is expected of them after high school, just as fifth grade followed fourth. I had to go to fifth grade, and sixth, and all the way through 12th, but I've done my time in school. I'm through. *Now* I can begin to get an education.

Source: John Hingeley, "I Hate School" from *Newsweek Education Program,* 1996. Copyright © 1996. Reprinted by permission of the author.

Chapter 3

Finding the Motivation

I think and think for months and years. Ninety-nine times the conclusion is false. The hundredth time I am right.

Albert Einstein

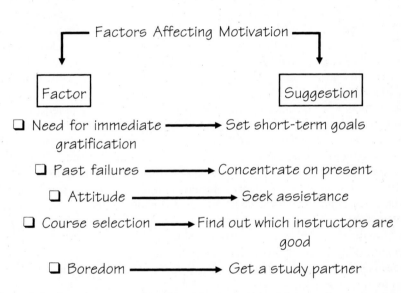

One of the keys to success in college is motivation. With motivation, you can accomplish many things that you may have thought were impossible; without it, you can cut your college career short. You probably know someone who is smart but who does not make good grades. Such students never do homework, rarely study for tests, and show little or no enthusiasm for what occurs in class. In other words, their performance is not in line with their potential. Working up to your potential—being the best that you can be—requires motivation.

Students who are motivated are, as a general rule, successful. They begin their college careers earning good grades and generally continue to do so. Conversely, students who start college unmotivated and therefore make lower grades may continue on that same path until they are either dismissed or become motivated. Success seems to beget success, and failure seems to beget failure. If you begin motivated and maintain your motivation as you progress through your degree program, you will reap the rewards of good grades and a positive self-image.

One of our students told us that it was difficult to earn high grades in college. She was right. In high school, you competed with students from a wider ability range than in college. In college, students are at least average or above average in intelligence and had above-average performance in high school. Therefore, in college you must be motivated in order to compete with students who are at least as intelligent, and maybe even more intelligent, than you are. Think of it this way: You would not have been admitted to your college unless someone felt you had the potential for success. You already possess the potential; now you must consciously provide the motivation. The two attributes go hand in hand. The remainder of this chapter will (1) examine some of the more important factors that affect motivation, and (2) offer some suggestions about how to become motivated and maintain that motivation.

Student Attitude and Responsibility

In college no one looks over your shoulder and tells you to do your homework or to study for tests. Professors want you to succeed, but they will not track you down to find out why you failed to turn in an assignment or why you did poorly on a test. College instructors rarely check to see who appears in class. In short, professors expect students to take responsibility for turning in assignments, doing well on tests, and attending classes. It is not professors' responsibility to motivate you; they expect you to be motivated already. Most instructors are willing to help you if you ask them, but do not expect pampering or sympathy if you are doing poorly yet never attend class.

This is one more major difference between high school and college. In high school, teachers, school administrators, and parents all assumed some responsibility for making sure you went to school, did assignments, and were successful in class. But in college, learning and doing your best in courses is 100 percent your responsibility. This is one of the ways in which college prepares you for your adult life; in a job or career, you are 100 percent responsible for what you do and how well you do it.

This is such an important ingredient to your success in college that we want to repeat the statement: *In college, learning and doing your best in courses is 100 percent your responsibility.* If you think a particular lecturer is boring, it is still your responsibility to go to class and find ways to stay connected with the lecture. If you are taking a course that is not related to your major or interests, you need to take responsibility for creating interest and motivation inside yourself. In this book, we will show you some ways to create interest and maintain attention, but your attitude and taking responsibility for your own learning are the most critical factors.

Immediate Gratification Versus Delayed Gratification

Students often find it difficult to become motivated for something that is two or four years away. It seems to be a universal psychological principle to have the attitude, "I want it, and I want it now!" This is why students who were only lukewarm about going to college when they graduated from high school often decide to find jobs and delay attending college—doing a job and receiving immediate gratification in the form of a paycheck wins out.

Because the big payoff in attending college comes down the road—better jobs, higher salaries, job security—students must look for short-term gratification in other ways in order to remain motivated. This gratification can take several forms: earning good grades, learning new information, meeting new people, and having new experiences. For some first-year students, college is their first time away from home, and thus they are motivated to show family and friends that they can succeed with their new freedom. For others, college follows several years of work experience and the growth of a desire to better one's self. In this situation, motivation may come from wanting to show an employer, wife, husband, or children that the person can be successful. No matter how you receive this gratification, take your accomplishments as they come. Rather than constantly thinking, "Four years from now is a long time!" consider the short term: "I'm really going to celebrate at the end of the term if I make a *B* in this class."

Even more immediate, try to maintain day-to-day motivation by studying first and playing later. Students who attend to their work on a daily basis tend to stay motivated to a higher degree than those who study in a catch-as-catch-can fashion. Even if you are a working student, try to plan your study time from week to week as a way of maintaining motivation.

If Necessary, Wipe Out the Past

As mentioned previously, it is important to get off on the right foot. However, for a variety of reasons many students do not. If you are one of those students who failed to make a good start or who somehow got off track, do not concentrate on blaming yourself! The worst thing you can do is to sit around and think about what an awful person you are and how you have failed. Move on; pick yourself up and try again; wipe out the past. Think positively, and don't dwell on the past but on the future instead. Imagine yourself in a new job as a result of your newfound motivation and success. Imagine yourself halfway through your coursework. Imagine yourself with a 3.0 grade-point average. Imagine yourself with a *B* in a difficult course. Imagine anything positive and nothing negative. Wipe out the past. Don't think about what you did or didn't do but about what you are *going* to do. Tell yourself, "I can," not "I failed."

Developing the Big M

Just as no one is born a Republican or a Democrat, no one is born with motivation. Motivation, like political persuasion, is developed and learned over a period of time. Unfortunately, there is no magic formula for developing it or for teaching it. Researchers really cannot explain why some people have motivation and some people do not, or why some people suddenly become motivated. We know that role models play a key part in the process. That is, if your parents are highly motivated and work hard, or if your peers tend to be motivated toward success, you stand a better chance of following in their footsteps. However, this is not always the case.

CALVIN AND HOBBES © 1988 Watterson. Dist. by UNIVERSAL PRESS
SYNDICATE. Reprinted with permission. All rights reserved.

Another thing that is known about the Big M is that it tends to compensate for some academic weaknesses. Students who, within reason, score lower on the SAT or ACT but who are motivated to learn and study as reflected by high school grade-point averages stand a better chance of being successful in college. In fact, a study by the New York Public Interest Research Group found that the SAT is only slightly better than random chance (50–50) in predicting students' college performance. One reason for this finding is that motivation is reflected much more in individuals' high school grades accumulated over four years than in one standardized test score taken at one point in time (such as the SAT).

If you are not motivated to do well in college, one of the things that you should do immediately is to examine the reasons why you are attending college. Most of the students we have worked with who have not done well did not really want to be in college. Some were there because their parents forced them to go; others were there because they were too unmotivated to work, so they saw college as a way to delay taking responsibility for themselves. Even older students who decide to go to college some years after they have graduated from high school often attend because of family pressure or job boredom, rather than because their goal is to obtain a college degree. Motivation is highest when you are doing something because you want to do it.

Another reason students are unmotivated is that they cannot choose a major. Many students who begin college without a career focus lose motivation. Again, family members often enter the picture negatively in this situation by getting frustrated when John changes majors and thus loses credits every term. Also frustrated, John gives up and loses his motivation. In this situation, no one wins. This is not to say that everyone should know exactly what he or she wants to major in, and that highly motivated people never change majors. The point is that if you have no idea what you want to major in, you should get help during your first year or two. Most college campuses offer assistance and counseling to students to help them to become more focused on a career choice. Even if you can begin by identifying a general area—"I know that I want to major in business"—it then becomes easier to identify what aspect of business will most interest you. Often, the feeling that you are doing something to explore different careers will motivate you to want to do well in your courses.

Maintaining a Positive Attitude

It is rare—and sad—that individuals who have managed to survive twelve years of formal education cannot objectively evaluate themselves positively. Most of us have been conditioned to stand up and take notice of the things we have done wrong, while virtually ignoring the things we have done right. It is the rare teacher who will compliment students for getting five out of ten answers correct because that is only 50 percent—and we all know that 50 percent is equivalent to the letter grade of *F*. What we have heard over and over is that we got five wrong, not five right. In the workplace, similar scenarios occur. Bosses rarely pat employees on the back for a job well done, but employees certainly find out if they have done something wrong. With so many negative encounters in school, at work, and even at home, it is not surprising that so many students enter college with negative opinions of themselves, particularly with negative opinions of themselves as learners.

If this has been your experience, try to be aware of it. Think about all the times that someone pointed out your mistakes, and learn from them. In everything you do, try to find something positive that you have done or learned as a result of the experience. Maximize your successes and downplay your failures. Learning from your failures is one way to maintain a positive attitude. Ignore neither your successes nor your failures, but do not dwell on the negatives.

If you are having academic trouble, do something about it. Just taking any of the following actions is often enough to restore or maintain a positive attitude:

- Talk to your professor to find out what you are doing wrong in terms of class and test preparation.
- If your professor is not helpful, see if your campus has a learning center or tutorial services.
- Seek the assistance of others in your class by forming a study group (see Chapter 2).
- Trade services with someone who needs help in a subject in which you are strong.
- If you can afford it, pay for a tutor; nothing helps you improve more rapidly (either mentally or physically) than having to pay for it.

Getting help when you are in academic trouble is important. It is a fact of life that in order to maintain a positive attitude and motivation you must have more academic successes than failures. Remember what we said earlier: Success begets success. Hence the sooner you get help, begin experiencing academic success, and view yourself in a positive light, the sooner you will be motivated to maintain that success.

Selecting Courses: What's in It for You?

The courses you select play a key role in your level of motivation. Because of this, there are several factors to keep in mind as you register for your classes.

1. *If possible, select at least one course every term in which you have a relatively high degree of interest.* Usually this is not so much of a problem once you get into your major area of study because most students are more interested in their major. However, core courses—those introductory or basic courses that all students are required to take—are a different matter. It makes sense that the higher the interest, the higher the motivation.

2. *Once you decide on the courses you want to take, ask around about professors.* Keep in mind that the easiest professor is not necessarily the best. Try to get instructors who generate interest in their subject matter, care about

students' learning, are good lecturers, and give fair and well-written exams. Remember that a good professor can often compensate for what would normally be boring subject matter. A good instructor can also change your perceptions about what is boring. If you like a subject or if you like the professor, your motivation will usually be higher.

3. *Do not overload your schedule.* Nothing affects motivation more severely than having no time for simple relaxation and fun. Students who have such a difficult schedule that they have no time to themselves or for socializing often become frustrated, angry, and ultimately unmotivated. (We will discuss scheduling more when we introduce time management in the next chapter.) Be reasonable in scheduling so that you can comfortably fit everything in. If you work or have a family, it is particularly important that you think about other obligations when you are registering for courses.

4. *The underloaded schedule can be equally problematic.* Students who have too much unstructured time either become bored or fritter away large blocks of time. For students with too much time on their hands, going to *any* class often becomes a chore. In addition, having too light a load one term often forces students to overload their schedule the next. The moral of the story is to strike a balance when you schedule your courses.

Fighting Boredom

Another key reason students lack motivation or become unmotivated is that they view most of their courses as boring. As stated earlier, if you have selected your courses wisely, that should take care of part of the problem. However, even the most cautious and selective students sometimes select losers or, in some instances, may have little of interest to choose from when registering for classes.

Should you find yourself in this unfortunate position, there are several things you can do, most of them psychological, to stay motivated through the term.

1. *Most courses do have some interesting aspects. Search for these aspects by trying to personalize them in some way.* Using your own experiences to make what you read and study more applicable to your own life may lessen the boredom. One student made information on Social Security interesting by thinking what it must be like for his grandparents to live on their fixed income. It made him start thinking about the importance of some kind of supplemental retirement plan, something the average nineteen-year-old probably does not ponder with any degree of regularity.

2. *A really boring class is more easily tolerated if you study with someone.* The old adage "Misery loves company" is certainly true. Divide the workload by developing rehearsal strategies for the tests (see Chapter 10) and share them with the people with whom you study. Although you will still have to read the material, attend class, and take good notes, dividing the work and studying with others help improve motivation.

3. *Study uninteresting course material in small doses by giving it daily attention and, as much as possible, studying it first.* Many students make the mis-

take of either putting off the boring class until they are so far behind that it is very difficult to catch up or studying their interesting classes first with good intentions of getting to their boring class last. More often than not, students manage to avoid the boring class by using excuses such as "I'm tired" or "I promise myself I'll get to it tomorrow." If either of these scenarios sounds familiar, shift your studying priorities.

Finally, if all else fails, try the psychological game of "It only lasts one term, and I can do anything for that period of time." Try to put the time period in perspective. For example, if your school is on a quarter system, what are ten weeks out of an entire lifetime? Remember that time is relative; in the big picture, a term of school is only a tiny fragment of your life.

Key Ideas

Motivation is probably the most important aspect of being a successful student. Those who are adequately motivated have a stronger likelihood of success in college and in life than those who are smart but unmotivated. Because motivation is something that is learned rather than biologically transmitted from parent to child, anyone who is unmotivated can *become* motivated; anyone who is already motivated can maintain that motivation with a little effort. There are numerous ways to acquire and maintain motivation. For example:

1. Set short-term goals for yourself so that you receive some kind of immediate gratification.
2. If you have not been very motivated in the past, turn over a new leaf. Put failures behind you and concentrate on your newfound successes.
3. If you are not motivated, examine the reasons why.
4. Make sure that you have career goals or are at least exploring the possibilities.
5. Maintain a positive attitude about yourself as a learner.
6. Select your courses and plan your schedule with care to maximize motivation.
7. Try to personalize learning to make it more interesting.

▮ Two Scenarios to Write About and Discuss

Think about these scenarios and the questions that follow them, and write down your ideas. Then discuss your answers with others in your class.

Scenario I

You are having a lot of trouble keeping up with all the reading and assignments for your classes. Part of the problem seems to be that you are not very interested in the courses. You keep putting off doing any of the work as long as you can, then when you do study, you feel overwhelmed.

What ideas from this chapter could you use to build up your interest and motivation? What might you do differently next term so you do not repeat the same problem?

Scenario 2

Your roommate, who wants to major in computer sciences, has slept late and missed the first class of the day for six weeks in a row. This class is an introductory course in American literature. Your roommate says, "Why should I go to classes that are not part of my major field? I'm not interested in American lit. at all. Besides, we covered some of that in high school. They should just let us take courses we're interested in."

What do you think of your roommate's arguments? What reasons could you suggest for going to class? Are there ways that your roommate could create interest in the course content? How else might your roommate take more responsibility for his or her learning?

Application Exercises (DTT)

1. Write about your level of motivation. Which aspects of this chapter apply to you? What might you do to either maintain or improve your motivation?

2. Interview a classmate about his or her motivation. When is your classmate most highly motivated? How is he or she like or different from you in the area of motivation?

3. Keep a motivation diary for a minimum of one week. Write in this diary on a daily basis, and discuss when and why you are extremely motivated, moderately motivated, and unmotivated. Share this diary with classmates for similar experiences.

4. Read the article "First Born, Later Born" at the end of this chapter. It is about the theory that birth order—whether you are the oldest, middle, or youngest child in a family—influences us in many ways. What differences are suggested in the article? Do you and your friends fit the descriptions of first-born and later-born? Do you agree with the scientists who believe that birth order causes these differences? Or do you agree with scientists who argue against the importance of birth order? What does this article suggest about motivation? What motivates a firstborn? A later-born? What does this suggest about *your* motivations?

5. Read the article "For $6,000 . . ." at the end of this chapter. Write a "response" entry for your journal about the article. (Response journals are described in Chapter 1.) Discuss your response with others in your class.

Application Exercise (Your Courses)

Write a journal entry that focuses on a course in which you were extremely motivated and on one in which you had a low degree of motivation. What were the elements of each? What caused the difference in your level of motivation? What would you do to compensate for low motivation now?

Selection from a Magazine

First Born, Later Born, Rebel or Reactionary?

Geoffrey Cowley

A new book says it's due to your place in the family structure.

When twenty-two-year-old Charles Darwin set out in 1831 to circle the globe on the HMS Beagle, his mind lay squarely in the mainstream. He assumed that life forms were fixed entities, each one handcrafted by God for its special place in nature. But during his travels, Darwin started noticing things that didn't fit the paradigm. Why, he wondered, would finches and iguanas assume distinct but related forms on adjacent islands? And when Darwin proposed a revolutionary solution—that all nature's variety stems from a simple process that preserves useful variations and discards harmful ones—the authorities were appalled. "A scientific mistake," thundered Louis Agassiz, then the world's leading naturalist—"untrue in its facts . . . and mischievous in its tendency."

What drives people like Darwin to stick pins in conventional wisdom? And why do radical innovations so enrage people like Agassiz? To Frank Sulloway, a science historian at MIT, it's no coincidence that Darwin was the fifth of six kids in his family, or that Agassiz was the firstborn in his. Sulloway has spent two decades gathering data on thousands of people involved in historic controversies—from the Copernican revolution to the Protestant Reformation—and running statistical tests to see what sets rebels apart from reactionaries. His findings . . . suggest that "the foremost engine of historical change" is not the church, state, or economy but family structure. Sulloway makes a compelling case that firstborns, whatever their age, sex, class, or nationality, specialize in defending the status quo while later-borns specialize in toppling it. Indeed, he says, people with the same birthranks have more in common with each other than they do with their own siblings.

It's an audacious claim (Sulloway himself is a later-born), and not one that social scientists will flock to embrace. Birth-order research, for all its intuitive appeal, has a reputation for flakiness. "Both laypeople and experts tend to over-interpret the importance of birth order," says Joseph Rodgers, a psychologist at the University of Oklahoma. "There are very few birth-order effects." In a 1983 review of 2,000 studies dating to the 1940s, the Swiss psychologists Cecile Ernst and Jules Angst declared that since most had failed to control for variables like social class and family size, none could be taken seriously. Sulloway agrees that much of the past research has been marred by weak hypotheses and poor methods. But his own study tackles many of the issues left unresolved by earlier ones, and some experts are raving about it. "It's a monumental work of scholarship," says Sarah Blaffer Hardy, an anthropologist at the University of California, Davis. "I think it will change the way all of us think about ourselves and our families."

Most of us already have a seat-of-the-pants sense of how birthrank affects personality. Firstborns are by reputation the list makers and control freaks. "Show me a librarian who's not a firstborn," says pop psychologist Kevin Leman, author of *The Birth Order Book* and *Growing Up First Born.* "They live by the Dewey Decimal System." Firstborns are supposedly at home in trades like accounting and architecture—and maybe airline piloting. Walter Cronkite, Peter Jennings, and Ted Koppel are all firstborns or only children. Chevy Chase, Danny DeVito, and Jay Leno are last-borns. Psychologists have theorized about sibling differences since the 1920s, when Freud's estranged disciple Alfred Adler alleged that firstborns spend their lives getting over their displacement by younger brothers and sisters. But the models have been vague enough to accommodate almost any real-world observation—or its opposite. Adler, for example, argued that last-borns are often spoiled and lazy because they don't have younger siblings challenging them. He also characterized them as go-getters, hardened by incessant competition with their elders. Take your pick.

Sulloway starts not by spinning random hypotheses but by thinking about the Darwinian pressures that foster sibling competition throughout the natural world. Parental support is often the key to a youngster's survival—and siblings are often the primary obstacle. When food is scarce, chicks in a nest may gang up to murder the youngest member of the brood, without a peep of parental protest. Humans harbor similar propensities. Many societies accord firstborns higher status than later-borns, and some still condone killing a newborn in times of scarcity, just to ensure an older child's survival. Sibling competition may take different forms in the New Jersey suburbs than it does among peasants facing starvation. But firstborns and later-borns still confront very different pressures and opportunities. And by Sulloway's reckoning, their experiences should foster very different qualities of character.

How, exactly, should they differ? Firstborns, who grow up knowing they're "bigger, stronger, and smarter than their younger siblings," should be more assertive and dominant. They should also be more jealous and status-conscious, having seen their untrammeled turf invaded by newcomers. Their early experience as parents' lieutenants should make them more conscientious than later-borns. And the favoritism they enjoy should leave them more closely wedded to their parents' values and standards. Later-borns, since they can't get their way by force or bluster, should be more sociable and agreeable. And their lesser stake in the established family order should leave them more open to novelty and innovation.

Sulloway has found ingenious ways of testing these hypotheses. By sifting through the 2,000 studies that Ernst and Angst discarded in 1983, he found 196 in which researchers had factored out differences in social class and family size before looking for birth-order effects. And those studies, which included nearly 121,000 participants, supported his predictions about each of the five personality dimensions that psychological tests look for. Birth order was a lousy predictor of extroversion, a category so broad that it could encompass both a firstborn's assertiveness and a later-born's backslapping sociability. But most studies found that firstborns were more neurotic than were later-borns, and more conscientious (as in responsible, organized, and achievement-oriented). Later-borns were consistently deemed more agreeable, and they were overwhelmingly more open to experience. People without siblings fell somewhere between firstborns and later-borns on most personality measures, but they were no more open to experience than were firstborns.

So far, so good. But did these psychological tests say anything about how people would behave out in the world? That's where Sulloway's historical surveys come into play. To get at the roots of real-life radicalism, he compiled biographical data on 6,566 people who have played public roles in scientific or political controversies over the past five centuries. By having panels of historians rate these players on their resistance or receptivity to the innovations they confronted, he was able to plot their "openness to experience" in relation to everything from birth order to age, sex, race, temperament, social class, family size, and even the tenor of their family relationships.

In one case after another, the influence of birth order is remarkable. Later-borns were more likely than firstborns were to support each of the sixty-one liberal causes Sulloway surveyed, from the Protestant Reformation to the American civil-rights movement. Indeed birth order rivaled race as a predictor of who would support the abolition of slavery during the mid-1800s. Firstborns and later-borns differ more in their styles of thought than in their core beliefs— liberals can be rigidly doctrinaire and conservatives can be open to new ways of thinking. But the last-borns in Sulloway's survey were eighteen times more likely to take up left-wing causes than to get involved in conservative ones, such as the temperance movement. Not surprisingly, Mahatma Gandhi and Martin Luther King Jr. were all later-borns, as were Leon Trotsky, Fidel Castro, Yasir Arafat, and Ho Chi Minh. Rush Limbaugh, George Wallace, and Newt Gingrich are all firstborns.

The pattern was just as clear when Sulloway examined twenty-eight scientific controversies. Later-borns were five times more likely than firstborns were to support the Copernican and Darwinian revolutions—and nine times more likely to embrace phrenology, a wacky 19th-century fad that involved divining character from the shape of a person's skull. By contrast, Sulloway found that "conservative innovations," such as the eugenics movement, have consistently been spearheaded by firstborns and opposed by later-borns.

Are You a Rebel?

Later-borns are said to be more receptive to unconventional thinking. How do you match up? In section one, find the description closest to yours and enter the numerical value in the box. For each item in section two, enter the numerical value indicated, then add or subtract. The resulting score suggests your receptivity to unorthodox ideas.

Section one

Under age 30	Firstborns	Middle	Last-borns
Social conservatives	14	40	49
Social moderates	48	77	84
Social liberals	75	92	96
Age 30 to 59			
Social conservatives	6	22	26
Social moderates	25	58	66
Social liberals	52	82	86
Age 60 or over			
Social conservatives	3	12	15
Social moderates	15	44	50
Social liberals	36	72	76

Enter your score here

Section two

1. Pronounced conflict with parent
   Firstborns add 30; later-borns add 10
2. Gender
   Women add 5; men no adjustment
3. Pronounced shyness
   Firstborns add 20; middle-borns no adjustment;
   last-borns subtract 15
4. Early loss of a parent
   Firstborn who acted as surrogate subtract 15;
   later-born raised by surrogate add 15
5. Race
   Minorities add 10

Add all entries: this is your final score

Your rebel score: −12 to 24 = intolerant of new ideas; 25 to 61 = resistant; 62 to 99 = supportive; 100 to 136 = enthusiastic

Source: "Born to Rebel" by Frank J. Sulloway

This isn't to say that birth order is all that counts in life, or even in the contentious worlds of science and politics. "These are statistical patterns, not physical laws," says Harvard evolutionist Ernst Mayr. "There are always exceptions." Isaac Newton was a firstborn, for example, and Adolf Hitler wasn't. Sulloway is the first to admit that the effects of birth order can be offset, exaggerated or even overridden by other factors. Indeed, he devotes much of [a] new book to plotting the ways in which different influences interact. Gender has a huge and obvious impact on personality. But studies have found that firstborn girls are typically more confident, assertive, and verbally aggressive than their younger brothers or sisters are. By the same token, age makes most people less open-minded, regardless of their birthrank. Within Sulloway's sample, young later-borns were more than twice as likely as elderly ones were to embrace the idea of evolution during the 19th century. But eighty-year-old later-borns were still more receptive than thirty-year-old firstborns.

Like age, certain features of a person's innate temperament can mask the effects of birth order. Congenital shyness, for example, tends to minimize birth-order differences. By placing a damper on other aspects of character, it makes firstborns less arch and later-borns less outwardly subversive. Likewise, extroversion tends to magnify the contrast. It might lead a firstborn to become a drill sergeant instead of a bank teller, and a last-born to do stand-up comedy instead of writing poems. Conflict with a parent can also offset a firstborn's conformist ways. Once estranged from the familial status quo and pushed into the underdog role, says Sulloway, anyone becomes more radical.

Sulloway's findings are sure to strike a chord with lay readers, but social scientists may not appreciate his chutzpah. In the years since Ernst and Angst declared birth order meaningless, few researchers have bothered to look at it, and many of those who have tried have been disappointed. In a recent book titled *Birth Order and Political Behavior,* Alfred University political scientist Steven Peterson and two colleagues describe how they analyzed a huge list of eminent figures to see if it was dominated by firstborns. When they came up dry, they assumed there was nothing left to study. "There are always some people who are going to say, 'Gee, you just didn't look at enough variables'," says Peterson's collaborator Alan Arwine. "It's like trying to kill a vampire." But Arwine and Peterson's findings don't contradict Sulloway's. They merely answer a less interesting question. "The question isn't whether firstborns are more eminent than later-borns," Sulloway insists. "Eminence isn't even a personality trait. It's an outcome. What's interesting is that firstborns and later-borns become eminent in different ways."

Other critics will dismiss Sulloway's whole approach. "From what I read, it's not scientific," says Toni Falbo, a professor of educational psychology at the University of Texas at Austin. "He looks at special cases. If you're looking at special cases, particularly in history, you can find a case that fits almost any hypothesis you want." By her logic, history is just an endless series of special cases, not a lawful process that can be illuminated through hypothesis testing. Sulloway's real accomplishment is to show that's not the case. His "special cases" span five centuries and many countries, yet they repeatedly confirm his predictions. "Frank attacks questions that could not be more contingent," says John Tooby, an anthropologist at the University of California, Santa Barbara— "why some countries ended up Protestant, why France resisted Darwinism, who ended up in which faction in the French National Assembly—and shows that they fit into larger patterns."

Sulloway doesn't claim to have solved any ultimate questions. He plans to expand his database, test new predictions, and publish a revised edition of the book every five years or so. "The publisher put that in my contract," he says. "It was the only way I could make myself stop and publish this." Anyone who can stomach a revolution should be glad that he did.

For $6,000, You Get a Pencil
with the Answers Included

Adam Rogers

Federal agents break up a cheating ring charged with beating graduate-school entrance exams

It was a sweet little scam, as the Feds tell it. Prospective students respond to an ad promising a "unique" method that guarantees high scores on several standardized tests required for entry by most graduate schools. They have to pay up to $6,000 and get to Los Angeles. On the day of the exam, confederates in New York take the test and, taking advantage of the three-hour time difference, phone the West Coast ringleader with the answers. In L.A., the paying clients then receive the answers, carefully inscribed in a secret code on the side of pencils. The guarantee is good: They ace their tests.

Three years into the con, it went sour. According to Mark Godsey, an assistant U.S. attorney, one of the clients for the Oct. 19 Graduate Management Admission Test was an undercover postal inspector. A week later, federal agents charged Po Chieng Ma, the owner of the American Test Center in El Monte, Calif., with two counts of mail and wire fraud. . . . If convicted, Ma faces up to ten years in prison and a hefty fine. But now, critics of the Educational Testing Service, which administers the tests, want to know how ETS could have missed the scheme for so long. And university deans are preparing for bad news, trying to decide what to do if they find that one of their students was an exam cheater.

Ma's alleged plan wasn't entirely new. Four years ago ETS broke up a less well organized (though apparently successful) effort to hack the Scholastic Aptitude Test, another ETS product, using the time-zone quirk. But Ma is also accused of providing fake identities for the expert test-takers in New York and taking the tests himself a few times. He's apparently no stranger to aliases—the Feds swore out their complaint against "George Kobayashi," the name used in the scam, but he was incarcerated as Ma. The authorities didn't get that worked out until Thursday afternoon, when they tried to arraign Kobayashi and learned he didn't exist.

According to the complaint, Ma would pick up his clients at Los Angeles International Airport in a black Mercedes the day before the test and drive them to a hotel. There, Ma laid out the plan and had the undercover agent sign a confession, which Ma threatened to send to ETS if he didn't get his $6,000 on time. The next day Ma and his staff drove their clients to various testing locations around L.A., spread out so their impending high scores wouldn't arouse suspicions. The agent reported that Ma rode along with two carloads of clients to a local university campus where the test was to be administered. In the parking lot, Ma took a call on a cellular phone and then announced the essay questions. He proved to be correct. During a break, the agent went outside and Ma gave him the coded pencils. The undercover op finished the test, though his score has not been released.

How could such a scam go on for so long? "ETS has been told repeatedly about this security hole for ten years, by me, and done nothing about it," says John Katzman, president of The Princeton Review, a major test-preparation company. Katzman and representatives of his main competitor, Kaplan Educational Centers (which is owned by *Newsweek*'s corporate parent, The *Washington Post*), say that ETS has consistently ignored or confounded their attempts to alert it to security problems. ETS denies those charges. "There are many instances where we have thwarted and foiled efforts to compromise test security that never received the notoriety that this one has," says Stanford von Mayrhauser, ETS's general counsel. David Wilson, president of the Graduate Management Admission Council, which sponsors the GMAT, says that the Postal Service uncovered the scheme by following up on a tip from ETS security, whose scoring algorithms picked up unusual performance by one of the alleged cheaters. That student blew the whistle to the Feds. Neither von Mayrhauser nor Wilson would discuss plans for specific security changes.

There's one group very worried about its security: the customers who took part in the alleged scam. What happens to Ma's clients, some of whom are already in graduate school? Godsey says he can't discuss how many other people might be involved or what kind of action could be taken against them. But von Mayrhauser says ETS could cancel scores and notify schools. "It would be a very serious character and integrity violation that might well involve separation from the program," says George Parker, director of the M.B.A. program at Stanford University.

But if the fix has been in for three years, as the Feds allege, then a few cheaters might have already graduated. "I think you're probably facing something like a statute-of-limitations problem," Parker says. "The number of degrees that are revoked is very small." In other words, if they've made it through the system and into the work force, they may be home free. Unless a dormant conscience proves hard to live with.

Chapter 4

Finding the Time

Winning is a habit. Unfortunately, so is losing.

Vince Lombardi

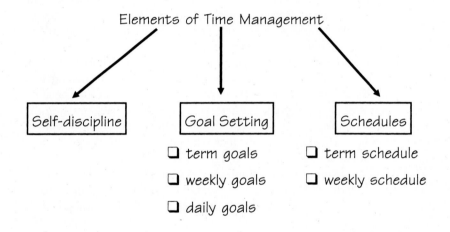

After motivation, the next most important characteristic that college students can possess is the ability to manage their time in an effective manner. Do you know people who are chronically late for everything? No matter how hard these individuals might try, they never seem to get anywhere on time. And if you are a person who is always punctual, people like this probably drive you crazy.

This chapter examines some ways to help you manage your time so that even if you are chronically late, you can follow these hints to use your time more effectively. If you already tend to be on time for things, the information in this chapter may help you to budget your time even more efficiently.

Self-Discipline

Up through high school, most students have parents who keep after them to do their schoolwork. You probably hated to hear questions such as "Is your homework done?" or "Did you study for that big history test?" Perhaps worse yet were the threats: "No, you cannot have the car until your homework is completed" or "You know what will happen if you don't get all *B*'s on your report card. You'll never get into college." Sound familiar? But as much as you may have hated these reminders, they probably served a purpose of which you were unaware—they kept you on task. For whatever reasons, parental pressure helped you get things done, and your parents could be at least partly responsible for your presence in college. But today is a different story.

One of our students told us that it was very hard for her to become self-disciplined once she arrived at college. Her parents had always kept her on track. She was from a relatively large family that saw the value in, and the importance of, an education. Hence, on every school night, between 7:00 P.M. and 9:00 P.M., the television was turned off, and everyone in the house studied. Mom and Dad read, and if the children didn't have any written homework, they studied or read. But when Barbara got to college, there was no one there to force her to study. At first she rationalized that she was only taking three classes, not six as in high school, so there really was not any need to spend two or more hours every night preparing for class. She pledged a sorority, got involved in other clubs, had a very active social life, and, in general, was having a marvelous time. However, after she took her first tests, Barbara's grades were not so marvelous—two *D*'s and an *F*.

Barbara's motivation to get organized so that she could improve her grades was initially still due to her parents. She kept thinking about how disappointed they were going to be in her, but she also realized that she was disappointed in herself. She knew that she was capable of doing the work, but that she had not yet managed to find the self-discipline needed to get the job done. She frittered away large amounts of time, planned no set study schedule, and had an unbalanced proportion of play-to-study time. It was only when Barbara motivated herself and learned how to use her time to her advantage that she was able to turn things around. And although her grades that first term were not great (she managed to pull all *C*'s), she went on to become a Dean's List student.

Unfortunately, not every student's story ends as positively as Barbara's. Many students never manage to develop that first step of self-discipline, nor do they learn the art of budgeting their time wisely. Sometimes it is difficult to remember that everyone has the same number of hours in a day. Although some have more activities to cram into those twenty-four hours, everyone has to learn how to manage his or her time efficiently to be successful. If you are willing to exhibit some self-discipline, you can take steps to ensure that you have adequate time for all of your activities.

Setting Goals

In the chapter on motivation, we discussed taking responsibility for your learning and the importance of goal-setting. We made the point that it was easier to maintain motivation once you have relatively clear goals and continue to set new goals once the old ones have been achieved. The same idea holds true when discussing time-management issues. Students who manage their time efficiently and effectively generally have set goals for themselves and are willing to modify their lifestyles in order to achieve those goals.

When most students enter college, their most obvious aim is to obtain a degree. But such a long-term goal is not sufficient. College students need to set goals for each term, goals for each week, and still smaller goals for each day. That is why it is important to write down your goals. At the beginning of each term, set several goals for yourself. Goals such as "I want to make all *B*'s in my classes" or "This term my goal is to give daily attention to each of my classes" help you to stay focused. Hang your list of goals in a prominent place. Share your goals with friends and family. Make your goals realistic, so that you do not set yourself up for failure. If you have three extremely difficult courses, maybe you need to modify your goals to be happy with two *C*'s and one *B*, rather than all *B*'s. Also remember that because these goals are more global in nature, set only a few goals. Two or three overall goals for a term would be reasonable; eight or ten would be too many.

Once you have defined your goals for the term, reset weekly goals each week. These goals should be more specific than the term goals but should, in some way, reflect the term goals. For instance, if one of your term goals was to receive a grade of *B* in your psychology class, one of your weekly goal sheets for the class might be:

Weekly Goal Sheet

1. Start to do research for psychology paper (due in three weeks).

2. Read and annotate Chapters 4 and 6.

3. Make concept cards and maps for Chapters 1–3 in preparation for a test in two weeks.

Notice several things about these goals. First, this student knows the importance of preparing for tests and beginning to write papers early. Second, she knows the differences between reading, studying, and reviewing. Note that she is just beginning to read two of the chapters, but for the chapters that she has already read, she is ready to make a variety of rehearsal strategies. Finally, if she carries out these goals, she is working toward that overall goal of receiving at least a *B* grade in the psychology course. (Later chapters will deal with each of these issues.)

The final type of goals that you should set are daily goals. Daily goals are best done in the form of what many call "To Do" lists. These lists should be made either just before you go to bed or right before you get started for the day. Put your lists on 3 × 5 cards and then paperclip them to your notebook or put them in your pocket or purse. Many people think that the only individuals who use "To Do" lists are those with poor memories. Not so. Students are busy people who have numerous responsibilities to juggle. Without some sort of daily plan, they often leave important things undone. Most students do not mean to forget; it is just that there are so many activities that forgetting is easy to do.

The "To Do" list also lets you see what you have already accomplished and what you have yet to do. Therefore, try to prioritize your list, putting those things you *must* get done at the top; place lower-priority items further down the list. As you complete your tasks, cross them off and proceed to the next item on the list. It may be only a psychological phenomenon, but it gives you a sense of accomplishment when you can see all of the things that you have managed to get done. If you still have tasks left on your list at the end of the day, make them your top-priority items for the following day. You will be surprised that once you become used to setting goals and making "To Do" lists, it will be difficult to stop.

Once again, your daily goals should reflect your overall goals as well as your weekly goals. In addition, most students like to include activities on their lists other than those that are course related. If we continue with the example we used previously, a daily "To Do" list for the psychology class might be:

To Do

1. Spend one hour in library (psychology research).

2. Read and annotate Chapter 4.

3. Map Chapter 1.

4. Do laundry (I have no clean clothes).

5. Call home before my parents disown me.

6. Sorority meeting tonight.

It is important for everyone to have goals. When you no longer have goals, it is more difficult to get things done and certainly more difficult to manage your time. The next section will help you become a more efficient student, with enough time to accomplish all of your goals. As a means of supplementing goals and arranging specific times to meet all of your goals, we will discuss scheduling.

Schedules

Because everyone has twenty-four hours a day in which to get things accomplished, it seems reasonable to think that you should be able to get everything done in that period of time. But for most people, time always seems too fleeting. If we start by examining realistically the amount of time we have, it is easy to see how much of it we waste. An average student's daily accounted-for time may look something like this:

Sleep	8 hours
Class	3 hours
Eating	2 hours
Total	13 hours

That still leaves eleven hours every day for obligations other than eating, sleeping, and attending class. The point of this example is to show that each of us probably has plenty to time to take care of all of our obligations; it is just that we do not do a very good job of budgeting that time. Even students who work three or four hours a day still have seven or eight hours for studying and recreation. But it takes some effort to manage time so that you can fit everything in.

Another way to think about the amount of time you should be devoting to being a student is to think about it as being your job. Most people who work full-time are expected to put in forty hours a week on the job. As a full-time student, you should also think about putting in forty hours a week in student-related activities. You can spread your forty hours any way you like. For example, some students are really tired by the time Friday rolls around and know that they are not able to accomplish anything school-related at that time. But after a bit of rest on Saturday, they feel rejuvenated enough to spend several hours Sunday afternoon or evening staying on top of their schoolwork. As mentioned earlier, use your own rhythms to organize your time, but use the "forty-hour workweek" as a good rule of thumb as you devise your schedule. This should not only guarantee your success as a student, but also help you move toward the world of work later on.

Term Schedules

You have seen the importance of goal-setting. Now let us examine how to get everything accomplished as a way of meeting those goals.

You will need to construct two types of schedules in order to organize and budget your time wisely: a term schedule and a weekly schedule. Just before each term begins, after you have your class schedule and know what additional obligations you will have, make a schedule for the term.

The schedule should follow a format such as that presented in Figure 4.1. To make your term schedule, first block out all of your set obligations—that is, things you must do. This includes being in class, sleeping, working (if you have a job), eating, going to religious services—any obligation that is set and that you are relatively sure will remain stable throughout the term. If you plan to work but are not sure how many hours weekly or daily, estimate as best as you can.

Next, look for blocks of time and fill in other obligations that require consistent attention yet are more flexible in terms of when they can be inserted into your day. These activities would include studying, spending time with friends, or miscellaneous activities such as doing laundry, cleaning your room or apartment, or shopping. Make sure that you include things that are often oversights. For example, if you have a favorite television show that you simply must watch, make sure that you include it. Finally, check your schedule for balance. Answer the following questions:

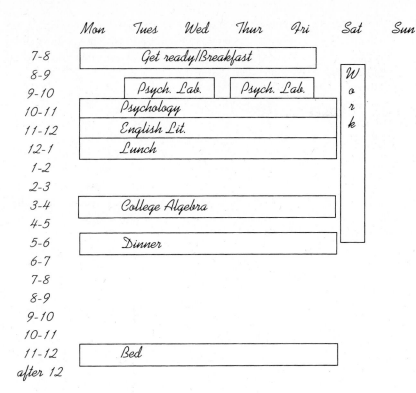

Figure 4.1 Scheduling Blocks of Time

1. Do you have an adequate amount of study time?
2. Do you have an adequate amount of recreation time?
3. Is there a balance between study time and recreation time?
4. How much time is unexplained—time during which nothing is being done?
5. Have you left enough time for miscellaneous activities?
6. Have you built in some flexible time in case of an emergency?

Your final schedule should resemble the one shown in Figure 4.2.

Just as your term goals should be realistic, your schedule should follow suit. Keep in mind that you are making the schedule for yourself, not to impress someone else. An unrealistic schedule that you have little intention of following serves no purpose. Remember that the aim of the schedule is to help you to organize your time more efficiently and effectively so that you can accomplish everything.

After you have made and feel comfortable with your overall schedule for the term, try it out during the first week or so of classes. Determine its shortcomings. Is one of your classes much easier or harder than you anticipated?

Does your boss want you to work additional or fewer hours? Is your recreation time adequate? Are you allowing too much time for play and not enough time for work? After you think about these and other modifications that you need to make, you are ready to prepare weekly schedules.

Weekly Schedules

You will make a weekly schedule in the same way you made your term schedule—that is, by blocking out all of your set obligations and then filling in study time, recreation time, and so forth. The major difference between the two types of schedules is that you can be considerably more specific with the weekly schedule. For instance, rather than just blocking in study time, you can actually earmark study time for a particular subject or add more time for rehearsing and reviewing several days prior to a big exam.

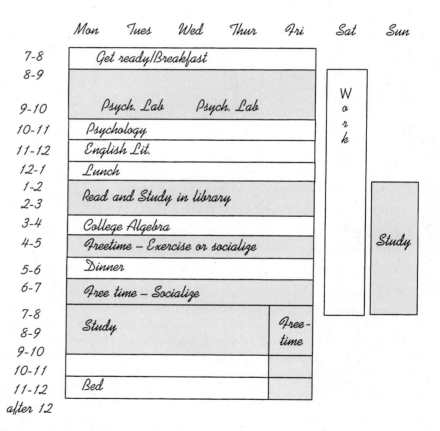

Figure 4.2 Fleshing Out Your Schedule

Here are a few guidelines to help you set your weekly schedule:

- *On average, schedule two to three hours of study time for every hour of class time.* Courses vary greatly in this respect, but if you are unsure about how much time to study for a course, start by scheduling in three hours of study per hour of class.

- *Schedule study time for your most difficult courses at times when you are most alert.* Everyone has "power periods" when he or she seems to learn best. Use these periods to tackle the most difficult classes.

- *Schedule your study time based on your ability to concentrate.* Students have different concentration spans. If you find you can concentrate for forty-five minutes at a time, then schedule your time in forty-five-minute blocks, with a fifteen-minute break between blocks. The length of each block is not that important, as long as you give yourself enough total time on each course. What is important is that you maintain a high level of concentration during your blocks of study time.

- *If you have a long period of study time, use it to study for different classes.* Your concentration will be better if you switch topics every hour or so. How often you switch will depend upon your own ability to concentrate.

- *Set aside time to prepare for lectures.* Review the reading for a class right before the lecture on that topic; you will find the lecture much easier to follow. Also, set aside time as soon after a lecture as possible to review your notes, make additions, and apply some study techniques. (These are covered in Chapter 5 on note taking in lectures.)

- *Distribute your time spent on each class.* Your memory of material will be limited if you read the material only once. For example, rather than spending two hours at one time reading and studying material, it is better to spend one hour today reading, half an hour tomorrow reviewing, fifteen minutes the following day reviewing, and fifteen minutes at the end of the week reviewing. You will still study a total of two hours, but you will find that your understanding and memory of the information are much greater.

Once you use this initial schedule for a week or two, you will want to make adjustments based on the actual class demands.

The weekly schedule also enables you to make adjustments for more studying during midterm week, for example, but it still allows you to see what you must give up in order to finish all of your needed studying. Look at the weekly schedule in Figure 4.3 and compare it to the term schedule. How are they alike? How are they different?

Your weekly schedules should be used in conjunction with your daily "To Do" lists. Remember that the "To Do" lists are very specific about the tasks you need to accomplish on any given day. The "To Do" list is the most specific of the goals and schedules that you set for yourself.

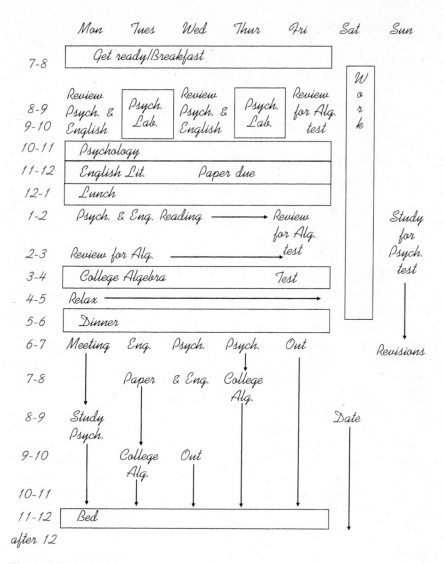

Figure 4.3 Example of a Weekly Schedule

Key Ideas

In this chapter we have seen that, in order to manage your time efficiently and effectively, it is important to set long- and short-term goals. It is also important to construct and stick to an overall schedule. Keep the following ideas in mind when scheduling:

- In order to be successful in college, you must be self-disciplined.
- At the beginning of each term, set two to four overall goals.

- Set weekly goals that are related to, but more specific than, the overall goals.
- Make daily "To Do" lists to help you organize each day.
- At the beginning of the term, make an overall schedule.
- Supplement your term schedule with weekly schedules.

■ A Scenario to Write About and Discuss

Your schedule for next semester includes the following courses and activities:

1) Introduction to Sociology: a large lecture class; meets Tuesdays and Thursdays from 10:00 A.M. to 12:00 P.M.; your discussion section meets on Thursday from 3:00 P.M. to 4:30 P.M.; the class has a lot of assigned textbook reading; your grade is based on two major tests.

2) English Composition II: a small, intensive writing class; meets Monday, Wednesday, and Friday from 1:00 P.M. TO 2:00 P.M.; the class has writing assignments that are begun in class and finished for homework; your grade is based on these papers and on one large, final term paper.

3) Issues in American Life: an interdisciplinary course that has the reputation of being very interesting, although there is a lot of work; the class meets on Wednesdays, 9:00 A.M. to 11:00 A.M. for a lecture and on Mondays and Fridays, 9:00 A.M. to 10:30 A.M., in small discussion sections; the class reading includes one textbook, a dozen articles, and two novels; your grade is based on weekly quizzes, given on Fridays, and a final exam.

4) Survey of Nineteenth Century Art and Ideas: a course with the reputation of being easy and not requiring a lot of outside work; the class meets Monday and Wednesday from 3:00 P.M. to 5:00 P.M. with a requirement to spend an additional hour per week doing research in area museums; the class reading is a selection of short articles and essays, put together in a "course-pack" by the instructor; your grade is based on four short papers, spread throughout the term, that express your opinion about some aspect of art and culture.

In addition to the courses, you have ten hours a week that you have to dedicate to an extracurricular activity (it might be a work-study job, community service, a club, or an athletic team—you choose.)

Based on the guidelines on pages 61–62, plan a weekly schedule (like the one shown in Figure 4.3). You can make a copy of the blank schedule provided in Figure 4.4.

First, schedule the class times, decide how many hours to spend on each course, and block out time appropriate for the course. Schedule your extracurricular activities. Include time for your social life.

When you are done, discuss the schedule with others in your class. Discuss the differences in each of your schedules. Discuss why you decided to arrange your schedule the way you did. After seeing how other students solved this scheduling problem, are there changes you would make in yours?

Application Exercises (DTT and Your Courses)

1. Using the blank schedule in Figure 4.4 as a model, make a term schedule.
2. Each week that you need to modify your schedule, make a new weekly schedule.
3. Set three goals for yourself for this term.
4. Try making "To Do" lists every day for a week. Then write a journal entry about how the lists helped, hindered, or failed to have any influence on helping you to organize your time more efficiently and effectively.

	Mon	Tues	Wed	Thur	Fri	Sat	Sun
7-8							
8-9							
9-10							
10-11							
11-12							
12-1							
2-3							
3-4							
4-5							
5-6							
6-7							
7-8							
8-9							
9-10							
10-11							
11-12							
after 12							

Figure 4.4 Blank Schedule

Critical Thinking

This chapter mentioned "power periods," times during a day when you seem best able to concentrate and study. Reflect on why your power periods occur when they do. Here are some questions to guide your thinking:

1. Do others in your family share the same power periods? Do you think this trait is inherited? Why or why not?

2. Do you know people with opposite power periods (for example, "morning people" versus "night owls")? Are they different in other ways? Are there any conclusions you could draw about the time of people's power periods and their personalities?

3. Are there things you do that affect your power periods? Does the amount of sleep you get change the time or intensity of your power periods? Does caffeine or sugar influence the periods? How?

4. Are there other factors that seem to influence power periods (for example, seasons of the year)? Try to come up with five other factors.

Based on your thinking, develop a plan to increase your ability to concentrate for longer periods of time.

Chapter 5

Taking Notes from Lectures

I'm a great believer in luck, and I find the harder I work
the more I have of it.

Thomas Jefferson

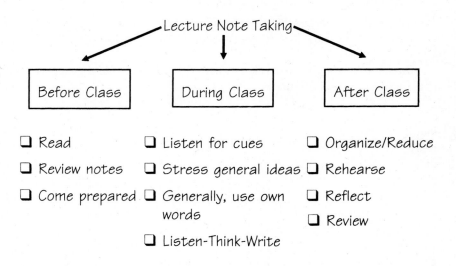

The Split-Page Method
====================
The Split-Page Method

The **BCA** method of studying textbooks, described in detail in Section II, suggests that what you do *before* and *after* reading is as important to your learning as the reading itself. This idea is true for all learning, including learning information from lectures. In this chapter, we will show you the *split-page method* of taking lecture notes. This method gives you a structure to use before, during, and after a lecture to make your learning more powerful.

Most college professors require that you read the text in order to gain certain information about a topic. They use lectures to supply additional information and to expound on topics introduced in the text. If all you do is read the text and show up for class occasionally, you'll find yourself in trouble at exam time. The method of taking notes outlined in this chapter will help you to review and study.

This chapter discusses strategies to use to help you to understand, annotate, and remember the information better. How you use these strategies will depend partly on the kind of lecture you are attending.

Types of Lectures

Large Lecture (50–500 People)

Professors with large classes can't spend time interacting with individual students, answering questions, or gearing the lecture to a particular interest. They tend to begin class on time, follow a prepared outline, move quickly through material, invite little student input or questioning, and end promptly. These professors often use overhead transparencies or the chalkboard to make important points. The strategies in this chapter will help you take notes effectively in such a setting. Pay attention to the ideas that will help you sustain interest and attention because it is very easy to lose concentration during a large lecture.

Small Lecture (10–50 People)

Small lectures tend to be more informal. Professors can pay more attention to individual students, and they can gear the lecture speed to the abilities of the particular group of students. You usually find more opportunity for questions, discussions, and demonstrations, which makes it easier for you to sustain your concentration and interest. At the same time, it is harder for you to miss class or to be inattentive or unprepared without being noticed. For these small lectures, then, *prepare* through reading and reviewing, *participate,* and *maintain your interest and attention.*

Discussion Group (As an Adjunct to the Lecture)

Lecture classes—especially large ones—often break up into discussion groups; the lecture might be held once a week for two hours and a discussion group held once a week for one hour. Although discussion groups are usually taught by teaching assistants (T. A.'s), they are almost always planned or coordinated by the professor.

Some students think that discussion groups are not really an important part of the course and that they are only for students who have trouble understanding the lecture. Although sometimes this may be true, for the most part the discussion groups are very important for *all* students. Discussion classes usually include other information, examples, and demonstrations that will help you understand the course better—and that will probably be on a test. Because professors often provide T.A.'s lists of discussion questions and topics, these classes give you an opportunity to practice answering sample test questions. In discussion classes, you can ask questions and clarify information as well. Attendance at, and participation in, the discussion sessions are often as important a part of the course as going to the lecture or reading the textbook. Remember to *prepare* for discussion classes by reading and reviewing, *participate,* and *remain alert for new information.*

Laboratories

Many courses, especially those in the sciences, have required laboratory experiences. While labs are not lecture situations, they are usually adjuncts to the lectures, in much the same way the discussion groups are adjuncts. Like discussion groups, labs help you to explore and learn the material in more interactive ways. For some students, the hands-on experience of a lab is the best way for them to learn and remember material. The professor usually arranges labs around particular concepts or facts that are especially important or that are difficult to understand without a direct experience. For these reasons, we strongly recommend that you complete all the labs that go with a class, whether they are required or not.

Since labs are usually based on material covered in your textbook or in class lectures, it is important that you read and review the related lecture notes and textbook sections *before* you complete the lab. Also, review the lab procedures or the experiment entirely before you begin doing it. As you complete the lab, take notes on what you are learning, on how it relates to the course, and on questions that arise. If you are having trouble doing the lab assignment, don't be afraid to ask for help. Professors expect that many students will have some trouble, and they or their T.A.'s are usually available to give assistance. After you finish the lab, try to relate what you learned to your lecture notes and textbook reading, and make sure you review your lab notes before a test. If the professor arranged a lab around a concept or set of facts, you can bet the professor considers those concepts and facts important—and will test you on them.

Before the Lecture

The following tips will help you to prepare for an upcoming lecture:

1. *Read the text.* Reading your text gives you the general information that your professor expects you to have. Read the text before the lecture so that you can ask any questions about topics that you did not understand fully. Remember, your text annotations can flag information that you did not understand. If you wait until after the lecture to read the chapter, you may not realize that you don't understand something until it is too late. You may get further and further

behind and eventually become so lost that it becomes impossible to catch up. This is especially likely with highly technical material that is taught sequentially, because in order to grasp Chapter 2, you must first understand Chapter 1, and so on.

2. *Review the previous lecture notes.* If possible, reread your notes for five or ten minutes immediately before class; this will refresh your memory and get your mind ready for the lecture. Note anything that you do not understand, because many professors will address questions from the previous lecture right at the beginning of class. Before the lecture, read the text to become familiar with the material the lecture will cover, and review your lecture notes to refresh your memory of what has already been covered.

3. *Arrive on time, and get a good seat.* Coming to class late not only interrupts the lecture for others but also puts you at a disadvantage. Once you sit down, you'll need another several minutes to get ready to take notes. By this time, you may have missed important information, or you may be unable to make sense of what the professor is saying. By arriving early you can select a seat close to the front, which is to your advantage for two reasons:

(a) It keeps your attention focused on the lecture. You can see the chalkboard and clearly hear what the professor is saying.

(b) Students who sit in the front tend to ask more questions, and the instructor gets to know them better. Students who may be on the border between getting an *A* and a *B* or a *B* and a *C* may receive the higher grade if they have shown interest and enthusiasm.

4. *Be prepared.* Use a loose-leaf notebook rather than one that is spiral bound. Loose-leaf notebooks make it easier for you to add information and class handouts. At study time you can spread out your notes, which will help you to gain a coherent picture of a whole section, chapter, or course.

Divide your paper so that you have about a two-inch margin on the left, as shown in Figure 5.1. Use this wide margin after the lecture to record major ideas or questions.

Date your notes and number the pages. These notations are easy to refer to at a later date.

Staying Connected: Listening to Lectures

While you are getting accustomed to your professor's style of lecturing, pay attention to the following clues. Even though each professor has his or her own lecture style, these clues will indicate when information is important.

1. *Look for obvious clues.* If professors say, "This is important information to remember," "Pay particular attention to . . . ," or "Make sure you understand the handouts," believe them. You will probably see the material again on

60's (cont'd)

JFK economics more gov. spending + tax cuts ↓ led to ↓ Inflation *def.: prices rose too fast ex. @ price-fixing Infl. controlled led to ↓ Social programs	Kennedy (JFK) concentrated 1st on foreign policy & the economy ① Strengthen economy: — more government spending ⒠ invest in space program as way to stimulate economy ⒠ urban renewal — tax cuts — businesses and individuals results — business boomed; unemployment dropped 2% points ② Good economy = inflation *def — inflation — when prices for goods and services increase too fast —JFK tried to keep inflation under control ⒠ set informal wage & price guidelines; US Steel ignored and JFK attacked them, accused of price-fixing; they backed down and JFK finally neg. noninflationary wage agreement w/whole steel industry — Inflation slowed; economy cont'd to grow ③ With economy strong, JFK could push for social programs — civil rights — antipoverty

Figure 5.1 Sample Lecture Notes Using the Split-Page Method

the exam. Look for information that professors write on the chalkboard or otherwise emphasize—for example, via slides or an overhead projector. Don't ignore these clues; use them to guide your test preparation. (See Chapter 12.)

2. *Write down spellings and definitions.* If a professor writes a new term on the chalkboard and defines it, put both the spelling and definition in your notes correctly. For example, the words *ectoplasm* and *endoplasm* do not differ much in spelling, but their meanings differ drastically. If you're unsure of something, ask your instructor to clarify it; other students may be unsure as well.

3. *Note any repetition and extended comment.* When a professor repeats a comment several times or gives it a considerable amount of attention during the lecture or class discussion, include the comment in your notes. A well-written exam should reflect the amount of class time spent on a particular idea.

4. *Copy lists.* Include any lists of items in your notes. For example, if the professor says, "The three major causes of the Revolutionary War were . . ." or "There were several reasons why . . . ," write this information down. Although

CALVIN AND HOBBES © 1990 Watterson. Dist. by UNIVERSAL PRESS SYNDI-CATE. Reprinted with permission. All rights reserved.

you may not see the information in the *exact* form on the exam, you should still know it. "The three major causes of the Revolutionary War" may become the following essay question:

> Three major causes of the Revolutionary War were discussed in lecture. Which of these causes made the most significant contribution to the war's beginning? Discuss in terms of the politics, persons, ideologies, and places involved.

In order to answer this question, you must first know what the causes were!

5. *Listen for superlatives.* Phrases such as "*most* important," "*greatest* contribution," "*fewest* students," and "*best* example" all contain superlatives; include them in your notes.

6. *Hear changes in volume and speech rate.* Individuals tend to talk more loudly and slowly when the information is important. In fact, instructors often

pause after they have made a key point in order to give you time to write. Use these clues as aids to what you should include in your notes and what you should omit.

Staying Connected: Taking Notes During the Lecture

Our method for taking notes may differ somewhat from what you are used to, but if you practice it you will find it to be very effective. Most note-taking systems emphasize an outline form; this method does not.

Take notes only on the right-hand side of pages (see Figure 5.1). Don't cramp your notes; skip a line or two to show where one idea ends and another begins. Take your notes in simple paragraph form rather than in an outline. Students who try to take notes in outline form often concentrate more on the format than on the content. Don't worry too much about form; content is what's important. Use the following guidelines for taking notes:

1. *Stress general ideas.* Write down only enough details and examples so that you will be able to understand the information later. Be selective; you can't write down everything. Focus your attention on general ideas and fill in the necessary details later.

2. *Put most things in your own words.* Notice that we said *most* things. Definitions of new terms should always be in the lecturer's exact words, because an *and* or an *or* can change the whole meaning. Math, chemistry, physics, or statistics formulas must be exact, too. Nevertheless, putting most lecture information in your own words shows that you understand the material and will make it easier for you to study from your notes.

3. *Listen first, think second, write last.* Some students make the mistake of listening and then writing, leaving out the thinking step. If you listen to what is said and then think about what is important, you probably will be much more selective in your note taking and will find it easier to decipher your notes at study time.

4. *Remain alert and ask questions.* If you are unsure of a concept the professor presents, ask for clarification or explanation. Try to clear up the misunderstanding immediately. Although a large lecture class may make this approach impossible, most large lecture courses break down into smaller groups at which students can ask questions and discuss the answers. If you have to wait to ask your question, make sure that you mark it in your notes so that you don't forget to bring it up later.

After the Lecture

Once you have left the lecture, you still have work to do. Take time to go over your notes daily, or you'll have a difficult time when exam day arrives. Include lecture notes in your daily review just as you do text material (see Chapter 11), and review your notes as soon after the lecture as possible. Chapter 4 discussed scheduling your time, and suggested blocking out time *before* a lecture to review the reading and the previous lecture's notes and *after* each lecture to organize and review. The following tips will help you fix the lecture material more firmly in your mind:

1. *Organize and reduce your notes.* Before you went to the lecture, you divided your notebook page and left a two-inch margin on the left-hand side; now is the time to use it. As soon after the lecture as possible, annotate the major ideas (a few key words will suffice) in this margin (see Figure 5.1). This process is very similar to the text annotation discussed in Chapter 9. Some students prefer test-prediction questions about the key ideas in the margin; others like a combination of both types of annotations. Use either or both procedures to locate information easily. When you are reviewing, cover up the right-hand side of the page where you wrote your notes, leaving only the key words, phrases, or questions exposed. Then go through and see how much you can remember about each major idea in your notes. In addition, go through and reduce the material in your notes, if possible. Use a highlighter to mark important information. When you study, ignore anything that you have not highlighted.

2. *Rehearse the material.* Spend some time, soon after the lecture, in rehearsal. Go over the information, rehearse it, and discuss it with classmates. Some students prefer to copy their notes over again, this time including only the most important information. This process helps to get the material into long-term memory as well as reduce further the amount to be learned; but this can be time-consuming. Experiment to see which is the most efficient and effective method for you.

3. *Reflect on what you have written.* Think about what you have written. Do you actually understand everything? If not, seek out sources (either people or printed material) that can clarify any misunderstandings. If you don't reflect upon your notes, you will probably memorize a lot of facts that won't help you very much on a test. Ask yourself memory, interpretation, and application questions about the material. This procedure will force you to think about how everything fits together—the text, the lecture notes, and any additional reading.

4. *Review your notes.* Review your lecture notes each day. If you did a good job taking and reducing notes, you will probably have to spend only fifteen to twenty minutes each evening. Review your lecture notes, using the rehearsal strategies you have chosen, along with your annotations from the related text material. (Annotation and rehearsal strategies are discussed in detail in Chapters 9 and 10.) See how much overlap there is between text and lectures, and keep that overlap in mind as you further reduce and consolidate information to study for a test. If you do review daily, make sure that the night before an exam the material is fixed in your mind. You won't have to cram if you have done a little bit each evening.

Taking good lecture notes is a real skill for college students. If you practice this method, you will have a set of notes that is easy to learn from. Good notes should stand the test of time: A month or even a year later they should still make sense to you.

Figure 5.1 presents a sample of what your notes should look like. Notice that the major headings are in the left-hand margin and the actual class notes are to the right. Abbreviations were used (you can probably think of others) and, although the writing is quite legible, punctuation was omitted.

Key Ideas

1. Taking good lecture notes is a three-step process, encompassing what you do before the lecture, during the lecture, and after the lecture.

2. Be prepared when you go to class. Read the text before the lecture. Make sure that your paper is ready.

3. During the lecture, *listen* attentively for key points. *Think* about what the lecturer said. *Write* in simple paragraph form, leaving the left-hand margin blank.

4. After the lecture, use the left-hand margin to annotate key ideas or to predict test questions. Review your notes as soon as possible.

■ A Scenario to Write About and Discuss

You are in an introductory course that includes two large lectures and one discussion group each week. The lectures, for 200 students, are held in an auditorium. The professor is a fairly interesting speaker, and she uses lots of overheads to illustrate her main points. She also speaks quickly and covers material at a rapid rate. Her lectures each week are usually on the same topics as the assigned textbook reading for the week, although she covers material and gives examples that are not in the textbook. In other words, she assumes the students have read and remembered the assigned textbook material, so she can quickly expand on what was in the text. The discussion groups are taught by a graduate student. Each week, a particular topic is discussed, followed by time to ask questions about what was in the textbook or the lecture.

You are having a difficult time in this class. It is a required course and you are not very interested in the subject. You also find the lectures difficult to follow. Your note taking does not keep up with the speed of the lecture. When you look over your notes before a test, you cannot remember why you wrote some things down; other parts of your notes do not make sense.

Based on the ideas in this chapter, how might you change your studying to be more effective? Consider what you might change in: (a) how and when you read the textbook assignments; (b) what you might do right before the lecture begins; (c) where you might sit in the lecture hall; (d) how you could make better decisions about what to write in your notes so you can keep up; (e) what you might do right after the lecture to help your learning; (f) how you could use the discussion section to your best advantage; and (g) how you could consolidate and review your notes. Also, consider how you could develop more motivation for learning the material.

Write down your ideas and then discuss them with other students in your class.

Application Exercises
(DTT or Your Courses)

1. If you are taking a core class at the same time as you are using this text, practice taking notes using the method we described. Ask your instructor and peers to evaluate the format and content of your notes.

2. If you are not taking a core course, try to arrange to visit one (a psychology or sociology class would be best). Practice taking notes using the method discussed in this chapter. You may not be able to follow all of the procedures (such as reading the text before the lecture), but attending sample lectures will give you practice in listening for key ideas and putting your notes into the correct format.

3. Practice taking notes on documentary television shows. The television program "60 Minutes" provides an excellent opportunity for you to practice your note-taking skills.

Chapter 6

Vocabulary Development

How often misused words generate misleading thoughts.

Herbert Spencer

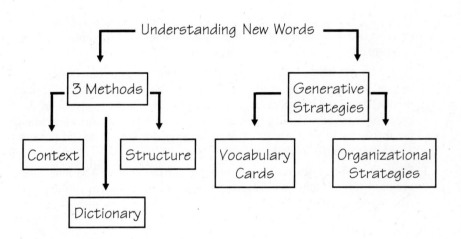

Of all the strategies presented in *Developing Textbook Thinking,* vocabulary strategies are probably the most difficult to write about, because it is hard to have much impact on your vocabulary in a brief period of time, such as a quarter or semester. The study strategies outlined in the following chapters—guidelines for taking textbook notes and test preparation techniques—are all relatively easy to learn with just a little practice. Increasing your vocabulary, however, like becoming a better reader, is a lifelong process. Although we are primarily concerned in this chapter with generative vocabulary strategies that you can use in your courses and in reading your texts, you can also apply many of the strategies to learning new words that you encounter in your pleasure reading. In other words, the goal of this chapter is not to teach you hundreds of new words. Rather, we want to expose you to more generative strategies that you can use on your own.

Vocabulary development in your courses (often referred to as *content-specific vocabulary*) actually focuses on five different areas:

1. Determining the meanings of unfamiliar words as you read a textbook or listen to a lecture.

2. Learning a new, specialized meaning for a familiar word as it is used in the text or lecture.

3. Understanding a new concept (which may be conveyed by more than one word). A concept is more complex than just a word, and so it is necessary to learn several elements for each concept.

4. Remembering new words, new definitions, and new concepts.

5. Extending your new knowledge to other words and concepts.

As Chapter 7 will discuss, different disciplines stress different types of vocabulary development. The social sciences, for example, tend to have *familiar* words with new, specialized meanings, whereas the physical sciences tend to use *new* words with specialized meanings; and all disciplines rely on major concepts to organize information.

Understanding New Words and New Definitions

As you read or listen to lectures, you will come across unfamiliar words. For example, in the article "The Psychology of Memory," that appears in the textbook selections section at the end of this book, the terms *encoding* and *engram* may be unfamiliar to you. You will also see familiar words used in ways that do not fit your understanding of those words, perhaps because the word has a special meaning in that subject area. For example in "The Psychology of Memory," the terms *decay* and *chunking* are used. You have certainly heard the word *decay,* which means to rot or to lose strength. And you also have used the word *chunk,* as in buying a chunk or a piece of cheese or spending a chunk of money. But you probably have not heard of either of these words used in the specialized way that psychologists use them. You might have a fuzzy notion of what it means for a memory to "decay" or how you can expand your memory through "chunking," but without reading the chapter and listening to your professor lecture on these topics, you would have a difficult time accurately and precisely defining these terms. Whether a term is unfamiliar to you, or a familiar term has a specialized definition, you have three tasks to perform with the term:

1. *You have to decide whether the term is important to learn.* You may come across many new words, and you must decide which ones you need to learn and which ones you can let slip by. Have you seen or heard the word before—enough to know it is relatively commonplace? Is the word used more than once in the book or lecture? Is the word necessary for understanding a main idea or a major supporting detail? If the answer to any of these questions is yes, you need to understand the meaning of the word.

2. *Once you have identified a term as important to learn, you need to determine the level of understanding that is necessary.* If you need only a low-level understanding, learning a definition that enables you to pass a couple of items on an exam may be appropriate. However, if knowledge of the word is imperative to learning other new terms or if the word is in some way related to your major area of study, it would be important for you to have more of a conceptual understanding. As you will see, memorizing a definition and learning the word at a conceptual level are two very different processes and require different strategies.

3. *If the word is important, you need to apply a strategy to help you to understand the word as you are reading or listening.* The last part is especially important. Your studying will be much less effective if you have to stop several times per page to ponder a word or to consult a dictionary. If you can quickly figure out the new word so that you can keep reading, your efficiency and effectiveness will be much greater.

When unlocking the meaning of new words, you can use three key methods: context, structure, and the dictionary. Previous editions of *Developing Textbook Thinking* suggested that students should first try the context, then use the dictionary, then analyze the structure, and, finally, sound out the word. Newer research and our own experiences in working with students, however, suggest that no one particular order works best in all situations. Hence we now suggest that, within the guidelines that follow, you use your own judgment about the best method or combination of methods, depending on the level of word meaning that you need to have. That said, it is important to realize that when context clues are available (either obvious clues or those that aren't so obvious), it would be in your best interest to use them. In the examples provided later in this chapter, you will see examples of context providing a considerable amount of information and examples of context not being all that helpful. When you come across a new word (or a familiar word with a new meaning), you should do any or all of the following, not necessarily in any particular order:

- Use the *context*—the phrase, sentence, or paragraph in which the word occurs—*and sound out the word*. Often you can understand the word just by sounding it out and then examining the context, without disrupting the flow of your reading. You may have heard the term used before, perhaps in a lecture, and already have some knowledge of what it means. This knowledge, in combination with what you can figure out from the context, the dictionary, and the structure, will help you gain a fuller understanding of the term.

- Examine the *structure,* or the word parts. Word parts include prefixes, suffixes, and root words. Especially in the physical sciences, words tend to be related to each other structurally. You can unlock the meanings of words and often remember them better if you examine their structure.

- Consult the *dictionary.* A dictionary will give you the authoritative definition, as well as the pronunciation of a term. It will also give you alternative, but related, definitions and can help you determine the structure of the word. Related definitions can aid in remembering a term and in extending what you learn about the term to other words or other uses of the same term. If the textbook has a glossary, consult it first, because the author will often give you the definition of the term as it is used in the textbook. Note also that sometimes the dictionary definition, especially for content-specific terms, may not provide as clear a definition as you need.

Using Context

Using context to figure out the meaning of an unfamiliar word is important for three reasons:

1. If you can use context to figure out meaning, you do not have to interrupt your reading to look up the word. Your studying will be more efficient, and you are less likely to forget what you have learned because you did not interrupt yourself.

2. Many of the words in the various subject areas have specialized definitions. A word's context gives you the most accurate idea of this specialized usage.

3. You will run across many words with which you are unfamiliar in your textbook reading. Some of these words are important and occur several times in a text. Other words, less important to your understanding of the subject, may appear only once or twice. The important words are the ones you should learn, and because they are used several times, you may have several different word contexts that will help you to determine their meanings. If you come across a new term several times and still do not know what it means from the context, *then* you should look it up.

Context Clues

Learning to use a word's context and content clues is one way to improve your vocabulary. You will not necessarily get the exact meaning of a word just from seeing it in one context; but if you use the context each time a word occurs, you often can get a more and more precise understanding of the word. You also will not always find direct context clues every time you see an unfamiliar word. But when they do occur, context clues are good shortcuts to more efficient reading.

Context clues signal a definition in four main ways:

1. Synonyms
2. Antonyms and contrasts
3. Examples and illustrations
4. Opinion and tone

Synonyms

The most common context clue is a *synonym,* a word similar in meaning to the unfamiliar word you have encountered in your reading. Synonyms appear especially when a new term is being introduced, because the textbook author wants you to understand the word. The clue word may not have exactly the same meaning as the word for which you seek a definition, but it may be close enough to give you an approximate definition. Here are examples of synonyms from the textbook selections at the end of this book:

> Memorizing clusters or groups are called chunks, and the process of grouping items into such units is called chunking. ("The Psychology of Memory," p. 273)

Note that *chunks* and *chunking* have specialized meanings here and are synonymous with units or groupings.

> *Computer networks* (systems that link multiple computers through phone lines or satellite) allow marketers to interface with data sources and customers with almost instantaneous information about products and sales performance. ("Information Systems and Marketing Research" p. 398)

In this example, the synonym is cued by the use of parentheses. Thus *computer networks* is synonymous with "systems that link multiple computers through phone lines or satellite."

> Societies that are "tight" (where members share the same language, religion, and social customs) tend to be rigid and intolerant of those who veer from the norm. ("Human Diversity" p. 356)

Note that the word "tight" as used in this context has a specialized meaning and is synonymous to societies where members have shared language, religion, and social customs. The author cues you to the fact that he is using a synonym by the parentheses. He also cues you that "tight" has a specialized meaning by using quotation marks.

Antonyms and Contrasts

Occasionally an author may use an *antonym*—a word or phrase with an opposite meaning—to suggest the meaning of an unfamiliar word. This often occurs when an author contrasts two ideas or attitudes. Here are examples from the textbook selections at the end of this book:

> Whereas the online information services (such as CompuServe and America Online) limit their services to subscribers, the Internet permits the exchange of e-mail, global discussion through public forums . . . and just about everything in between. . . . ("Information Systems and Marketing Research" p. 398)

In the example, the word *whereas* should immediately provide you with the cue that you will read about a contrast. Here the author is contrasting information services with the Internet, indicating that one limits their services and the other provides expansive services.

> . . . [P]eople who grow up in individualistic countries see themselves as entities that are *independent*—distinct, autonomous, self-contained, and endowed with unique dispositions. By contrast, people from collectivist countries hold an *interdependent* view of the self as part of a larger social network that includes family, coworkers, friends, and others with whom they are socially connected. ("Human Diversity" p. 356)

This example is an interesting one since it incorporates the use of both synonyms and antonyms. The goal of the author is to contrast *independent views* with *interdependent views*. *"By contrast"* cues you to the fact that the two views are antonymous rather than synonymous. In addition, the author also defines *independent* for you and cues you by using a dash. In this example, then, you are given a definition of one of the terms and are also shown how the two terms are different.

> Research shows that retention of material processed at "shallow" levels is very poor, but retention of material processed at "deep" levels is good. ("The Psychology of Memory," p. 273)

Here the author contrasts the two different levels of process by telling what they are and by contrasting them—hence also telling you what they aren't. Words such as *but* and *however* cue you to this type of context clue.

Examples and Illustrations

The meaning of an unfamiliar word may be suggested by examples and illustrations. The examples and illustrations taken together may provide several clues to meaning, although no one word by itself gives a definition. The following excerpts use examples and illustrations.

> The result was "the *Freedom Summer* of 1964." Led by SNCC's Bob Moses, whites and blacks went to Mississippi to open "Freedom Schools" and to encourage African-Americans to register to vote. The Freedom Schools taught basic literacy and black history, stressed black pride and achievements. They also tutored African-Americans on the Mississippi voter literacy tests. ("Great Promises, Bitter Disappointments, 1960–1968" p. 297)

Freedom Summer is defined here by providing several of the different programs that went on during the summer of 1964. The author is trying to show that *Freedom Summer* was not just about one thing that happened. Rather, he attempts to characterize this period by explaining some of the programs and goals of the "Freedom Schools." It would be difficult to get an idea of the scope of *Freedom Summer* simply by reading one sentence.

He proposed a system of *particulate inheritance* in which heritable characteristics were controlled by individual "units." Mendel assumed (correctly,
as it turned out) that each plant had two such units for each trait. Mendel
called each unit a "Merkmal," the German word for "character." Today we
call these units *genes,* and we know that the cells of the pea plant carry two
genes for most characteristics. ("Genetics: The Science of Inheritance"
p. 377)

Note that in this example, *particulate inheritance* is characterized through a
description, rather than a definition. Note also that this description was initially
tied to the pea plant (which Mendel was studying when he made his famous
discovery). Through this illustration we can see that each plant had two genes
for each characteristic.

Opinion and Tone

The last kind of context clue is more indirect and, consequently, more difficult
to rely on with accuracy. The writer's tone, attitude toward the subject, and
opinions may provide a clue for an unfamiliar word.

Read the following account of the integration of "Ole Miss" and think
about the tone the author uses:

Integrating southern universities threatened to provoke wholesale slaughter.
Some desegregated painlessly, but the University of Mississippi ("Ole
Miss") became a volcano. A twenty-nine-year-old air force veteran, James
Meredith, encountered violent opposition when he attempted to register in
October 1962. In the end President Kennedy was forced to send in four hundred federal marshals and three thousand troops to enroll Meredith in his
first class—in colonial American history. He ultimately graduated, with a
sheepskin that cost the lives of two men, scores of injuries, and some 4 million taxpayer dollars. (*The American Pageant*, 9th ed., 1991)

Now read the second account of the same event. Think about the tone of
this excerpt as well.

A year later James Meredith integrated the University of Mississippi.
Meredith, an air force veteran and student at a black college, heard
Kennedy's inaugural speech and decided to transfer to Mississippi, knowing
Governor Ross Barnett had vowed to go to jail before allowing blacks to enroll. Robert Kennedy sent five hundred federal marshals to guard Meredith,
hoping a show of force would prevent violence. The tactic did not work.
Thousands of white students and nonstudents attacked Meredith and the
marshals. Two people were killed and 166 marshals were wounded before
5,000 army troops arrived and restored order. Protected by federal forces,
Meredith finished the year, and in May, the University of Mississippi had its
first African-American graduate. ("Great Promises, Bitter Disappointments,
1960–1968")

How do you think these two accounts differ in tone? Which account appears to be more biased? Think about the language used in each piece and how that language sets the tone. For example, in the first account, words such as "wholesale slaughter," "volcano," and "violent opposition" lead the reader to believe that the authors had some pretty strong feelings about this incident. What kind of feelings did they have? Contrast that with the second account where the language used appears to be much more neutral and unbiased.

Discovering Meaning through Context

A word's context can reveal its meaning in several ways:

1. *The actual definition may be given right after the word is introduced.* Watch for punctuation signals such as parentheses, dashes, or commas and word signals, such as *or, like, that is, in other words, such as,* and *consists of.* These types of context clues are usually the easiest to identify. The following examples illustrate this use of context:

   Radar (*ra*dio *de*tecting *a*nd *r*anging) is used to detect and monitor precipitation, especially that of severe storms. ("Weather Forecasting" p. 335)

   On-site computer interviewing, a variation of the mall intercept interview, consists of respondents completing a self-administered questionnaire displayed on a computer monitor. ("Information Systems and Marketing," p. 398)

   In the recognition method you are shown an item and asked whether you have seen it before. ("The Psychology of Memory," p. 273)

   Notice that in each example, the definition follows the unfamiliar word. Each also uses punctuation or word signals.

2. *Watch for an example of how a concept is applied.* The following excerpt gives an example of proactive interference. The example is helpful in understanding the concept more fully.

   Two kinds of interference have been identified: proactive interference and retroactive interference. *Proactive interference* occurs when your memory for something you learned recently is interfered with by some previously learned material. In preparing for exams, if you study sociology and then psychology, your memory for the psychological material may be interfered with by the sociological material you learned first, because of *proactive interference.* ("The Psychology of Memory," p. 273)

   Notice that the author gives a clue ("occurs when") to alert the reader that he will discuss how the concept is applied.

3. *Use additional information to help you to draw inferences—educated guesses—about the meaning of a word.* The example that follows forces you to draw inferences:

" MY INSTRUCTOR SAID MY VOCABULARY WAS EXECRABLE. I WONDER WHAT HE MEANT BY THAT?"

A Republican victory would have been difficult even for Eisenhower, whose health and age, and the *Twenty-second Amendment,* prevented him from running for a third term. ("Great Promises, Bitter Disappointments, 1960–1968" p. 297)

In this example, you must infer what the *Twenty-second Amendment* did. You know that it has nothing to do with health and age, so you have to infer that it was something else. The clue here is that the amendment prevented him from running for a third term, inferring that he had already served two terms as president. Thus you should be able to conclude that the *Twenty-second Amendment* to the Constitution prevents presidents from running for a third term.

4. *Meaning may be revealed through an extended discussion of a term or concept.* An extended discussion provides a particular meaning for the term—not only what it is, but also what situations relate to it, what its limits are, how it came into being, and so forth. Such discussions are often used for words that are familiar to the reader but that have a limited or specific meaning in a given subject. For example:

A *family* is defined by many sociologists as the smallest social grouping of individuals, usually related by kinship or proximity, who assume specific roles and function cooperatively for mutual benefits or purposes. A family, then, is more than one individual, but it is viewed as the smallest grouping that can be identified. The family may consist of parents, children, and other relatives, or it may include close friends or neighbors who are not related but who assume family roles (such as a neighbor who looks after children after school). Generally, members of a functioning family live close to each other and interact often. Hence, grandparents who live far from their children and grandchildren, and see them only occasionally, do not actually function, except on occasion, as "family" members. Family members also assume specific societally determined roles. These roles vary by culture and even subculture, and may vary depending on the purposes for the family unit. Within a culture, for example, there may be very specific roles for such family members as mother, eldest child, or aunt. A nonrelated person could assume any of these roles and enable the family unit to function in the culture by carrying out that role. Note, too, that the roles of family members change according to the tasks at hand, but, overall, all work together for some common purpose. Last, this definition allows a person to belong to more than one family at the same time.

In this example, a very common word, family, is given a specific and limited definition. The first sentence gives a formal definition, and the rest of the paragraph is extended discussion. This discussion is designed to help the reader to understand the specialized definition that the author is using for the word.

In brief, authors often provide "helps" that clarify the meaning of words, making it unnecessary to consult a dictionary. Writers give these clues by including familiar words with the unfamiliar word. Sometimes you have to read several sentences, a paragraph, several paragraphs, or even an entire chapter to extract an accurate definition. Sometimes the clue will be readily apparent, and determining the meaning of the unfamiliar word will be easy. Also remember that context clues are often signaled by punctuation marks, such as commas, dashes, or parentheses.

In many instances, however, context provides either no clues or at least not enough information to get a clear idea of what the word means. For example, based on the following context, could you define feminism?

Feminism, or "the woman question" as it is called, seems to come to the forefront and then subside at various times throughout Western history.

Or try to explain Kennedy's New Frontier, based on the context in which it is used in the following excerpt:

Drawing on a legacy of Franklin Roosevelt, he challenged the nation to enter a *New Frontier,* to improve the overall quality of life of all Americans, and to re-energize American foreign policy to stand fast against the Communist threat. ("Great Promises, Bitter Disappointments, 1960–1968," p. 297)

Although context can help, and it should certainly be used whenever possible, you probably will have to go beyond context use, especially if you need to obtain a more conceptual understanding of what a word means.

Application Exercises (DTT)

The sentences that follow are taken from the textbook selections in the appendix. In each sentence or paragraph, the author defines a term using the context. Read each example, noting the italicized term. Then, in your own words, write a definition for the term in the space provided, and circle any cue words or punctuation.

1. A *rain gauge* is an open container that automatically weighs and records the accumulated precipitation.

   A *rain gauge* is used for _____

   _____

2. A *population,* or "universe," includes all the elements, units, or individuals that are of interest to researchers for a specific study.

   In research, a *population* is _____

   _____

3. To spur economic recovery, Kennedy turned to "new economics" as advocated by Walter Heller, his chairman of the Council of Economic Advisors, and called for more government spending and business and income-tax cuts. The defense budget was the first beneficiary, growing by almost 20 percent. Kennedy also asked Congress for a modest domestic program that included increases in social security coverage and benefits and in the minimum wage, an extension of unemployment insurance, a housing and urban renewal bill, and aid to education.

   "New Economics" according to Kennedy was _____

   _____

   _____

4. One of Ebbinghaus's discoveries was that the first and last syllables on the list were typically recalled more easily than the ones in the middle. In a long list, he found that he was more likely to be able to recall the first one or two and the last one or two but was more likely to forget the items in the middle of the list. This effect has been called the *serial-position effect.*

   The *serial-position effect* is: _____

   _____

   _____

5. The original plants involved in the cross are known as the *parental,* or P, generation.

   Parental plants are _____

   _____

   _____

6. As people live in increasingly complex *industrialized societies*—compared, for example, to a life of food gathering among desert nomads—there are more groups to identify with . . . which means less loyalty to any one group and more of a focus on personal rather than collective goals.
Industrialized societies are _____

_____

7. Marketers often begin the marketing research process by gathering *secondary data*. They may use available reports and other information from both internal and external sources to study a marketing problem.
Secondary data are _____

_____

8. *Encoding* is the process of changing physical scenes and events into the form of information that can be stored in memory.
Encoding is _____

_____

9. In the affairs of day-to-day living, each culture operates according to its own explicit rules of contact, or *social norms*.
Social norms are _____

_____

10. Torn between the need to fit in and a desire to retain their own heritage, ethnic-group members differ in the way they manage *acculturation*—the process by which persons are changed by their immersion in a new culture.
Acculturation is _____

_____

11. He [Lyndon Johnson] was famous for his *"treatment,"* in which he would overpower people by putting his face inches from theirs, sometimes grabbing their lapels, and overwhelming them with a barrage of facts, fictions, humor, and threats.
Lyndon Johnson's *"treatment"* was _____

_____

12. Of the many obstacles that confront ethnic minorities in any culture, the most vicious is *discrimination*—behavior directed against persons because of their affiliation with a social group.
Discrimination is _____

_____

Application Exercise (Your Texts)

As you read a chapter in one of your textbooks, write down the major new words you encounter. Be sure to include any words that are italicized or are otherwise highlighted by the author. Carefully read the sentences around each new word to see how the author uses the context to define it.

1. List each word.

2. Give your definition of the word, based on your best guess from the context.

3. Identify what type of context clue the author uses.

Using the Dictionary

As stated earlier, knowing only one method for determining what a word means is not enough. Although using context clues is a good place to start, especially when unknown words or terms are from content-specific texts, context clues still may not give you enough information to learn the word at a conceptual level. Therefore, you need to be able to use and interpret dictionary definitions. In addition, recent research indicates that when dictionaries provide strong definitions, students learn words significantly better than they would if they were given strong contexts. The key issue here, however, is that the dictionary definitions must provide adequate information.

Anyone who has ever used a dictionary knows that its definitions can often be more hindrance than help or, at best, provide little information about what a word means. The definition of the word *gaffe* below is a good example.

> **gaffe:** clumsy social error; faux pas

If you had no idea what a gaffe was before you looked the word up in this dictionary, your knowledge of an accurate and precise meaning probably didn't improve considerably after reading this definition! This definition gives you no idea as to what kinds of social errors are gaffes and what kinds are not. In addition, *faux pas,* which is used to define *gaffe,* isn't even English! What this definition fails to convey is that a gaffe is generally something that is spoken: spilling food on your shirt during a formal banquet would not be considered a gaffe, although it is a social error. However, remarking to a stranger at this banquet that the guest of honor has terrible taste in clothes and then discovering that the stranger is related to the guest of honor *would* be considered a gaffe.

Characteristics of Strong Definitions

Not all dictionary definitions are as poor as the preceding example. But because lexicographers (individuals who compile dictionaries) are limited by space, definitions tend to help the most when you already have some knowledge, however vague, of what the word means. In order to be able to use the dictionary to its fullest extent, you must understand that some definitions will be clearer and stronger than others. A strong definition has the following five characteristics:

1. The definition does not use another form of the same word in the definition. For example, defining *retrieval* as "the act of retrieving" gives no information about the meaning of the unknown word.

2. The definition uses precise language that has a high degree of explaining power. Vague language often fails to represent the word.

3. The definition should be written so that readers are not likely to substitute an incorrect synonym for the target word. The definition of the word *gaffe,* in our example, is poorly written because readers are apt to use incorrect synonyms for it.

4. Definitions that provide several pieces of information should also offer some guidance about the way these pieces of information should be integrated. For example, the definition of *exacerbate* is "to increase the severity, violence, or bitterness of; aggravate," but the definition fails to communicate the kinds of things that can or cannot be exacerbated.

5. When necessary, definitions should provide examples so that readers can see proper usage of the word, particularly in situations in which it may be easy to misinterpret the stated definition.

In other words, be aware of the strength of the definition you use. If the definition is strong, you should come away with a fairly good idea of what the word means, particularly if you are also using context. Because we feel strongly that all college students should own a good dictionary and use it as part of studying, we have three additional cautions:

1. *Always use the dictionary definitions in conjunction with the context.* You are looking for a definition of the word as it is used in the textbook or lecture. Refer to the context to help you to choose the right definition and to increase your understanding of exactly how the word is used in the subject you are studying.

2. *Use a dictionary that is current.* Many of the terms you will be studying may be relatively new, and older dictionaries may not have the current definitions. For example, older dictionaries do not have the correct definitions for *web* as used in the "Information Systems and Marketing Research" selection in the appendix, or *NEXRAD* as used in the "Weather Forecasting" selection.

3. *Use a dictionary that presents definitions in a way that you understand.* Looking up a word is useless if you don't understand the definition. Before you purchase a dictionary, spend time looking at different dictionaries and comparing the way they give definitions. Your purpose in looking up a word is to understand it, so make sure your dictionary presents definitions that you understand.

The Dictionary Entry

Entries (words and their definitions) in the dictionary include several types of information. Although dictionaries differ somewhat in this regard, most have certain standard parts.

The following entry for the word *recall,* taken from "The Psychology of Memory" selection, serves as an example for what a typical dictionary entry might include and the way in which it might be organized. Keep in mind that dictionaries differ somewhat in the arrangement of information in the entry, so check the user's guide or the introduction for each dictionary's policies.

In order to select the correct dictionary definition, we need to know the context in which the word is used. *Recall* is introduced in the following context:

> One method that provides a measure of forgetting is the *recall method.* In the recall method you are asked to reproduce exactly what you have read or seen.

Now examine the organization of the dictionary definition.[1] We will return to the definition later to determine its strength and to determine which specific definition fits the context.

1 2 3 5	

re•call (rĭ-kôl′) *tr.v.* **-called, -cal•ling, -calls. 1.** To ask or order to return: *re-called all workers who had been laid off.* **2.** To summon back to awareness of or concern with the subject or situation at hand. **3.** To remember; recol- lect. **4.** To cancel, take back, or revoke. **5.** To bring back; restore. (*n.*) (*also* rē′kôl′). **1.** The act of recalling of summoning back, esp. an official order to return. **2.** A signal, as a bugle call, used to summon servicemen back to their posts. **3.** The ability to remember information or experience. **4.** The act of re- voking. **5. a.** The procedure by which a public official may be removed from office by popular vote. **b.** The right to employ this procedure. **6.** A re- quest by the manufacturer of a product specified as defective for its return to the dealer for necessary repairs or adjustments—**re′call′a•ble** *adj.*

6   4

7

The *recall* entry contains four types of information common to most dictionary entries:

1. The word is *written out* to show divisions between the syllables.

2. *Pronunciation* immediately follows the word. This tells you which syllable is accented and how the letters, especially the vowels, sound. If special pro- nunciation symbols are used, explanations and examples of the symbols are usually listed in the user's guide or in the front or back of the dictionary.

3. The *part of speech* generally comes next. In this case, *tr.v.* means that the most common way *recall* is used is as a transitive verb. Again, check your

dictionary for what the abbreviations mean, as they may vary from dictionary to dictionary.

4. Next comes the *list of definitions.* As a general rule, most dictionaries list the most frequently used definition first, but such is not always the case. Consult your dictionary so that you know its format. In addition, for specialized terms, such as those you study in a textbook, the first definition is often *not* the one used by the textbook author. Read all of the definitions in order to find the one that best matches the context.

This entry also contains three additional kinds of information that many entries may not have:

5. The *word or a form of that word used in an example sentence or phrase.* In the case of *recall,* the first definition reads: "To ask or order to return: *recalled all workers who had been laid off."* Examples such as this one are helpful because they provide another context for the word. The more contexts in which you read a word, the greater your understanding of the word.

6. The word may function as *more than one part of speech;* for example, the *n.* in the middle of this entry indicates that *recall* can be used not only as a transitive verb but also as a noun, although this usage occurs less frequently. Note that the numbering of the definitions begins at 1 again and that the pronunciation of the word differs slightly when it is used as a noun. Only words that can be more than one part of speech would be organized in this manner.

7. The final piece of information that is provided, when appropriate, is the *different forms the word can take* when endings, or *suffixes,* are added. In this case, the noun *recall* becomes the adjective *recallable* when the suffix *-able* is added.

Our final note about information that can be found in dictionary entries: A piece of information usually found in definitions, although not present in the *recall* example, is some information on the word's etymology. A word's etymology explains where the word came from: the country from which the word originated, its root word (the word that it was derived from), or both. In the case of the word *imagery* in the following definition,[2] the portion of the entry marked 8 shows where you generally find this information. *Imagery* comes from the Old French ("OFr.") word *imagerie.*

> **Im•age•ry** (im′ij-rē) *n., pl.* **-ries. 1.** Mental pictures or images. **2. a.** The use of figures of speech or vivid descriptions in writing or speaking to produce mental images. **b.** A metaphoric representation, as in music, art, or motion pictures. **3. a.** Representative images, particularly statues or icons. **b.** The art of making such images. [ME *imagerie* < OFr. < *image,* image.]

8 ─────────────────────────────────────

In addition to the elements already discussed, dictionary entries may also include:

8. Sentences or phrases that show how a particular definition of the word is used in context.

9. Specialized definitions from particular fields, with the fields identified.

10. Synonyms and antonyms for the word (usually given at the very end of the definitions).

For example, in a text on computers you would expect to see *hardware* used in this context:

> . . . computer hardware (the physical parts of a computer system) varies widely in performance. . . .

Even though you are looking for the definition of the term as used by the author, you can gain knowledge about the term by also looking at the other definitions. For example, read the definitions for *hardware* in the following entry:[3]

> **hard·ware** (hârd′•wâr′) *n.* **1.** Metal goods and utensils such as locks, tools, and cutlery. **2.** *Technology.* **a.** A computer and the associated physical equipment directly involved in the performance of communications or data-processing functions. **b.** Broadly, machines and other physical equipment directly involved in performing an industrial, technological, or military function. **3.** *Informal.* Weapons; especially, military weapons. **4.** *Informal & Regional.* A pistol or pistols; a six-gun.

You can see that definition 2.a is the one used in the computer text. At the same time, by looking at the other definitions, you can see that *hardware* is used in many contexts. What seems to be similar across contexts is that "hardware" is a tool of some kind and that it is made of metal or some other durable substance. Seeing these similarities may help you to understand and remember that *hardware* refers to the tools of the computer that are durable or hard.

Application Exercises (DTT)

The following excerpt, taken from the "Psychology of Memory" selection in the appendix, uses the word *decay.* Read the dictionary entry[4] that follows, select the definition that best fits the use of the word in this context, and answer the questions about it.

> The *decay theory* states that memories weaken spontaneously as time passes; that is, they "decay."

de•cay (dĭ-kā′) *v.* **-cayed, -cay•ing, -cays.**—*intr.* **1.** *Biol.* To decompose; rot. **2.** *Physics.* To disintegrate or diminish by radioactive decay. **3.** *Aerospace.* To decrease in orbit, as an artificial satellite. **4.** To fall into ruin. **5.** *Pathol.* To decline in health or vigor; waste away. **6.** To decline from a state of normality, excellence, or prosperity.—*tr.* To cause to decay.—*n.* **1.** The destruction or decomposition of organic matter as a result of bacterial or fungal action; rot. **2.** Radioactive decay. **3.** The decrease in orbital altitude of an artificial satellite due to conditions such as atmospheric drag. **4.** A gradual deterioration to an inferior state, as of health or mental capability. [ME *decayen* < AN *decair* < VLat. *ˌdecadere* : Lat. *de-*, down + Lat. *cadere*, to fall.]

1. Which of the dictionary definitions best defines *decay* as used in this example? Why? _____

   _____

   _____

   _____

2. As what parts of speech can *decay* be used? _____

   _____

   As what part of speech is *decay* used in our example? _____

   _____

   _____

3. Would you consider this dictionary definition of *decay* adequate? Why or why not? _____

   _____

   _____

4. According to the dictionary entry, which use of *decay* would appear to be most common? Why? _____

   _____

   _____

5. Based on the context and the dictionary definition, write your own version of an adequate definition of *decay*. _____

   _____

   _____

Application Exercises (Your Texts)

Find several words with which you are unfamiliar from textbooks in your other courses. Look up each of these words in the dictionary and determine if the definitions provided are adequate or inadequate. What can you do if you cannot determine their meanings from the dictionary?

Using Structure

The third way in which you can gain knowledge about unknown words and other related words is through knowing something about the word's structure. *Structure* refers to the prefixes, roots or base words, and suffixes that help you to determine what a word means. Because word parts generally retain consistent meanings in words, knowing the meaning of a particular prefix, root, or suffix can often help unlock the meanings of other unknown words. For example, in the appendix selection from a biology text, the section titled "Genetics: The Science of Inheritance" (p. 377) defines *filial* as follows:

> The original plants involved in the cross are know as the *parental,* or P, generation. The seeds produced from this first cross Mendel called the *first filial,* or F1, generation (*filial* comes from the Latin root for "son").

Now look at this section from a dictionary:[5]

fil·i·al (fĭl′ē-əl) *adj.* **1.** Of, relating to, or befitting a son or daughter. **2.** Having or assuming the relationship of child or offspring to parent. **3.** *Genet.* Of or relating to a generation or the sequence of generations following the parental generation. [ME < OFr. < LLat. *filiālis* < Lat. *filius,* son. See **dhē(i)-**.] — **fil′i·al·ly** *adv.*

fil·i·a·tion (fĭl′ē-ā′shən) *n.* **1.** The condition or fact of being the child of a certain parent. **2.** A line of descent; derivation. **3.a.** The act or fact of forming a new branch, as of a society or language group. **b.** The branch thus formed.

fil·i·bus·ter (fĭl′ə-bŭs′tər) *n.* **1.a.** The use of obstructionist tactics, esp. prolonged speechmaking, in order to delay legislative action. **b.** An instance of the use of this delaying tactic. **2.** An adventurer who engages in a private military action in a foreign country. — *v.* **-tered, -ter·ing, -ters.** — *intr.* **1.** To use obstructionist tactics in a legislative body. **2.** To take part in a private military action in a foreign country. — *tr.* To use obstructionist tactics against (a legislative measure, for example). [< Sp. *filibustero,* freebooter < Fr. *flibustier* < Du. *vrijbuiter,* pirate. See FREEBOOTER.] — **fil′i·bus′ter·er** *n.*

fil·i·form (fĭl′ə-fôrm′, fī′lə-) *adj.* Having the form of or resembling a thread or filament. [Lat. *filum,* thread; see **gʷhī-** + -FORM.]

fil·i·gree (fĭl′ĭ-grē′) *n.* **1.** Delicate and intricate ornamental work made of gold, silver, or other fine twisted wire. **2.a.** An intricate, delicate, or fanciful ornamentation. **b.** A design resembling such ornamentation. — *tr.v.* **-greed, -gree·ing, -grees.** To decorate with or as if with filigree. [Alteration of Fr. *filigrane* < Ital. *filigrana :* Lat. *filum,* thread; see **gʷhī-** + Lat. *grānum,* grain; see **grə-no-**.]

fil·ing (fī′lĭng) *n.* **1.** A particle or shaving removed by a file. **2.** The act or an instance of using a file.

fil·i·o·pi·e·tis·tic (fĭl′ē-ō-pī′ĭ-tĭs′tĭk) *adj.* Of or relating to an often immoderate reverence for forebears or tradition. [Lat. *filius,* son; see FILIAL + PIETISTIC.]

Fil·i·pi·no (fĭl′ə-pē′nō) *n., pl.* **-nos. 1.** A native or inhabitant of the Philippines. **2.** The Austronesian language based on Tagalog that draws its lexicon from other Philippine languages and is the official language of the Philippines. — *adj.* Of or relating to the Philippines or its peoples, languages, or cultures. [Sp. < *(Islas) Filipinas,* Philippine (Islands).]

This list of words taken directly from the dictionary begins with the word *filial,* the same word used in the biology excerpt. Note that not only does this definition provide you with a general definition of this word, but definition 3 gives you the definition specifically as it relates to genetics. The definition also tells you about the Latin root *filius,* which means son.

Now look down this list of words a bit further. Do you see any other words that are based on this same Latin root? How can you distinguish those words that are derived from this root from those that are not? The words *filiation* and *filiopietistic* are from *filial* while the others are not. Both of these words have something to do with descendents or forebearers while the others do not. The point here is to be careful when assuming words may be from the same root just because the first few letters are the same.

Application Exercises (DTT)

Two examples of terms from the selections in the appendix follow. First, the term is used in the context of the original textbook. Then a dictionary listing that includes the term is given.

Read the sentences in which each word is used; then read the dictionary entry. Also examine the structure of the word and look at any other words on the dictionary page that use the same structure. Last, answer the questions after each example.

1. "When you repress a memory, you block it from consciousness. It is possible that certain memories are too painful to relive and so are forgotten. According to Freud, *repression* is a major psychological defense we all use against anxiety. We repress painful experiences in order not to feel the anxiety that would accompany their memories." ("The Psychology of Memory," p. 273) Look at the following dictionary definitions:[6]

> **re•press** (rĭ-prĕs') *v.* **-pressed. -press•ing. -press•es.—***tr.* **1.** To hold back: restrain: *repress a laugh.* **2.** To suppress: quell: *repress a rebellion.* **3.** *Psychoanal.* To exclude (memories, for example) from the conscious mind.—*intr.* To take repressive action. [ME *repressen* < Lat. *reprimere* : *re-,* back—*premere,* to press.]—**re•press′er** *n.*—**re•press′i•bil′i•ty** *n.*—**re•press′i•ble** *adj.*
> **re•pres•sion** (rĭ•prĕsh′ən) *n.* **1. a.** The act of repressing. **b.** The state of being repressed. **2.** *Psychoanal.* The unconscious exclusion of painful impulses, desires, or fears from the conscious mind.—**re•pres′sion•ist** *adj.*
> **re•pres•sive** (rĭ-prĕs′iv) *adj.* Causing or inclined to cause repression: *a repressive dictatorship.*—**re•pres′sive•ly** *adv.*—**re•pres′sive•ness** *n.*
> **re•pres•sor** (rĭ-prĕs′ər) *n.* **1.** One that represses. **2.** *Biol.* A chemical compound that prevents the synthesis of a protein by interfering with the action of DNA.

(a) Reading the entry for *repression:*
How many syllables are in the word? _____

What part of speech is the word? _____

(b) Matching the context and the definition:
Only three definitions for the term are given. Which one is the same as the definition the author uses in the context? _____

_____

What additional information do you get from the dictionary definition?

_____

_____

(c) Using the structure:
There are other words on the dictionary page that use *repress* as a word part. How does the word *repress* help describe the meaning of *repression?*

_____

_____

2. From a cognitive standpoint, it [discrimination] can often be traced to *stereotypes*—simplistic beliefs that associate whole groups of people with certain, sometimes unflattering traits. ("Human Diversity," p. 356) Now look at this group of dictionary definitions:[7]

ster·e·o (stĕr′ē-ō′, stîr′-) *n., pl.* **-os. 1.a.** A stereophonic sound-reproduction system. **b.** Stereophonic sound. **2.** A stereotype. **3.** A stereoscopic system or photograph. *— adj.* **1.** Stereophonic. **2.** Stereoscopic.
stereo– *pref.* **1.** Solid; solid body: *stereotropism.* **2.** Three-dimensional: *stereoscope.* [Gk. < *stereos,* solid. See **ster-¹•**.]
ster·e·o·bate (stĕr′ē-ō-bāt′, stîr′-) *n. Archit.* **1.** See **stylobate. 2.** The foundation of a stone building, its top course sometimes being a stylobate. [Lat. *stereobatēs* < Gk. **stereobatēs : stereos,* solid; see STEREO– + *-batēs,* walker (< *bainein,* to go; see **gʷā-***).]
ster·e·o·chem·is·try (stĕr′ē-ō-kĕm′ĭ-strē, stîr′-) *n.* The branch of chemistry that deals with spatial arrangements of atoms in molecules and the chemical and physical effects of these arrangements. — **ster′e·o·chem′i·cal** (-ĭ-kəl) *adj.*
ster·e·o·chro·my (stĕr′ē-ə-krō′mē, stîr′-) *n., pl.* **-mies.** The art or process of mural painting with pigments mixed with water glass. — **ster′e·o·chrome′** *n.* — **ster′e·o·chro′mic** *adj.* — **ster′e·o·chro′mi·cal·ly** *adv.*
ster·e·o·gram (stĕr′ē-ə-grăm′, stîr′-) *n.* **1.** A picture or diagram that gives the impression of solidity. **2.** A stereograph.
ster·e·o·graph (stĕr′ē-ə-grăf′, stîr′-) *n.* Two stereoscopic pictures or one picture with two superposed stereoscopic images, designed to give a three-dimensional effect when viewed through a stereoscope or special glasses. — *tr.v.* **-graphed. -graph·ing. -graphs.** To make a stereographic picture of.
ster·e·og·ra·phy (stĕr′ē-ŏg′rə-fē, stîr′-) *n.* **1.** The art or technique of depicting solid bodies on a plane surface. **2.** Photography that involves the use of stereoscopic equipment. — **ster′e·o·graph′ic** (-ə-grăf′ĭk), **ster′e·o·graph′i·cal** (-ĭ-kəl) *adj.* — **ster′e·o·graph′i·cal·ly** *adv.*
ster·e·o·i·so·mer (stĕr′ē-ō-ī′sə-mər, stîr′-) *n.* One of a set of isomers whose molecules have the same atoms bonded to each other but differ in the way these atoms are arranged in space.

ster·e·o·i·som·er·ism (stĕr′ē-ō-ī-sŏm′ə-rĭz′əm, stîr′-) *n.* Isomerism due to differences in the spatial arrangement of atoms in a molecule. — **ster′e·o·i′so·mer′ic** (-ī′-sə-mĕr′-ĭk) *adj.*

ster·e·ol·o·gy (stĕr′ē-ŏl′ə-jē, stîr′-) *n.* The study of three-dimensional properties of objects or matter usu. observed two-dimensionally. — **ster′e·o·log′ic** (-ə-lŏj′ĭk), **ster′e·o·log′i·cal** (-ĭ-kəl) *adj.* — **ster′e·ol′o·gist** *n.*

ster·e·o·phon·ic (stĕr′ē-ə-fŏn′ĭk, stîr′-) *adj.* Of or used in a sound-reproduction system that uses two or more separate channels to give a more natural distribution of sound. — **ster′e·o·phon′i·cal·ly** *adv.* — **ster′e·oph′on·y** (-ē-ŏf′ə-nē) *n.*

ster·e·op·sis (stĕr′ē-ŏp′sĭs, stîr′-) *n.* Stereoscopic vision.

ster·e·op·ti·con (stĕr′ē-ŏp′tĭ-kŏn′, stîr′-) *n.* A magic lantern, esp. one with two projectors arranged so as to produce dissolving views. [New Latin : STEREO- + Gk. *optikon*, neut. of *optikos*, optic; see OPTIC.]

ster·e·o·scope (stĕr′ē-ə-skōp′, stîr′-) *n.* An instrument with two eyepieces used to impart a three-dimensional effect to two photographs of the same scene from slightly different angles.

ster·e·o·scop·ic (stĕr′ē-ə-skŏp′ĭk, stîr′-) *adj.* **1.** Of or relating to stereoscopy. **2.** Of or relating to a stereoscope. — **ster′e·o·scop′i·cal·ly** *adv.*

ster·e·os·co·py (stĕr′ē-ŏs′kə-pē, stîr′-) *n.* **1.** The viewing of objects as three-dimensional. **2.** The technique of making or using stereoscopes and stereoscopic slides.

ster·e·o·tax·is (stĕr′ē-ə-tăk′sĭs, stîr′-) *n.* **1.** A method in neurosurgery and neurological research for locating points within the brain using an external three-dimensional frame of reference usu. based on the Cartesian coordinate system. **2.** Movement of an organism in response to contact with a solid body. — **ster′e·o·tac′tic** (-tăk′tĭk) *adj.*

ster·e·ot·ro·pism (stĕr′ē-ŏt′rə-pĭz′əm, stîr′-) *n.* See **thigmotropism.** — **ster′e·o·trop′ic** (-ē-ə-trŏp′ĭk) *adj.*

ster·e·o·type (stĕr′ē-ə-tīp′, stîr′-) *n.* **1.** A conventional, formulaic, and oversimplified conception or image. **2.** One seen as embodying or conforming to a stereotype. **3.** *Print.* A metal printing plate cast from a matrix molded from a raised printing surface. — *tr.v.* **-typed, -typ·ing, -types. 1.** To make a stereotype of. **2.** To characterize by a stereotype. **3.** To give a fixed, unvarying form to. **4.** To print from a stereotype. [Fr. *stéréotype*, stereotype printing : *stéréo-*, solid (< Gk. *stereo-*; see STEREO-) + *type*, printing type (< OFr., symbol < LLat. *typus*; see TYPE).] — **ster′e·o·typ′er** *n.* — **ster′e·o·typ′ic** (-tĭp′ĭk), **ster′e·o·typ′i·cal** (-ĭ-kəl) *adj.* — **ster′e·o·typ′i·cal·ly** *adv.*

ster·e·o·typed (stĕr′ē-ə-tīpt′, stîr′-) *adj.* **1.** Lacking originality or creativity. **2.** *Print.* Made from stereotype plates.

(a) Reading the entry for *stereotypes:*

How many syllables are in the word? _____

What part of speech is the word? _____

How is the word commonly used? _____

_____

What are the two word parts that make up the word?

_____ + _____

(b) Matching the context and the definition:

Several definitions for the term are given. Which one is the same as the definition the author uses in the context? _____

What additional information do you get from the dictionary definition?

_____

_____

(c) Using the structure:
There are other words on the dictionary page that use *stereo* as a word part. How does the word-part *stereo* help describe the meaning of *stereotypes?*

_____

_____

What other word that uses *stereo* is most familiar to you?

_____

How does the structure make this word's definition similar to the definition of *stereotypes?*

_____

_____

Application Exercises (Your Texts)

Choose two difficult terms from your textbook. For each, complete the following:

Term 1: _____

Name of course in which the term is used: _____

Read the context the author uses with the term.

1. What do you think the word means? _____

_____

Look up the word in a dictionary.

2. How many syllables are in the word? _____

3. What part of speech is the word? _____

4. In what phrase is the word most commonly used? (Your dictionary may not give examples.) _____

_____

5. What are the word parts that make up the word? (Your word may not have identified word parts.) _____

_____

6. If only one definition is given, is it the same as the definition the author uses in the context? _____

What additional information do you get from the dictionary definition?

_____

_____

If more than one definition is given, which definition is closest to how the word is used by the textbook author? _____

_____

7. If the word is made up of word parts, how does each of the word parts help to describe the meaning of the word? _____

_____

_____

8. What other word that uses one of the word parts is most familiar to you?

_____

Term 2: _____

Name of course in which the term is used: _____

Read the context the author uses with the term.

1. What do you think the word means? _____

_____

Look up the word in a dictionary.

2. How many syllables are in the word? _____

3. What part of speech is the word? _____

4. In what phrase is the word most commonly used? (Your dictionary may not give examples.) _____

_____

5. What are the word parts that make up the word? (Your word may not have identified word parts.)

_____

6. If only one definition is given, is it the same as the definition the author uses in the context? _____

What additional information do you get from the dictionary definition?

_____

_____

If more than one definition is given, which definition is closest to how the word is used by the textbook author? _____

_____

7. If the word is made up of word parts, how does each of the word parts help to describe the meaning of the word?

_____

_____

Generative Vocabulary Strategies

It is not enough to be aware of the different methods—context, dictionary, and structure—that can help you to determine what a word means. The key is to be able to increase your vocabulary and to know words beyond merely memorizing a dictionary or textbook definition. Students should have a systematic way of building their vocabularies that can combine the three different methods. The simplest and easiest way to build your vocabulary is through learning and using a variety of generative vocabulary strategies. By *generative* we mean *strategies that you can use on your own to increase your understanding of words.*

The best way to increase your vocabulary is through reading. Those of you using this text who have read the most probably also have the best vocabularies. But if you haven't been a reader, it's never too late to work at improving your knowledge of words. The sheer fact that you are in college and thus will be required to do a considerable amount of reading and critical thinking puts you in a position to be able to increase your vocabulary as part of what is already assigned in your other college classes. The purpose of this section, then, is to provide some strategies for continuously and systematically increasing your understanding of new words.

Vocabulary Cards

Perhaps the most widely used, as well as the most efficient, generative strategy is *vocabulary cards*. Students generally like using vocabulary cards because they are portable and can be grouped and reordered to make learning and remembering the words easier.

If you want to work seriously on improving your vocabulary using the vocabulary-card strategy, the first thing you should remember is always to read your texts with a stack of 3 × 5 notecards beside you. (This strategy can be modified slightly to include words you find in nontext reading, also.) When you encounter an unknown word or term, or a term that you are somewhat familiar with but think that you will need to know more about for a test, jot it down on a card. (See Figure 6.1 for an example of a content-specific vocabulary card.) Complete the card immediately or when you have completed your reading.

Front

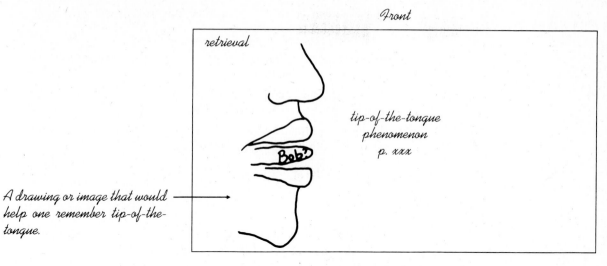

retrieval

tip-of-the-tongue
phenomenon
p. xxx

A drawing or image that would
help one remember tip-of-the-
tongue.

Back

A frustrating experience where you know that you have a particular
memory for something, but you are unable to retrieve it.

Ex You are trying to remember the name of an actor in a
movie. You can see his face and even recall that his
last name has 3 syllables and begins with a "T". Two
days later his name comes to you!

Figure 6.1 A Vocabulary Card

Some students find it intrusive to interrupt their reading to complete the card;
others find that it negatively influences their comprehension if they continue
reading without a clear understanding of the unfamiliar term. Try it both ways
to see which feels more comfortable for you. Some students wait to complete
words that do not negatively influence comprehension, but immediately look
up those that do.

Whichever way you choose, complete your cards in the following manner:

- Write the new word or term in the middle of the front of the card.
- Under the word, write the page number the word appears on so that you can locate the word in context.
- In the upper left-hand corner, write a general word that will help you to categorize the information on the new vocabulary word.
- In the lower right-hand corner, put a mnemonic that will help you to remember the word's meaning (*mnemonics* are discussed in Chapter 11).
- Turn the card over and record the meaning of the word as presented by your text. If the term is not clearly defined in the chapter, consult your lecture notes, a dictionary, a glossary (if your text has one), or your professor (if the meaning still is not clear).
- If appropriate, also be sure that you include applications or examples of the term; at the college level, instructors often expect you to go beyond simply memorizing a term's meaning. Including examples and applications moves you toward a more conceptual understanding of the word.

Once you have completed your cards for a particular chapter, you can easily use them when you study. Using the term in the upper left-hand corner of each card, you can group the words for easier study, separate out those that you know from those that you don't know, and rehearse the words blindly. (Chapter 2 mentioned rehearsal as an active strategy to use after reading, and Chapters 10 and 11 will discuss rehearsal further.) Making and using vocabulary cards helps you to learn vocabulary in any kind of reading situation, but the technique is especially useful in courses such as biology, psychology, chemistry, sociology, and physical science, all of which introduce many new terms.

Organizational Strategies

As mentioned earlier, complete word knowledge requires more than just memorizing a dictionary or even a text- or content-specific definition. Memorizing definitions and learning words in isolation do not get at the conceptual meaning of a word, nor do these methods show how words and concepts are related to one another. Several generative strategies are useful if you are expected to know how concepts interrelate. The list-group-label strategy is representative of such strategies. Chapter 10 will discuss some additional organizational strategies that can be modified so that you can use them with key terms presented in your texts.

As an example of how to use this strategy, we will use several new terms introduced in "The Psychology of Memory" selection in the appendix. You will encounter the following terms during your reading:

duplex theory of memory	rehearsal
elaborative rehearsal	maintenance rehearsal
deep processing	short-term memory
long-term memory	transfer
levels-of-processing theory of memory	shallow processing

You know that on the test you will be expected to know how these terms are related. After you have your list, first group similar terms together. You could then group and label the list of words in the following manner:

Duplex Theory of Memory	**Levels-of-Processing Theory of Memory**
short-term memory	shallow processing
long-term memory	deep processing
rehearsal	maintenance rehearsal
transfer	elaborative rehearsal

From this grouping it is easy to see which concepts go with which key label. Define and give examples for each of the key labels (*duplex theory of memory* and *levels-of-processing theory of memory*) and for each of the other concepts that are associated with the labels. Do this either by using the vocabulary-card method discussed earlier or by putting the information in chart or map form. (See Chapter 10 for additional information on charts and maps.)

The major advantage of using generative strategies to improve your knowledge of vocabulary is that you can easily test yourself on the material. If you fall into the trap of thinking that you know something without doing serious self-testing, you may enter a classroom testing situation without having a real understanding of what you know and what you *don't* know. Students who memorize without understanding often become confused during exams and mix up information. If this has happened to you, engaging in this type of self-testing and rehearsal is particularly important.

Key Ideas

1. Use the dictionary, context, and structure—not necessarily in any particular order—to help you to figure out the meaning of words that are unknown to you.

2. Context clues signal a definition in four main ways: They (1) provide synonyms, (2) provide antonyms and contrasts, (3) give examples and illustrations, and (4) offer opinion and tone.

3. Dictionary definitions have varying degrees of strength. The stronger the definition, the more helpful it will be.

4. Structure refers to knowledge of a word's prefix, root, and suffix. Knowing these word parts can help you to figure out a word's meaning.

5. Generative strategies can help you to determine and remember the meaning of unknown words on your own. Generative strategies include vocabulary cards and a variety of organizing strategies such as word maps and list-group-label.

■ A Scenario to Write About and Discuss

You are in a history course where a considerable amount of material is presented at a quick pace in class. The reading load is also considerable—about 150 pages per week, most of it taken from original sources. Even the general textbook is difficult to understand. Most of your difficulty with this class seems to stem from the fact that the vocabulary is difficult. There are many new terms that you must learn quickly, but there are also many general vocabulary words used both in the reading and lecture that are unfamiliar to you. What can you do to help yourself in this course? What are some approaches you might take to help you with the general words as well as with the course-related words? What might happen if you continue to ignore the problems you are having with the vocabulary?

Vocabulary Exercises for an Article: "A Colony in the Sky"

Read the following magazine selection, "A Colony in the Sky." Note that twenty-one words with which you might be unfamiliar have been underlined. Make vocabulary cards, using the procedure outlined in this chapter, for the words you don't know. Then answer the questions that follow the article. For your convenience, the words are listed here in the order they are presented in the article.

bounding	cyanobacteria
exhilarating	spiral
habitats	biosphere
fascinated	presumptuous
savannah	extinction
superficial	outlandish
"terraformed"; terraform; terraforming	steward
hypothetical	sustainability; sustainable
transformations	contemplate

Selection from a Magazine

A Colony in the Sky

Kim Stanley Robinson

After humans get to Mars, they'll start doing what comes naturally—turning it into another Earth.

One day early in the next century, several people will land on Mars. They will put on spacesuits and leave their vehicle, <u>bounding</u> over red rocks under a pink sky. After this <u>exhilarating</u> day, seen on Earth by billions, they will move into a cluster of <u>habitats</u> already on site. They will spend a year living there making scientific studies, and then they will return to Earth. Another team will cycle in. Back at home we will start to take the base for granted. Nevertheless, something very big will have begun.

The initial crossing to Mars will be made for a great number of reasons, some of them solid (to see if there really are fossil bacteria there), some of them not (to look for Elvis). Most of the reasons will be scientific and practical: The more we know about the solar system's other planets, the better we will understand Earth, and the safer we will be. It's not heroic but it makes sense, and it is important. Even if these were the only reasons, they would be good enough to send us.

But Mars will never remain just a research site to sharpen Earth management skills. We've been <u>fascinated</u> by the red wanderer ever since our days on the <u>savannah</u>, and even if life at the research station proves to be quite ordinary, the videos they send back will show us a magnificent world of volcanoes and canyons, icecaps and sand dunes, wind and weather. These wild new landscapes will also look somewhat familiar, especially in comparison to the bone-white moon. This familiar quality is not just <u>superficial</u>, for Mars does resemble Earth in several important ways—general size, presence of water, length of day, range of temperatures—so many similarities, in fact, that some people are beginning to ask if it might be possible to make Mars even more like Earth than it is now. And that's the question that will shift us to the next level of our fascination with the place: the idea that we could live there, that Mars could be "<u>terraformed</u>."

To <u>terraform</u> means to alter a planet's surface until Earth's life forms can survive there. It's a <u>hypothetical</u> discipline at this point, born in science-fiction stories. But in the last thirty years a number of scientists have taken up the concept. Their studies make it clear that the process would be somewhat slower than the cork-popping <u>transformations</u> seen in some recent sci-fi movies; in reality, it would take centuries. But it is an idea that operates within physical reality as we know it. It's possible to do it.

The recipe is simple. Add nitrogen and oxygen to the atmosphere; pump water to the surface; cook for decades, spicing first with cyanobacteria, then with all the rest of Earth's plants and animals, adding them in the order they evolved here. Mars is blessed with all the ingredients called for in the recipe; indeed, Mars turns out to be perfect for terraforming. So, because we have all the life forms here at hand, we can try replaying evolution at extreme fast forward.

Of course it will be more complex than the recipe—it always is. And the process will certainly spiral out of our control. Eventually, however, if all goes well, we will have helped to start a new biosphere. Think of that! It's hard to know how even to characterize such an activity. It would be something like growing a garden or creating a wilderness or building a cathedral or flying seeds over an ocean to drop them on a new island. It would be unlike anything else, a new thing in history.

Some people may believe that such a project is too large or slow or presumptuous for humanity to undertake. But consider our current situation on Earth. There are nearly six billion of us now, and the number may double, though we have no good idea how many of us the Earth can support. Many larger species are in danger of extinction unless we protect them from us. We have rearranged much of the land, and we have altered the atmosphere to the point where the global climate in the future will be a matter of legislation and industrial practice. In other words, we are already starting to terraform Earth by necessity to keep it livable. Given this situation, the attempt to terraform Mars does not look so outlandish. Doing it could be regarded as a valuable experiment, with Mars as a giant lab or university, in which we learn how to steward a planet's biosphere for long-term sustainability.

Long term indeed! Terraforming Mars would take 300 years at least. It's not a time scale we often think about, and it does seem unlikely that any society could persist in anything for so long. Luckily, the process will not depend on our consistent backing, but on the people who settle there and pursue it as their own closest interest.

As for us, here on Earth in the age of the quarterly statement, it is probably a good thing occasionally to contemplate a really long-term project. Humanity's existence on this Earth is a long-term project, after all, and it's important to remember what that means. People will be living here 500 years from now, and they will be our relatives. These distant children of ours deserve to be given a livable planet to care for in their turn. For their sake we need to work out a sustainable way of life on Earth. Going to Mars will be part of that larger environmental project, and terraforming it will be an education that we will apply at home as we learn it—pausing, from time to time, to look up at our wilderness garden in the sky.

Source: Kim Stanley Robinson, "A Colony in the Sky," from *Newsweek,* September 21, 1996. Copyright © 1996 by Kim Stanley Robinson. Used by permission of Kim Stanley Robinson c/o Ralph M. Vicinanza, Ltd.

Application Exercises

Using your vocabulary cards, complete the following exercises. If you have problems completing these exercises, your cards may not be complete enough to be very useful.

1. What happened when you looked up the word *terraform* in the dictionary? What do you find when you look up this word?

    _____

    Why do you suppose you have encountered this problem? _____

    Write a definition in your own words for *terraform*. _____

    _____

    _____

    What part of speech is *terraform?* _____

2. In the article "A Colony in the Sky," the author said that ". . . the process will *spiral* out of control." What does *spiral* mean in this context?

    _____

    _____

3. Give an example of a *hypothetical* situation other than the one described in the article. _____

    _____

4. Where might you find a *savannah?* _____

    _____

5. In order to make the planet Mars like Earth, why would it be important to add *cyanobacteria?* _____

    _____

6. What does the author mean when she states that we need to "learn how to *steward* a planet's *biosphere* . . . ?" _____

    _____

7. Why might some people think that the Mars project is too *presumptuous?*

    _____

8. Give an example of something that is *extinct* or faces the danger of *extinction.* _____

    _____

Notes

1. Copyright © 1991 by Houghton Mifflin Company. Reproduced by permission from *The American Heritage Dictionary, Second College Edition.*

2. Ibid.

3. Ibid.

4. Ibid.

5. Copyright © 1997 by Houghton Mifflin Company. Reproduced by permission from *The American Heritage College Dictionary, Third Edition.*

6. Copyright © 1991 by Houghton Mifflin Company. Reproduced by permission from *The American Heritage College Dictionary. Second College Edition.*

7. Copyright © 1997 by Houghton Mifflin Company. Reproduced by permission from *The American Heritage College Dictionary, Third Edition.*

Chapter 7

Flexibility and Efficiency in Studying

Personally, I'm always ready to learn,
although I do not always like being taught.

Winston Churchill

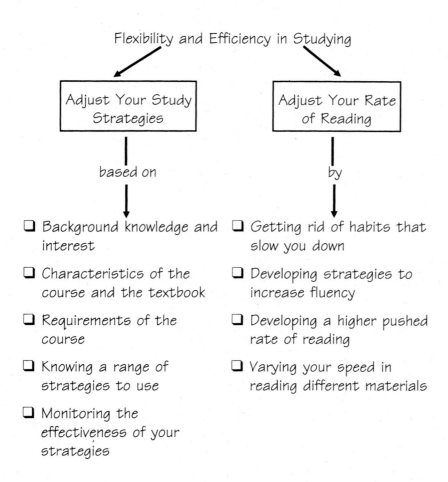

Flexibility and Efficiency in Studying

Adjust Your Study Strategies

Adjust Your Rate of Reading

based on

by

❑ Background knowledge and interest

❑ Characteristics of the course and the textbook

❑ Requirements of the course

❑ Knowing a range of strategies to use

❑ Monitoring the effectiveness of your strategies

❑ Getting rid of habits that slow you down

❑ Developing strategies to increase fluency

❑ Developing a higher pushed rate of reading

❑ Varying your speed in reading different materials

In earlier chapters, we discussed becoming aware of reading and studying habits and developing ways to have the motivation, the time, and the organization to study effectively. There is another important aspect of efficient and effective studying—flexibility.

Flexibility in studying includes:

- adjusting your reading speed
- deciding what kinds of information to isolate and learn
- deciding what kinds of study strategies to use with the textbook and with the lectures and discussions
- asking yourself different types of questions in preparation for a test
- deciding how often to review

Flexibility allows you to spend more time, with more intensive study strategies, on the classes that are the most difficult for you. You can do this by spending less time and energy on the classes that you find easy.

To be flexible, adjust your reading and study strategies to each task, and have several strategies from which to choose. The next several sections of this text will cover a variety of strategies for reading, studying, note taking, and test taking that will help to increase your flexibility.

In addition to developing a range of study strategies, becoming flexible requires you to assess your own background knowledge and interest. You also have to consider the types of studying required by the textbook, the instructor, and the tasks your instructor expects you to carry out. So, as you move from course to course, your tasks, and thus the way you will need to study, will change.

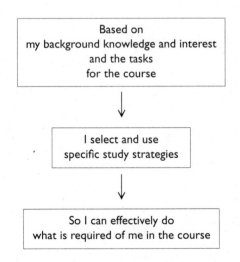

Figure 7.1 Developing Flexibility

Background Knowledge and Interest

How much background knowledge you have in a subject affects how easy or difficult a course will be for you. You don't learn new information in a void or from scratch; you learn it by linking new information with information you already know. The more you know about a topic, the fewer new linkages you have to make, and the easier it is to make the new linkages.

As an example, suppose you read a newspaper account of a basketball game. If you knew a great deal about basketball, you already knew the rules in detail, the teams that played, who the key players were, and what you might expect them to do. All you had to learn was who won, by how many points, and what the key plays were. You could read the article very quickly—by skimming over what you knew already and reading only the information about that particular game.

On the other hand, if you knew only a little about basketball, you might have to learn the team names and the player names in addition to who won and how. This would be slower reading, and there would probably be more new information than you could learn by reading the article only once.

If you know *nothing* about basketball, the article might prove impossible to read. You might have to ask someone for information or read about the rules and scoring before you could make sense of the article. And even then, it would take several readings and extensive study to learn as much as our first reader knew just by skimming the article.

Authors make assumptions about the amount and type of background information their readers have. If you have more background knowledge than the author of a textbook assumes, the book will be easy to read and study. If you have less background knowledge, the book may be very difficult, unless you can use similar, related knowledge to help you. In either case, you can make use of your background knowledge only if you

1. determine what type and amount of background information the author assumes you have

2. call the appropriate background knowledge to mind before you start reading so you can use it to link the new information in your memory

Chapter 8, which focuses on strategies to use before you read, discusses ways to bring your background knowledge to mind. The next part of this chapter will help you to determine what the author expects by looking at the typical characteristics of textbooks.

Characteristics of Textbooks

In addition to using your background knowledge, you must also have knowledge about differences among textbooks from a variety of disciplines, because such knowledge promotes effective and efficient learning. As you take different courses in college and read the required texts, you will notice some basic differences among them. The selections in this textbook are representative of texts in the social sciences, biological and physical sciences, and humanities. Actually, even within each of these three areas, textbooks have differing characteristics. Some examples of academic disciplines and subdivisions of those disciplines include the following:*

Humanities

Language
Literature
Philosophy and Theology
Fine Arts
    Architecture
    Theater
    Art
    Music

Social Sciences

Social Orientation
    Sociology
    Social Work
    Psychology
Business
    Economics
    Accounting
    Business Administration
Study of Ancient Humans
    Anthropology
    Archaeology
Education

Political Orientation
    Law
    History
    Political Science

Sciences

Exact Sciences
    Mathematics
    Physics
    Chemistry
    Computer Science
Biological Sciences
    Biology
    Agriculture
    Medicine
    Forestry
    Botany
    Zoology
True Physical Sciences
    Astronomy
    Engineering
    Geology

With so many subareas and courses, it is difficult to generalize about the characteristics of each. However, the three main subject areas can be contrasted in several ways. The following sections compare humanities, social science, and science texts in six different areas:

- new terminology

- major ideas and emphases

- text organization

* The categorization system we suggest is certainly not the only one you might use. Differences among texts do exist, and those differences affect the choice of study methods.

- use of typographical aids
- assumptions about background knowledge
- tests

New Terminology

Humanities texts (and especially literature texts) tend to have little new terminology. The texts do, however, present difficulties in understanding dialects, foreign expressions, and archaic (old or outdated) usages of words. The texts also use words in symbolic or metaphoric ways, and interpreting the symbolism can pose problems for many students.

In social science and fine arts texts, familiar words may have new and specialized meanings. This tendency can create problems, because you may already know one general meaning for a word (such as *class* or *mobility*), and therefore you may think that you know the new, specialized meaning when you really do not.

Science texts tend to introduce new terms and new definitions, often very rapidly. This tendency creates a double demand on your memory. You also may have problems if the textbook authors later use the new words in defining other words. If you didn't learn the first word, you will have trouble understanding later terms and more complicated concepts.

Major Ideas and Emphases

Humanities texts, especially literature texts, tend to stress such points as the author's purpose, symbolism, characters, and the mood or tone of a selection, thus requiring students to think critically about what they read. These topics are rarely stated directly in the selection and must be discovered by the student.

Social science texts tend to stress particular theories or slants with supporting evidence. Because it is so difficult to prove much about people and social institutions, social scientists rely on theories about what happens in a society. Social science texts can often confuse students about what is fact and what is theory or opinion.

In science texts, proven principles of basic importance and well-researched (but not proven) theories tend to be stressed as facts. In addition, science texts stress relationships between and among ideas.

Text Organization

Humanities texts, especially literature texts, usually present information in story, drama, essay, or poem format. The text may be organized by time period, type of literature, themes of literature, or world regions. Generally, such texts use few instructional aids (such as graphs, charts, or diagrams).

Social science texts are often topical; the text or its chapters are divided into topics and subtopics of roughly equal importance. You could open many texts to, say, Chapter 12 and read and understand it as easily as Chapter 1, because each topic stands on its own. Other social science texts follow some other, logical order. For example, history texts usually follow chronological order. Political science texts may be organized according to the regions of a country. In such cases, you need information from previous chapters in order to understand the chapter you are currently reading. Social science texts also tend to use headings, subheadings, italicized words, and other typographical aids to help you follow the author's organization of the material.

Science texts are almost always sequential. You have to study chapters in a particular order, because one chapter in a section usually builds on the one before. Science texts may present broad concepts and then elaborate on specific areas, or they may present specific information that leads to broad concepts. These texts also use many headings, subheadings, and italicized words, breaking the reading into small chunks to make it easier to understand.

Use of Typographical and Instructional Aids

Typographical aids, such as headings, subheadings, and italicized or boldfaced words, are signposts that make learning easier. Examples of instructional aids are charts, graphs, photographs, and diagrams, all of which summarize information or present new information more clearly than a textual description alone could have.

Humanities texts rarely use charts, graphs, or diagrams, but they often use photographs. Even then, the pictures usually are included to set a tone, to build interest, or to illustrate something particular in the text; they rarely present new information and thus are not extremely important in studying. Other humanities texts assume that you have some knowledge of the sequence of historical events.

Social science texts use all of these aids at one time or another. In many texts, they serve to create interest or to illustrate graphically some point in the text. In such cases, they are not vital to study. In other cases, such aids add new information or summarize information from the textual discussion. In these instances, you should study these aids.

Science texts use many instructional aids. These aids almost always present additional information or summarize a great deal of text information (for example, a diagram of an amoeba can summarize two pages of description). In science texts, you should study these aids carefully in order to understand the material thoroughly.

Assumptions About Background Knowledge

Literature texts typically assume that you have some knowledge of the basic structure of stories, essays, plays, and poems. More important, they often assume that you are able to determine the symbolism used, to recognize figurative language (such as metaphors and similes), and to interpret the author's purpose, tone, or mood. Literature texts sometimes assume that you learned these skills in high school and that you can think critically about what you are reading. If you have not already learned these skills, you may find literature texts difficult to read and comprehend thoroughly.

Social science texts assume that you have some understanding of how people and societies function. Authors assume, for example, that you can read a one-sentence definition of "social stratification" and understand what is meant because you have experience with living in a society. In some cases, an author assumes that you know what was covered in a previous chapter or course. They also assume that you can distinguish between theories and proven facts.

Science texts tend to assume that you have a working understanding of scientific inquiry—how basic laws, facts, and principles are discovered and the relationship between basic principles and their supporting proofs. In addition, authors typically assume that you have background knowledge from previous chapters in their book, from high school courses or from other college courses. These assumptions make reviewing a vital part of studying scientific material. Finally, science texts assume that you can quickly decode new and unusual words and understand their meaning. Authors often use a new word in the very next sentence to define yet another word.

Tests

Many, but not all, humanities tests use essay questions. At the beginning of the course, ask your instructors what type of tests they plan to give.

Social science tests tend to combine multiple-choice, short-answer, and essay questions. Again, ask your instructors for particulars.

Science tests tend to be multiple choice, short answer, or labeling, because in science courses, the stress is on facts and exactness. Here again, check with your instructor.

■ A Scenario to Write About and Discuss

Suppose that you are taking a chemistry course, an English literature course, and a sociology course this term. Based on the general differences among texts for these courses, how would you study each subject differently? Specifically, what would you do differently with each textbook in terms of (a) reading the textbook; (b) marking the textbook or taking notes; (c) studying for a test? Review pages 117–121 to get ideas on how such textbooks might differ.

Application Exercises (DTT)

1. Use "The Psychology of Memory" selection in the appendix to complete the exercise at the end of this section. First, preview the text selection by applying these steps:

   (a) Read the title.

   (b) Read the headings and subheadings.

   (c) Skim and look for italicized or underlined words or phrases.

   (d) Look at any pictures or figures and read the captions.

   While previewing, try to answer the following questions:

   - What is difficult about this selection?
   - How is the material organized?
   - How is the information conveyed?
   - What prior knowledge would you need in order to read and study the selection?
   - What types of questions would you expect from such materials?

   After previewing and skimming the selection, complete the Application Exercise on pages 123–125. Keep in mind that your answers to the questions on this exercise should be based on your familiarity or unfamiliarity with the topic, as well as on the actual presentation of the topic.

2. Using the section "Weather Forecasting" in the appendix, do the following:

   (a) Survey the chapter.

   (b) List the characteristics of "Weather Forecasting" using the six factors discussed in this chapter. Give examples.

   (c) Compare your list with the generalizations about science texts. Does this chapter follow the generalizations? Explain.

Application Exercises (Your Courses)

Use the first ten to fifteen pages of one chapter from one of your textbooks to complete the exercise on pages 123–125.

Preview the text selection by applying these steps:

(a) Read the title.

(b) Read the headings and subheadings.

(c) Skim and look for italicized or underlined words or phrases.

(d) Look at any pictures or figures and read the captions.

While previewing, try to answer the following questions:

- What is difficult about this selection?
- How is the material organized?

- How is the information conveyed?
- What prior knowledge would you need in order to read and study the selection?
- What types of questions would you expect from such materials?

After previewing and skimming the selection, complete the Application Exercises that follow. Keep in mind that your answers to the questions on these exercises should be based on your familiarity or unfamiliarity with each topic, as well as on the actual presentation of the topic.

Application Exercises for Textbook Characteristics

Chapter Title: _____

Check the items that describe this textbook selection. Try to give one specific example for each item checked.

1. What is difficult about this passage?

_____ Unfamiliar terms; uses dialect

   Example: _____

_____ Terms I am familiar with that have specialized meanings

   Example: _____

_____ Lots of new terms or ideas introduced rapidly

   Example: _____

_____ General descriptions that are hard to understand

   Example: _____

_____ Very specific descriptions that are hard to memorize

   Example: _____

_____ A need to understand symbolism

   Example: _____

_____ Pictures or figures difficult to understand

   Example: _____

_____ Other (specify) _____

2. How is the material organized? What kinds of typographical or reading aids are given?

_____ Headings and subheadings

  Example: _____

_____ New terms italicized

  Example: _____

_____ New terms underlined

  Example: _____

_____ Figures used to illustrate points

  Example: _____

_____ Other (specify) _____

3. How is the information conveyed?

_____ Chronologically (by time)

  Example: _____

_____ From large topics to smaller topics

  Example: _____

_____ Different sections on topics of equal importance

  Example: _____

_____ Typical story format

  Example: _____

_____ Uses primarily explanation

  Example: _____

_____ Uses scientific proofs

  Example: _____

4. What would you need to know beforehand to read and study such a selection?

  _____

5. What types of test questions would you expect to cover such a passage?
  _____ (a) Multiple choice
  _____ (b) True/false
  _____ (c) Short answer
  _____ (d) Essay
  _____ (e) Questions testing for knowledge that a person can memorize

_____ (f) Questions testing how well a person can use what he or she has learned

Write one question that you predict could be used on a test covering this selection:

_____

_____

_____

Developing Reading-Rate Fluency and Flexibility

Most people, including students, read all material—magazines, novels, and textbooks—at the same rate of speed. This practice is a waste of time as well as inefficient. Because 85 percent of all courses in college involve reading, it is advantageous for students not only to increase their reading rate but also to develop some flexibility in their rate.

It is a fallacy that the more slowly you read the more you comprehend. In fact, reading very slowly can *inhibit* comprehension rather than enhance it. Think of it this way: If you are reading only 100 or 150 words per minute, you are reading less a word at a time (a rate that is even slower than you speak); it takes extra work for the brain to make sense of the incoming visual stimuli, and you also may forget the start of a passage by the time you get to the end.

The concept of reading rate, then, actually encompasses two related but not identical issues: flexibility and fluency. *Flexibility* is the ability to adjust your rate to the kind of material you are reading, just as you adjust your studying to meet the demands of each course. You should read a magazine more rapidly than your biology text, for example. Flexibility is also the ability to vary your rate throughout a chapter. You may read relatively quickly easier material, material in which you have adequate background knowledge, and material that your instructor tells you is not very important. You may read difficult or unfamiliar concepts within that same chapter more slowly.

Fluency, in contrast, means increasing your rate while enhancing your comprehension. It makes little sense to "read" 400 words per minute and yet understand only 40 percent of what you have read. In developing reading fluency, rate and comprehension go together.

Reading slowly and reading all types of materials at the same rate are actually just bad habits; therefore, you can break them with effort and practice. We do not intend to teach speed-reading in this book, but we will discuss some of these bad habits and the remedies for them. We will also suggest ways to increase your speed in reading easy material. With practice, this should give you one more tool for flexibility in your studying.

Reading Habits That Slow You Down

Several common problems can inhibit your reading rate. These problems, fortunately, are relatively easy to correct with practice. Think about what you do when you read silently to see if you do any of these things.

Are You an Auditory Reader?

Most people learned to read by sounding out words and reading out loud. Although this can be a good way to learn to read, it can create "auditory readers"—people who believe reading means *hearing* every single word. If you have to hear every word on the page, you will never read any faster than you can talk. Auditory readers may move their lips during reading, move vocal chords, or subvocalize.

Lip-reading means taking time to form each word with your lips. If you lip-read, you are not reading any faster than your lips can move. To correct this problem, place your finger lightly on your lips while you are reading. You can cure yourself of lip-reading by making a conscious effort to hold your lips still.

"READING SKILLS ARE VERY IMPORTANT. THAT'S HOW YOU FIND OUT WHAT'S GOING TO BE ON TV."

PHI DELTA KAPPAN

Sometimes people move their lips while reading a passage that is extremely difficult to comprehend or when their concentration is poor. Even if you lip-read infrequently, you should still try to eliminate it completely, but your problem is less serious than that of the person who lip-reads all the time.

Moving your vocal chords occurs when you partially activate your vocal cords during reading. This means that you form words in your throat rather than with your lips. In order to determine if you habitually move your vocal chords, put your fingers lightly on your throat as you read silently. If you feel vibrations, you are moving your vocal chords. To correct this habit, keep your fingers on your throat as you read, and make a conscious effort not to form the words in your throat. As long as you move your vocal chords on *every* word, you cannot read any faster than you speak.

Subvocalization means that you don't move your lips or vocal chords, but you still "hear" every word in your mind. If you feel uncomfortable when you don't hear every word (even words such as *the* and *and*) in your mind while you're reading, you are a subvocalizer. For most material, you don't need to hear every word. Instead, try to understand key words and phrases. If you subvocalize, practice key-word reading and phrase reading to break the habit. (We will discuss these techniques in the next section of this chapter.)

Remember that your goal in reading is to be efficient and effective. If you find that subvocalizing or even lip-reading helps you to understand difficult material, then you should subvocalize or lip-read *that type* of material. However, you will lose your efficiency if you subvocalize or lip-read *everything*. Vary your reading strategy to fit the material you are reading.

Do You Regress During Reading?

Regression is the process of going back and rereading a word, phrase, or sentence that you thought you missed the first time through. Because written information is usually repeated, regression is rarely necessary. Although infrequent regressions do not slow reading rate very much, readers who habitually regress often lack confidence in their ability to comprehend. Regression is by far the most difficult habit to break. People with this habit tend to lose their concentration easily, because they are programmed to go back and reread.

For an example of how inefficient regression can be, read this sentence:

Memories can be thought of as consisting of information, rather than of physical objects such as houses.

If you frequently regress, you "read" the sentence something like this:

Memories can be thought of memories can be thought of as consisting consisting of information, rather than of physical physical objects physical objects such as houses houses.

Not only does it take you much longer to read the second "sentence," it is also much harder for you to comprehend. Regression affects your efficiency and your effectiveness.

Regression often results from losing concentration when you read. Some of the techniques in the next section will help you maintain concentration. For many students, losing concentration and regressing have simply become bad habits. Regression is a difficult habit to break because over a period of years you have allowed yourself *to fail to understand* what you read the first time because you could (and did) always go back and reread. Have you ever been looking at a textbook and realized you have "read" several pages but haven't gotten anything out of it? So you go back and reread those pages.

To break the regression habit, convince yourself that you *have to understand the first time through*. Move your finger under the line of print as you read, or cover the lines you have already read with an index card so you cannot regress to previous lines. In time, you will find that you understand more information the first time you read it, because your mind now knows it cannot go back and reread.

Another effective technique for eliminating this bad habit involves gradually decreasing the problem. Keep a piece of paper by you when you read. As soon as you realize you've lost concentration, make a mark on the paper. You might have 25 marks for the chapter you read today; try to have only 23 marks tomorrow, 20 the next day, and so on. By keeping track of regressions, you will find that you do begin to decrease the number of times they occur. You will also find you become aware of losing concentration much sooner—you won't "read" several pages before realizing it. Thus this technique helps you decrease both the number of times you regress and how much you regress each time.

Do You Move Your Eyes at One Speed?

Another habit that slows readers down occurs when they move their eyes from left to right across the line at a certain speed, and then move their eyes *at the same slow speed* from right to left, down to the beginning of the next line. When you go from one line to the next, of course, you aren't reading anything; you're just waiting (even for a second) for your eyes to get to the next line. Waiting interrupts your comprehension of the material, and it may break your concentration. At the least, you are slowing yourself down.

To see if you have this habit, time yourself as you read a page of text in your normal way. Then read another page that is from the same source and is about the same length. This time, purposefully move your eyes as quickly as possible from the end of each line to the beginning of the next. Then read the next line at your regular speed. (Don't worry if you lose some comprehension at this point; your mind is busy thinking about a "fast return-sweep.") Time yourself using this fast return-sweep and see if you read the second page more rapidly. Some of our students found that their reading speed doubled if they just increased the speed of the return-sweep. Not only did they save time in the return-sweep, they also found that they moved more quickly across the lines they read because they had a sense of momentum.

To work on breaking this slow return-sweep habit, practice increasing the speed of your return-sweep. Practice on materials that are light reading for you. Most students find that their comprehension decreases at first, but once they develop the habit of a fast return-sweep and stop thinking about doing it, their comprehension returns to its normal level. You are replacing a bad habit (going between lines as slowly as you read across lines) with a new, efficient habit (a fast return-sweep).

Strategies to Increase Fluency

Most speed-reading techniques are based on two facts about reading and readers: First, our eyes can see clearly and our minds can comprehend more than one word at a time. Second, written material almost always conveys meaning in phrases, not in single words; within phrases (or chunks of meaning), some words are more important than others.

Fast reading involves taking advantage of these two facts by using several techniques. The three strategies we have found to be easiest and most helpful in quick reading are *increasing the speed of your eye movements, key-word reading,* and *phrase reading.* Although these three strategies are basically the same—they all involve reading chunks of meaning rather than each individual word—we have found that different strategies work for different students. Try out each strategy to see which works best for you. Then use that strategy in your speed-reading practice.

Increasing the Speed of Your Eye Movements

When you read, your eyes do *not* move steadily across a line. (If you doubt this, watch people's eyes move when they read.) Instead, your eyes jump from point to point across the line. At each point, they stop and focus ("fixate") so you can read. A very slower reader stops and focuses on every single word. By putting a dot where the eye fixates, we can show how this slow reader goes over a line of text:

A very slow reader stops and focuses on every word.
• • • • • • • • • •

You can increase speed by expanding the number of words you focus on at one time (increasing your "eye-span") and by stopping and focusing less frequently (decreasing your "fixations"). First, try focusing on two words at once:

A very slow reader stops and focuses on every word.
• • • • • •

Your eye-span is about twice as great and your fixations are half as many. Then, focus on three or four words at once:

A very slow reader stops and focuses on every word.

$\bullet$ $\bullet$ $\bullet$

We have found that three or four words per fixation is the maximum for most students just beginning to use this technique.

Try this strategy on Part 1 of the article about Malcolm X at the end of this chapter. Start by reading the way you normally do. Then, after a paragraph, start fixating on pairs of words. Then, after a few paragraphs, start fixating on three or four words at a time. When you have finished, jot down the main ideas of the article. Your comprehension is probably decreased as you increased your eye-span. This is normal because you are focusing on the mechanics of moving your eyes. As you continue to try this strategy on materials, however, and the mechanics become a habit, your comprehension will increase.

Key-Word Reading

With the previous strategy you may have found that you focused on, and read, key words. *Key words* are the words in a sentence or phrase that carry the meaning. (Key-word reading and the key-word method of memorizing information that will be presented in Chapter 11 are not the same.) Other words signal the key words (for example, *the* has no meaning; it signals that a noun—a key word—is coming up in the text.)

Key-word readers say the key words to themselves. Students who tend to subvocalize often find key-word reading to be the most effective method because they can still subvocalize some of the words. A key-word reader might subvocalize the example sentence like this:

A very (slow) (reader) (stops) and (focuses) on (every) (word.)

or like this:

A very slow (reader) (stops) and (focuses) on every (word.)

Try this exercise: Quickly read through the following paragraph[1] and circle the key words.

> About a year ago, as Spike Lee tells it, he was setting up a rally scene for *Malcolm X* on a Harlem street when an empty car suddenly came hurtling toward him and his crew. Although the car crashed before injuring anyone, its interior chilled the blood. "Someone," says Lee, "had tied a brick to the accelerator and gunned it in our direction." No one ever found out who-dunit—but talk about symbolic moments. If getting a movie made sometimes resembles the art of war, the making of this film was a two-year display of Spike Lee's audacity, ingenuity, and sheer endurance.

Which words did you circle? You probably circled nouns, verbs, and some of the adjectives and adverbs. The words you circled are probably the longer words. Compare those you and other students circled. You probably circled many, but not all, of the same words.

When you key-word read, you quickly go through the passage and subvocalize only those words you perceive as key. The trick in key-word reading is that *your eyes see* and *your mind reads*—without subvocalizing—the words that *surround* the key word. So it doesn't make a difference if you identify the same key words as another student. It only matters that you identify and subvocalize enough key words to comprehend the meaning of the material.

Try this strategy on Part 2 of the article about Malcolm X at the end of this chapter. Begin by reading in your normal way. Then, after a paragraph, start key-word reading. If, after another paragraph, you feel that you are losing too much comprehension, slow down and read more key words. If, on the other hand, your comprehension seems fine, speed up and read (subvocalize) fewer key words. When you have finished, jot down the main ideas of the article.

Phrase Reading

Phrase reading is very similar to key-word reading. In fact, when you key-word read, you are probably reading phrases; you subvocalize the key word and your eyes and mind simultaneously process the words next to the key word and complete the phrase. This occurs because your mind is always trying to make sense out of things. In written language, the sense—the meaning—is carried in phrases or chunks.

We could divide our example sentence into meaning chunks like this:

A very slow reader | stops and focuses | on every word.

or like this:

A very | slow reader | stops and | focuses | on every word |.

Try this exercise: Quickly scan through the following paragraphs[2] and put a slash mark at the end of each phrase (or each meaning chunk).

Upon winning the director's job after a public campaign arguing that Malcolm's story could be filmed only by an African-American, Lee found himself under attack from black nationalists who questioned his ability to portray their hero correctly. Nation of Islam head Louis Farrakhan was most concerned about how the film would treat spiritual leader Elijah Muhammad, from whom Malcolm X broke after a bitter dispute. "I will wait and see what is done and how it's done," Farrakhan told Lee.

Meanwhile, the director clashed with his studio, over both the epic length and the budget. Lee wanted $33 million; Warner Bros. agreed to put up only $20 million. After picking up $8 million more by selling the foreign rights, Lee began shooting, hoping that Warner would make up the shortfall. When it didn't, and the project went $5 million overbudget, the bond company that insured it took financial control of production.

Compare how you and other students divided the text. As in key-word reading, there is no "correct" way to divide a text into meaning chunks. Your goal is to focus on and process groups of words rather than individual words. The length of the grouping depends upon you and on such factors as your familiarity with the topic and your goals.

When you phrase-read, you quickly go through the passage and let your eyes stop and focus in the middle of each phrase. Your eye-span takes in, and your mind processes, the entire chunk at once. Although you may find yourself subvocalizing a few words, you are trying, in phrase reading, not to subvocalize at all. This can be very difficult for students who rely heavily on subvocalization; for them, key-word reading seems to work better. But for some students, phrase reading is easier and less disruptive of comprehension than key-word reading. Practice both strategies and decide which works better for you.

Try this strategy on Part 3 of the article about Malcolm X at the end of this chapter. Start by reading in your normal way. Then, after a paragraph, start phrase reading. Let your eyes stop and focus only a few times per line and try to see and process chunks of print. If, after another paragraph, you feel that you are losing too much comprehension, slow down and read smaller chunks. If, on the other hand, your comprehension seems fine, speed up and read larger chunks. When you have finished, jot down the main ideas of the article.

Push Yourself to Read Faster

We have discussed eliminating habits that slow your reading rate. We have also covered three related strategies for increasing your reading rate: increasing the speed of your eye movements, key-word reading, and phrase reading. The key to increasing your fluency and flexibility, however, is practice. We have found that the best way to increase your rate is to practice "pushed reading" regularly.

Pushed reading is not speed-reading. You may have heard of commercial speed-reading programs that promise, "You, too, can read 1,200 words per minute" or "Read a 500-page novel in only an hour." Both of these promises are nonsense; although you may be able to skim at 1,200 words per minute or skim the novel in an hour, you are not physiologically capable of reading that fast—no one is! The human eye is capable of taking in, at the very most, only 600 to 700 words per minute. It takes special techniques and lots of practice to read and comprehend at that speed. People who read at such rates generally do so with easy material and on topics with which they are familiar—*not* with college textbooks.

At the same time, if you do begin to read easy materials at a pushed rate of speed, your speed with other materials, such as textbooks, also increases. Your *pushed rate* is the rate at which you force yourself to read at an uncomfortable rate. So by practicing increasing your pushed rate of reading, your *study rate* (the slow and careful rate you use with textbooks) also increases. In the end, you will have more flexibility in studying because you can use different rates for different materials.

The best way to increase your pushed rate is to *practice* pushing. To start, try the following exercise: Find a newspaper or magazine article that interests you. Read it as fast as you can. Then write a brief summary of what you remember. Now select another article of approximately the same length and interest level. Read it at your normal rate, and write a brief summary. Compare your two summaries for both the amount of information you remembered and its accuracy. You were probably able to remember almost as much information from the article you read rapidly as from the article you read slowly. This exercise shows that you are capable of understanding at a pushed rate of speed. A pushed rate of speed is faster than your normal rate, but you can still understand much of what you read. If you were to push yourself even faster, you would still comprehend at least some of the article.

To increase your fluency and flexibility, practice pushed reading for fifteen minutes every day. The following are guidelines to help you.

1. Use relatively easy, high-interest material—not a textbook and not something on which you will be tested. Newspaper or magazine articles work well.

2. For ten minutes, read the material as quickly as you can without losing too much comprehension.

3. To check for comprehension, stop after each article or section and try to list five major ideas from what you read. If you can't list five, you need to slow down a little. If you have more than five, you can push yourself faster.

4. For the last five minutes, once you have established a good pace, make a timed reading. Have a friend time you for five minutes, or use a tape recorder on which you have recorded a "start" signal and, after five minutes, a "stop" signal. Put a pencil mark on the word on which you start and another at the point where you stop five minutes later. Count the number of words between the marks and divide by 5 to get your words-per-minute rate.

5. Each time you do this, graph the results in Figure 7.2. Try to keep increasing your rate, but do not exceed the speed at which you can remember five main points from what you read.

Remember the following key factors as you work on the bad habits that slow you down and begin to increase your pushed rate:

1. *Select material that is easy and of high interest.* Because you probably will notice a decrease in comprehension at first, it is best to begin with easy material. With practice, your comprehension will improve to keep pace with your rate, but the initial drop in comprehension and memory is natural.

2. *Increasing fluency and developing rate flexibility do not happen overnight.* Resign yourself to the fact that it is going to take time. With a concerted

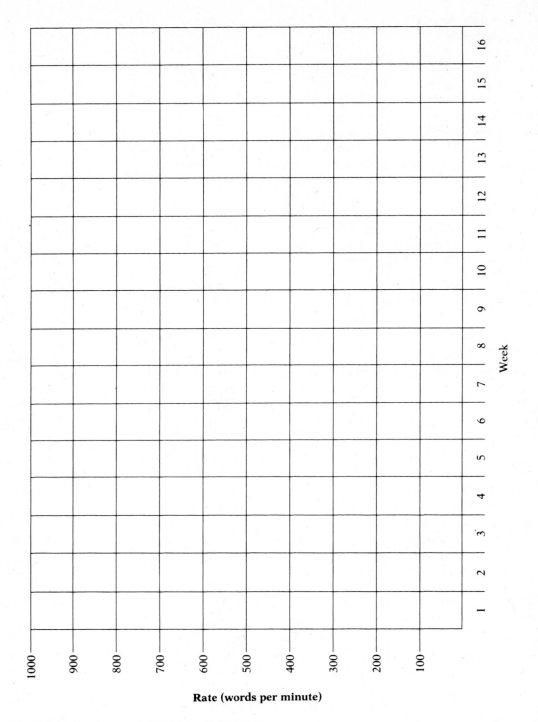

Rate (words per minute)

Figure 7.2 Grid for Charting Reading-Rate Progress

effort, most students can at least double their reading rate in six to eight weeks while maintaining comprehension.

3. *Practice reading at your pushed rate for at least fifteen minutes every day.* Most students can find this much time to devote to working on their rates. If possible, try to practice at the same time every day. If it becomes part of your schedule, you will do it automatically. Also, increases in your rate will motivate you to work harder.

4. *Don't give up.* Some students become discouraged at first because they find it extremely difficult to change their reading habits. Students also become discouraged by the initial drop in comprehension, and they fall back to believing the fallacy that in order to comprehend you must read slowly. Just try to remember that the difficulty you may experience in the beginning is natural and that, given time and practice, you *will* be able to increase your rate.

In addition to practicing pushed reading, you might set other goals to increase your fluency and flexibility. Base your goals on the habits that especially slow you down and on that one technique that seemed to work best in reading more rapidly. Your goals chart might look like the one in Figure 7.3.

Flexibility

Developing reading-rate fluency is only part of the picture. Earlier we mentioned the importance of developing rate flexibility—that is, adjusting your rate according to the type of material you are reading. Several factors affect the rate at which you read printed material. The most obvious is the difficulty of the material, a factor that is tied strongly to the amount of interest and background knowledge you have about a particular topic. For example, many first-year college students find chemistry to be a difficult subject because they have taken only one previous chemistry course and therefore have little background knowledge. It is also probably safe to assume that many students do not have a strong interest in chemistry. Students who find a subject difficult because they lack interest or background knowledge will have to read the material more slowly than students who know a lot about the topic and who are very interested in it.

Another important factor affecting rate flexibility is the purpose of your reading. A magazine article or a newspaper should be read relatively quickly, for two reasons:

1. *These materials generally are written at a much lower reading level than textbooks are.* Most newspapers, for example, are written so that anyone with a sixth-grade education can read and understand them. Although magazines may be slightly more difficult to read than newspapers, they are still relatively simple, and simple material can be read quickly.

What I'll do to increase fluency	Day 1	Day 2	Day 3	Day 4	Day 5	Day 6	Day 7
Push-read for 15 minutes							
Practice not sub-vocalizing for 5 min-utes							
Read a textbook chapter with 50% fewer re-gressions							
Practice key-word reading on the news-paper I read							

Figure 7.3 Sample Goals Chart

2. *In most cases, you read magazines and newspapers for pleasure.* Your major goal is not to remember everything. You might decide to read an article to learn about a new computer or the results of a local election, but you are not going to be tested on it. You are simply reading to gather some information that seems relevant, important, or interesting to you. Two weeks, two days, two hours, or even two minutes later, you may be unable to recall the information—but you aren't expected to.

Textbooks also require rate flexibility. Take a few minutes and glance through the sample chapters in the appendix. Most students will be able to determine almost immediately which chapters they will have to read more slowly. Typically, the more technical the text, the more slowly you will need to read it. However, also keep in mind that background knowledge plays a major role in how quickly you can read something. Therefore, if you have a considerable amount of prior knowledge on a topic, even if the topic is technical, you probably can read it relatively quickly.

By developing flexibility with your reading speed, you can be more efficient and effective in your studying.

Key Ideas

1. A key to using your study time wisely is to adjust your study strategies to each class and textbook.

2. The strategies you use and the amount of time you spend on a course will depend upon

   - your background knowledge and interest in the subject;
   - the characteristics of the course and the textbook;
   - what you have to do with the information in the course;
   - your knowledge of a range of study strategies; and
   - your ability to monitor how well your strategies are working and adjusting those strategies, if needed.

3. College texts can be divided into three major disciplines: humanities, social sciences, and biological and physical sciences. These types of texts differ in six areas; by understanding the differences among texts, you can better determine the appropriate study strategies to use.

4. Reading-rate flexibility means adjusting your rate according to the type of material you are reading, the difficulty or complexity of the material, and the amount of prior knowledge you have about the material.

5. Eliminating habits that slow you down will help you develop speed and flexibility.

6. Three related strategies for increasing your reading rate are increasing the speed of your eye movements, key-word reading, and phrase reading.

7. The key to increasing your fluency and flexibility is practice. Pushed reading and setting goals are two ways to practice.

8. Changing your speed of reading for different materials will increase your effectiveness and efficiency.

A Scenario to Write About and Discuss

Suppose that you have gone to the learning center on your campus at the recommendation of your history professor. He believes that you are having trouble in his course because you do not seem to have enough time for all of the reading. At the center, you take a test to determine your reading rate and comprehension. You find out that your rate is 180 words per minute and that your comprehension on this material is 80 percent. What kind of program do you think would best benefit you? Describe a plan that would assist you in improving your rate so that you could get through all of the reading and studying needed in your history course.

Application Exercises (DTT)

1. To give you an idea of your rate on a fairly easy, interesting magazine article, read the following selection, "The Date Who Rapes." Then determine your rate and take the comprehension check to see how well you understood it.

2. Use this rate as your base rate. Pushing your rate on easier narrative material will increase your rate on more complex content material, as well. After practicing pushing your rate for a few weeks, you can repeat this exercise to determine how much you have improved.

Selection from a Magazine

The Date Who Rapes

Mention the word "rape" and most people picture a sinister, masked figure jumping out of an alley or breaking through the bedroom window. But in reality the circumstances are not usually that dramatic: A rape occurs every seven minutes in the United States, and, more often than not, the victim knows her assailant. Indeed, she often knows him quite well: He may be a professional colleague, an old family friend, an ex-lover, or the man who has lived next door for years. All these "nice" criminals add up to one grim statistic: According to law-enforcement officials and rape-treatment counselors, "acquaintance rape"—or "date rape," as it is popularly known—accounts for about 60 percent of all reported rapes. And the true percentage may be far higher, since only an estimated 10 percent of all rapes are ever reported, and victims of date rape are especially reluctant to report the crime to the police.

There is good reason that date rape remains a little-discussed crime—and a source of guilt and shame to its victims. Often, the people who have knowledge of the incident—including family, friends, and jurors—suspect that the woman did something to "ask for it." Observes Gail Abarbanel, a social worker and director of the Rape Treatment Center in Santa Monica, Calif.: "Most people are very understanding if a stranger breaks into your house with a gun and rapes you, but if you say you made a date with the rapist, they always wonder how far you went before you said no."

Weekends: There are several factors that make acquaintance rape different from sexual assault by a stranger, says Abarbanel, who is compiling the first major study comparing the two types of assault. Based on long interviews with 600 victims, the report describes a number of telltale characteristics that set date rape apart. While assaults by strangers occur at all times of day, every day, and usually in the victim's home, acquaintance rapes cluster on weekends, between 10 P.M. and 2 A.M., and generally take place on the assailant's turf. They often last longer than stranger rapes, sometimes stretching over four hours, but are less likely to involve lethal weapons; instead, the date rapist uses verbal threats and his own physical strength to intimidate and overpower his victim.

The sharpest distinction Abarbanel and other rape counselors have found is in the response of victims to the two different types of attack. Typically, women who have been raped by strangers develop fears of the unfamiliar, but date rape is "a triple-barreled assault," says Emily Chandler, director of psychiatric nursing at Boston City Hospital. Not only is the woman assaulted physically and emotionally, explains Ann Burgess, a psychiatric nurse at the University of Pennsylvania, [but] her sense of trust and integrity in friendship is also destroyed. A college student who was fixed up by a close sorority sister with a blind date who raped her asked Abarbanel, "How do I know whom to trust any more?" Many women also feel betrayed by their own judgment. "They think they no longer know how to tell the good guys from the bad guys," Abarbanel says. The other overwhelming emotion experienced by victims who were raped on an actual date is guilt. "Because she initially wanted to be with the man," observes Teddie Melhart, a Texas psychiatric social worker, "she thinks, 'It's all my fault.'"

Many victims report that their attackers have a Jekyll-and-Hyde personality, turning in an instant from a charming escort into an aggressive assailant. Some date rapists convince themselves that the women were willing participants. A year ago, Grace Benson, 28, an attractive Houstonian, says she was raped twice in one evening by her stockbroker date. When he was finished, reports Benson, who has filed criminal charges against her alleged assailant, he spoke to her tenderly about having babies and let her leave his house only after arranging another date.

Young People: Acquaintance rape is a crime that happens most frequently to young people; the majority of victims are between the ages of 15 and 24. In a preliminary study done by the National Center for the Prevention of Rape in Rockville, Md., 92 percent of teen-age victims said they were acquainted with their attackers. Cheryl, 15, is one such case. She had known Joey, 19, for years; he was her older brother's best friend. When he dropped by one afternoon while she was alone in the family's Florida home, Cheryl left him downstairs to wait for her brother and went up to her room. But Joey soon followed her and shoved her down on the bed. "I kept trying to push him off me," recalls the thin, blond youngster, "but he kept saying, 'Come on, you know what's happening.'"

Other surveys of this age group reveal disturbing attitudes about acquaintance rape that may contribute to the scope of the problem. In 1981 a study of 432 teens by the University of California at Los Angeles found that 54 percent of the boys and 42 percent of the girls believed forced sexual intercourse was permissible under some circumstances. In a 1982 Auburn University (Ala.) study of college men, 61 percent said they had touched a woman against her will.

Indeed, in rape-education sessions with students in Washington, D.C., public high schools, a number of boys told members of the D.C. Rape Crisis Center that they never consider themselves a rapist if they force a girl to have sex at the end of a date. "The whole time I'm thinking that she expects to have sex," one boy declared, "I'd be a real wimp if I let her get away."

To help change the attitudes of young people who tacitly condone acquaintance rape and to provide practical advice on preventing attacks, antirape groups offer lectures and workshops in high-school classrooms and on college campuses. At Stanford University, incoming freshmen are introduced to the perils of date rape at seminars held in their residence halls. In a similar program at the University of Florida in Gainesville, policewoman Martha Varnes warns women that some rapists show up at student watering holes and dorm parties, looking for likely victims.

Ordeal: A date-rape victim who decides to press charges against her attacker may face a second grueling ordeal when she comes up against the criminal-justice system. In fact, some prosecutors discourage women from bringing charges against attackers they knew beforehand by emphasizing the slim chance of conviction. Victims are also sometimes required to take a lie-detector test. "These are the toughest cases," asserts Jacqueline Connor, until recently the Los Angeles deputy district attorney in charge of sex crimes. "It amounts to legal rape."

But over the last decade, thanks largely to the efforts of women's groups and an increased number of female district attorneys and judges, law-enforcement agencies and courts in some jurisdictions have grown not only more compassionate in the handling of all types of rape cases, but also more effective in prosecuting them. Scott Harshbarger, a Boston-area district attorney, reports that date rape is now accorded high priority by his department, which pushes for prosecutions and works closely with police, hospitals, and members of rape-counseling groups who provide support for victims.

The seriousness of date rape is also gaining recognition. At a recent Los Angeles Policy Academy training session devoted specifically to the crime, a new recruit made a snide, suggestive remark to a victim about the bar where she worked. The tough, red-faced sergeant in charge let him have it. "It doesn't make any difference if she was a dancer or a secretary or a nun," he told the aspiring officer. "She's a victim. Police should become comrades in arms for revenge." Perhaps even more encouraging is the case of the date rapist—a junior at the University of Southern California—who was so distraught over what happened that he has become active in campus antirape groups. "I want other people to be aware that this sort of thing can happen," he explains, "and that it happens a lot more than most people ever imagine. It just has to stop."

Time ÷ Words = WPM   1,336 words

_____ Time

_____ Words per minute (WPM)

Application Exercise for "The Date Who Rapes"

1. The majority of date-rape victims are in their
    (a) early 30s.
    (b) early teens.
    (c) midteens to early 20s.
    (d) late 20s to mid-30s.

2. Which of the following is *not* characteristic of date rape?
    (a) It takes place on the assailant's turf.
    (b) It occurs on weekdays.
    (c) It lasts longer than stranger rape.
    (d) The rapist does not use dangerous weapons.

3. One reason why date rape is rarely discussed is that
    (a) its victims feel guilt and shame.
    (b) it does not occur as frequently as stranger rape.
    (c) assailants are rarely brought to trial.
    (d) counselors are not trained to deal with the victims.

4. Many victims of date rape do not press charges because
    (a) prosecutors discourage the practice.
    (b) the chances of conviction are slim.
    (c) they may have to take a lie detector test.
    (d) all of the above.

5. This article suggests that the incidence of date rape will
    (a) decline significantly.
    (b) remain about the same.
    (c) decline a little.
    (d) continue to increase.

6. Many date rapists convince themselves that
    (a) their victim is a willing participant.
    (b) they are in love with their victim.
    (c) their victim "asked for it."
    (d) all of the above.

7. In order to change the attitudes of young people about date rape,
    (a) the assailants are being sent to juvenile court.
    (b) lectures and workshops are being offered.
    (c) cases are being televised.
    (d) the assailants are being convicted and sent to prison.

8. Those who have had the biggest influence in drawing attention to the way rape cases are handed are
    (a) police officers.
    (b) female judges.
    (c) district attorneys.
    (d) women's groups.

9. A study conducted at Auburn University found that _____ percent of college men had touched a woman against her will.
    (a) 41
    (b) 51
    (c) 61
    (d) 71

10. Date rape accounts for about _____ percent of all reported cases.
    (a) 40
    (b) 50
    (c) 60
    (d) 70

    _____ WPM
    _____ Percent correct

11. Summarize this article. Use the summarization steps discussed in Chapter 1.

Answers to Questions on "The Date Who Rapes"

1. c	6. a
2. b	7. b
3. a	8. d
4. d	9. c
5. d	10. c

Selection from a Magazine

Malcolm X

Part I

Directions: Use this portion of the article to try the eye-span strategy described earlier in the chapter. When you are finished, jot down the main points of what you read. This will give you an idea of how much your comprehension was affected by this strategy.

The black martyred hero still haunts our
conscience. A new film burnishes the myth.

X . . . X . . . X . . . X . . . X/Now that Malcolm's dead . . . /We all love Malcolm;/Malcolm's alive . . . /Though His body's been Dead/Damn near Thirty Years Now . . . /Yes . . . I'm sure Malcolm lives/His name scrawled all over/Drug peddler's backs/X . . . X . . . X marks the spot/X . . . Gang Violence/X . . . Babies having babies/X . . . Illiteracy is kool/I'm sure Brother Malcolm loves/The way his philosophy/Is held in those young black fists/Delivering fiery resolve/To trivial issues . . .

As a black kid growing up in Harlem, poet Benson Wheeler heard only about The Bad Malcolm X. He went with his family to see Malcolm speak once, and he remembers they seemed frightened by the tall, red-haired mulatto who called white people devils. For years after Malcolm X was killed in 1965, Wheeler had an image of a "reefer-smoking, gun-carrying ex-con, a mad, angry Black Muslim." Then he went to college and read Malcolm's speeches and autobiography. There, he discovered The Good Malcolm—the eloquent advocate of black "enlightenment," self-respect, and self-reliance. Now a performance artist and community activist in Boston, Wheeler tries to capture that Malcolm in his rough-edged street poetry. But around the neighborhood, he sees a lot more interest in X clothes than in Malcolm's ideas. "The large majority of folks don't know where to tell you to find a copy of 'Malcolm X Speaks'," he says. "But ask them about an X hat: You can get one on every corner."

In life, Malcolm X was a numbers runner, thief, prison convert, antiwhite demagogue, and, finally, globe-trotting seeker of a new multiracial truth. In death, he's become a martyr, a myth, and a fashion statement. Now director Spike Lee and actor Denzel Washington are about to turn him into something even more improbable: Malcolm the Matinee Idol. Lee's much-awaited three-hour twenty-one-minute movie, "Malcolm X," won't be in theaters until next week, but already it's given rise to a media and marketing blitz that's part history lesson, part retailing bonanza. At least six national magazines have already put Malcolm, Spike, or Denzel on their covers. In the next year, several new biographies and a PBS documentary are due out. Lee himself has written a companion volume, "By Any Means Necessary—The Trials and Tribulations of the Making of 'Malcolm X'," about the hurdles he faced in bringing his $34 million project to the screen. Looking to cash in on the inevitable boom in caps and T-shirts, Spike has even opened two new boutiques in Los Angeles to sell his own line of clothes.

Spinoffs: The movie's distributor, Warner Bros., is also pursuing any means necessary to maximize its return on Malcolm's memory, hiring Uni-World Group, one of the nation's largest black advertising firms, to market the movie to black consumers. But the studio whose parent company, Time Warner, took so much heat for distributing rapper Ice-T's incendiary "Cop Killer" is also mindful of the passionate emotions that Malcolm can still stir on both sides of the color line. To reassure older whites who may remember Malcolm only as a militant troublemaker, Warner Bros. has prepared movie trailers that portray the film character as a relative moderate. It has also scheduled special screenings for L.A. Mayor Tom Bradley and other city officials across the country to allay worries that "Malcolm X" might set off the kind of unrest that another Warner Bros. release, "New Jack City," did last year.

Within the black community, the sense of possessiveness over Malcolm's legacy is so intense that Lee came under attack simply for making the movie. Writer Amiri Baraka charged that Lee was too "bourgeois" to do justice to Malcolm's story. Others who have found Lee's earlier films a little too self-indulgent wondered whether he could tell Malcolm's story straight. Yet after almost two years of work, Lee has managed to produce a film that achieves the sweep of an old-fashioned Hollywood epic and still captures the complicated intellectual and personal odyssey chronicled in "The Autobiography of Malcolm X." Alex Haley, who coauthored the autobiography, saw a print of the movie before he died. "Malcolm would have loved this," he said.

Lee relies on a subsequent trail of investigative reporting to tell the story of Malcolm's brutal death. At the time, a group of Muslim extremists were found to have acted alone in gunning down Malcolm gangland style as he gave a Sunday-afternoon speech in Harlem's Audubon Ballroom on February 21, 1965. Yet later digging unearthed strong evidence of at least indirect orders from Malcolm's former mentor, Black Muslim leader Elijah Muhammad. Lee points strongly to the larger conspiracy and even hints that the FBI had knowledge of the plot and at best did little to prevent it. But Lee isn't out to play Oliver Stone and retry the case on the screen. He keeps his focus on Malcolm's life and his remarkable series of transformations. "It was that evolution that fascinated me," Lee says.

For all its appeal, Lee's movie can't fully explain why Malcolm X continues to be such a figure of fascination—why he still "haunts America's racist conscience," as Detroit-based scholar Paul Lee puts it. Recent surveys suggest that most whites today know and care little about Malcolm. Even among

African-Americans, a *Newsweek* poll found, only half have a clear knowledge of who he was and what he stood for. Yet, fully understood or not, Malcolm still holds a powerful grip on blacks' imagination. A majority of African-Americans—and an overwhelming 84 percent of young blacks—say they consider him a hero. Most rank him only after Martin Luther King in his importance to the black community today. And surprisingly, most who admire him say it's not because they think that blacks are worse off now or that today's black leadership is lacking. Clearly, many blacks believe that Malcolm's indictment of racist attitudes is still relevant today, but his appeal goes even deeper than that. To understand it, black scholars say, requires an appreciation of just how many things Malcolm X stood for. As Kansas City, Mo. mayor the Rev. Emanuel Cleaver puts it, he was a man with "ten different personalities and eleven messages to be learned from them."

Although there's been much talk of "a rediscovery" of Malcolm in recent years, black scholars insist that his influence never really faded. In fact, "Malcolm has always been popular within the black community," says Paul Lee, who served as a consultant on the movie. A decade before Martin Luther King's birthday became a national holiday, blacks in Washington, D.C. celebrated Malcolm X Day on May 19; for years, there have been similar unofficial commemorations in Philadelphia, Cleveland, and Harlem. Mayor Cleaver has 25-year-old memories of getting together with school friends to listen to and analyze records of Malcolm X's speeches. To hear young blacks today discussing Malcolm, Cleaver says, "is like the '60s all over again."

Part 2

Directions: Use this portion of the article to try the key-word strategy described earlier in the chapter. When you are finished, jot down the main ideas of what you read. This will give you an idea of how much your comprehension was affected by this strategy.

When Malcolm X was alive, he was portrayed in the national press mostly as an apostle of violence, a kind of vengeful antithesis to Martin Luther King and his creed of nonviolence. Yet unlike the Black Panther and later militant groups, Malcolm and his followers never made a fetish of preparing for armed conflict. Before he made his famous call for blacks in Harlem to form "rifle clubs," he consulted lawyers about just how far he should go in wording the statement. His real intent, many students of his speeches now agree, was not actually to supplant the pacifist tactics of Dr. King with a more violent battle plan; it was to offer a *psychological* alternative: a way of talking back, if not fighting back. As longtime Chicago political activist and friend of Malcolm's Timuel Black puts it, "Violence was not his theme, but his position was 'You don't turn the other cheek.'"

It was for that undaunted ability to talk back to The Man that so many blacks adored Malcolm, no matter what some thought of his more extremist rhetoric. At a time when most black folks had to weigh every word they said around white people, Malcolm stood up before crowds and TV cameras and uttered thoughts that most African-Americans gave voice to only in private: that whites would never really accept blacks as equals, and that the promise that blacks could get ahead if only they acted "more white" was a cruel illusion. Even more gratifying, Malcolm told off the white man with an eloquence, wit, and confidence that was a match for any white orator. "People were afraid of Malcolm, but they loved Malcolm," recalls Abdul Alkalimat, a Northeastern University professor who is writing a book on "How to Read Malcolm X." "They loved Malcolm as the young warrior who dared to say things."

Malcolm was able to talk so defiantly to white people partly because he didn't want anything from them. In Lee's film, there's a poignant moment when a well-meaning white student approaches Malcolm as he arrives to give a speech at Harvard University. She insists she's a good person despite being white, and asks what she can do to help his cause. "Nothing," Malcolm replies coldly, walking away. In the last year of his life, Malcolm was to rethink that position and express a willingness to cooperate with sympathetic whites. But even then, his message was that blacks had to stop waiting for whites to solve their problems and start helping themselves. Long before Jack Kemp or Daniel Patrick Moynihan entered the debate, Malcolm articulated the need for blacks to start their own businesses, break free of welfare, keep their families intact, and provide positive role models for black children.

He also emphasized the importance of instilling "self-esteem" in black kids decades before it became a trendy educational buzzword. It was Malcolm who insisted that blacks start calling themselves "Afro-Americans" as a symbol of pride in their roots and a spur to learn more about their history. In the period when he was a spokesman for the Black Muslim doctrine of racial separation, he portrayed it as a way for blacks to discover their own worth, free of the images of white beauty and success that pervade mainstream culture. Malcolm later abandoned full-scale separatism as impractical—but his notions about separate education still live on in the current debate over establishing special programs and schools for black inner-city kids. In Minneapolis, Dr. Willarene Beasley cites Malcolm as an influence in her push for an experimental all-black junior high school that is now part of the city school system.

Part 3

Directions: Use this portion of the article to try the phrase-reading strategy described earlier in the chapter. When you are finished, jot down the main ideas of what you read. This will give you an idea of how much your comprehension was affected by this strategy.

Black manhood: Asked to sum up what Malcolm and his message represented to them, blacks through the decades have come back to one word: "manhood." In the beautiful eulogy that actor Ossie Davis gave at Malcolm's funeral—and that he reads over newsreel footage at the end of Lee's movie—he proclaims, "Malcolm was our manhood, our living, black manhood! This was his meaning to his people." It was how Malcolm himself used to taunt white people: "I am the man you think you are." In an age when white men wanted to be John Wayne or Steve McQueen, Malcolm offered an image of black gunslinger to his people—a man who was gentle and upright with family and friends but fearless toward adversaries. Former Atlanta mayor Andrew Young recalls that simply seeing Malcolm in action had a therapeutic effect for many black people. "He did, really, what a psychiatrist does," Young says. "He made them proud of themselves and proud of being black."

When black kids in the inner cities put on their X caps, that's what they're identifying with, says Ojo, at 43 a kind of elder statesman in the Disciples street gang in Chicago. "They don't really know what Malcolm's message was. They just know that he was one of the first real outspoken black men." On the street, most kids have heard enough about Malcolm to know that he was one of them—a city punk who grew up poor, got in trouble, did time, and kicked drugs. Today, a staggering 23 percent of African-American males between the ages of 20 and 29 are in prison or on parole or probation, and millions more are only one more wrong move away. For them, Malcolm X is one of the few "role models" whose life stories have any resonance. As Rep. Maxine Waters, whose district includes South-Central L.A., . . . puts it, "They know [Malcolm] knew what the real deal was. He was a brother who had been in prison; he'd been on the streets."

If some young blacks now consider Malcolm X more of a hero than Martin Luther King, it's testimony to both the success and the failure of King's dream. King's crusade for legal equality and greater opportunity has made life better for millions of blacks, allowing them to get better jobs, move to the suburbs and enjoy many of the same comforts that white Americans do. But that exodus has had the cruel effect of making those left behind—the kind of poor urban blacks who grew up like Malcolm—even worse off. One reason for Malcolm X's enduring appeal "lies in the simple fact that we have not yet overcome," says Duke University professor C. Eric Lincoln, who was a friend of Malcolm's. "For many of the kids in the ghetto we are right back where we were. The few advances that have been made have not reached them. So if we didn't make it with King, what have we to lose? We might as well make it with Malcolm."

What are the chances that Spike Lee's movie will get through to those kids? The director is hoping that, at the very least, it will give them a greater understanding of what Malcolm X stood for, and of the role that education played in turning his life around. "We've got to turn this backward thinking around where ignorance is champion over intelligence," Lee says. "Young black kids being ridiculed by their peers for getting A's and speaking proper English: That's criminal." The movie ends by encouraging viewers to read "The

Autobiography of Malcolm X," and Warner Bros. plans to send a study guide to the movie to high-school teachers in America's 100 largest cities. In South-Central L.A., Congresswoman Waters hopes to form a reading group to study the book. And Malcolm X scholar Manning Marable of the University of Colorado at Boulder has called on Warner Bros. to donate 1 percent of the film's gross profit to set up public forums, archives, and an oral-history project to promote the study of Malcolm's life.

Stern advocate: Yet some black leaders are worried that the movie may serve only to turn Malcolm into more of a commodity. So many companies have taken to making caps, T-shirts, and other products with Malcolm's name or image on them that Malcolm's widow, Betty Shabazz, has hired a management group to seek license fees. The firm has already sued five companies and has hinted that it might be contemplating a lawsuit against Spike Lee's retailing operation. After seeing the movie, many kids will just want to rush out and buy the clothes, predicts Eric Ellison, a psychology major who runs an "Afro-centric" bookstore at Michigan State University and refuses to stock the X caps. The danger, says Harvard historian Henry Louis Gates, is of "a lot of people running around with X caps who ain't read the autobiography and ain't gonna read the autobiography. They've emptied [Malcolm] of his complexity."

Ultimately, the film's impact will depend on which of the many Malcolms it portrays will remain fixed in the audience's mind. Will it be the firebrand who goaded white people and talked up armed self-defense—the image of Malcolm that many kids have gotten from rappers like Public Enemy and KRS-One? Will it be the stern advocate of black self-discipline—the Malcolm who "would want young African-Americans to build a strong family, develop African-American economic institutions, devoutly practice a religion, and nurture the next generation," as black author Shelby Steele of San Jose State University puts it? Or will it be the impatient seeker of the last year of Malcolm's life—a phase, a bit too telescoped in Lee's version, when he was trying to intensify his fight against injustice while also reaching out to white Americans and other people of color around the world?

Or, in the end, should it be all three? For as historian Paul Lee points out, the real message of Malcolm's life is about "the ability to change." That, certainly, is the lesson that Ricky Troupe learned from Malcolm. At 15, Troupe came to L.A. as a ward of the court and all but dropped out of school and started to steal and deal drugs. One day he picked up "The Autobiography of Malcolm X." "I was just going to read a little part of it," he says, "[but] I stayed up all night trying to finish that book." It gave Troupe hope that if Malcolm could emerge from the streets and turn his life around, so could he. He went back to school, and now, at 21, he's pulling *A*'s in a paralegal program at a community college and hoping to get into a four-year program and eventually to law school. "I'm constantly setting high goals for myself," says Troupe. "That all ties into the effect Malcolm had on my life." It's a story that's still all too rare. But in today's Black America, it's tribute enough to Malcolm's legacy.

Notes

1. Harry P. Waters with Vern E. Smith, "Spike's Mo' Better Moviemaking Blues," *Newsweek,* November 16, 1992, p. 71. © 1992 Newsweek, Inc. All rights reserved. Reprinted by permission.

2. Ibid.

Part II

Developing the *BCA's* of College Reading and Study Strategies

Aim for the highest.

Andrew Carnegie

Abraham Maslow, a famous psychologist, once said, "If the only tool you have is a hammer, you will treat every problem like a nail." In studying, if the only tools you have are the old habits and techniques you learned in elementary and high school, you will probably read and study all your materials the same way, regardless of whether your methods are effective.

As you saw in Part I, the reading and studying demands of college texts can be diverse. Most of the ideas and techniques in Part II are built around the following learning principles:

- "Psyching up," or creating interest
- Using what you already know
- Intending to remember
- Anticipating test questions
- Being selective
- Creating meaningful organization
- Putting ideas in your own words
- Reducing information
- Finding personal application
- Monitoring your learning

By understanding and applying these key principles, you should be able to discover study techniques that work for you. Although there are some general study strategies you can use in most learning situations, the methods you devise should vary according to what you are studying. Don't try to memorize one or two techniques and use them in every study situation. Rather, use these strategies and your knowledge of key learning principles as a starting point, and modify them to meet your specific needs.

The principles and strategies we will discuss are built around the idea that what you do before and after you read is as important as the reading itself. In the first edition of *Developing Textbook Thinking,* we used a modified version of the SQ3R[1] method as a framework for studying. However, many students found the method rather overwhelming and time-consuming, and they balked at using it consistently. In the second edition, we tried to devise a studying framework, called PROR, that was less burdensome. In the third edition, we streamlined the **BCA** studying process even further and made it more "student friendly." In this fourth edition, we have continued to use the **BCA** approach because students and instructors alike gave us considerable positive feedback on it.

The **BCA**'s of studying—doing things **B**efore reading, staying **C**onnected during reading, and doing things **A**fter reading—also taking time to learn, but if you stick with it, you will benefit in the end. As you work through the exercises, apply the various ideas and techniques to college-level material and then decide which strategies, or combination of strategies, is most successful for you. Think constantly about how you can modify strategies to meet your needs. Take what you can from a strategy, alter it, and use it in the best possible way for you. Personalizing strategies is important if you want flexibility in studying.

The **BCA** system has three important aspects: First, it encourages you to modify strategies based on the text, the task, and your personal study quirks, rather than implementing each strategy or each part of the system in a lock-step fashion. Second, it focuses on learning the material in such a way that you can think critically about it and depend less on rote memorization. Hence information not only gets into your long-term memory more easily but also stays there longer and is easier to retrieve because you have learned it in an organized fashion. Third, self-monitoring and reflection are built into each stage. In other words, before proceeding from phase to phase—before reading, during connected reading, and after reading and studying—you monitor your readiness to continue and to reflect on what you have learned. Note as you read through the **BCA** overview that each phase ends with a question. If you can answer yes or supply the necessary facts to answer each question and if you can reflect on your answer with specific information, then you are ready to go on.

BCA's: A Method for Efficient and Effective Study

BCA = doing things **B**efore reading, staying **C**onnected during reading, and doing things **A**fter reading and studying

Before Reading

Activate prior knowledge as you get an idea of the chapter's focus.

- Read the title of the chapter, and think about what you already know about the topic.

- Read the headings and subheadings or the chapter outline, if one is included. Try to create an organizational scheme for the entire chapter. As you organize the information, continue to use the knowledge you already possess. This will help you think critically about your reading.

- Think about what might be difficult and what might be easy about learning the information in the chapter. Use this information to set learning and studying goals.

- Begin to formulate possible questions about key concepts that you might need to remember for a test.

- Ask yourself, Do I have a clear idea of what this chapter is about?

Staying Connected During Reading

Read and annotate the chapter in predesignated pieces or "chunks."

- Before beginning to read, set a goal for how much you will complete.

- Read and annotate the text one section at a time by isolating key concepts and supporting ideas and noting examples in the text's margins.

- Think about ideas, not just words.

- Continue to think about how the text information could be asked as test questions.

- Read actively and aggressively, with the intention of getting answers and remembering important information.

- Ask yourself, Am I understanding the information in this chapter? What is confusing to me?

After Reading: Studying

Write down the information that you will need to learn for the test. Say this information out loud in the form of talk-throughs.

- Isolate the important information by constructing rehearsal strategies such as maps, charts, and concept cards.
- Reread your text only to locate information that is unclear or that requires additional explanation.
- Formulate more specific test questions as you become familiar with the material.
- Talk through the important information in the chapter by covering up the answers to your test questions. Check your rehearsal strategies to see if you are correct.
- Ask yourself, Do I know this information well enough to score high on the test?

After Studying: Reviewing

After you have learned the information, keep it in your long-term memory by reviewing it. Say the information that you have already learned. Practice over several days.

- Reduce your rehearsal strategies each time you review. Use only a notecard with the major points listed one or two days prior to the test.
- Make sure that you can talk through supporting details and examples about your main points.
- Distribute your practice over several days. Do not cram.
- Try to predict more accurate test questions.
- Ask yourself, Specifically, what information do I know very well? What information do I not know as well?

Prior to discussing the principles and strategies in depth, let's quickly review the list of learning principles and the phases in the **BCA** study method to see the relationship between the two.

BCA's	*Principles*
Before reading	• Psych up
	• Use previous knowledge
	• Intend to remember
	• Anticipate test questions
Staying **C**onnected	• Be selective
	• Create meaningful organization
After reading: Studying	• Put ideas in your own words
	• Reduce the information
After studying: Reviewing	• Further reduce the information

- Find personal application
- Monitor your learning

Notes

1. F. P. Robinson, *Effective Study* (New York: Harper and Brothers, 1941).

Chapter 8

Before You Read

I would live to study, not study to live.

Sir Francis Bacon

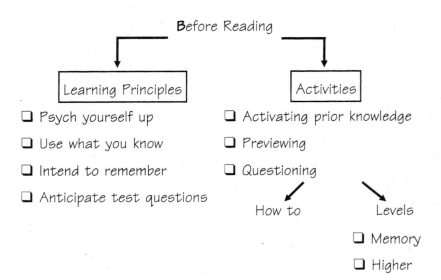

For students who do not have a wide repertoire of study and learning strategies, reading and studying can be passive processes. Students who practice passive reading sit at their desks, "read" the words, underline or highlight line after line, and, when they reach the end of the chapter, close the book and consider their studying complete. Passive study consists of "looking over" notes or rereading everything underlined in a text, generally the night before a test.

The study method presented in this text is an active approach to reading, studying, and learning. If carried out properly, this method forces you to be an active, involved reader, a reader who interacts with, thinks about, questions, and monitors the progress of each assignment.

When you use **BCA,** you engage in prereading activities designed to activate your prior knowledge and help you to organize information in some meaningful way. You establish goals, motivate yourself, and begin to monitor your understanding of the chapter before you actually begin reading.

Students who study passively often work hard to learn material. The BCAs show you ways to work smart as well as work hard. With practice, these strategies will make you an efficient learner. The first step is to use strategies *before* you read.

Learning Principles

Principle 1: Psyche Yourself Up, or Create Interest

In all likelihood, you can already effectively read and study material in which you have interest. In fact, you can probably actively read about sports, fashion, or lifestyles for an extended period of time. Subjects that interest you keep your attention and concentration and help you to remember the material later. However, you may not have developed such a keen interest in some college subjects. As you learn more about those subjects, your interest will develop naturally. But until that happens, you need to find ways to "psych yourself up," or create interest in the subject. Setting goals, asking questions, and annotating, among other techniques, are designed to help you to create interest and maintain concentration, even in materials that would be very dull otherwise.

Principle 2: Use What You Already Know

We know that people comprehend and remember new things not by starting from scratch with each new passage, but by building on what they already remember. In other words, you don't create a brand new "page" of memory for each thing your read. Instead, you take what you read and store it with information you already have. You insert some new lines in a page of existing memory.

You can read, comprehend, and remember information effectively and efficiently, if you actively use what you already know. It makes sense to review old information before starting on new, to bring to mind what you know about a topic before reading more about it. For example, if you are assigned to read a biology chapter on unicellular plants and animals, think back to that pond water you examined under a microscope in eleventh grade. Try to remember what you saw and what you learned. Add to your existing knowledge. Use the "page" you have in your mind as a basis for broadening your knowledge and increasing your understanding.

A grave mistake that many college students make is to treat each topic in each class as a bit of isolated information: Sociology has nothing to do with psychology, say, or psychology is unrelated to literature. Of course, these assumptions are false. What you learn in one class helps you in another. What you already know helps you continuously.

Another way to use what you already know is to try to relate your reading to your life or to the lives of your friends or relatives. Do you remember the student who wrote the journal entry on Social Security in Chapter 1? She found it difficult to maintain interest in Social Security because it would not affect her for forty or more years. But if she knew a relative or friend who was struggling to live on Social Security, the article might have been less boring to her.

Principle 3: Intend to Remember

You probably have been to a party at which someone told you his or her telephone number. If you didn't really intend to phone the person later, you rapidly forgot the number. In fact, you probably didn't even pay attention when the person gave it to you. However, if you did intend to call, you probably used all types of tricks to help you remember. You might have repeated the number several times, written it on the inside of a matchbook, or invented a memory device to help you remember it. As soon as you actually decide to remember something, you begin to do so.

The same principle applies to text reading. If you are reading the material only because it is assigned, then you probably don't intend to remember it. Consequently, you don't pay close attention and you don't make efforts to isolate, rehearse, consolidate, or apply information. Instead, you grit your teeth and plow through, heaving a sigh of relief when you're finished. By intending to remember information, you get your mind actively working on strategies to remember. You pay closer attention, you monitor your learning, you make connections with what you already know, and you use strategies to help fix the material in your memory.

Principle 4: Anticipate Test Questions

Your college career revolves around two things: learning, and the game of learning. It is not enough for you to learn the material in a class; you also have to perform well on tests, in discussions, and on papers you write. Because there is so much information to learn in any one class, you must be selective. You can best select what you want to know and what you anticipate will be on tests.

Selectivity involves being a good predictor. As you engage in activities before reading a chapter and begin to formulate questions, try to predict how your professor might test you on the material. Try to think like your professor by identifying the information that he or she feels is important. At first this will be difficult, but as you get to know your professors and become more attuned to their lecturing styles and exam formats, you will find it easier.

After absorbing the first four learning principles, you'll need to turn to the before-reading strategies that relate to these principles.

Before Reading

Why engage in activities before you read? For one thing, it is difficult to judge the importance of information if you're unaware of where the chapter is going. For example, the author might use an unusual term or introduce a concept early in the chapter. How important is it that you grasp that word or concept? You can't know unless you know whether the word or concept is used again or is elaborated upon later. Before-reading strategies improve learning by

- *providing a meaningful organization of the material to be learned.* As you read the headings and subheadings, you will see how to organize the chapter's major topics and subtopics.

- *giving you information about the chapter before you actually start to read.* It helps you to see where the chapter starts, where it ends, and the direction it will take. You will then be able to use what you already know about the chapter to help you to read and study better.

- *creating interest.* When you interact with text quickly, you almost always end up feeling that you missed a great deal of information. Cultivate this feeling of curiosity. Read the whole chapter in order to satisfy your curiosity and to fill in the gaps in your information.

- *allowing you to think critically while you read.* By previewing a chapter, you have an idea of where the author is going with information presented. You are then better able to judge the importance of information, to relate it to other knowledge you have, and to think critically about it.

Let's examine each aspect of before-reading activities.

Activating Prior Knowledge

Individuals, by virtue of possessing experiences unique unto themselves, can almost always call up some existing knowledge about a topic. Granted, you won't be an expert in all areas, nor will you have the accuracy in your information that you might have originally thought, but you will know something that can be useful in helping to understand the impending chapter. Think about the example of reading the newspaper article about the basketball game given in Chapter 7. Remember that the amount of knowledge you have affects how you will study the material.

When you activate existing knowledge, use the following guidelines:

- Read the title and ask yourself, What do I already know about this topic? Give yourself a moment to think about the knowledge you already have. If you have trouble doing this, try jotting down a list of terms or concepts that seem related to the title.

- Ask yourself, What would I like to know about this topic? Even if you would like to answer "nothing," come up with two or three ideas that have potential for future learning.

- Based on your prior knowledge, think about the kinds of strategies and approaches to learning that you might have to employ. For example, if you know very little about the topic, you will have to annotate more, create more detailed rehearsal strategies, and spend more time on the chapter than if you have a significant amount of knowledge about the topic.

After you have activated your prior knowledge, you are ready to get a "feel" for the chapter by previewing it.

Previewing

Think of the preview as a road map or game plan that will guide you through the chapter. The preview should give you a general idea of where the chapter begins and ends; it should not be an extremely detailed or lengthy process. Use the following steps when previewing the chapter:

- *Skim the chapter.* Skimming orients you to the information included. If the chapter is extremely long, you may want to read half, take a brief break, and then finish.

- *Read the title and activate prior knowledge,* as outlined previously. As strange as it may sound, some students neglect this very important step.

- *Read the chapter headings and subheadings.* This shows you how the chapter is organized, aids you in formulating questions during reading, and divides the chapter into logical learning units. You will also learn to use your background knowledge. By reading the chapter title, you began activating your general knowledge. The headings and subheadings will help to activate your specific knowledge.

- *Look over any charts, graphs, diagrams, or pictures.* These learning aids present a visual picture of important ideas in the chapter. Make sure you understand the information shown. Read each caption and all labels.

- *Note unfamiliar terms,* particularly those that are related to the discipline about which you are reading.

If time permits or if your background knowledge about the chapter is particularly weak, take the following steps:

- Read the summary at the end of the chapter (if it has one). Just as the introduction states the major points to be covered, the summary restates the ideas that the author deems important. The introduction tells you where the chapter will go; the summary tells you where it has been. Note what is said in the conclusion, so that when you read the whole chapter, you can read carefully for those major ideas, implant them firmly in your mind, and intend to remember them.

- If there are questions at the end of the chapter, read them; the author is asking for the most important information. Many students avoid reading the questions, only to find similar ones on a test.

- Stop and reflect for a couple of minutes before reading the entire chapter. Let what you have just found out about the chapter sink in. What do you know about this chapter? Do you understand how it progresses? Have you already begun to see the major ideas? How much can you remember simply from previewing? Think from the time you begin learning a chapter, and you will be able to understand and remember much of it.

The exact process that you follow when you preview depends on three factors: the type of material, your time constraints, and your previous knowledge. Modify your previewing procedure accordingly. However, don't skip the preview altogether. You will find some previewing steps more helpful than others. With previewing, as with the other strategies presented in this text, use what is most efficient and effective for you. Just be sure to preview in some manner.

Set Goals and Begin to Formulate Test Questions

Many students read a textbook or listen to a lecture merely to complete an assignment. If that is your only goal, you will find your work boring and tedious.

You will find yourself losing concentration and thinking about all the things you would rather be doing. You may find yourself disliking the text, the teacher, or the school for forcing you to do things that you have no desire to do. But if you can set other goals for yourself, you are more likely to maintain concentration and to understand and remember information. Set two kinds of goals—personal goals and textual goals.

1. *Personal goals* give you meaningful reasons to read chapters; they are closely tied to prior knowledge and experiences. For example, students in psychology classes always seem to read, understand, and remember the chapters on sex and on psychological abnormalities. Why? Because students have personal reasons for wanting to know about these topics. As they read, they are always looking for information to help them with their private lives (Why is my roommate so crazy? Is my anxiety a sign of abnormality?). Set personal goals even for chapters with less obvious personal meaning. After previewing a chapter, think for a moment about some personal questions the chapter may address.

2. *Textual goals* answer questions about the text. Initially, devise textual goals by asking questions based on the chapter's headings and subheadings. As you read each heading or subheading, pose questions to guide your reading; this type of prediction will start you thinking like your instructor. In other words, from the time you begin to familiarize yourself with the chapter through previewing, you should try to predict which questions your instructor might ask on the test. Even if your predictions are incorrect, you will have read more actively. Posing questions also alerts you to the author's organization of the subject matter and to what is and what is not important.

The easiest way to formulate questions is to turn headings or subheadings into questions. After all, the heading shows you the topic that the author decided was key for that section. Use the heading's actual words in your questions. Questions that ask who, what, when, where, why, or how are easy questions to begin with. Who, what, when, and where questions generally elicit factual information. Why and how questions call for broader, deeper levels of comprehension and critical thinking.

Although turning headings into questions is an easy way to form initial predictions, it can become counterproductive and tedious. Students who turn most headings into questions by using the word *what* are posing only memory-level questions that encourage lower-level thinking skills. This is a very passive activity. Instead, try to ask purposeful and useful questions that will guide your reading and aid your performance at test time. It is much better to ask a few good questions initially than it is to ask only "what" questions simply for the sake of carrying out this aspect of the **BCA** process.

Look at the following examples that are taken from the selections in the appendix. Which questions are good and which questions are not so good? Why?

Heading	**Questions**
Encoding (psychology)	What is encoding? Why is encoding important in the learning process?
Civil Rights and the Kennedys (history)	Why did civil rights become an important issue for the Kennedys? What did the Kennedys do for civil rights?
Acculturation and Ethnic Identity (sociology)	How are acculturation and ethnic identity different; how can they be the same? What is "acculturation"?
Mendel and the Birth of Genetics (biology)	Why is Mendel credited with the birth of genetics? When was the birth of genetics?

Notice that although all of the questions use the actual words from the headings or subheadings, each pair has a better question. For example, in the first pair of questions, Why is encoding important in the learning process? is the better of the two. It asks for more advanced levels of thinking and requires you to think about the relationship between encoding and learning. This question certainly might be one that your psychology professor would draw from to make test questions. In contrast, the other question, What is encoding? asks you merely to memorize a fact; this requires lower levels of thinking.

Remember that your questions should point to what is important in the text. It takes some trial and error to figure out how many and which types of questions to use with any one text. But because writers are quite consistent, once you have figured out the right questions for one section, you should be able to ask the same type and number of questions for future sections. Keep in mind that the best test of your predicting ability is your exam score. If it is high, your questions and the instructor's questions probably are a good match. However, if your exam score is not as high as you would like, reevaluate your prediction questions. (See Chapters 11 and 12 for more information on evaluating test performance.) Remember that asking questions

- *creates interest.* It makes you read for a very specific purpose.

- *helps with "intending to remember."* Your answers to the questions are what you have decided to remember, and you intend to remember them. But beware: Research shows that if you are a poor question predictor and concentrate only on trying to answer your predictions, you could miss vital information.[1] The exercises in this text will sharpen your ability to predict questions.

- *helps you to anticipate tests.* Once you start asking questions, you may be surprised by how many test items resemble the questions you asked yourself!
- *also helps you to think critically about information while you read.* This is especially true of higher-level questions.

Students who clearly understand and remember what they read are usually active readers. They do not simply take in words passively. Active readers question and reflect constantly as they proceed through a chapter. They pause, think about what they have just read, and formulate questions about what they have just read and what they are about to read. Active readers ask not only memory-level questions but also higher-level questions that require critical thinking.

Choose to ask one or both types of questions, depending on the kind of material to be read. An easy way to remember the two types is by the level of understanding required to answer them. Memory-level questions require you to memorize factual information, whereas higher-level questions require you to interpret and apply the information learned.

Memory-Level Questions

When you finish a passage, ask memory-level, or "reading-the-lines," questions to test your recall of the facts. Who? What? Where? When? and Why? questions will help you to make sure that you have all the facts straight. Some memory-level questions for the article "Born Happy?" at the end of this chapter might include:

- What does OGOD stand for?
- What is the difference between identical twins and fraternal twins?
- What is "heritability"?

Questions such as these are easy to form and to answer because the information is explicitly stated in the article. However, in order to do well on most exams, you will need to have a more in-depth understanding of the significance of the material when test time arrives.

Higher-Level or Critical-Thinking Questions

Higher-level questions require "reading between the lines" and "reading beyond the lines." Rather than merely remembering facts, you need to think, interpret, and apply your knowledge. Higher-level questions require you to analyze, judge, or generalize. Sometimes they have no single correct answer; instead, the answers lie in going beyond the text. For example, in the article

"Born Happy?," at the end of this chapter, you should ask higher-level questions that encourage your critical thinking such as:

- Why are identical twins used so often in studies of heredity?

- How was evidence collected to try to disprove the "one gene, one disorder" theories? Why did some scientists feel these were better studies?

- Which studies do I believe produced better evidence and why?

- What other evidence do I need to decide if happiness and other traits are or are not determined by genetics? What studies might be done to provide this evidence?

Another effective way to find higher-level information is to ask yourself, What, in my own words, are the most important ideas in this article?

Often a reader has to answer "I don't know" to higher-level questions. However, just because you can't answer applied questions does not mean that you haven't read and studied effectively; perhaps no one in the world yet knows the answers to such questions. The important thing is that by asking probing questions while you read, you will more clearly understand what you read, and you will remember it for longer periods of time.

To try out this reading and questioning technique, read "Born Happy?," thinking about the two levels of questions while you do so. Formulate some of your own questions as you go along. Pause for a moment and make sure you understand the major ideas. Finally, jot down some of your questions in the margins of the article and check to see if you have a few at the memory level and a few at the higher level. Check your questions against those suggested in the margin of the same article at the end of the chapter. Be careful not to write only memory-level questions.

Selection from a Magazine

Born Happy?

Sharon Begley

Geneticists have been claiming that DNA explains human traits as complex as schizophrenia, alcoholism, even happiness. Now the backlash has set in.

Scientists, like most mortals, grow attached to whichever theory works. For geneticists, it's a model that one researcher calls OGOD. It stands for "one gene, one disorder," and it means that a single gene causes, and is enough by itself to cause, a disease. Huntington's and cystic fibrosis are two single-gene diseases for which researchers have identified the culprit DNA; there are scores of others. But lately, the cries of "OGOD" from biology labs have not been whoops of victory in nabbing yet another disease gene. They have instead been cries of dismay as some researchers apply the OGOD model to traits and behaviors as complex as "novelty seeking" and schizophrenia. "Looking for single genes for complex behaviors reminds me of the old story of losing your wallet in a dark alley but looking for it under the street lamp because the light is better there," says Robert Plomin, a behavioral geneticist at the Institute of Psychiatry in London. Critics outside the field are even harsher. "Many of these 'results' [in behavioral genetics] disappear when you do the statistics right," psychologist Helena Kraemer of Stanford University told a recent meeting at the Institute of Medicine in Washington. "Fallacious methods are very common."

The latest offering in "the gene for . . ." sweepstakes is "happy DNA." In the journal *Nature Genetics,* molecular biologist Dean Hamer of the National Cancer Institute reviews studies suggesting that one's baseline level of happiness—the very small range within which one's happiness level fluctuates—is "largely a matter of heredity." Identical twins (who have exactly the same genes) are alike in their happiness level 44 percent of the time, according to studies at the University of Minnesota. Fraternal twins, who are no more genetically similar than other siblings, are alike only 8 percent of the time. "These data show that the broad heritability of well being is 40 to 50 percent," Hamer writes. Moreover, people's happiness levels seem extraordinarily stable through the years (*Newsweek,* July 29, 1996); they are affected neither by winning a lottery nor by becoming paralyzed. Studies of twins suggest that 80 percent of this stable component of happiness is heritable. "How you feel right now is about equally genetic and circumstantial," says Hamer. "But how you'll feel on average over the next ten years is fully 80 percent because of your genes." Though no one has identified genes wearing teeny smiles, Hamer suggests that a good place to look would be the DNA involved in the brain's "pleasure chemical," dopamine. This molecule is released in the brain after good food or good sex, for instance. "I don't think there will be *a* gene for happiness," Hamer says, "but rather many genes, each explaining maybe 1 percent" of someone's happiness level.

Critics argue that nongenetic reasons can explain why identical twins' happiness levels are more closely correlated than those of fraternal twins. Perhaps people who are treated better by society—by parents, teachers, store clerks, cops—are, all things being equal, happier than those treated shabbily, suggests Stanford's Kraemer. Perhaps, too, one is treated better if one is attractive, thin, or even-tempered. Or if one is not a member of a minority group. All of these traits are partly or completely under genetic control. Then is it not possible, Kraemer asks, that this thing called "happiness" is not itself genetic but is instead a proxy for traits that are? "Although a high heritability is being claimed," she says, "in fact the whole explanation may be environmental."

It would not be the first time that a genetic explanation collapsed. All sorts of complexities can trip up researchers. One of the biggest comes when scientists try, as Hamer does, to calculate "heritability," which is supposed to be a measure of how much of the variation in a trait from one person to the next is explained by genes. (What's not explained by genes is accounted for by people's different "environments," which include everything from obstetrical complications to education, relationships, and wealth.) A heritability of 100 percent means a trait is fully and only determined by genes. Eye color is 100 percent heritable; using chopsticks is presumably zero percent heritable. A common way to calculate heritability is through studies of twins. If identical twins are more alike in some trait than fraternal twins, then the trait is thought to have a high heritability. "But whenever you measure heritability this way, you are glossing over the fact that the similarity of environments for identical twins is much greater than it is for fraternal twins," says biologist Marcus Feldman of Stanford (whose own identical twins are now in medical school). Identicals often dress alike, are treated alike, and create their own secluded, two-person world. But fraternal twins, according to years of psychological studies, are typically no closer than other siblings. By failing to take into account that identicals share more environmental influences, argues Feldman, geneticists risk ascribing twins' similarities in happiness levels and other traits more to their genes than is warranted.

Genes for Complex Traits: Going, Going . . .

Initial excitement over the "discovery" of a gene for a behavior or complex trait has often turned to disappointment as other researchers have been unable to confirm the claims.

Gene	Identification Claimed	Current Status
Manic-depression	1987	Claim retracted. Other hints of links to a gene or genes persist.
Schizophrenia	1988	Numerous failures to replicate the results; one claim has been retracted, reports of seven other possible genes remain.
Alcoholism	1990	A 1993 review found no link between alcoholism and the purported gene.
Happiness	1996	Unresolved.
Novelty seeking	1996	Reported by two research teams. The only attempt at replication by other scientists failed to find the gene.
Neuroticism	1996	To be published later this year.

Over the last decade geneticists have reported finding genes causing schizophrenia, bipolar disorder (manic-depression), alcoholism, novelty seeking, and other complex traits. Few have held up (see table). Some, such as the claim for a schizophrenia gene, have been withdrawn; others have simply not been replicated (yet) by other scientists. In the latest such attempt, researchers led by psychologist Michael Pogue-Geile of the University of Pittsburgh searched the DNA of 287 twins, hunting for the gene that two separate research groups recently linked to novelty seeking, the yen for new experiences. "We didn't find anything," Pogue-Geile told *Newsweek* magazine; a paper describing the work is being submitted to a journal. Failure to replicate could mean that the effect of the novelty-seeking gene is too weak to be easily detected; it could also mean that the claim is wrong. Outright fraud seems to lie behind at least one claim of a gene for a complex trait.

Even the harshest critics do not deny that genes play some role in behaviors. Behavior, after all, comes from thought, which comes from the brain. The brain runs on neurotransmitters (chemicals that carry messages from one neuron to another) and receptors (sites on neurons at which neurotransmitters dock, like spacecraft on a space station). Both neurotransmitters and receptors are made according to instructions in genes. But it's a long way from these connections to "genes determine behavior." For one thing, environment influences which of the body's 100,000 or so genes are turned on: Like a computer hard drive loaded with programs, only the one opened by a click of the mouse runs. So it is with genes. Take schizophrenia. Someone growing up in bucolic environs may carry the exact same "schizophrenia" genes as a kid in South Central [Los Angeles]. Since stress increases the risk of schizophrenia, the denizen of the inner city will develop the disease but his country cousin will not, explains psychologist Irving Gottesman of the University of Virginia. If one twin is schizophrenic, his identical twin is schizophrenic only about 48 percent of the time: The environment has not "opened" his disease genes.

Because of such complications, behavioral genetics is moving from OGOD to the idea that no single gene is sufficient for a complex trait. Genes are propensities and probabilities, not destiny. But science has not heard the end of these claims. In July, at Jackson Laboratory in Bar Harbor, Maine, NCI's Hamer described his research on genes linked to neuroticism, a trait he called "much more heritable than [a susceptibility to] breast cancer." The gene is involved in the brain's serotonin system, he said. A paper on the "neurotic gene" will be published in the journal *Science*. . . . The public, and the press, will likely eat it up, as they have earlier claims of behavioral geneticists. As philosopher Philip Kitcher of the University of California, San Diego, says, "The seduction of a simple explanation for complicated problems is the strongest force driving this field." But keep your ears pricked. Cries of "OGOD" will continue to echo throughout the land.

Key Ideas

1. Activities that you carry out before reading are built around four important learning principles:

   - Psych yourself up.
   - Use what you already know.
   - Intend to remember.
   - Anticipate test questions.

2. Preview and question before reading a chapter thoroughly.

3. Previewing involves getting an overview of a chapter by

   - reading headings and subheadings.
   - looking at typographical aids.
   - noting difficult vocabulary.
   - recognizing the chapter organization.

4. Questioning involves formulating questions based on the important concepts presented in the text. Questions can be formulated by turning headings and subheadings into questions.

5. The two levels of questions are memory-level and higher-level, or critical-thinking, questions. Formulate both types for each chapter.

Application Exercises (DTT)

1. Using the article at the end of this chapter, "Unfinished Business: The Toll of Psychic Violence," write both memory-level and higher-level questions in the margins. One memory-level and one higher-level question have been posed for you.

2. Preview "The Psychology of Memory" selection in the appendix. Specifically explain the process you followed. Mention the prior knowledge you activated, how you previewed, the goals you set, and questions you predicted. Give page numbers when appropriate.

3. As you work through the selections in the appendix, answer the following questions after engaging in before-reading strategies to make sure that you are ready to proceed to the reading stage:

   (a) List three things that you already know about this selection.

   (b) How many major concepts are presented in this chapter? List them.

   (c) What appears difficult about this selection?

   (d) What appears easy about it?

   (e) How is this selection different from the last one you read?

   (f) What strategies might be appropriate to use when studying this chapter?

(g) What kind of test questions might you expect for this selection?

(h) Predict several memory-level and several higher-level questions on this chapter.

4. The following headings and subheadings are from the selections in the appendix. Using the headings as a guide, formulate questions that might provide important information to learn for a test. The first four are from the social sciences and the next two are from the physical/biological sciences.

Social Science

(a) "The Psychology of Memory"
Why You Forget
   Decay
   Interference
   Repression
   Amnesia
      Brain Injury
      The Case of the Anxious College Student

(b) "Great Promises, Bitter Disappointments, 1960–1968"
JFK and the New Frontier
   The New Frontier
   Civil Rights and the Kennedys
Flexible Response
   Vietnam
   Death in Dallas

(c) "Human Diversity"
Multicultural Perspectives
   Ethnic Diversity: A Fact of Life
   Acculturation and Ethnic Identity
   Discrimination
   Racism in America
      The Problem
      The Symptoms
      The Treatment

(d) "Information Systems and Marketing Research"
Marketing Research and Marketing Information Systems
Capitalizing on New Technologies for Marketing Research
   Databases
   Electronic Bulletin Boards
   Online Information Systems
   The Internet

Physical/Biological Science

(e) "Genetics: The Science of Inheritance"
　　Inheritance: A Problem
　　Mendel and the Birth of Genetics
　　　Mendel's First Experiments
　　　A Theory of Particulate Inheritance
　　　　The Punnett Square
　　　Dominance

(f) "Weather Forecasting"
　　The National Weather Service
　　Data Collection and Weather Observation
　　Folklore and the Weather

Application Exercises (Your Texts)

1. For a chapter in one of your texts, engage in before-reading activities by activating prior knowledge, previewing, setting goals, and formulating questions based on the information gained from the headings and sub-headings. Write out exactly what you did.

2. Prior to reading the chapter, write several memory-level and several higher-level or critical-thinking questions. (Save these questions for later use.)

3. As you engage in before-reading activities with chapters from different content areas, answer the following questions to ensure that you are ready to progress to the reading stage:

   (a) List three things that you already know about this chapter.

   (b) How many major concepts are presented in the chapter? List them.

   (c) What appears to be difficult about this chapter?

   (d) What appears to be easy about this chapter?

   (e) How is this chapter different from the last one you read?

   (f) What strategies might be appropriate to use when studying this chapter?

   (g) What kind of test questions might you expect for this chapter?

   (h) Predict several memory-level and several higher-level questions for this chapter.

Selection from a Magazine

Unfinished Business: The Toll of Psychic Violence

The changes brought by the civil rights movement since World War II have been extraordinary but shamefully inadequate. As someone who has spent all of his adult life conducting research on the damaging effects of racism and racial segregation on American children, I now find myself embarrassed. I'm embarrassed that even in my own field—education—the roots and symptoms of racism continue. Conflicts among some black and white students in school have grown worse, not better, in recent years. The whole idea of educational "progress" has been turned on its head.

What did Martin Luther King mean when he preached nonviolence?

When Martin Luther King preached nonviolence, many of his listeners thought he meant ending just *physical* violence. But he also meant *psychological* violence. This part of the civil rights lesson has not been fully learned in the postwar period. Despite the best efforts of many educators and social scientists, our system of education has never really absorbed the concept.

Consider the standards for college admissions. For the past half century, we have determined advancement by the grades of students in reading, writing, math, and other subjects, and by their performance on standardized tests. Ignorance in any of these areas can hold them back. By contrast, social sensitivity—an awareness of the needs of others—is rarely seen as part of the curriculum. Throughout the system, these social values are generally viewed as subjective interference with more objective indications of being well educated. Ignorance of decency and respect has rarely caused anyone to be flunked or kept out of college.

The history I witnessed seemed to offer something more. Before the *Brown vs. Board of Education* decision of 1954, 17 states and the District of Columbia had laws on the books requiring racially segregated schools. Most other states segregated schools by custom. When the lawyers of the NAACP brought this form of psychological violence before the United States Supreme Court, they won a receptive hearing. The court decided unanimously that to separate children in school "solely because of their race generates a feeling of inferiority as to their status in the community that may affect their hearts and minds in a way unlikely ever to be undone." The court then quoted the Kansas federal court: "Segregation of white and colored children in public schools has a detrimental effect upon the colored children."

How does racism affect nonminority groups?

And the decision went further. Significantly, the Appendix to the Appellants' Brief, which was prepared by me and other social scientists and submitted to the court by the NAACP lawyers, contained a section on the impact of racism and segregation on children of the *majority* group. The brief stated that,

"Those children who learn the prejudice of our society are also being taught to gain personal status in an unrealistic and nonadaptive way. The culture permits and at times encourages them to direct their feelings of hostility and aggression against whole groups of people perceived as weaker than themselves. Confusion, conflict, moral cynicism, and disrespect for authority may arise." That statement described a specific form of psychological violence.

Unfortunately, in the years since then we have not significantly modified the structure, function, or substance of American education. Beyond the failures to desegregate, we have not yet developed a technique by which reading, writing, mathematics, and the arts are seen as skills for fostering cooperation and for identifying with others. We have not yet made education a process whereby students are taught to respect the inalienable dignity of other human beings.

How can today's teachers learn from their predecessors' failings and work toward completing the unfinished business of one of history's great social movements? In order for education to be an instrument of nonviolence:

• Children must be helped to understand the genuine meaning of democracy from the earliest grades.

• Children must be helped to understand that one cannot keep others down without staying down with them.

• Children must be helped to understand social values, not just by word, but by their conduct, such as responding positively to the needs of their classmates.

• Children must be helped to understand the importance of empathy and respect. Those who are capable of meeting high academic standards can assist others who are not so fortunate. Students often learn basic academic skills more readily from their peers. Social sensitivity can be internalized as a genuine component of being educated. This is nonviolence in its truest sense.

By encouraging and rewarding empathetic behavior in all of our children—both minority and majority youth—we will be protecting them from ignorance and cruelty. We will be helping them to understand the commonality of being human. We will be *educating* them.

Source: Kenneth B. Clark, "Unfinished Business: The Toll of Psychic Violence." From *Newsweek,* January 11, 1993, p. 38. Copyright © 1993 by Newsweek, Inc. All rights reserved. Reprinted by permission.

Selection from a Magazine
(Annotated)

Born Happy?

Sharon Begley

Geneticists have been claiming that DNA explains human traits as complex as schizophrenia, alcoholism, even happiness. Now the backlash has set in.

How did researchers determine which diseases were from DNA?

Scientists, like most mortals, grow attached to whichever theory works. For geneticists, it's a model that one researcher calls OGOD. It stands for "one gene, one disorder," and it means that a single gene causes, and is enough by itself to cause, a disease. Huntington's and cystic fibrosis are two single-gene diseases for which researchers have identified the culprit DNA; there are scores of others. But lately, the cries of "OGOD" from biology labs have not been whoops of victory in nabbing yet another disease gene. They have instead been cries of dismay as some researchers apply the OGOD model to traits and behaviors as complex as "novelty seeking" and schizophrenia. "Looking for single genes for complex behaviors reminds me of the old story of losing your wallet in a dark alley but looking for it under the street lamp because the light is better there," says Robert Plomin, a behavioral geneticist at the Institute of Psychiatry in London. Critics outside the field are even harsher. "Many of these 'results' [in behavioral genetics] disappear when you do the statistics right," psychologist Helena Kraemer of Stanford University told a recent meeting at the Institute of Medicine in Washington. "Fallacious methods are very common."

What is "happy DNA"?

The latest offering in "the gene for . . ." sweepstakes is "happy DNA." In the journal *Nature Genetics,* molecular biologist Dean Hamer of the National Cancer Institute reviews studies suggesting that one's baseline level of happiness—the very small range within which one's happiness level fluctuates—is "largely a matter of heredity." Identical twins (who have exactly the same genes) are alike in their happiness level 44 percent of the time, according to studies at the University of Minnesota. Fraternal twins, who are no more genetically similar than other siblings, are alike only 8 percent of the time. "These data show that the broad heritability of well being is 40 to 50 percent," Hamer writes. Moreover, people's happiness levels seem extraordinarily stable through the years (*Newsweek,* July 29, 1996); they are affected neither by winning a lottery nor by becoming paralyzed. Studies of twins suggest that 80 percent of this stable component of happiness is heritable. "How you feel right now is about equally genetic and circumstantial," says Hamer. "But how you'll feel on average over the next ten years is fully 80 percent because of your genes." Though no one has identified genes wearing teeny smiles, Hamer suggests that a good place to look would be the DNA involved in the brain's "pleasure chemical," dopamine. This molecule is released in the brain after good food or good sex, for instance. "I don't think there will be *a* gene for happiness," Hamer says, "but rather many genes, each explaining maybe 1 percent" of someone's happiness level.

How did researchers determine that 80 percent of happiness is because of genes? What might disprove this theory?

Critics argue that nongenetic reasons can explain why identical twins' happiness levels are more closely correlated than those of fraternal twins. Perhaps people who are treated better by society—by parents, teachers, store clerks, cops—are, all things being equal, happier than those treated shabbily, suggests Stanford's Kraemer. Perhaps, too, one is treated better if one is attractive, thin, or even-tempered. Or if one is not a member of a minority group. All of these traits are partly or completely under genetic control. Then is it not possible, Kraemer asks, that this thing called "happiness" is not itself genetic but is instead a proxy for traits that are? "Although a high heritability is being claimed," she says, "in fact the whole explanation may be environmental."

It would not be the first time that a genetic explanation collapsed. All sorts of complexities can trip up researchers. One of the biggest comes when scientists try, as Hamer does, to calculate "heritability," which is supposed to be a measure of how much of the variation in a trait from one person to the next is explained by genes. (What's not explained by genes is accounted for by people's different "environments," which include everything from obstetrical complications to education, relationships, and wealth.) A heritability of 100 percent means a trait is fully and only determined by genes. Eye color is 100 percent heritable; using chopsticks is presumably zero percent heritable. A common way to calculate heritability is through studies of twins. If identical twins are more alike in some trait than fraternal twins, then the trait is thought to have a high heritability. "But whenever you measure heritability this way, you are glossing over the fact that the similarity of environments for identical twins is much greater than it is for fraternal twins," says biologist Marcus Feldman of Stanford (whose own identical twins are now in medical school). Identicals often dress alike, are treated alike, and create their own secluded, two-person world. But fraternal twins, according to years of psychological studies, are typically no closer than other siblings. By failing to take into account that identicals share more environmental influences, argues Feldman, geneticists risk ascribing twins' similarities in happiness levels and other traits more to their genes than is warranted.

What other reasons explain happiness?

Initial excitement over the "discovery" of a gene for a behavior or complex trait has often turned to disappointment as other researchers have been unable to confirm the claims.

Gene	Identification Claimed	Current Status
Manic-depression	1987	Claim retracted. Other hints of links to a gene or genes persist.
Schizophrenia	1988	Numerous failures to replicate the results; one claim has been retracted, reports of seven other possible genes remain.
Alcoholism	1990	A 1993 review found no link between alcoholism and the purported gene.
Happiness	1996	Unresolved.
Novelty seeking	1996	Reported by two research teams. The only attempt at replication by other scientists failed to find the gene.
Neuroticism	1996	To be published later this year.

Why have some findings changed over time?

Over the last decade geneticists have reported finding genes causing schizophrenia, bipolar disorder (manic-depression), alcoholism, novelty seeking, and other complex traits. Few have held up (see table). Some, such as the claim for a schizophrenia gene, have been withdrawn; others have simply not been replicated (yet) by other scientists. In the latest such attempt, researchers led by psychologist Michael Pogue-Gelei of the University of Pittsburgh searched the DNA of 287 twins, hunting for the gene that two separate research groups recently linked to novelty seeking, the yen for new experiences.

What is the connection between genes and behavior? How is environment a factor?

"We didn't find anything," Pogue-Gelei told *Newsweek* magazine; a paper describing the work is being submitted to a journal. Failure to replicate could mean that the effect of the novelty-seeking gene is too weak to be easily detected; it could also mean that the claim is wrong. Outright fraud seems to lie behind at least one claim of a gene for a complex trait.

Even the harshest critics do not deny that genes play some role in behaviors. Behavior, after all, comes from thought, which comes from the brain. The brain runs on neurotransmitters (chemicals that carry messages from one neuron to another) and receptors (sites on neurons at which neurotransmitters dock, like spacecraft on a space station). Both neurotransmitters and receptors are made according to instructions in genes. But it's a long way from these connections to "genes determine behavior." For one thing, environment influences which of the body's 100,000 or so genes are turned on: Like a computer hard drive loaded with programs, only the one opened by a click of the mouse runs. So it is with genes. Take schizophrenia. Someone growing up in bucolic environs may carry the exact same "schizophrenia" genes as a kid in South Central [Los Angeles]. Since stress increases the risk of schizophrenia, the denizen of the inner city will develop the disease but his country cousin will not, explains psychologist Irving Gottesman of the University of Virginia. If one twin is schizophrenic, his identical twin is schizophrenic only about 48 percent of the time: The environment has not "opened" his disease genes.

Because of such complications, behavioral genetics is moving from OGOD to the idea that no single gene is sufficient for a complex trait. Genes are propensities and probabilities, not destiny. But science has not heard the end of these claims. In July, at Jackson Laboratory in Bar Harbor, Maine, NCI's Hamer described his research on genes linked to neuroticism, a trait he called "much more heritable than [a susceptibility to] breast cancer." The gene is involved in the brain's serotonin system, he said. A paper on the "neurotic gene" will be published in the journal *Science*. . . . The public, and the press, will likely eat it up, as they have earlier claims of behavioral geneticists. As philosopher Philip Kitcher of the University of California, San Diego, says, "The seduction of a simple explanation for complicated problems is the strongest force driving this field." But keep your ears pricked. Cries of "OGOD" will continue to echo throughout the land.

What do I now believe is the connection between genes and happiness?

Source: Sharon Begley, "Born Happy?" *Newsweek,* October 14, 1996. Copyright © 1996, Newsweek, Inc. All rights reserved. Reprinted by permission.

Notes

1. T. Anderson and T. Biddle, "On Asking People Questions About What They Are Learning," in G. Bower, ed., *The Psychology of Learning and Motivation* (New York: Academic Press, 1975).

Chapter 9

Staying Connected During Reading

Learning without thought is labor lost.

Confucius

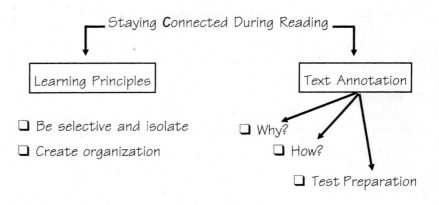

Learning Principles

In the last chapter, we discussed the importance of engaging in strategies *before* you read—activating prior knowledge, previewing, and predicting possible questions. We also outlined the four important learning principles that describe what you need to do before you begin to read a chapter in its entirety:

1. Psych yourself up.
2. Use what you already know.
3. Intend to remember.
4. Anticipate test questions.

There are also learning principles to guide your choice of study strategies *during* reading. These learning principles help you to stay connected while you're reading the text:

5. Be selective and isolate.
6. Create meaningful organization.

The process of text annotation, also discussed in this chapter, is based on these two learning principles.

Principle 5: Be Selective and Isolate

Each subject area presents a large quantity of material, but you are limited by the amount of time you can study and in the amount of information you can reasonably commit to memory. Therefore, in every phase of your reading and studying, you have to be selective. Selectivity is based on several interrelated factors:

- your background knowledge
- the amount of material and the way it is presented
- the types of information the text stresses
- the task you are expected to engage in or the types of exams, papers, discussions, and other performances you are expected to give

For example, if you had considerable background experience in the sciences in high school and did extremely well in those courses, you probably will have to annotate and study less in college science courses than someone with a limited science background.

However, in order to stay connected during reading, you cannot just select key information; you must also isolate it for later study. Isolating involves distinguishing key concepts from supporting details and selecting appropriate examples to depict key concepts. Isolating information is the first step in reducing the large amount of material presented in texts. Keep in mind that much of the information you read in a text chapter is unimportant. Think about isolation as a kind of filtering process: When you are finished, only the important material and the material that you did not already know remains.

Principle 5 is built into most of the study techniques presented in this text. Remember that you will have to study and reflect upon material in your various subject areas differently, depending upon how selective you need to be.

Principle 6: Create Meaningful Organization

Comprehending and retaining material are much easier when you have some organization in which to fit the material. After all, the human memory has limits. As stated in "The Psychology of Memory" selection in the appendix, many psychologists believe we have both "short-term" and "long-term" memory. Short-term memory helps to screen, select, and consolidate information for long-term memory. But short-term memory has an average limit of about seven items. In other words, we can store only about seven bits of information at a time in our short-term memory (which may explain why we have seven days in a week, seven digits in telephone numbers, seven deadly sins, and so on). Thus you can remember *photosynthesis* much more easily than *ostsptyhihones* because you remember the first as one "chunk" (one word) and the second as fourteen individual "chunks" (fourteen letters).

Read the following passage, and be prepared to tell what it is about.

> The procedure is actually quite simple. First you arrange things into different groups. Of course, one pile may be sufficient, depending on how much there is to do. If you have to go somewhere else due to lack of facilities, that is the next step; otherwise you are pretty well set. It is important not to overdo things. That is, it is better to do too few things at once than too many. In the short run this may not seem important, but complications can easily arise. A mistake can be expensive as well. At first the whole procedure will seem complicated. Soon, however, it will become just another facet of life. It is difficult to foresee any end to the necessity for this task in the immediate future, but then one never can tell. After the procedure is completed one arranges the materials into different groups again. Then they can be put into their appropriate places. Eventually they will be used once more and the whole cycle will then have to be repeated. However, this is part of life.[1]

Although all the words are familiar, and the sentences by themselves appear to make sense, the whole passage might not make sense to you because you have no meaningful organization for the information. But suppose that you entitled the passage "Doing the Laundry." Now read it again. See how all the information makes sense? The title enables you to apply meaningful organization to the passage. It makes sense because you know about doing the laundry and because all the sentences can be interpreted easily in that light.

Students who do not meaningfully organize while reading become detached and often fail to see how the ideas fit together. Rather than structuring their learning around major concepts, supporting details, and examples, these students try to memorize many small bits of information without ever seeing the "big picture." Students who approach the text in this fragmented manner often perform poorly on tests. Organization is important both for learning the material and for retrieving the information at test time.

Annotate Your Text

Information, whether written or spoken, tends to have two parts: major concepts and supporting details. Supporting details take the form of proofs, explanations, or examples. However, not every paragraph contains a major concept. Only about half of all the paragraphs in a text have a recognizable main idea.[2] Attempting to look for a major concept in every paragraph is an exercise in futility.

Although the major concepts are key to the text passage, they are not the
only part of learning. In most subjects, you also need to know important proofs,
explanations, or examples. This supporting information helps you to assess the
value of the major concept and to better understand its relationship to other ideas.
Conversely, you also shouldn't concentrate only on the supporting details, because they make little sense unless they are hooked into a major concept.

Don't interpret this to mean that you have to learn everything in the text.
First of all, that is impossible. Second, no one expects you to learn everything.
Instructors will tell you to learn just the "most important information." But
how do you identify what is most important?

To begin with, you must learn all of the major concepts stressed both in your text and in your professor's lectures. Although this may seem overwhelming, if you look for overlap between what your professor says and what your text says, you won't find the task that difficult. As we discussed in Chapter 5, most professors give clues as to important content and to whether test questions will be taken primarily from text, lectures, or both. Once you have determined the major concepts, you should learn as many supporting details and examples as you need to help you to understand and remember concepts and to pass tests. Being selective, then, depends upon being able to:

- differentiate major concepts from supporting details
- assess which major concepts are really important, somewhat important, or unimportant. If you have done a good job of previewing and formulating some possible questions (see Chapter 8), you should have some basis on which to select the most important ideas
- pick up cues from a text or a lecture that can help you to judge the importance of information. Pay particular attention to what your professor says in class
- monitor and reflect upon your own learning and background knowledge, so that you can judge how much supporting information you need. When you monitor your learning, you are continuously aware of what you know and don't know about a particular chapter. Reflection also helps you to stay connected

Annotating: A System of Text Marking

Text marking can be a difficult technique to learn. If you are a first-year college student, you probably have had little experience in marking books because most high schools forbid writing in texts. First-year college students often highlight as they read—in fact, they often highlight everything! It is not uncommon to open a student's psychology or sociology text and see pages of almost totally yellow, pink, or green text! Marking a text in this manner is certainly not a valuable study method and is actually no better than no marking at all. Such highlighting is a passive activity and does little, if anything, to aid in your comprehending and retaining important information.

The opposite problem can also arise; that is, students merely read the text without doing any kind of marking. Many used books are sold back to campus bookstores with few or random markings. Students who fail to mark their texts won't be able to use their books during test preparation unless they plan on doing an enormous amount of rereading. Because most college students don't have time for copious amounts of rereading, studying in this manner is neither efficient nor effective.

The system suggested in this text forces you to be selective in your marking and helps you to isolate key ideas in the text's margins, thus promoting active reading. Because the annotating system helps you to stay connected during reading by keeping you focused, it is also a very effective study aid. The following principles apply:

1. *Set aside your highlighters.* Use a pen or pencil to do your annotation. You cannot write with a highlighter, and annotating involves writing.

2. *Remember that when you mark your text, you should be able to use it to aid future reviewing.* Good annotations, like good lecture notes, stand the test of time. When it comes time to prepare for exams, you should be able to study using your annotations. You can also use the markings to create rehearsal techniques, as discussed in Chapter 10.

3. *Annotation involves writing rather than underlining.* It means writing important words and phrases in the margins of your text so that you can easily refer to them later to locate key words, names, dates, lists, and so on. Annotating also consists of jotting abbreviations (such as "def." for definition; "ex." for example; " * " for important; and " √ " for supporting details).

4. *Read and annotate a section at a time.* Use text headings and subheadings as stopping points. After reading and annotating a section, stop and think about the questions you posed as part of your preview (a technique described in Chapter 8). Can you answer those questions?

5. *Put the information in your own words.* Don't copy directly from the book unless you are annotating something that must be learned exactly as stated. An example of something that must be learned word for word might be a formula in a chemistry or physics text. Otherwise, even with most definitions, try to put the material into your own words. This indicates that you understand it. It also helps you to monitor your understanding. That is, if you can't write something in your own words, you probably do not understand it.

Notice that when you use the **BCA**'s of reading and studying, each new step builds on the previous one. Thus, in order for annotating to be most effective, you must first engage in activities before you read in order to activate prior knowledge, see how the chapter is organized, and get a general idea of the concepts. You must also formulate good questions and read to answer them. Then you must continue to restate and revise your questions and to pose new ones as you find out more about the chapter. Your questions can be the key to annotating a text properly. If you ask good questions, you should be able to do a good job of isolating important text information.

Notice also that you are actively involved in reflective reading. When you read actively, you remember more than when you read passively. Studying and reviewing become much less painful tasks. Although at this point you might think that these procedures require an inordinate amount of time, you will find that you will save time in the long run. As with anything in which you wish to become proficient, practice is the key.

Isolating Key Information

In order to do an adequate job of isolating important information by annotating, you must first be actively engaged in reading. You must also continuously monitor your understanding of the text. Remember to ask yourself, What is the author of the text saying? How does this information fit with my professor's lectures? Do I understand what I am reading? Am I selecting the key points? Annotating forces you to monitor, to select, and to reflect, because you write the ideas in your own words.

By now you probably have gotten the message about annotating and writing key points in the text's margins, but let's examine some specific kinds of information you should target. Annotate:

def.

- *definitions for content-specific terms and concepts.* Some texts isolate key terms in the margins. A word to the wise: Be careful not to overlook these marginal definitions. It doesn't hurt to annotate the isolated definitions.

ex.
eg.
i.e.

- *examples that illustrate theories, experiments, and so forth.* Many students overlook examples, only to find them on tests. If you understand the examples in the book, you should be able to generate new examples on your own.

JFK (1962)

- *names/dates/events.* Names, dates, and events are important in history courses and in certain humanities and social-science courses, but a word of caution: Make sure that names and dates aren't the only information that you annotate. In high school, students often become accustomed to memorizing names and dates because that is what is asked for on tests. Because college often requires you to think at a higher level, names, dates, and events are only a small part of what you are expected to learn. When annotating names, dates, and events, be sure to think of their significance and the context in which they are embedded.

3 reasons for x
1.
2.
3.

- *lists or characteristics.* Watch for cues such as "There are three major reasons for . . ." or "Four features distinguishing Theory X from Theory Y are. . . ." Annotate these reasons or features and make sure that you number them.

cause → effect
1.
2.
3.

- *causes/effects and likenesses/differences.* Cause/effect and likeness/difference information makes for good essay questions. Remember that a cause comes before an effect and that there is usually a chain of events. Hence, what initially was an effect may be the cause of a subsequent event.

Most students prefer to read a paragraph or two and then annotate. Better yet, train yourself to read an entire section and then go back and annotate. How do you know if something is important enough to annotate unless you have read it first? However, many students find it difficult to read larger chunks of text and then go back and annotate. Try to avoid annotating as you read. Students who do this usually copy exactly from the text rather than putting the information in their own words. They almost always annotate too much. If you find that it is taking you forever to annotate your chapter, you are probably marking as you read and marking too much. Instead, read a piece of text, think about the key information, and then annotate.

In addition to annotating, some students also like to underline. If you do a good job of annotating, underlining really isn't necessary. However, if you want to underline in addition to (not in place of) annotating, follow a few guidelines: First, annotate. Then go back and underline the information that you annotated; this will identify material that further explains your annotations in case you need to clarify your understanding by rereading. In other words, if the material was not important enough to annotate, it should not be underlined. Remember to underline with a pen, not a highlighter.

When students initially begin to annotate they may have difficulty organizing the information in the text's margins. Many make random annotations that follow no organizational pattern. Look at the sample annotations at the end of this chapter. Note that in the marketing excerpt, the annotations are organized mainly around definitions of different types of databases and examples of each type.

Now examine the skeletal annotations for the psychology excerpt. The organization shows that this portion of the text focuses on three memory processes. This specific section addresses only encoding; it provides a definition, an example, and information about brief and permanent memory coding.

In both excerpts, the way the annotations are organized makes it easy to see at a glance how the key ideas relate to each other and how supporting details relate to the key ideas.

But what if you are required to read a text that has margins too small for annotating? One solution is to purchase a package of Post-it notes (those tiny pieces of paper that have a sticky strip on one side) and write your annotations on them. Then you can simply stick the Post-its on the appropriate pages so that you have good annotations for future study. When using this approach, you might also want to put the page number on the Post-it note in case it falls off.

Using Your Annotations for Test Preparation

If you have annotated properly, you have already taken a big step in preparing for the exam. Once you have annotated in your own words, reflected upon the key concepts, and monitored your understanding, you have started to put key information into long-term memory. Now you are ready to use those annotations as part of several test-preparation strategies. One strategy is to study your annotations directly. To use this method, follow these procedures:

1. *Cover the actual text.* You want to avoid large amounts of rereading and instead concentrate only on the annotations.

2. *Read your annotations.* Explain each theory; give examples of each experiment. Be sure that you know the information thoroughly. Students often

make the mistake of learning only the names of three important theories or two important reasons. Make sure that you understand the basis of those theories and why certain battles were important. Ask yourself, Do my annotations make sense? Do I understand what I have annotated?

3. *Reread the text only if you cannot explain your annotations.* This is where underlining can be helpful. Find the section of the text that explains the annotation and reread only that part. If you have underlined, read only the underlining that explains the annotation. Do not waste precious time reading unrelated material; stay focused on the particular information you are seeking.

4. *Talk through all of your annotations,* marking in some way those that you know and those that will require additional study.

5. *Think about the overlap between your text annotations and lecture notes.*

Now that you have an idea of what annotation entails and how to annotate, let's look at some examples. Excerpts from three different selections that appear in the appendix serve as models for you to follow. The marketing excerpt, which we will discuss in detail, has been completely annotated for you, but the psychology and history excerpts are only partially annotated so that you can practice on them.

Notice several features of the marketing annotation. First, the annotations basically consist of definitions and examples, the way this portion of the text is organized. This type of organization makes annotating fairly easy. Second, note that the three types of databases are numbered to cue you that there is more than one type. Finally, note that abbreviations are used whenever possible. For example, *database* is abbreviated *db* and *information* is *info.* The annotations are legible and can easily be used in studying. Abbreviations have been used when appropriate to make the annotating more efficient. The key information has been isolated in the margins so that when it comes time to prepare for the test, self-recitation will be easy.

Now look at the skeletal annotations for the psychology selection. Although these annotations are obviously incomplete (you will finish them when you do the application exercises at the end of the chapter), the organization and the key ideas are readily apparent. Note that encoding is subsumed under memory processes; there are two additional memory processes that are mentioned but not discussed in this section of text.

Finally, examine the skeletal annotations for the history selection. Students often have a difficult time annotating history because every little fact seems important. Rather than writing down every little fact in the margins, note that these skeletal annotations cue you to be aware of concepts rather than isolated facts. Note also that these annotations should reflect how everything is related to "The New Frontier," one of the chapter headings.

Key Ideas

1. Annotating is a good way to stay connected during the reading process.
2. Annotating is derived from two key learning principles: being selective and creating meaningful organization.
3. Use the information gleaned from previewing and the questions formulated for each section to help you in selecting the main ideas.
4. Read to answer your questions and to discover other important information your questions may have missed.
5. Annotate as you read.
6. After you have read a section, think about it. Attempt to recall its most important information by answering your questions.
7. Use your annotations to prepare for exams.

Application Exercises (DTT)

1. Complete the annotations for the excerpt from the psychology text entitled "The Psychology of Memory." Make sure that you fill in the three memory processes, the definition, and the example. Complete any additional information about the implications and complete the section on how brief memories differ from permanent ones. Use the annotation checklist at the end of the chapter to evaluate your markings. Finally, compare your annotations with the excerpt at the end of the chapter.

2. Complete the annotations for the excerpt from the history text entitled "Great Promises, Bitter Disappointments, 1960–1968." As you complete the annotations, pay particular attention to the three factors that were targeted for "change and activism." Note words such as *but* and *however.* Words such as these are important and ones that students often gloss over in their reading and annotating. Use the annotation checklist at the end of the chapter to evaluate your markings.

3. Later, as you work through the chapters in the appendix, under the direction of your instructor, annotate each one using the methods discussed in this chapter. As you annotate, indicate which information will be important to remember for a test. If appropriate, make notes on charts and graphs. Then complete the application exercises at the end of each chapter to give you practice in reading and studying. Remember to read and annotate one section at a time. Use the following annotation checklist to evaluate your markings.

Annotation Checklist

____ I have focused my annotations on key ideas rather than on details.
____ I have annotated in my own words. I did not copy directly from the book.

_____ I have annotated in a brief and telegraphic nature.

_____ I have marked the graphic aids.

_____ I have annotated specific examples because they could reappear on a test.

_____ I have enumerated the specific facts, characteristics, causes, events, and so forth.

_____ I have developed some symbols of my own and have used them consistently.

_____ I have organized my annotations logically.

_____ I have annotated this chapter perfectly.

_____ I need special assistance on my annotations for this chapter.

On a scale of 1–10, I give my annotations a _____.

Application Exercise (Your Texts)

Using the suggestions given in this chapter, annotate a chapter or two from several of your texts. Try to practice your annotations on texts from two different areas—that is, a science text and a social-science or humanities text. Compare your markings. What kinds of information did you mark in each? What were the emphases? Discuss with your instructor any problems you had annotating. Use the annotation checklist at the end of the chapter to evaluate your annotations.

Selection from a Marketing Text (Annotated)

Capitalizing on New Technologies for Marketing Research

Databases

database (db)
(def) info. arranged for easy access & retrieval
(purpose) provides info used to make decisions
eg sales reports
articles
Commercial dbs also available via telephone or CD-ROMs
eg CompuServe

A **database** is a collection of information arranged for easy access and retrieval. Databases allow marketers to tap into an abundance of information useful in making marketing decisions: internal sales reports, newspaper articles, company news releases, government economic reports, bibliographies, and more, often accessed through a computer system.

Many marketing researchers use commercial databases developed by information research firms to obtain useful information for marketing decisions. Commercial online databases are accessible via a telephone hookup for a fee. They can also be obtained in printed form or on computer compact discs (CD-ROMs). In most commercial databases, the user typically does a computer search on a key word, topic, or company, and the database service generates abstracts, articles, or reports that can then be printed out. Accessing multiple reports or a complete article may cost extra.

CompuServe, for example, has a special neighborhood report option that provides summaries of demographics for any ZIP code in the United States. In addition, a menu allows the researcher to select demographic, sales potential, or neighborhood reports, but these carry a surcharge. For example, two sales potential reports for the automotive parts market cost approximately $100. Medical/health insurance data for a ZIP code in Ohio costs $25. CENDATA, another database available through CompuServe, allows marketers to access 1990 U.S. Census Bureau data in both tabular and report form. It also lists names, addresses, and phone numbers for local, regional, and national census offices. CENDATA supplies statewide population and housing characteristics for variables such as income, education, and language spoken, as well as others.

Information provided by a single firm on household demographics, purchases, television viewing behavior, and responses to promotions such as coupons and free samples is called **single-source data.** For example, Behavior Scan, offered by Information Resources, Inc., screens about 60,000 households in twenty-six U.S. markets. This single-source information service monitors consumer household televisions and records the programs and commercials watched. When consumers from these households shop in stores equipped with scanning registers, they present Hotline cards (similar to credit cards) to cashiers. This enables each customer's identification to be electronically coded so that the firm can track each product the customer purchases.

Many marketers also develop their own databases. An example is NSS, a firm that markets software to banks. Facing a challenge of qualifying thousands of new sales leads, NSS developed a database program to track customers and prospects according to specified criteria. NSS's database provides detailed data that ranks prospects in terms of those who can make a buying decision within a year and those who can make one within two years or more. Such information gives NSS greater control in managing its sales force.

Source: From *Marketing: Concepts and Strategies,* Tenth Edition by Pride and Ferrell. Copyright © 1991 by Houghton Mifflin Company. Used by permission of Houghton Mifflin Company.

Selection from a Psychology Text

The Psychology of Memory

Memory Processes

How are you able to remember past experiences and events? Since you do not have a camera in your mind, how can you remember a picture? Since you do

Margin notes:

single-source data
(def) info given by one firm
eg—Behavior scan has data on
TV watching

private dbs
(def) mkters who dev own db
eg NSS

Memory Processes
Remembering = 3 processes
  1.
  2.
  3.

not record music with your brain, how can you remember a song once heard? Human memory is still a mysterious process that we know relatively little about. Logically, however, we know that remembering requires at least three processes: getting information in the mind, retaining it, and then getting it out. These processes are called encoding, storage, and retrieval.

① *Encoding*
ⓓⓔⓕ

Encoding

Memories are not the same as real events: I do not have actual music in my mind; my house is not actually in my head. Memories can be thought of as consisting of information, rather than of physical objects such as houses. **Encoding** is the process of changing physical scenes and events into the form of information that can be stored in memory. This "form" of information used in recording memories is the memory code. Thus the process of encoding consists of changing the physical energy in the environment (for example, a sound) into memory codes.

ⓔ𝓍 What is this code? Evidence shows that memories of recent letters or words are often encoded into labels or sounds. . . . In a complex experiment designed to test the capacity of memory, Sperling allowed participants one very brief glance at a group of twelve letters printed on a card, then asked them to name as many letters as they could remember. On the average, they were able to name only four or five letters. But the errors that they made were very interesting. Although the letters were presented visually, the participants tended to confuse letters that *sounded* alike; for example, they would mix up D and E or B and C. This finding indicates something about the nature of the memory code in this task: People must be encoding what the letters sound like, and then storing the sound codes. If people encoded what the letters looked like, they would have made more confusions among letters that looked alike than among letters that sounded alike. Other experimenters have confirmed that errors made in recalling visually presented items tend to be acoustically related (related by sound) to the missed item. That is, people are more likely to confuse E with C (an acoustic confusion) than they are to confuse E with F (a visual confusion).

ⓘ𝓂𝓅𝓁𝒾𝒸𝒶𝓉𝒾𝑜𝓃𝓈 These brief memories of recent events are sometimes encoded into the spoken sounds of letters or words.

More permanent memories are not influenced so much by sound similarity. The memory for material that is highly practiced tends to be influenced more by semantic similarity—similarity in meaning. Apparently, material that is more permanently stored in memory is encoded into meanings rather than into sounds. Since you can remember pictures of all sorts—even abstract designs—it is clear that the sound code and the meaning code are not the only memory codes we have available. An image code is also used.

Brief memories =

Permanent memories =

Source: From *Introductory Psychology* by Morris K. Holland. Copyright © 1981 by D. C. Heath and Company. Used by permission of Houghton Mifflin Company.

Selection from a History Text
(Annotated)

The New Frontier

The weather in Washington was frigid when Kennedy gave his inaugural address, but his speech fired the imagination of the nation. Speaking in idealistic terms, avoiding any mention of specific programs, he promised to march against "the common enemies of man: tyranny, poverty, disease, and war itself." He asked all Americans to participate, exhorting them to "ask not what your country can do for you—ask what you can do for your country."

JFK's program
Focus:
*Change & activism through
1. Appointments

Kennedy's staff and cabinet kept up the image of change and activism. Recruiting from businesses and universities, he appointed men and women whom one reporter dubbed the "best and the brightest." Rhodes scholars and Harvard professors were prominent, including historian Arthur Schlesinger, economist John Kenneth Galbraith (both personal advisers), McGeorge Bundy (national security director), and Dean Rusk (secretary of state). Ford Motor Company's president, Robert McNamara, was tapped for secretary of defense. In a controversial move, Kennedy gave the position of attorney general to his younger brother Robert. John Kennedy praised his choices as men with "know-how," experienced in solving problems. Not everyone, however, was convinced. Referring to the lack of political background among appointees, Speaker of the House Sam Rayburn remarked that he would "feel a whole lot better . . . if just one of them had run for sheriff once."

Rayburn had noted a critical point. Kennedy and his staff wanted to be activists, leading the nation along new paths of liberalism, but Congress was likely to be an obstacle. Democrats had lost twenty-one seats in the House in the 1960 election, and since 1937 many congressional Democrats had voted with Republicans to prevent any notable expansion of the New Deal. It would be "very difficult" to pass controversial legislation, Kennedy told his staff, and so he decided to delay civil rights and social legislation and instead concentrate on shaping foreign policy and improving the economy.

2. JFK wanted liberalism
BUT

To spur economic recovery, Kennedy turned to "new economics" as advocated by Walter Heller, his chairman of the Council of Economic Advisers, and called for more government spending and business and income-tax cuts. The defense budget was the first beneficiary, growing by almost 20 percent ($6 billion). Kennedy also asked Congress for a modest domestic program that included increases in social security coverage and benefits and in the minimum wage, and extension of unemployment insurance, a housing and **urban renewal** bill, and aid to education. By the autumn of 1961, Congress had passed all but the education bill and tax cuts. Meanwhile, the economy was also re-

3. Economics

urban renewal Effort to revitalize rundown city centers by providing federal funding for the construction of apartment houses, office buildings, and public facilities.

bounding from the "Eisenhower recession" as unemployment fell by 2 percent from a 1960 high of 7 percent.

HOWEVER
New problem =

The booming economy, however, created a new problem: inflation. Fearful of slowing economic growth, Kennedy established informal price and wage guidelines for businesses and labor unions. Most accepted the president's formulas, but in early 1962 United States Steel and a few other steel makers raised their prices above Kennedy's ceiling. He took it as a personal insult and lashed out at U.S. Steel. Announcing that the new price was not in the public interest, he told the Federal Trade Commission and FBI to investigate the steel maker for possible **price fixing** and other fraudulent business practices, and he threatened to reduce its government contracts. Facing an angry president and being undersold by other steel companies, Roger Blough, president of U.S. Steel, retreated and lowered prices. Kennedy gloried in the victory but allowed steel prices to rise the following year. As 1962 ended, the White House boasted that the economy was strong and that forty of fifty-four bills had been passed in the first 170 days of Kennedy's administration. When liberals complained about the lack of civil rights legislation and new social programs, Kennedy hid behind the Republican–southern/conservative Democratic coalition. "There is no sense in raising hell and then not being successful," he told them. He promised a liberal package for 1963 and 1964, including a civil rights bill and programs to attack poverty.

1962 record

Source: From *Making America* by Berkin, Miller, Cherny, and Gormly. Copyright © 1995 by Houghton Mifflin Company. Used by permission of Houghton Mifflin Company.

Selection from a Psychology Text (Annotated)

The Psychology of Memory

Memory Processes

Memory Processes

Remembering = 3 processes
1. Encoding—getting info in
2. Storage—keeping info in
3. Retrieval—getting info out

How are you able to remember past experiences and events? Since you do not have a camera in your mind, how can you remember a picture? Since you do not record music with your brain, how can you remember a song once heard? Human memory is still a mysterious process that we know relatively little about. Logically, however, we know that remembering requires at least three processes: getting information in the mind, retaining it, and then getting it out. These processes are called encoding, storage, and retrieval.

price fixing   Illegal mutual agreements among competing firms to hold prices at a certain level; the price is usually somewhat inflated so that all firms will make larger profits.

Encoding

Memories are not the same as real events: I do not have actual music in my mind; my house is not actually in my head. Memories can be thought of as consisting of information, rather than of physical objects such as houses. **Encoding** is the process of changing physical scenes and events into the form of information that can be stored in memory. This "form" of information used in recording memories is the memory code. Thus the process of encoding consists of changing the physical energy in the environment (for example, a sound) into memory codes.

What is this code? Evidence shows that memories of recent letters or words are often encoded into labels or sounds. . . . In a complex experiment designed to test the capacity of memory, Sperling allowed participants one very brief glance at a group of twelve letters printed on a card, then asked them to name as many letters as they could remember. On the average, they were able to name only four or five letters. But the errors that they made were very interesting. Although the letters were presented visually, the participants tended to confuse letters that *sounded* alike; for example, they would mix up D and E or B and C. This finding indicates something about the nature of the memory code in this task: People must be encoding what the letters sound like, and then storing the sound codes. If people encoded what the letters looked like, they would have made more confusions among letters that looked alike than among letters that sounded alike. Other experimenters have confirmed that errors made in recalling visually presented items tend to be acoustically related (related by sound) to the missed item. That is, people are more likely to confuse E with C (an acoustic confusion) than they are to confuse E with F (a visual confusion). These brief memories of recent events are sometimes encoded into the spoken sounds of letters or words.

More permanent memories are not influenced so much by sound similarity. The memory for material that is highly practiced tends to be influenced more by semantic similarity—similarity in meaning. Apparently, material that is more permanently stored in memory is encoded into meanings rather than into sounds. Since you can remember pictures of all sorts—even abstract designs—it is clear that the sound code and the meaning code are not the only memory codes we have available. An image code is also used.

Source: From *Introductory Psychology* by Morris K. Holland. Copyright © 1981 by D. C. Heath and Company. Used by permission of Houghton Mifflin Company.

Notes

1. J. D. Bransford, *Human Cognition: Learning, Understanding, and Remembering* (Belmont, Calif.: Wadsworth Publishing Company, 1979), pp. 134–35.

2. R. R. Braddock, R. Lloyd-Jones, and L. Schoer, *Research in Written Composition* (Champaign, Ill.: National Council of Teachers of English, 1963), pp. 13–14.

3. Developed by M. L. Simpson and S. L. Nist.

Margin notes:

① Encoding
(def)—changing occurrences into a form that can be stored
—the form is a kind of memory code.

(Ex) of memory code = Sperling's exp. in which subjects confused letters that sound alike although letters were presented visually.

Exp. showed that letter sound was encoded over visual likenesses

Like results found only in brief memory research
Permanent memories more influenced by meaning
—meaning more easily encoded than sound

Chapter 10

After You Read: Studying

Nothing is particularly hard if you divide it into small jobs.

Henry Ford

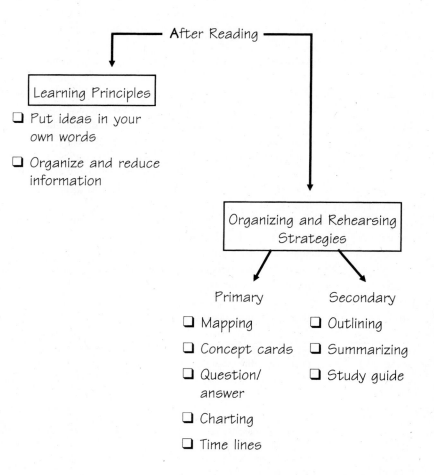

Perhaps the most important phase of studying occurs after you read a text or hear a lecture. We forget very rapidly almost everything we read or hear unless we make efforts to remember. Therefore, if you merely read a chapter, even if you intend to remember it, chances are that you will forget most of it by the next day, and you will have wasted a great deal of time in the process.

Think about the following situation. You look up the number for your dentist in the telephone directory so that you can call and make an appointment for your semiannual checkup. Right after you look up the number, your roommate interrupts to ask about a psychology assignment that is due at the end of the week. After you finish explaining the assignment (it took less than one minute), you return to make your phone call. What do you think has happened?

Unless you frequently call your dentist, you probably will have forgotten the phone number. Why? Because the only thing you did was get the information into short-term memory. You probably didn't try to learn the number because you thought you were going to call right away.

Now think about the implications the dentist scenario has for textbook learning. If the only thing you do is to begin on the first page of the chapter, read to the end, and close your book, how much of the material are you going to remember? Probably not very much, because you need to interact actively with the text's information and "chunk it" into meaningful units to remember it. Unless you use additional strategies, you will probably have to reread the complete chapter before a test, just as you would have to look up your dentist's telephone number again. By spending some time immediately after you read to organize the material and perform rehearsal strategies, you will improve your memory up to three times. You'll spend a little more time but remember so much more—a much more effective use of your time!

The organizing and rehearsing phase of the **BCA** method, which occurs after you have read and annotated your text, is based on several new learning principles (as well as those already mentioned).

Learning Principles

Principle 7: Put Ideas in Your Own Words

If you simply *read* a textbook chapter, you will probably remember less than one-third of it by the following week. And in two months, you will remember only about 14 percent of it—hardly enough to help you to do well on a test. In order to transfer a greater portion of the material you read from your short-term to long-term memory, you must do something active and reflective with the

CALVIN AND HOBBES © 1989 Watterson. Dist. by UNIVERSAL PRESS
SYNDICATE. Reprinted with permission. All rights reserved.

information to help "fix" it in your memory. If you take time after reading each section of the chapter to organize and rehearse the information, more of it goes into long-term memory. If you rehearse, you will probably remember 80 percent of what you read after a week has passed and 70 percent after two months!

Ensure the greatest amount of understanding by rehearsing *in your own words*. The previous chapter discussed the importance of putting information in your own words when you annotate. The same principle holds true for rehearsing: If you can put the important material in your own words, you probably understand it and thus will be better able to remember and retrieve it at test time.

Principle 8: Organize and Reduce the Information

Because it is impossible to remember everything you read or hear, rehearsal techniques serve to organize and reduce the material to a reasonable amount. The strategies discussed in this chapter will make your job easier. Becoming proficient in organizing and reducing both lecture notes and text is a necessity if you want to do well on tests. Students often defeat themselves by trying to learn too much material through memorizing many isolated facts. They are not going to do very well on exams because they are unable to synthesize information. It is therefore imperative for you to learn a variety of rehearsal strategies, so that you can put new information in your own words, organize it, and reduce it to an amount that can feasibly be rehearsed and remembered.

Rehearsal Strategies

The next section will present numerous rehearsal strategies that will help you to organize and reduce information. These strategies are divided into two key types—primary rehearsal techniques and secondary rehearsal techniques. Primary strategies are more efficient and effective and can be used in a variety of learning situations. Primary strategies focus on self-recitation and self-testing; that is, each strategy, in some way, provides questions or cues to help you learn but conceals the "answers" as a check to see if you actually know the information. For example, concept cards have only the term and a memory cue on the front; you cannot see the definition or example because it is on the back. The memory cue should spark the definition and any other important information that you should remember. You say the definition and give the example. Then you turn over your card to check for accuracy. In other words, primary rehearsal strategies have a built-in monitoring element. You receive immediate feedback as to whether your answer is correct.

Secondary strategies, which are more traditional rehearsal devices, don't have a monitoring element built in. They may have worked for your high school classes, but they are probably neither as efficient nor as effective as the primary strategies. However, they can serve learning purposes in specific situations for specific types of students. Although we recommend that you use primary strategies most of the time, in some instances you may want to use secondary techniques.

As you work through the different rehearsal strategies, remember that it is all right to modify and personalize them, so that they work for you. Try each strategy out as it is presented in the text, and then modify it to meet the needs of a particular course, professor, or your own studying behaviors. These strategies are supposed to help you to isolate and learn through self-testing the information so that you can learn the material thoroughly, retrieve it, and perform well on a test.

Primary Rehearsal Strategies

Mapping

Some material, especially material that contains a lot of new terminology or requires a lot of organizing, can be better understood and remembered if you can actually see the relationships in the material. These graphic representations are sometimes called *maps* or *graphic organizers.* Maps, such as those at the beginning of each chapter of this text, show how ideas and terms are related, and this helps you to comprehend and memorize material. For example, these techniques might help you to learn the biology selection in the appendix. "Genetics: The Science of Inheritance" includes a lot of new terminology; you might find it difficult to keep all of the terms straight. Mapping should both improve your comprehension and aid your memory and retrieval.

When constructing your map, first preview the section and ask questions to guide your reading, as outlined in Chapter 8, and then read the section. Immediately after you read and annotate, jot down a list that includes the key terms and/or concepts. Make a map that includes most or all of what you listed. You probably will have to construct more than one map to cover all of the important material. Also, if you do a good job of annotating your text, the annotations can take the place of the list from which you can draw the key terms and/or concepts.

Figure 10.1 shows a generic map. In making your map, decide on a single key term or concept and put it in the middle. Then decide what class that term

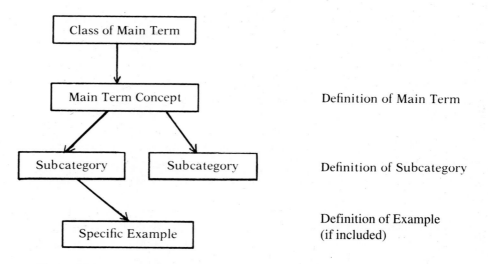

Figure 10.1 Example of a Generic Map

Source: Drawn from P. D. Pearson and D. D. Johnson, *Teaching Reading Comprehension* (New York: Holt, Rinehart and Winston, 1974).

or concept belongs in, and put the class above the key term. List the definition(s) of the key term. List and put the class above the key term next to it. Next place any subcategories of terms or concepts below the key term. Finally, if further clarification is necessary, put specific examples lowest on the map, with their definitions out to the side.

The way you actually construct your map may differ slightly from the method described here; in fact, you can map in many different ways. The main point is to graphically organize the relationships among concepts, terms, and examples. As you study, try mapping the information in different ways. By making up your own type of map, you rehearse, consolidate, and give the information the organization that is most meaningful to you.

Now let's look at an example. Read the following paragraphs, taken from the biology selection in the appendix,[1] and then map the concepts. Remember, you can construct your map in any way you want to, as long as the relationships are clearly delineated.

A Theory of Particulate Inheritance

At first, these results must have seemed every bit as confusing as the blue and yellow parakeets mentioned in the opening pages of this chapter. But Mendel was able to explain them. He proposed a system of **particulate inheritance** in which heritable characteristics were controlled by individual "units." Mendel assumed (correctly, as it turned out) that each plant had two such units for each trait. Mendel called each unit a "Merkmal," the German word for "character." Today we call these units **genes,** and we know that the cells of the pea plant carry two genes for most characteristics. If we represent the units with symbols, we might use P for Mendel's purple-flower character and p for the white-flower character.

P and p are known as **alleles,** which are alternative forms of a single gene, in this case the gene for flower color. In Mendel's first cross, the original, true-breeding purple-flowered parent would have been PP, and the original white-flowered plant would have been pp.

One of Mendel's most extraordinary insights was the realization that when organisms produce their reproductive cells, or **gametes,** each gamete carries only one allele for each gene. Therefore, the two alleles for each gene are **segregated** from each other when gametes are formed. In Mendel's experiment, for example, the F_1 generation received an allele for purple flowers from one parent and an allele for white flowers from the other parent. In this way, each parent makes an individual genetic contribution to its offspring.

Compare your map to the one in Figure 10.2. Although this map is very simplistic, it gives you an idea of basic organization and lets you see how the concepts are related.

Now let's examine a longer piece of text more similar to the kinds of information you would need to map. Obviously, you should not make a map for every paragraph; doing so would lead to fragmented learning and would defeat

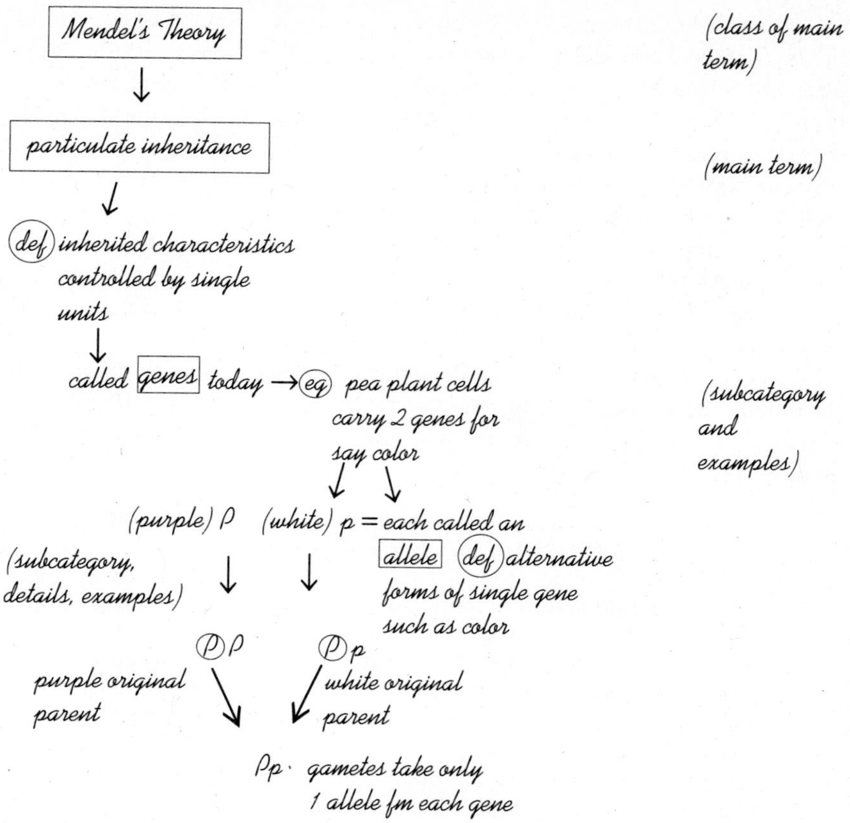

Mendel's Theory — (class of main term)

↓

particulate inheritance — (main term)

↓

(def) inherited characteristics controlled by single units

↓

called [genes] today → (eg) pea plant cells carry 2 genes for say color — (subcategory and examples)

(purple) P   (white) p = each called an [allele] (def) alternative forms of single gene such as color — (subcategory, details, examples)

(P) P purple original parent

(P) p white original parent

Pp · gametes take only 1 allele fm each gene

Figure 10.2 Map of a Paragraph from a Biology Text

the purpose of devising maps. Instead, map sections from the text or key concepts. Figure 10.3 shows a partially completed map depicting the three memory processes drawn from the selection "The Psychology of Memory" in the appendix. Note that there are three key elements to the map: encoding, storage, and retrieval. Each concept also has certain key information organized under it. It is easy to see from the map that there are two different kinds of memory codes, each used under different circumstances.

When using your maps to rehearse, cover up everything except the key concepts. Say the information that goes with each concept, and then immediately check to see if you are correct. If not, re-cover the material and try again. Once you say the information correctly, say it several times to put it into long-term memory.

Application Exercises (DTT)

1. Complete the map on the three memory processes in Figure 10.3. The first process has been completed for you. Finish "Storage" and "Retrieval" in a

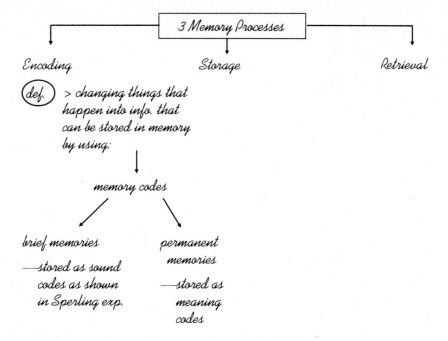

Figure 10.3 Partially Completed Map from "The Psychology of Memory" Excerpt

similar fashion. Remember to make your map more detailed if your background knowledge in this area is weak.

2. Construct a map of the measures of forgetting also presented in "The Psychology of Memory" selection.

3. Map appropriate sections of the appendix selections as your instructor assigns.

Application Exercise (Your Texts)

Find appropriate segments to map from your college texts. Discuss these maps with your instructor. Remember to map entire sections or concepts, rather than just paragraphs.

Concept Cards

Another primary rehearsal strategy that you can do after you read is to make concept cards. Concept cards lend themselves well to studying and learning factual material, although some students are able to modify the cards so that they can use them with more conceptual ideas. You have probably used concept cards without actually calling them that. The procedure is quite simple: Write the term, person, concept, or the like on one side of an index card and its definition, description, or related idea on the reverse side. Often it helps if you use some sort of a mnemonic device, or memory technique (see Chapter 11), to help you to remember what the concept means. For example, if you wanted to learn the term *chunking* from "The Psychology of Memory" selection in the appendix, your card might look like the one in Figure 10.4. On the front of the card are the term, a mnemonic device (in this case a simple drawing) to help you to remember what the word means, a key term in the upper right-hand corner for organizing purposes, the reading selection associated with the term, and the page number. On the back are the definition, any additional information, and an example.

Front

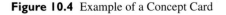

Storage

Chunking

("The Psychology of Memory")
p 273

Back

— The process of grouping items together (usually in groups of 3 or 4) in order to make learning easier.
— Can recall 7 ± 2 chunks of info. that was seen once

ex   Grouping of phone numbers & Social Security numbers (e.g., 546-7816) would be learned as 2 chunks, not 7.

Figure 10.4 Example of a Concept Card

Concept cards present several advantages:

1. As you learn the terms or concepts, *you can separate out those cards* so that you have one pile of cards on material that you know and another on material that you need to study further.

2. *The cards are easy to carry around* in case you have fifteen or twenty minutes free or want to review during lunch or between classes. Concept cards are particularly valuable in courses such as biology or psychology, in which many new terms are introduced rapidly.

3. Although concept cards are generally recommended for use with factual material, they *also can be valuable for key essay responses.* Pulling together the information from several cards can form the basis for a good essay answer. For example, the marketing selection in the appendix presents numerous terms that deal with information systems. Many of these terms could be organized and used to answer the following essay question:

Discuss and be sure to give examples of the ways information systems can be used in marketing research. Evaluate the effectiveness of each of these systems.

4. *Concept cards can help organize ideas by using the concepts to create maps.* To form maps, use the key word in the upper right-hand corner as your guide. First group together all cards that have the same key term. Then arrange the cards so that it is easy to see which terms are related and how they are related. In the appendix selection "The Psychology of Memory," (pages 273–296), for example, you could organize the cards that have terms related to forgetting, as shown in Figure 10.5.

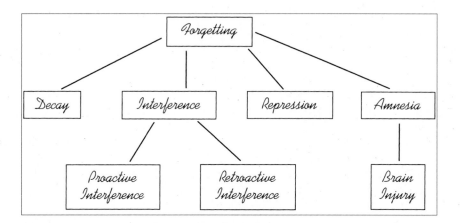

Figure 10.5 Concept Cards Showing Related Terms

Application Exercises (DTT)

1. For the psychology selection in the appendix, make concept cards for the section on forgetting. (The cards you will need to complete are shown in Figure 10.5.)

2. Using the terms from the biology selection in the appendix, make a minimum of ten concept cards. Remember to include mnemonics and examples. After you have completed your cards, try to organize them into a map.

3. For which selections or parts of selections in the appendix would concept cards be most appropriate? Why?

Application Exercise (Your Texts)

Using your college texts, make concept cards for new terms or concepts. When appropriate, use your cards to help you to predict and answer essay questions or to organize key terms into maps. Discuss your concept cards with your instructor.

Question/Answer

The third primary rehearsal strategy that you can use after you read is the question/answer technique. The quickest way to carry out this strategy is to look up from your book after each section and answer the prereading questions you posed for that section. Use your own words, and refer to the book only to check yourself. Stopping after each section and rehearsing the answers will help you to check your memory and comprehension.

The drawback to merely rehearsing the answers is that you have nothing written down that you can use later for review. A second purpose for rehearsing is to reduce the amount of information for later study. Recall the discussion on annotating in Chapter 9: Proper text marking reduces the amount of information you must learn and guides your question/answer sessions. Instead of having to reread entire sections, you can simply review your questions and answers, your notes, and the annotated material. This technique allows you to review only about one-third of the information in a chapter, but it is *key* information and will usually remind you of other supporting information in the section. Rehearsing, therefore, involves putting information into your own words and organizing, consolidating, and reflecting upon the information for later study.

The second way to use questions and answers, then, is to write them out; this gives you reduced information in a very easy and adaptable framework for later study and review.

To use the question/answer technique effectively, examine the format in Figure 10.6 and then follow these four steps:

1. *Before* you read each section, predict some possible test questions, as outlined in Chapter 8.

2. *After* you read each section, on the left-hand side of a sheet of paper write down several key questions. Be sure you leave enough room to write down complete answers.

3. *After* you read each section, close the book and write answers to the questions in your own words on the right-hand side of the paper.

4. *Refer* to the book to answer any questions you could not answer before, to check your other answers, and to answer any questions you may have answered inadequately.

Questions	*Answers*
1. Define the "tip-of-the-tongue" phenomenon. Why does this phenomenon occur?	1. Knowing that you know something (e.g., a person's name or the first letter of the thing you're trying to remember) but being unable to retrieve it. Tip-of-the-tongue occurs because you can't locate the information because of the way it has been "filed."
2. Describe Lashley's rat experiments. What was the purpose of the experiments and what were his findings?	
3. Explain the duplex theory of memory.	
4. Explain the levels-of-processing theory.	
5. What are the similarities and differences between the 2 memory theories?	

Figure 10.6 Question/Answer Technique on "Memory"

When you go back to rehearse the section, use the following five steps:

1. Cover up your answers or fold your paper back.

2. Ask yourself each question that you have written down, and try to answer it.

3. Check each answer against what you wrote. If you were right, put a check next to your question so that you won't need to spend more time rehearsing it until you do a comprehensive review.

4. If you were wrong, cover up the answer, ask yourself the question again, and rehearse the answer. When you are finished with all of the questions, go back to the ones you missed the first time and go over them again. Correctly answer each missed question three times. This technique will prevent you from remembering your wrong answer.

5. If you don't understand your answers or if you feel you need to study the topic further, return to your book and review the section. Then add any new information to your original answer. (See Figure 10.6.)

The question/answer technique initially may seem a bit burdensome or time-consuming. But as with most of the other rehearsal strategies in this chapter, students will find that it suits them some of the time and with certain kinds of materials and tasks. This strategy forces you to predict test questions. But don't fall into the trap of writing all memory-level questions; write some higher-level questions as well, so that the technique is appropriate for both objective and essay tests. Notice that only one of the questions in Figure 10.6 begins with the word *what*. The remainder of the questions all begin with the higher-level terms such as *describe* or *explain*.

Application Exercises (DTT)

1. Complete the question/answer technique started for you in Figure 10.6. Write at least five additional questions and answer them. Make sure that you use the correct format.

2. Select an appropriate section of the "Great Promises, Bitter Disappointments, 1960–1968" selection in the appendix and write ten good questions. Make sure you write a blend of memory- and higher-level questions. Then answer your questions. Check the format you used. Did you put the questions on the left and the answers on the right so that you can monitor your learning?

3. What other selections or parts of selections from the appendix would be appropriate for using the question/answer technique?

4. As you preread, annotate, and organize the selections in the appendix, use the question/answer technique appropriately. Discuss with your instructor

the effectiveness of your questions and answers. If you have a study partner, go over your questions and answers with him or her.

Application Exercise (Your Texts)

Use the question/answer technique for a chapter or a portion of a chapter of one of your college texts. Use the questions with your study group as a way to check for understanding of the chapter.

Compare/Contrast Charting

Another primary rehearsal strategy that you can use after you read is compare/contrast charting. If you are reading a text that contains information on which an instructor might test you by asking for similarities and differences, charting is a good approach. Suppose you have completed reading "The Psychology of Memory" from the appendix selections. Your professor has told you to make sure that you can compare and contrast the duplex theory of memory with the levels-of-processing theory. Your chart might be set up something like the one in Figure 10.7.

Note that the two theories—duplex and levels-of-processing—are listed horizontally on the chart. Categories for which they can be compared or contrasted are listed vertically. When you do charting, think about the categories for which you can compare or contrast subjects. Some students err by trying to compare apples with oranges, using *however* as a catchall connector. For example, for an essay comparing and contrasting these two theories, you might include the following statement, based on your chart, as part of your essay answer:

> Although both theories of memory systems consider rehearsal to be important, the similarities of these two systems appear to end there. The duplex theory suggests that there are two distinct and separate systems, short-term memory and long-term memory, while the levels-of-processing theory emphasizes processes rather than separate systems. The duplex theory purports that information is moved from short-term memory to long-term memory through rehearsal. In other words, the more something is rehearsed, the greater chance it has of getting into long-term memory. However, in the levels-of-processing theory, it is the nature of rehearsal, either maintenance rehearsal or elaborative rehearsal, that makes information difficult or easy to remember.

The most difficult part of creating charts is figuring out which categories you should include. Remember what we said earlier: You can't compare apples and oranges. Thus you want to select categories for which there is something important to say about each concept that you are charting. In the history selection in the appendix, "Great Promises, Bitter Disappointments, 1960–1968," the presidencies of both John Kennedy and Lyndon Johnson are described.

Theories-of-Memory System		
	Duplex Theory	*Levels-of-Processing Theory*
Overall Beliefs (Description)	There are 2 mem. systems: ① Short-term Memory (STM)— Stores info. for only several seconds, has a very limited capacity- holds only 7±2 new pieces of info; keep info. in STM through rehearsal ② Long-term Memory (LTM) holds info. for long periods of time; info. can last for months or decades; is transferred from STM by rehearsal; can have retrieval problems getting info out of LTM	Emphasizes different mem- ory processes: — Memory is limited b/c of the way it is processed; the way we process determines how well something is remembered —3 levels lowest ← ① process shape ② " letters or sound highest ← ③ " meaning —Rehearsal helps process info to deeper levels: ① Maintenance rehearsal — role repetition ② Elaborative rehearsal — associating what you want to remember w/something meaningful
Major Similarity	Both use rehearsal in some way	
Major Difference	Parts vs. processes	

Figure 10.7 Compare/Contrast Chart for Theories of Memory

A history professor might think it important for you to be able to compare and contrast these two presidents on a number of factors. Your chart might look like Figure 10.8 with the presidents' names on the horizontal (across) axis:

Categories	JFK	LBJ

Figure 10.8 Comparison–Contrast for the Presidencies of John F. Kennedy and Lyndon B. Johnson

Now you need to brainstorm some categories—categories that might be appropriate for both presidents. Factors such as background, legislation passed, civil rights record, and role in Vietnam War would certainly be good categories to start with. Put these categories and any others you can think of on the vertical (up-and-down) axis. Now you are ready to complete the chart.

Although you may have to return to your text or lecture notes for clarification, compare/contrast charting briefly indicates the most important information. Use the charts immediately before a test as retrieval cues to help you to think through the important material. Remember that one of the key learning principles is reducing information. Charting not only helps in this but also highlights major similarities and differences. This technique is most appropriate in situations in which you need to compare or contrast, but it is probably *not* appropriate in situations in which you need to learn a great deal of factual material (for example, in biology and chemistry). And the charting strategy is rarely appropriate for an entire chapter; rather, use it only for specific sections of text or lecture notes in which theories, ideas, concepts, and the like are compared or contrasted.

Application Exercises (DTT)

1. Chart another appropriate part of "The Psychology of Memory" from the appendix. If you have a study partner, discuss the categories you selected with him or her.

2. As you work through the selections in the appendix, chart appropriate parts as your instructor assigns them.

Application Exercise (Your Texts)

Using your college texts, find several sections of chapters that would be appropriate for charting. Chart these sections or concepts and discuss them with your instructor. Use them to predict and answer both objective questions and essay questions.

Time Lines

The final primary rehearsal strategy that you can use after you read is time lines. Time lines function exactly as their name implies: They help fix events at a certain place in time. They can encompass relatively brief periods of time, as would a time line showing the expansion of the Vietnam War in the early 1960s, or they can cover decades or centuries, as would a time line depicting the civil rights movement. Time lines are easy to make and work extremely well in a history or humanities course.

To construct your time line, first decide on the period of time you want it to encompass. Then, using regular notebook paper, put the beginning date in the left-hand margin as shown in Figure 10.9. Write in the event that occurred on that date. Continue writing key dates down the left-hand margin and key events next to the date.

To rehearse using your time line, simply fold back or cover up the events and use only the date as a cue. If you do not know the event that is associated with a date, look at the event several times and then try to say it blindly. Do this for each date/event to ensure that you have learned the chronology of events accurately.

Application Exercises (DTT)

1. When it is time to work on the "Great Promises, Bitter Disappointments, 1960–1968" selection in the appendix, complete the chart in Figure 10.8 and the time line in Figure 10.9. Check with your instructor to see how much detail is expected. Use your time line to talk through the chronological events. Remember to fold back the part of the paper containing the "answer" and use only the date as a cue.

1960–1962	*Crisis in Laos; in long run resulted in "flexible response" whereby $ was spent on conventional forces in S. E. Asia*
Late 1961	*Kennedy orders sharp increase in military advisers in S. Vietnam*
Nov. 1963	*Kennedy administration encourages successful coup against Diem; 1500 American troops present in Vietnam by Kennedy's death*
Feb. 1965	
Mar. 1965	
End 1965	
1966	
1967	
Jan. 1968	

Figure 10.9 Time Line of Action in Vietnam During Kennedy and Johnson Administrations

2. For which other selections from the appendix would a time line be appropriate for some concepts? (Remember that time lines are best suited to chronological events.)

3. After practicing all of the primary rehearsal strategies, which one(s) do you feel most comfortable with? Why? Write a journal entry that addresses these two questions.

Application Exercise (Your Texts)

Apply the time-line strategy to one of your college texts. Because this strategy is best for situations in which events are presented chronologically, you may not be able to apply it to any of your current texts. If such is the case, complete the preceding exercises designed for *DTT.*

Selecting the Most Appropriate Strategies

After reading Chapters 8, 9, and 10, you should realize that engaging in strategies before, during, and after reading requires some decisions. Some students will need more extensive and involved before-reading activities; others will require only minimal previewing. Likewise, some students will need to annotate considerably more information in order to stay connected and to isolate more key concepts in the text's margins. Keep in mind that both before-reading techniques and annotating depend heavily on your background knowledge and on the density of the material.

As you progress to the third phase of studying, which occurs after you read, your continued interaction with and reflection upon the text and your decisions about which strategies to use depend more heavily on the text itself. As noted in this chapter, some strategies are most efficiently and effectively used with factual material or for courses in which you must memorize numerous new terms—biology, chemistry, and psychology, for instance. Other strategies are best suited for learning information with higher-level applications or syntheses. Strategies such as compare/contrast charting and the question/answer technique help you to predict higher-level questions and to isolate the appropriate information to study from this type of text. Still other strategies, such as time lines, are used only in very specific situations. Although a time line may be appropriate for learning chronological events, it would be inappropriate for trying to understand key terms. Mapping is the strategy appropriate for many different kinds of information; maps not only isolate important information but also organize the information around major ideas.

You will find useful and will continue to employ some primary rehearsal strategies long after you complete this course. Other strategies you may try out here and never use again. The important thing is that you have been exposed to many strategies and have learned the circumstances under which each is most efficient and effective. You will probably need to modify strategies to meet your individual needs. This is a positive route as long as the modification helps you learn and remember the information. And each primary rehearsal strategy has built in a monitoring and self-regulatory element that should help you prepare for exams.

Secondary Rehearsal Strategies

Outlining

Outlining is a means of numbering and indenting to show major concepts, major supporting details, and examples. Outlining reveals the way the information is organized. Even though outlining a chapter can be the most complete rehearsal strategy, it is very time-consuming and often less effective than other strategies. We include it here as an alternative, because many students find it useful on complex material; it forces them to go through the material slowly and carefully.

If you are a student who finds outlining a valuable learning strategy, keep the following ideas in mind; they may help you to improve your efficiency. As with highlighting, many students outline while they read a section for the first time. This practice may help them to concentrate, but it does not help them to be selective. It is not as helpful for remembering as outlining is *after* reading a section for the first time.

Students often include too much detail in their outlines. Remember that one of the reasons for rehearsing is to reduce the amount of information you need to review. Use only key words or phrases. Don't write complete sentences, and include only information that you do not already know. If graphic examples are used, include a key word or phrase from the example. Graphic examples serve as good "memory hooks." Because examples are often easier to remember than the main points, include them (very briefly) in your outline so that they will "hook" your memory for the main points.

In short, outline after you have read a section once, reducing the information as much as possible. Take the four steps that follow (note that they are similar to those followed for mapping):

1. Preview the chapter. Formulate questions.

2. Read one section at a time to answer questions and to find other major information. Annotate *as* you read in order to stay connected.

3. Answer your questions to yourself.

4. Check the text to make sure your answers are correct. Then construct an outline, using your own words and organization. Let your annotations guide you.

The outline of the biology selection found in the appendix reduces the complex information to key terms.

Outline for the Portion of "Human Diversity" Selection

I. Cross-Cultural Perspectives
   A. Intro.
      1. Almost six billion people in world BUT no culture dominates
      2. Humans diverse in terms of
         a. geography
         b. languages
         c. religions
   B. Cultural Diversity
      1. Diverse in food choices
         a. e.g.—Greece—olive oil, lemon, oregano
         b. e.g.—Mexico—tomatoes, chili peppers
      2. Diverse in customs
         a. e.g.—Iraq—barter & negotiation
         b. e.g.—India—leave food on plate
         c. Even eating utensils differ
      3. Social norms
         a. U.S. vs Japan—U.S. teaches children independence; Japan teaches conformity
   C. Individualism & Collectivism
      1. Individualism—definition—when society values self-reliance, independence, & personal goals
         a. e.g.—U.S., Australia, Canada
      2. Collectivism—definition—when society values interdependence, social values, and team playing
         a. e.g.—Taiwan, China, Venezuela
      3. Three factors that determine what a culture will be (researcher–Triandis)
         a. complexity
         b. affluence
         c. heterogeneity

Summarizing

Summarizing a section of a textbook is usually effective if the section is not particularly detailed, if you already know most of the material, or if you use the summary as a secondary technique, usually as you review.

A summary states the most important points and a few major supporting details. A summary should be as brief as possible; it actually gets you to consolidate a great deal of information into a few sentences or phrases. For this reason, a summary is not effective for detailed information with which you are unfamiliar; it is almost impossible to be brief in such a situation.

Summaries are perhaps most useful as a secondary rehearsal strategy. First, annotate the text as you study the material. Then, when you go back to review what you marked, write a brief summary after each section. The summary forces you to rehearse the information and, therefore, remember it.

Writing summaries is an especially good idea when you know you will have essay questions on a test. Essays usually require you to take a great deal of information and organize it concisely in new ways (see Chapter 12). Preparing summaries for each question helps you to prepare for tests and to fulfill the principle of test-anticipation.

This section will focus on summarizing as a secondary rehearsal strategy. You can also use it as a primary rehearsal strategy with some types of materials—for example, social science—if you know the tests will contain essay questions. However, in most cases, other strategies are probably more efficient and effective.

To use summarizing as a secondary rehearsal strategy, do the following:

1. Review the text section by section—by posing questions, answering them, and checking your answers against what you had annotated or against your notes.

2. When you are finished with each section, ask yourself, What were the most important points in this section? Write these points down first either as phrases or sentences.

3. Ask yourself, What are the two or three major supporting details? Write these points down next.

4. Ask yourself, Were there any graphic examples that will help me to remember the major details? If there were, jot them down.

5. Put the information into your own words.

Remember that you are trying to be as brief as possible; you don't have to write an essay or follow typical grammatical rules. Simply listing major points will produce a summary.

Imagine that your summary is a news brief. When a reporter writes a news brief, she needs to be short and concise, but she cannot be *too* brief, because she is trying to get a clear message across. Imagine that your summary is a news brief to yourself. You are preparing it now and will review it in a few weeks. Don't make it long and involved, but don't make it so short that you will not understand the message several weeks later.

What follows is a brief summary of the same information from the portion of "Human Diversity" that was outlined earlier. Note that much of the information is stated identically; it is simply put into a different form.

> Humans are so diverse in terms of geo., lang., & relig. that there is no dominant culture, even though there are almost 6 bill. people in world. Cultures are diverse in terms of food choices (e.g., Greeks use lots of olive oil & lemon; Mexicans use tomatoes and chili peppers), customs (e.g., Iraqis barter; Indians leave a bit of food on plate), & social norms (e.g., U.S. teaches kids to be independent; Japan teaches conformity). Some cultures such as U.S. & Australia practice individualism. It is when society values self-reliance & personal goals. Some such as China & Venezuela practice collectivism. It is when society values social harmony and team playing. 3 factors determine what a culture will be (Triandis): complexity, affluence, heterogeneity.

Making a Study Guide

The last secondary rehearsal strategy we will discuss is the study guide. A study guide tells you exactly how to study the information. In high school you may have had teachers who gave you a study guide that contained reading instructions, questions, and perhaps summaries of your text. But you can make up the study guide yourself, giving yourself directions on how best to study the chapter later. Decide what you should and should not review; in this way, you are rehearsing the chapter.

You can make a study guide either by annotating in the margin of the book or by writing notes on a separate sheet of paper. (The margin of the book is preferable, because it lets you refer back to the text easily.) Comments you can make to yourself in the study guide would include:

- rereading directions ("read this paragraph very carefully"; "details—read if unclear"; "skim this section")
- test-prediction questions ("Why did LBJ allow the Vietnam War to escalate?")
- terms to review (*alleles, first filial*)
- summary notes to remind you of major information ("This could also be in the form of a map.")
- cross-references to other parts of the text or to your lecture notes ("Explained in lecture.")

Follow your study guide when you review. Use your directions to reread portions of the text, answer questions, or define terms. Then, as you begin to feel that you have mastered material, cross out your study-guide notes for that material. As you go along, you reduce the amount you have to review because you are transferring the information to your memory.

Using this study-guide technique as a secondary rehearsal strategy, you first annotate a chapter and then make study notes the first time you review. A study guide is useful as a primary rehearsal strategy with material that is not too complex or with which you are already somewhat familiar.

Key Ideas

1. After-reading activities in the form of organizing and rehearsing strategies are based on two key learning principles: putting ideas into your own words and reducing the information to be learned.

2. Rehearsal strategies can improve your memory by up to three times.

3. Primary rehearsal strategies are mapping, concept cards, question/answer technique, compare/contrast charting, and time lines.

4. Secondary rehearsal strategies are outlining, summarizing, and making a study guide.

5. The rehearsal strategies you use most frequently depend on

   - the type of material you are studying.
   - your background knowledge of the material.
   - your instructor' s test questions.
   - your own learning preferences.

6. Using rehearsal strategies forces you to be an organized, active reader.

7. Experiment with different strategies in the selections in the appendix to find out which strategies work best for you.

Application Exercises (DTT)

1. Use the first one-third of "The Psychology of Memory," up to the heading "Memories in the Brain," and try out two of the secondary rehearsal strategies. Try to select two that are most appropriate for this part of the selection. For other types of material, different rehearsal strategies may be more appropriate. You will find this selection in the appendix of this text.

2. Write a journal entry (see Chapter 1) that discusses which secondary strategies you think are most beneficial for both "Human Diversity" and

"Great Promises, Bitter Disappointments, 1960–1968," two selections in the appendix. Explain why you selected the strategies that you did.

Application Exercise (Your Texts)

Try out one of the secondary rehearsal strategies on your own text. The strategy you select depends on the courses in which you are enrolled.

Notes

1. From *Biology: Discovering Life,* Second Edition by Levine and Miller. Copyright © 1994 by D. C. Heath and Company. Used by permission of Houghton Mifflin Company.

Chapter 11

After You Study: Reviewing

Plan your work for today and every day, then work your plan.

Norman Vincent Peale

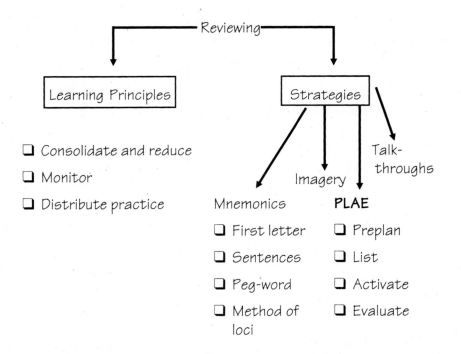

Once you have rehearsed after reading, you must complete a final phase: reviewing. You review after you have completed the major part of studying. Reviewing improves your memory for an exam. Many students wait until just before a test to review and then find that because there is too much material to review thoroughly, they have to stay up all night. However, if they would take that "cramming" time and spread it out over the term, reviewing a little bit at a time, they would remember much more and do better on the test. Reviewing is based on three final learning principles: further consolidating or reducing, monitoring learning, and distributing study time.

Learning Principles

Principle 9: Further Consolidate or Reduce

When you are suddenly interrupted while you're studying, you tend to forget some of what you were reading. Often you remember what you studied a minute or more before the interruption but not what you studied *immediately* before the interruption. (This same kind of forgetting can happen to people who are in accidents.) We forget because our minds need time to sort and consolidate information before we can remember it. The interrupted student or accident victim has had no opportunity to consolidate, and thus he or she cannot transfer the information to long-term memory.

To consolidate, organize the material, rehearse it and reflect upon it, and give yourself time to commit it to memory. Take all the pieces of information and put them together (con-*solid*-ating them) into larger, meaningful units. Students have to read and study a lot of material, so it is vital that they allow time for consolidation.

Principle 10: Monitor Learning

Many college students have difficulty monitoring their learning. In fact, college students may have greater problems monitoring than any other aspect of learning. Although monitoring is important during every learning phase, it is particularly important when preparing for tests. It is precisely at this time, however, that students often fail to pinpoint and verbalize their level of exam preparedness.

Being able to monitor your learning involves three key processes: First, *determine that you really understand the information.* Students who can effectively monitor their progress can verbalize what they have learned by telling you their strong and weak areas of knowledge. For example, a friend might say that she understood everything in the "Information Systems and Marketing Research" selection except the section on sampling. Second, *once you have targeted what you don't understand, decide how you can learn this information better.* The friend in the example might find someone to explain these concepts to her and subsequently construct a map or a chart illustrating the different types of sampling. Finally, *predict the grade you will receive on the exam.* You should be able to predict within at least one letter grade; students with good monitoring skills can predict their grades even more accurately. If you leave the test and predict that you scored a *B* on the exam and you actually scored a *C,* your prediction was relatively accurate. However, if you predicted a *B* and then you found out that you failed the test, you need to work on monitoring your learning. Later in this chapter we will provide some monitoring pointers.

Principle II: Distribute Study Time

As mentioned earlier, you forget material that you do not rehearse and review. To effectively learn all the information in your college classes, distribute your study time, or as a student once told us, "study every subject every day." What a smart piece of advice! Discover your best study times, determine how long you can reasonably study at one time, and, most important, manage your study time (as discussed in Chapter 4) so that you can rehearse and review material several times. Because each time you review the same material you learn more of it, later reviews can be briefer than earlier reviews. It is much more effective to study a chapter for one hour today, half an hour tomorrow, fifteen minutes the next day, and fifteen minutes before the test (a total of two hours) than it is to study the same chapter for two hours all at once, with no review. You spend the same amount of time, but your comprehension and memory for the material are roughly three to four times better if you distribute your study than if you cram.

Reviewing

Reviewing material can be very tedious unless you have some goal in mind (a goal, for example, is to study for tomorrow's test). Reviewing is usually a passive process; students just "look over" their texts or lecture notes. The four tricks to effective reviewing are:

1. Make the process more active.
2. Set goals for each reviewing session.
3. Continually consolidate information.
4. Actively rehearse.

Try to distribute your study time and consolidate information so that you can review each chapter a little less each day with fewer notes and cues. By test time you should have all the information down to two or three notecards with key concepts on them to help to cue retrieval.

To distribute study time and be more active when reviewing, use the techniques discussed throughout this text. For example, first preview a chapter and formulate your prediction questions. If the chapter is long, divide it in half; read and annotate half one night and half the next night. The following day, use your annotations to apply the appropriate rehearsal strategies. Finally, study your rehearsal strategies, further reducing and consolidating when possible. By now you should be studying only about one-tenth of the original information.

Each day you will have less to review because you have continued to consolidate. For example, if you have used the question/answer technique, check off the questions you can already answer and concentrate instead on those that

"It's funny. There are some things you think you'll remember as long as you live, but the minute you get out of college you forget them."

give you trouble. As you become comfortable with particular material, continue to check it off. If you have used concept cards, remember that you can divide the cards into two piles—those containing material that you know and those with material you don't know. Don't completely ignore known information, but concentrate on the material that is most difficult for you.

A word of caution: Be careful about getting a false sense of what you know and what you don't know. Simply "looking over" information rarely puts it into long-term memory. Fix the material in your mind by talking it through (a later section will discuss more about talk-throughs). When you use the cues from your rehearsal strategies or from your lecture notes, speak the information aloud or teach it to someone else as proof that you do know it.

Strategies to Help in Reviewing

Talk-Throughs

Talk-throughs are an important means of monitoring your level of understanding and determining whether you are ready for an exam. Talk-throughs can be your biggest asset in determining what you know. To do talk-throughs, use the following guidelines:

1. Preread and annotate the text information as it is assigned by your instructor.

2. Use your annotations after you have read to develop rehearsal strategies such as maps, concept cards, or charts. Make sure that you use the proper self-testing format when you construct your strategies.

3. Cover up the key information on your rehearsal strategies, leaving only the cues or major points revealed. Without looking, repeat aloud to yourself— or, better yet, to your study partner—what you know about the major points.

4. Uncover the supporting information to see how much you remembered and how precise you were. If you are working with a partner, she or he should check to see how much you knew. Say aloud at least three times the information you did not know or that you omitted. Then try to talk through the point again. Repeat this process until your knowledge is precise and you feel very comfortable with the amount of information you know. Being precise as well as accurate is crucial when conducting talk-throughs.

In talk-throughs, your cues or concepts become key; those small pieces of information should spark your memory for additional supporting details, facts, and examples. Many students make the mistake of talking through only the "big picture." For example, knowing that there are two memory theories— duplex and levels-of-processing—will not be much help in passing your psychology test. You also need to know the characteristics of each and be prepared to compare, contrast, explain, or discuss them.

What follows are two talk-throughs of the duplex theory of memory. Which one is better? Why?

Talk-Through A

The duplex theory says that there are two memory systems that help us remember information. Short-term memory is short and lasts only a couple of seconds. Long-term memory is much longer and can last for more than a week. Rehearsing information helps keep it in short-term memory for a long period of time. Sometimes it is difficult to retrieve information from long-term memory, but short-term memory does not have this problem. You use long-term memory only when you take a test.

Talk-Through B

The duplex theory of memory states that there are two separate memory systems, short-term memory and long-term memory. Short-term memory has several characteristics. They include:

1. It holds information for only about 30 seconds.
2. Repeating information helps it stay in short-term memory (an example would be repeating a telephone number several times in order to remember it).

3. It has limited capacity, which means it can hold only five to seven pieces of new information at a time.

Long-term memory also has several characteristics. They include:

1. Information stored in long-term memory has no limits on how long it can be held there.
2. We often have problems getting information out of long-term memory, even though we know that it is there (this is called the tip-of-the-tongue phenomenon).
3. After information enters short-term memory, it is either lost or transferred to long-term memory.

The student who did talk-through B did a much more comprehensive and precise job than the student who did talk-through A. Although most of the information in talk-through A is correct (with the exception of the last sentence—you also use short-term memory when you take a test), this student does not make the grade when it comes to completeness and precision. It is almost as if the student in talk-through A had memorized a couple of pieces of information for both short- and long-term memory, rather than learning it completely. In addition, talk-through A lacks precision; saying that short-term memory is short means nothing—you need to tell *how* short.

As your test gets closer and closer, the amount of notes you need to study from should steadily decrease. One or two days prior to the test, all you should need to study from are one or two 3 × 5 cards. Only the key concepts, along with some appropriate mnemonics, should be listed on the cards. (Figure 11.1 shows what your cards for the test on "The Psychology of Memory" selection might look like.) Use this card to practice your talk-throughs. If you can use just the concepts on the card as cues and be very precise in talking through the information, you are probably ready for the test.

Mnemonic Devices

Although being successful in college courses requires much more than memorizing facts, some memorizing will be necessary. Mnemonic devices can be valuable for memorizing certain types of factual material.

When you were in elementary school, you probably learned sayings such as:

* *I* before *e* except after *c,* or in words sounding like *a,* as in *neighbor* or *weigh.*
* Thirty days have September, April, June, and November. All the rest have 31, except February, which has 28, and 29 on leap year.

As early as first grade, children learn to spell *arithmetic* by memorizing the following sentence: *A rat in Tom's house may eat Tom's ice cream.* All of these examples are mnemonic devices—sayings or procedures that help people to remember an idea, list, or the like.

Memory Process
 Encoding
 Storage
  Chunking
 Retrieval
  "filing system"
  tip-of-the-tongue phen.
 Photographic Memory
  eidetic imagery (Ex +
   Luria exp.)
Engram (Lashley)
RNA
Penfield exps.
Theories of memory
 Duplex
  STM
  LTM
 Levels of Processing
  Rehearsal
   Maintenance Rehearsal
   Elaborative Rehearsal

Duplicative Theory
Reconstructive Theory
Forgetting
 Measures of forgetting
  Recall
  Recognition
  Relearning
 Why we forget
  Decay
  Interference
   Proactive
   Retroactive
  Repression (Freud)
  Amnesia
  Brain Injury
Principle of orderly associa-
tion

Figure 11.1 Sample 3 × 5 Cards for "The Psychology of Memory" Selection

Suppose you wanted a technique for memorizing the different types of sampling, as outlined in the marketing selection in the appendix. You can do this in several ways:

1. *Take the first letter of each of the components and make them spell a nonsense word.* The types of sampling are random, stratified, area, and quota. There are several combinations of letters that you might use:

RAQS   (pronounced "racks")
RASQ   (pronounced "rask")
QARS   (pronounced "kwars")

Using the first letter of each of the words and making them spell something can activate your retrieval system at test time. If you can make the sound of your nonsense word connect with the meaning of the targeted concept, so much the better.

2. *Use the terms to form a nonsense sentence.* Remember that the sentence need make sense only to you. For example, you could remember some of the types of sampling by using the following sentence:

When I asked RANDOM people in the STRATIFIED AREA to QUOTE a famous person, they thought I was odd.

The words RANDOM and STRATIFIED in the sentence obviously cue you to two of the four different types of sampling. AREA cues you to area sampling and QUOTE cues you to quota.

Because mnemonic devices are especially useful for learning lists of information, they may be useful for subjects (such as biology) that require more memorization. Notice that the previous example also forms a rather odd image in your mind. You can almost see yourself standing in a huge open area, such as the Grand Canyon, with many different levels (stratified), asking random people to quote (quota) a famous person. Images, which we will discuss in the next section, can also be valuable retrieval cues. The application exercise at the end of this section will give you practice in memorizing information from a biology test.

3. The *peg-word method* is particularly useful for learning new terms. It is a word-association technique that requires you first to learn the following rhyme:

One	is	a	bun.
Two	is	a	shoe.
Three	is	a	tree.
Four	is	a	door.
Five	is	a	hive.
Six	is	a	stick.
Seven	is		heaven
Eight	is	a	gate.
Nine	is	a	line.
Ten	is	a	hen.

Use the peg words to retrieve information. For example, let's return to the types of sampling. For "quota" you could image lots of hot dogs and hamburgers on buns ("One is a bun") and you are allowed to eat only a certain number or quota. For "stratified" you could image levels and levels of different shoe boxes ("Two is a shoe"). For "area" you could image trees in an extremely large area. All that was in front of you, for as far as you could see, is trees ("Three is a tree"). All that was in front of you, for as far as you could see, is trees ("Three is a tree"). Finally, for random, think of the game show where contestants select a door at "random" ("Four is a door"). Sometimes they receive a good prize and sometimes they get zapped! You can learn hundreds of peg words; simply invent as many of them as you have items to memorize.

4. To use the *method of loci*, imagine a familiar setting—perhaps your living room, dorm room, or street. Then "walk" this familiar path in your mind. As you walk, attach a word or concept to a particular familiar location. These paths can be as bizarre as necessary because they are personal aids to help you remember.

For the types of sampling, you might walk through different parts of your home. For example:

> I *randomly* select the bedroom to walk into, probably because it is such a large *area*. I could have chosen another *area* such as the family room or kitchen. I look into my closet and notice that someone has *stratified* all of my shoes, putting them in neat rows, by color. As I look at all of these shoes, I'm sure that my mother would be appalled that I owned so many. If she were paying for the shoes, she would have put a *quota* on the number of pairs I owned!

Note that in this example, you also can cue yourself to the meaning of the term as well as the term itself. For example, the definition of *stratified* sampling is "a population that is divided into groups according to a common characteristic and then a probability sample (random sample) is drawn." In the example, the shoes are stratified into neat rows, by color.

The method of loci relies heavily on the use of outrageous imagery. In fact, the more outrageous the image, the easier it is to remember the information.

As strange as some of these techniques may sound, they actually work, and they can be fun to create. Try them out on the application exercises, and see which methods you feel comfortable with.

Imagery

Imagery has been an aid to memory and retrieval since the time of the ancient Greeks. Prominent early Greeks, such as Plato and Aristotle, felt that the mind was "a waxen tablet" of sorts on which all experiences, ideas, and concepts were stored and retrieved as images. Although few psychologists would suggest that information is stored solely as images, imagery is widely accepted as a valuable learning and retrieval tool. Both the method of loci and the peg-word techniques use imagery. College students who use imagery outperform those who do not, particularly on tasks such as learning new terms.

Suppose you are preparing for a psychology test on phobias. Your test will ask you to define several phobias (a memory-level task). Here is a list of phobias that you have been asked to learn:

Acrophobia	fear of heights
Aerophobia	fear of flying
Agoraphobia	fear of open spaces
Amaxophobia	fear of driving
Anthrophobia	fear of people
Aquaphobia	fear of water
Claustrophobia	fear of closed spaces
Dementophobia	fear of insanity
Mikrophobia	fear of germs
Phonophobia	fear of speaking aloud

Although you could learn these words by traditional means (that is, by saying or writing them over and over), you would save a considerable amount of time if you were to devise imaging techniques instead. Let's describe some images that might help you to remember the first few words. Remember, you can formulate your own images, but here are some that have worked for others:

Acrophobia—fear of heights. Think of an *acrobat* very high off the ground, perhaps swinging on a trapeze. It is his first time performing without a net.

Aerophobia—fear of flying. Image flying in an *airplane.* See yourself in the seat. Imagine what it would feel like to fly in a bad storm.

Agoraphobia—fear of open spaces. Think of the word *agora,* the Greek word for market place. The Greek open markets were large open places that were also used as gathering places. Imagine yourself lost among the many people and you cannot find your way out.

Many students find it easy to learn lists of new terms if they use personalized images, and the images need not make sense to anyone else. Incorporating imagery into other rehearsal and review strategies can be an extremely powerful learning tool.

Application Exercises (DTT)

1. The terms *proactive interference* and *retroactive interference* are discussed in the selection "The Psychology of Memory" in the appendix. Students often confuse these two terms. Create a mnemonic device or image to help you to differentiate the terms.

2. How could you use imagery to more easily remember information about genetics discussed in the biology selection in the appendix? Discuss these images with your classmates or draw them to help you remember better.

Application Exercise (Your Texts)

From one of your own courses, find information that you could learn by using mnemonics. Do the same with imagery.

The PLAE Model

By now you probably are quite aware that learning the maximum amount of information and doing well on exams require considerably more than passively reading and "looking over" the material. Studying for an hour the night before a high-school test was probably enough to earn a decent grade, but to be academically successful in college you must begin to prepare well in advance of any exam. Professors expect you to possess the needed study strategies and to extract from text and lectures information that will be asked on an exam. As a general rule, cramming does not work consistently in a college setting. You must learn not only which study strategies work best for you in specific courses but also how to budget your time so that you can prepare adequately for tests.

The following approach to planning for tests is unique because it is task specific. Many college study-skills texts recommend using a block schedule: Plan everything you do, from morning until night, for each day of the week. Although we did discuss scheduling earlier in the text, for most students it is a passive activity. They may fill out a schedule, but they usually don't follow it, and they don't set specific study goals for particular study sessions. A study plan must be task specific; that is, you must know how many study sessions you need, what your goals will be for each session, and what the professor expects from you in the testing situation. A study plan must also have a built-in monitoring component that allows you to check your level of understanding. A good plan includes time for reflecting on the task at hand, on how you are preparing for the task, and on what you will do if you don't understand the material.

The **PLAE**[1] model—**P**replan, **L**ist, **A**ctivate, **E**valuate—can help you to prepare for exams so that you feel confident in your ability to do well. The **PLAE** procedure will put you well on your way to becoming an independent learner who can regulate his or her own learning. Before discussing particulars, let's first address the assumptions students generally have about studying and test preparation versus the assumptions inherent in **PLAE.**

1. *Students generally assume that reading and studying are synonymous terms.* Some students even say, "Gee, I'd better start studying. I have a test the day after tomorrow, and I haven't even read the chapters yet." The **PLAE** model takes a different focus: It assumes that all reading has been completed *before* studying begins. Therefore, reading chapters is not even addressed in any of **PLAE**'s stages. You may need to refer to your text to clarify information or to rehearse or review your annotations, but you should be finished with the reading before you begin using **PLAE.**

2. *Many students study by "looking at" important material.* Students who do this usually score rather poorly. When they "look at" material, they passively go through the text or their notes and look, underline, or read. They generally learn little new information because merely looking at material does not transfer it into long-term memory. Studying with **PLAE** involves active, self-testing processes that help you to define what you know and what requires additional study. Studying this way is hard work and requires active involvement and concentration, but it will enable you to learn a significant amount of material.

3. *Most students prepare for every test in the same manner.* They study for a literature test using the same strategies as for a biology exam; they prepare for an essay test in the same way as for an objective test. Students who cling to this method often do poorly, even though they may study for many hours. **PLAE**, however, assumes that studying is task specific. The model requires you to know what kind of test will be given (if you're not sure, ask your instructor), the grade you hope to receive, and specific strategies to use in certain disciplines.

4. *Many students assume that the total amount of study time equals success.* Students often assume that ten hours of test preparation the night before a test is equal to two hours of preparation on each of five nights. Many hours of study the night before an exam may work out on occasion, but a steady diet of cramming will eventually show up in your grades. The key to **PLAE** is *distributed practice*—spreading your test preparation over a number of days, with concentrated periods of time allotted for studying. Distributed practice helps you not only to perform better on the test but also to remember the information long after the test. For courses in which the final exam is cumulative, you will certainly benefit from retaining course material over an entire term.

5. *Students rarely use their test score as diagnostic information.* To most students, the grade is the only thing that matters. If they did well, the test paper is generally tucked away neatly in the back of their notebook; if they did poorly, the exam may wind up in the trash. **PLAE** suggests that you use your test papers as diagnostic information for future planning. Be aware of the items you missed. (Were they factual or inferential items? Were they taken from the text or from lecture notes?) By noting the types of items missed, you can modify future studying and improve poor grades.

As stated earlier, the four stages to the **PLAE** model are **P**replan, **L**ist, **A**ctivate, and **E**valuate.

Stage 1: Preplan

Preplanning focuses on defining tasks or problems and setting goals by asking yourself a series of questions:

1. When is the test? (date, day, time)

2. Specifically, what are my other obligations that week?

3. What does the test cover?

4. How many items or questions will be on the test?

5. What kind of test will it be?

6. What type of questions will be asked? Factual or memory-level questions? Inferential or applied?

7. How much does the test count in the total evaluation process?

8. What grade do I hope to get?

9. How much time do I need to spend studying, rehearsing, and reviewing?

10. How will this study change my regular schedule? (Explain how you will find this extra time.)

You should be able to answer the first seven questions by carefully reading your syllabus or course outline or by asking your professor. Most professors will respond as long as you ask them in the proper manner; in fact, they usually view such questions positively. It's questions such as "What's on the next test?" that professors disdain. Questions 8–10 require a commitment on your part. Answering these questions honestly should give you a good idea of what your task is and how much time you must allot to preparing for the exam.

Stage 2: List

Listing requires you to determine how to carry out the task or to solve your problem, and how to turn this strategic decision-making process into an ideal plan. Because mature learners realize that no single study approach will work equally well on all types of material, they plan each task specifically, depending on the subject matter and the type of test. In stage 2, identify the specifics of your study plan by answering some questions and engaging in several activities:

1. *List* the rehearsal strategies you will use for this particular test. Then explain *why* you feel that these strategies are the most appropriate.

   Strategies   *Why They Are Appropriate*

   (a)

   (b)

2. Complete a plan of study by answering the following questions:

   (a) What strategy(ies) will I use?

   (b) When and where will I study?

   (c) How long do I plan to study?

   (d) Did I reach my goal?

3. Check your plan of study and ask yourself these questions:

   (a) Have I distributed my study time over several days?

(b) Did I schedule blocks of time to review my annotations and preview the chapter again?

(c) Did I schedule at least two blocks of time to test myself on the key concepts? for a friend to test me?

Figure 11.2 shows that, as part of stage 2, you actually write down your plan of action. In order to write your plan, you must first think about it; this helps you to arrange your studying time realistically. Remember, most students have good intentions; they want to do well on tests. However, time slips away easily; putting your plan on paper will make you more aware of what you need to get accomplished.

Note that in Figure 11.2 each study session has a specific goal to learn X information. Simply stating that you will use your concept cards to study the chapter is not specific enough. Rather, work toward a narrower goal. If your goal is to learn all about the different aspects of memory theory, stick with your studying until you feel comfortable that you truly understand that particular information.

Note the importance that review plays in the study plan. Notice that each study session begins with a review of the information learned in the last session. Take ten to fifteen minutes to talk through and reflect on the key concepts. If you can't remember part of the material, go back to your rehearsal strategies immediately and look up what you need to know. Then move on to the new information. Unlike filling out a weekly schedule, the listing process should be active, flexible, and task specific.

Stage 3: Activate

Once you have listed your plan of action, you are ready to activate the plan. Monitor the plan by asking yourself another series of questions:

1. Am I following my list (plan)?

2. If not, why not? What is interfering? Which obligations did I not account for?

3. How can I make modifications without sacrificing my original goals?

4. Do I understand and remember the concepts? Are my selected strategies working?

5. If not, why not? Should I select another strategy or change my distribution of study time?

If the plan is not working, you may have to return to stage 1 or 2 and modify your original plan. This is not too difficult if you begin preparing early, but if you wait until two days before the test to begin to prepare, modification will be impossible.

This is why monitoring is such a key element of the **PLAE** model. Keep-

What Will I Do?	When? (date, time) Where?	For How Long?	Reached Goal?
Organize + review all annotations, rehearsal strategies + lecture notes.	Oct. 11, 1:00 library	2 hrs.	
Study chapt. 1. Use annotations and related lecture notes.	Oct. 14, 6:00 library	1 hr.	
Review chapt. 1. Study Chapt. 2. Use annotations, 2/A, and related lecture notes. Start 3 × 5 card of major concepts.	Oct. 15, 1:00 library	1 1/2 hrs.	
Review 1 + 2 by doing talk-through Study chapt. 4. Use annotations, 2/A, + related lecture notes.	Oct. 17, 7:00 room	1 1/2 hrs.	
Review 1, 2, + 4 by doing talk-throughs. Study 5. Use annotations, charts, + related lecture notes. Finish 3 × 5 card.	Oct. 19, 7:00 room	2 hrs.	
Prepare for essay questions. Review handouts.	Oct. 20, 1:00 library	1 1/2 hrs.	
Do talk-throughs with study partner. Check for precision in answers.	Oct. 21, 7:00 room	2 hrs.	
Review everything doing talk-throughs using 3 × 5 card.	Oct. 22, 6:00 library	1 hr.	
	Total Hours	12 1/2 hrs.	

Figure 11.2 Example of a Plan of Study Using PLAE (Stage 2)

ing your finger on your level of understanding will help you to avoid pushing the panic button two days before the test. Monitoring enables you to get assistance or to alter your studying tactics early on in the test-preparation game.

Stage 4: Evaluate

Evaluate your performance on the exam when you get it back. Careful monitoring during the earlier stages should prevent most problems, but you may feel confident of your knowledge before the test, only to have your confidence shaken when you receive your grade. The evaluation stage is crucial to preparing for future exams. Rather than looking at your grade or score as the end product, view it as a way to collect information that will help you to study for subsequent exams. Ask yourself the following questions for each missed item:

1. Why did I miss the item? Was it because I didn't know the answer to the question?

2. If I didn't know the answer, where did the concept come from? lecture? handout? films?

3. What type of question was it? factual? vocabulary? application? example?

4. Is there a pattern to my errors?

5. Did I select study strategies appropriate to the demands of the test? If not, which other strategies should I employ next time?

The information obtained from the evaluating stage of **PLAE** should then provide information for modification in preparing for the next exam. The **PLAE** procedure is cyclical, because it provides feedback for future planning.

As an example of how **PLAE** works, imagine that you are enrolled in an introductory history class. Your first exam is approaching, and you want to do well. You decide to use **PLAE** to prepare effectively. Look at the example worksheets (which you can use as a model) to see how you might carry out the first two **PLAE** stages—preplanning and listing. Then use the **PLAE** checklist at the end of this chapter to evaluate your plan.

PLAE Stages 1 and 2 Worksheet

Preplanning Stage

1. When is the test? (date, day of week, time)
   Oct. 23 (about 2 weeks away), 3rd period

2. Specifically, what are my other obligations that week?
   I have a biology lab report due that same day.

3. What does the test cover?
   4 chapters (1, 2, 4, & 5), all lecture notes, and 3 handouts

4. How many items or questions will there be on the test?
   50 items

5. What kind of test will it be?
   Objective, multiple-choice, and true/false, plus 2 essay questions

6. What type of questions will be asked? Factual or memory-level questions? higher-level?
   About 40% memory + 60% higher-level

7. How much does the test count in the total evaluation process?
   About 20%

8. What grade do I hope to get?
   A or B+

9. How much time do I need to spend studying, rehearsing, and reviewing?
   About 10 hours, spread over several study sessions

10. How will this amount of study time change my regular schedule? (Explain how you will find this extra time.)
    I need to add 2 hours since I usually spend about 8 hours weekly.

Listing Stage

1. *List* the rehearsal strategies that you will utilize for this particular test. Then explain *why* these strategies will be the most appropriate for this particular test.

Strategies	**Why They Are Appropriate**
(a) *Question/answer (focus on higher-level)*	*Most of the test will be analysis & synthesis; I tend to be a good predictor.*
(b) *charting*	*To compare/contrast presidents.*

2. Complete the plan of study below.

3. Check your plan of study and ask yourself these questions:

   (a) Have I distributed my study time over several days? ✓

   (b) Did I schedule blocks of time to review my annotations and to review the chapter again? ✓

   (c) Did I schedule at least two blocks of time to test myself on the key concepts? for a friend to test me? ✓

Stage 4: Evaluating

(Questions to ask myself once I see my exam's score)

1. Was the test what I expected?
   Yes

2. Did I follow my plan for studying? If not, what events or situations interfered with my carrying out the plan?
   For the most part, I didn't spend as much time on the talk-throughs as I should have.

3. How many hours did I study? Were those hours distributed or massed?
   About 10. Distributed

4. What types of questions did I miss? detail and example? key ideas? vocabulary? applications?

—*some detail questions, but mostly application questions*

5. Did I miss any questions because I misread them? How many?

Only 1

6. Did I miss questions because I didn't know or recognize the information? If so, where did that information come from: <u>lectures?</u> textbooks? handouts? films?

I recognized the information; I just couldn't remember it!

7. Is there a pattern to my errors on the test? (Check the appropriate ones below.)

   ✓   I missed questions on my lecture notes. *(4)*

   ✓   I missed questions that should have been in my annotations of the textbook's key ideas and <u>examples.</u> *(2)*

   ✓   I missed questions from handouts or films or outside readings.

   ✓   I missed questions about key vocabulary.

   ✓   I missed questions that asked me to make applications to new situations. *(2)*

   ✓   I missed questions because I failed to read the item carefully or overlooked key words such as *except*.

8. Did I select the most appropriate study strategies for this test? If not, which ones would be more appropriate next time?

Yes, but I'll need to spend more time on lecture information and be more precise.

9. For the next test on *Nov 12,* I will do the following things to change my pattern of study:

Lecture notes   *More time for essay preparation*
Talk-throughs
Time lines

I will continue doing these things that helped me:

Charts
Studying annotations
Taking good lecture notes

To put this plan into operation, check off each task as you accomplish it and monitor how your studying is progressing. For example, if you feel you are weak on the essay portion of the test, budget an additional hour for practice or check with your professor to see if your predictions of essay questions are accurate. If you carry out your designated plan, you should feel confident about how you will do.

Suppose that a week later you get your test back and receive a *B*, which is a good grade for your first exam. When evaluating your test, you find that you misread one question and missed four lecture-notes questions, two dealing with examples and two dealing with applications. Your essay lacked enough specifics for full credit. (You knew that the essay would be your weakest area.) From the evaluation, you decide that you spent enough time studying but that you needed to concentrate on predicting higher-level questions and on planning and writing essay questions to include more details. You decide to modify your plan slightly as you prepare for the next exam, which is three weeks away.

Just as you must practice and apply the **BCA** studying method to be effective, you must apply the **PLAE** method in a variety of settings. Simply memorizing the steps will do little to enhance your performance; you must practice in order to use the model efficiently and effectively. Remember, distribute your study time over a period of days and monitor your understanding. By using **PLAE** and beginning your preparation well in advance of the test, you should be quite successful.

Key Ideas

1. Reviewing, which is done after studying, is based on three learning principles:
   (a) further consolidation of information
   (b) distributing your study over time, which increases learning efficiency
   (c) monitoring your learning

2. Daily reviewing increases learning efficiency.

3. Mnemonic devices, peg words, the method of loci, and imagery are personalized reviewing aids.

4. The **PLAE** model of planning—**P**replan, **L**ist, **A**ctivate, and **E**valuate— should be used as a task-specific method for distributing your study time.

5. Doing talk-throughs using 3×5 cards with the major concepts listed is a good way to review for tests.

Application Exercises (DTT)

1. Make photocopies of the **PLAE** forms on the following pages. Use one of them to make a study plan for "The Psychology of Memory" selection from the appendix; save the other copies for later. Use the **PLAE** model in this chapter as a guide. Remember to use the appropriate rehearsal strategies, and be prepared to tell why you selected those strategies.

2. As you study the other selections from the appendix, make a study plan using the **PLAE** model as a guide.

Application Exercises (Your Courses)

For your next major test, make a study plan using the **PLAE** model. When your test is returned to you, evaluate your performance. Make adjustments in your studying as needed.

PLAE Model

Preplanning Stage

1. When is the test? (date, day, time)

2. Specifically, what are my other obligations that week?

3. What does the test cover?

4. How many items or questions will be on the test?

5. What kind of test will it be?

6. What type of questions will be asked? Factual or memory-level questions? Higher-level?

7. How much does the test count in the total evaluation process?

8. What grade do I hope to get?

9. How much time do I need to spend studying, rehearsing, and reviewing?

10. How will this study change my regular schedule? (Explain how you will find this extra time.)

Listing Stage

1. *List* the rehearsal strategies that you will utilize for this particular test. Then explain *why* these strategies will be the most appropriate for this particular test.

      Strategies   ***Why They Are Appropriate***

  (a)

  (b)

2. Complete the plan of study that follows.
3. Check your plan of study and ask yourself these questions:
   (a) Have I distributed my study time over several days?
   (b) Did I schedule blocks of time to review my annotations and to review the chapter again?
   (c) Did I schedule at least two blocks of time to test myself on the key concepts? for a friend to test me?

Activating Stage

What Will I Do?	When? (date, time) Where?	For How Long?	Why?

**Total Hours** _____

Evaluating Stage

(Questions to ask myself once I see my exam's score)

1. Was the test what I expected?

2. Did I follow my plan for studying? If not, what events or situations interfered with my carrying out the plan?

3. How many hours did I study? Were those hours distributed or massed?

4. What types of questions did I miss? detail and example? key ideas? vocabulary? applications?

5. Did I miss any questions because I misread them? How many?

6. Did I miss questions because I didn't know or recognize the information? If so, where did that information come from? lectures? textbooks? handouts? films?

7. Is there a pattern to my errors on the test? (Check the appropriate ones below.)

_____ I missed questions on my lecture notes.

_____ I missed questions that should have been in my annotations of the textbook's key ideas and examples.

_____ I missed questions from handouts or films or outside readings.

_____ I missed questions about key vocabulary.

_____ I missed questions that asked me to make applications to new situations.

_____ I missed questions because I failed to read the item carefully or overlooked key words such as *except.*

8. Did I select the most appropriate study strategies for this text? If not, which ones would be more appropriate next time?

9. For the next test on _____, I will do the following things to change my pattern of study:

I will continue doing these things that helped me:

Notes

1. M. L. Simpson and S. L. Nist, "PLAE: A Model for Planning Successful Independent Learning," *Journal of Reading,* Vol. 28, pp. 218–23.

Chapter 12

Pulling Everything Together: Preparing for Examinations

> With regard to excellence, it is not enough to know;
> we must try to have and use it.
>
> *Aristotle*

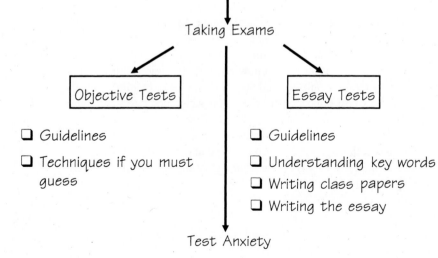

Preparing for Exams

- ❏ Know the academic task
- ❏ Review systematically over time
- ❏ Reduce information to study
- ❏ Predict exam questions
- ❏ Use PORPE
(Predict, Organize, Rehearse, Practice, Evaluate)

Taking Exams

Objective Tests

- ❏ Guidelines
- ❏ Techniques if you must guess

Essay Tests

- ❏ Guidelines
- ❏ Understanding key words
- ❏ Writing class papers
- ❏ Writing the essay

Test Anxiety

General Preparation Guidelines

It is a fact of life that the majority of college students are concerned about grades. Everyone wants to do well, and to most students being successful means making good grades. However, students should also consider how much they learned in a course. Those who get a *C* in a difficult course in which they learned a lot are probably more successful than those who get an *A* in "Basketweaving 101." Nevertheless, could the students who received the *C* in the more difficult course have made better grades if they had studied more, or harder, or differently? The answer is probably yes.

This section gives you suggestions for preparing for classroom tests. We will discuss general preparation guidelines, give specific ideas for taking both objective and essay exams, and present suggestions for reducing test anxiety. We also briefly discuss writing papers. As you read this chapter, keep in mind the reading and studying strategies you have applied throughout this text. At one time or another, they all come to bear in preparing for examinations.

Some "laws of the land" need repeating here. At the beginning of each college term, develop a daily schedule that allows time for class preparation, study, review, recreation, eating, and sleeping. Your ability to adhere to the plan will be a measure of your success (see Chapter 4).

A study area conducive to learning is important. Make sure your area has good light. Before the term starts, have all the necessary texts, study guides, outlines, dictionaries and other reference books, paper, pads, notebooks, and pens in your study area, so that you can concentrate without interruption.

Although rehearsing and reviewing are distinct activities, they are equally important: allocate time for both in your daily schedule. *Rehearsing* is learning new material. *Reviewing* strengthens the retention of this new knowledge.

You forget most rapidly immediately after you've learned something. Therefore, review and recall soon after you've studied. After each class, go over the main points for ten to fifteen minutes to reinforce them in your memory. This makes reviewing for exams much quicker and simpler.

Don't tax your memory or stamina. Research shows that most people can absorb and retain just so much knowledge at one time. With practice you can determine your own capacity and attention. It is important to learn day by day and week by week, but each period of study scheduled into your plan should be followed by recreation, a meal, or other activity (see Chapters 4 and 11).

Take legible class and study notes. Annotate in the margins and underline your textbook throughout the term so that you will be able to review for weekly quizzes or final exams with a minimum of strain (see Chapters 9 and 11).

Know the Academic Task

An important aspect of exam preparation is the *academic task*—that is, knowing what the professor wants and expects from you so that you can study the material efficiently and effectively. Let's say that for a core course in American history, you know that there will be four tests and a final exam. Two of the tests will be on the books that won't be covered in class, and the other two tests and the final exam will cover material from the main American history text and from the professor's lectures. All of these tests and the final will have essay questions.

This gives you some information on academic task. You know that you will have to learn the main text and lecture notes for two tests and the final exam, and read and synthesize on your own for the other two exams. You also know that your professor will expect the information in the form of essay answers.

This information would give you a start in test preparation, but you should constantly look for additional clues your professor might formally or informally pass along. Many students enter a college history course with what might be termed a "high school model" of what history is: In high school, most students were expected to memorize names, dates, people, and key events without having to put them into historical perspective. But what if your college professor said things such as "Facts are important only as they are used to support a more conceptual understanding of a historical event" or "You must be able to discuss the historical significance and place it in some sort of historical context"? These comments send clear signals that your professor expects an academic task far different from the one your high school teacher expected.

Your professor may also tell you the format he or she expects for your essay. Some professors are very specific about wanting an introductory paragraph, generalizations followed by supporting arguments, and a concluding summary paragraph. Other professors may have equally high expectations of the academic task, but they may fail to communicate them. With these professors, you might have to wait for your first test results before you can determine exactly what they expect.

Therefore, gather as much information about the academic task as you can. If a professor fails to give what you consider to be fair guidelines, ask politely for additional information. If you don't know what professors expect, you can't select and apply the best study strategies.

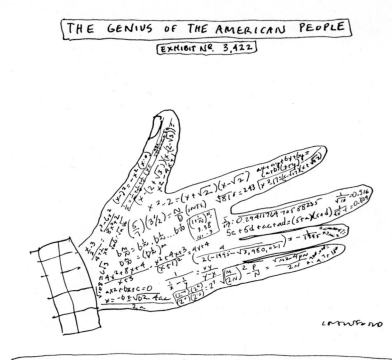

THE GENIUS OF THE AMERICAN PEOPLE

EXHIBIT Nº 3,122

RANDY CUNNINGHAM'S "NOTES" FOR THE ALGEBRA FINAL

Tips on Reviewing for an Exam

If you have applied yourself during the term, preparing for exams becomes largely a question of reviewing. If you have been working consistently, you won't need as much time as you might think. Review for weekly quizzes should take no more than fifteen minutes; for an hour-long midterm, two to three hours; and for a final examination, five to eight hours.

The **PLAE** model (in Chapter 11) gave you an overall framework to plan your time and study strategies for a test. Remember that one key to effective studying is distributing your study time. **PLAE** provides one way to distribute your review for a test over several days or weeks. The following tips will also help you to prepare effectively:

1. *Carefully schedule your preparation for a final exam.* Spread it out over the two weeks before exam day, especially if you will have a cumulative exam. Using **PLAE,** organize a plan that interferes as little as possible with your regular study for ongoing classes. Keep in mind, however, that the last two weeks of the term tend to be very draining. Professors are often rushing to complete everything on the syllabus, long-term projects tend to be due, and all of your final exams occur in the same week. Therefore, be prepared to feel some pres-

sure near the end of the term, and allow time for rest and relaxation, with no longer than one to one-and-a-half hours of review at a time. Your mind needs to take breaks.

2. *Plan your review systematically and consistently.* Use your chapter annotating, rehearsal strategies, and lecture notes. Separate the information you know from what you don't know. If certain points are difficult for you to remember, reread those specific points in the textbook and then concentrate on the rehearsal strategy for that information. Otherwise, stick with your notes and strategies and do as little rereading as possible. Don't plan to learn something for the first time.

3. *Make summary notes to reduce information.* Notecards are good for summarizing because they are easily transportable. Briefly summarize the main points of class notes and text annotations. Group your summaries or key terms under broad headings so that you can see relationships among concepts; this will help to reinforce major ideas and important details. These summary notes can also serve as a self-test toward the end of your preparation for exams. See if you remember the main points under each of the broad headings. As you go, ask yourself what, when, why, how, and so forth.

4. *Try to predict exam questions.* Be alert throughout the term to the emphasis instructors put on certain topics, aspects, or ideas. They often give clues to points that are important or that particularly need review. Consider what types of questions you might be asked. Unlike high school teachers, who often ask memory-level questions, college professors frequently include a variety of higher-level questions on exams. (Chapter 8 covered these types of questions and how they test both your memory for information and your understanding of how that information applies and relates to new situations.) Try to predict higher-level exam questions by beginning your questions with "why," "how," or "discuss."

Pay attention to the form of testing the professor uses. Objective tests (multiple-choice, true/false, or matching) usually test your knowledge of facts, whereas essay questions tend to require more in-depth understanding of the topic.

5. *Ask your professors what they recommend for preexamination work.* Use their comments as a guide, but don't try to outguess them.

6. *Group reviewing can be helpful, but it should not take the place of working on your own* (see Chapter 2). Limit discussions of significant points and possible test questions to thirty to forty-five minutes, with no more than four or five people in the group.

7. *Avoid cramming.* If you have followed a regular schedule of study and review, you shouldn't have to cram. Remember, forgetting takes place most rapidly immediately after learning. If you do have to cram, be selective; don't attempt an exhaustive review.

Follow these general guidelines when you are preparing for either objective or essay exams, but remember that studying for an objective test differs from studying for an essay test. The two sections that follow present some suggestions to help you prepare for and take objective and essay exams, respectively.

Objective Tests

An objective test can include any or all of the following types of questions:

- multiple-choice
- matching
- fill-in-the-blanks
- true/false

Chapter 7 noted that professors in certain disciplines are more apt to give objective tests. Tests in biological science, introductory psychology, and physical science usually lean toward multiple-choice formats. However, some may require a combination of essay and objective items. Ask your instructor what you can expect.

Pointers for Taking Objective Tests

Many students are their own worst enemies in testing situations. The guidelines that follow may help you to determine the answer the professor is looking for. As you work through the items, keep asking yourself, What answer does Professor *X* want? These nine pointers should help you determine the "correct" answer:

1. *Anticipate the answer* rather than look for it. Prediction works for formulating answers as well as for formulating questions. Many students read the stem of the item and then search the answer choices for the one that might be right. This approach can be confusing. Instead, cover up the answer choices and see if you can predict the responses. Then look to see if your response is there.

2. *Consider all of the alternatives.* Even though you are predicting, you still need to read all of the choices. Your exact prediction will probably not be listed; so read each response carefully and then make your choice.

3. *Use logical reasoning.* Eliminate answer choices that just aren't plausible. You may then be able to "reason" the correct answer by thinking to yourself, If *a* is correct, then . . . or If *c* is correct, then. . . . Again, keep in mind the answer your instructor wants.

4. *Use information from other questions and options.* Look at the whole test. Often information given in, say, question 4 on the multiple-choice part can help you to answer question 18 in the true/false section. Don't view each item in isolation.

5. *Look for specific determiners.* Exact terms such as *all, always, must, never,* and indefinite terms such as *hardly ever, seldom, sometimes, frequently,* and *usually* can be dead giveaways. For example, few things in this world *always* occur. Thus if you had a true/false question that read, "Chemical imbalances are always the cause of paranoid schizophrenia," the word *always* should

be a strong clue that this item is false. Even if you did not know the causes of schizophrenia, you could *guess* that there is no single proven cause. See how the meaning of this question changes by replacing *always* with *frequently:* "Chemical imbalances are frequently the cause of paranoid schizophrenia." Now the statement would be true.

6. *Balance points against each other.* Do this especially for multiple-choice items in which you are asked to give the "major reason" or the "best example." All of the choices may be reasons why an event occurred or examples of the applications of a particular theory, but which one is the *major* reason or the *best* example? As suggested earlier, predict your answer, consider the alternatives, and then choose.

7. *If there is no penalty for guessing, then guess,* if you're not sure. On multiple-choice exams, you have a one-in-four or one-in-five chance of being correct. On true/false items, you have a one-in-two chance of being correct. With matching, the odds decrease considerably, but you should still put down *some* answer. It is very foolish to leave objective questions blank, so weigh the alternatives and make your best guess. (The next section will discuss how to make an educated guess.)

8. *Go with your first hunch,* if all the choices seem equally likely to be correct. Unless you pick up additional information to make you change your mind, stick with that first choice. Many students get upset with themselves when they discover that they initially had correct responses for several items but at the last minute changed them.

9. *Answer the questions that you know first.* This procedure serves two purposes. First, it gives you confidence (this is why tests such as the SAT and the ACT put easier items at the beginning). Second, you can gain information that may help you on questions about which you are unsure.

The bottom line is this: Attempt to choose the responses that the professor or test-maker intended. To do this, you must think and reason effectively, and predict accurately. Remembering these nine points will help you.

If You *Must* Guess . . .

If you apply the strategies outlined in this text, you should enter most testing situations feeling confident and secure. You have surveyed your text, predicted questions, annotated important information, and used the appropriate rehearsal strategies. Using the **PLAE** model, you have developed a study plan that includes blocks of time for study and review. However, on the rare occasions on which you didn't adequately prepare for an exam, you will have to guess at answers to objective questions. The six tips that follow should be used *only* when you are in a bind and must guess. Keep in mind that most of these tips will help you only on tests that are not carefully constructed. Because most college professors have been trained in test construction or use tests supplied by publishers, these hints may not be extremely useful in many situations. But take them as a *last-ditch effort* to make the best guess you can. Remember, on objective (especially multiple-choice and true/false) tests, never leave items blank unless there is a penalty for guessing.

1. When you are forced to rely on sheer guesswork, *one of the answer positions (a, b, c, or d) is usually a better guess than others.* Most writers of multiple-choice tests tend to favor one or two positions over others. Out of 100 questions, *a* might be the correct answer for 32 items, *b* for 20, *c* for 27, and *d* for 21. If you are forced to guess on such a test, you are better off guessing *a* or *c*. The difference is not very great in these cases, but on some exams as many as half the correct answers are in the same position. Keep in mind, however, that on a well-constructed test each answer choice should be used equally. Therefore, on a 100-item test, *a, b, c,* and *d* should each be used about twenty-five times. Use this information to your advantage in guessing situations to determine whether your test is well or poorly constructed.

2. *Avoid answers that repeat important words in the question.* Many test writers routinely include wrong answers that repeat terms in the question just to distract wild guessers; for example:

The reference process of meaning

_____ (a) suggests that words refer to symbols.
_____ (b) connects a symbol with an object.
_____ (c) suggests that words are not arbitrary.
_____ (d) relies on an S-R theory.

The wild guesser who chooses *a* because of the words *reference* and *refer* is not likely to have picked a bargain (The correct answer is *b*.)

3. If one answer is definitely longer than the other choices, *the longer answer is more likely to be the correct one.* Instructors often feel that they need to include enough information to make the answer choice clear. For example:

Public opinions that are fluid

_____ (a) change very little.
_____ (b) exist as potential.
_____ (c) can change dramatically as a result of events.
_____ (d) have not crystallized.

Note that *c,* the correct answer, is longer than the other three choices and has the determiner, "can change."

4. In a carelessly written exam, you may be able to *eliminate on grammatical grounds one or more of the possible answers,* although you would rarely see this on a college exam. For example:

Acromegaly is an

_____ (a) decrease in the size of an adult's jaw, hands, and feet.
_____ (b) decrease in growth hormones.

_____ (c) increase in the size of an adult's jaw, hands, and feet.

_____ (d) increase in growth hormones.

Both *a* and *b* can be eliminated because *an* cannot be used before a word beginning with a consonant.

5. For problem questions in a multiple-choice format, look for *answers having numerical relationships* to the numbers stated in the problem, either by multiplication, division, addition, or subtraction. For example:

A and B are two points in an electrical field. If 6.0 joules of work are done in moving 2.0 coulombs of electric charge from point A to point B, then the potential difference between points A and B is

_____ (a) 1.5 volts.

_____ (b) 2.0 volts.

_____ (c) 3.0 volts.

_____ (d) 12.0 volts.

The numbers given in the problem are 6.0 and 2.0. Of the possible answers, only *c* and *d* are simple mathematical combinations of these numbers. Therefore, it is likely that one of them is the correct answer. Choice *b* should be eliminated because it repeats one of the numbers stated in the problem.

6. *Learning information from one test question to answer others* is a test-taking technique that can be extremely useful. This technique is more difficult to apply than any previously described, because learning from the test itself cannot be applied routinely and mechanically. One reason you should routinely read over the test before beginning to answer any of the items is to see if any of the items are related.

Application Exercise (DTT)

By now you should have applied the study methods from this text to the selection in the appendix, "Great Promises, Bitter Disappointments, 1960–1968." Now apply the discussion of pointers for taking objective tests to the sample test that follows. This exercise should also serve to prepare you for an actual test on "Great Promises, Bitter Disappointments, 1960–1968."

Multiple Choice

1. Which of the following events did *not* help shift popular support from the Republicans to the Democrats in the 1960 election?

    a) John F. Kennedy's age and religion

    b) the Soviet launching of Sputnik

    c) a soaring national debt

    d) Eisenhower's age and leadership

2. Kennedy's efforts to spur economic recovery included
   a) increases in business and income taxes to raise money for government programs.
   b) cutbacks in spending for domestic programs.
   c) greater government spending in defense.
   d) lifting of informal wages and price controls.

3. The "freedom riders"
   a) were acting outside of the federal law and Supreme Court rulings.
   b) met with a minimum of resistance in the South.
   c) used tactics substantially different from sit-ins and boycotts.
   d) forced the federal government to enforce a desegregation ruling.

4. Kennedy's civil rights bills were
   a) defeated by Republicans and southern Democrats.
   b) passed as a result of the 1963 March on Washington.
   c) not passed until after his assassination.
   d) abandoned by Lyndon Johnson.

5. The doctrine of "flexible response" was all of the following *except*
   a) an effort to respond to economic inequalities, nationalism, and revolution in the Third World.
   b) a rationale for Kennedy to sharply increase American military involvement in Vietnam.
   c) a set of policies designed to stop the spread of communism in developing countries.
   d) the motivation for a tactical Allied withdrawal from Berlin.

6. The Bay of Pigs invasion was
   a) an escalation of the war in Southeast Asia.
   b) quickly crushed when popular support did not materialize.
   c) first conceived by the Kennedy administration.
   d) in direct response to the Soviets putting nuclear warheads in Cuba.

7. In which of the following confrontations with the Soviet Union was the United States considered victorious?
   a) the Cuban missile crisis
   b) the Bay of Pigs
   c) the Berlin crisis
   d) winning the "hearts and minds" of the Third World

8. Ngo Dinh Diem was

    a) strong supporter of democratic ideals.

    b) opposed by the largely Catholic bureaucracy.

    c) opposed by political reformers and some of the military.

    d) supported by the United States until after the 1963 coup.

9. The "Freedom Summer of 1964"

    a) focused voting registration efforts in South Carolina and Georgia.

    b) included setting up literacy classes to increase the numbers of eligible voters.

    c) was largely nonviolent.

    d) occurred as a result of the passage of the Voting Rights Act.

10. The Kerner Commission report

    a) put the primary blame for urban riots on the racist attitudes of white America.

    b) put the primary blame for urban riots on groups such as the Black Panthers and Black Muslims.

    c) described an America in which integration was leading, although slowly, to one inclusive society.

    d) was a result of outrage over the assassination of Dr. Martin Luther King, Jr.

Matching

____ 1. Nuclear missiles in Cuba

____ 2. "Segregation forever"

____ 3. "New Frontier"

____ 4. Nonviolent resistance

____ 5. "Great Society"

(a) Stokely Carmichael
(b) John F. Kennedy
(c) Charles de Gaulle
(d) Martin Luther King, Jr.
(e) Barry Goldwater
(f) Lyndon Johnson
(g) Dwight D. Eisenhower
(h) Nikita Khrushchev
(i) George Wallace

Answers to Sample Test Items

Multiple Choice

1. a   6. b
2. d   7. a
3. d   8. c
4. c   9. b
5. d   10. a

Matching

1. h
2. i
3. b

4. d
5. f

Essay Tests

Both the preparation for and the approach to taking essay tests differ considerably from those for objective tests. Professors use essay exams to test your knowledge on a broad topic. Essay questions tend to test your ability to answer higher-level questions. Your success in college depends on your proficiency in taking both essay and objective tests.

Preparing for Essay Tests

The strategy for essay-exam preparation can also be used for preparing for short-answer or identification questions. This strategy relies heavily on your ability to predict questions that might be asked on the actual exam. This kind of prediction is generally not very difficult, if you have read and annotated your text properly, paid attention in class, taken good lecture notes, and rehearsed and reviewed consistently. If you have kept up in class, you should be able to predict at least some of the questions.

The strategy we suggest is called **PORPE**—**P**redict, **O**rganize, **R**ehearse, **P**ractice, and **E**valuate.[1] These five procedures take the following form:

1. *Predict (two or three days before the test):* From your reading, annotating, lecture notes, and study strategies, predict enough essay questions to cover the material. Write questions that cover larger issues, and include some of the higher-level type questions.

In addition to your notes, you can get prediction questions from

- the syllabus
- the chapter questions or study guides
- "retired tests"
- chapter boldface headings or italicized words
- ideas the instructor stresses in lectures

2. *Organize (two days before the exam):* Organize the key ideas and major details for each of your predicted questions. Use an outline, map, or jot list, making sure you list each key idea and its supporting details. Be concise, but include all of the important ideas and facts from the course handouts, readings, and lectures.

3. *Rehearse (two days before the exam):* Review and learn the organization to each predicted question.

- First, test yourself on the main ideas. Continue going over them until you know all the main ideas and can say them without looking at your outline, map, or jot list.

- Next, go over the main ideas one at a time, and review all of the supporting details for each idea. As you rehearse each one, repeat the main idea and details aloud until you can do so without looking at your paper. Also look for the relationships between the main ideas.

- Last, rehearse your list of main ideas and details again the next day. You may find that you have forgotten some points. Keep rehearsing until you again can go through the whole list without looking at your notes.

4. *Practice (a day or two before the exam):* When you have finished the previous stage, practice writing answers to the predicted questions. Write from memory, as if you were really taking the exam. If you have trouble answering one of the questions, go back and rehearse your main ideas and details again; then write the answer from memory.

5. *Evaluate (one day before the exam):* Reread your answers and make sure you included all the main ideas and details from your outline, map, or jot list. If you missed many points, rehearse and practice writing again.

Once you have all of the main ideas and important details included, honestly evaluate how you presented your answer. Use the questions in the following list as a guide. If you can answer *yes* to all the questions, you are ready for the exam. If any of the questions are answered *no,* work on revising the answer.

Checklist for Evaluating Essay Answers

Answer yes or no to the following questions:

1. Did I directly answer the question that was asked?

2. Did I have an introductory sentence that related the essay question and/or took a position on the question?

3. Did I organize the answer so that key ideas or points were obvious?

4. Did I include relevant details or examples to prove and clarify each idea?

5. Did I use transitions in the answer to cue the reader? (e.g., "First . . . ," "Another major idea . . . ," "Equally important . . . ," "Finally . . .")

6. Did my answer make sense and demonstrate a knowledge of the material?

Although your predicted essay questions may not always match perfectly with those of your instructor, chances are at least some of the material you prepared will be included on the test. As you repeat this preparation process, your predictions will conform more and more with your instructor's questions. Even if your questions do differ from the instructor's, by using **PORPE** you can usually modify what you prepared to answer the instructor's questions.

Taking Essay Tests

Certain guidelines for taking essay tests are helpful. Keep these seven suggestions in mind to increase your performance on an essay exam:

1. *Be prepared.* No amount of proficiency in stating, developing, and evaluating ideas can take the place of knowledge. Professors can easily spot an answer that has no supporting statements. Filling a page with empty words doesn't necessarily constitute an answer. Only studying will help you to write an essay answer with substance.

2. *Read all the essay questions through.* Jot down points beside each question as they occur to you, especially if you are given a choice of questions to answer such as, "Answer any three of the following five questions." The brief lists also get you thinking, and you are less apt to leave important information out of your answer.

3. *Answer the questions that you know most about first.* As on objective tests, this procedure builds your confidence and stimulates thought; it may also help you to think of information that you will need to answer the remaining items. Make sure that you number the questions, especially if you answer them out of order; professors don't like to search for your answers.

4. *Allow time to answer all of the questions.* You must be able to budget your time. If the class is 50 minutes long and you have three questions to answer, spend about 10 to 15 minutes on each question, leaving some time at the end of the period to proofread. When you are writing hurriedly, it is easy to leave out or misspell words and endings.

5. *Bring out the structure and logic of your main ideas in your writing.* A good answer includes the following:

- a first sentence that restates the question
- a listing of the major ideas to be covered in the essay
- for each main point, a general statement followed by relevant supporting details
- transitions between the main points to give coherence
- a brief concluding statement

Writing each answer in this manner will make you more organized in your thinking. The student who writes disorganized essay answers risks losing points.

6. *If pressed for time, answer your last question in outline form.* If you haven't adequately budgeted your time, outlining the remaining question(s) will at least indicate to your professor your knowledge of the answer. Although you probably won't receive full credit for your effort, you may get partial credit.

7. *Avoid rambling.* Get to the point. A professor who has thirty or forty students in a class, each of whom has answered three essay questions, is not going to be thrilled by an answer that goes on and on and is devoid of pertinent information. Say what you have to say in a structured manner, as explained in point 5, and move on to the next question. Remember, it is quality, not quantity, that counts.

In summary, practice making up your own essay questions and writing out the answers. Try to predict essay questions and answer them, or get together with a classmate and answer each other's questions. Prediction not only gives you practice in structuring an answer but also serves as a rehearsal strategy. If you can reach two goals using one procedure, so much the better.

The following application puts you in the professor's place. Using what you have learned about writing answers to essay items, particularly the way in which good answers should be constructed, give each of the answers a grade. (By the way, the following are actual student responses.)

A Scenario to Write About and Discuss

For an example of what you might expect as a typical essay question in a western civilization course, read the following item. Student responses come after the question; one student received an *A,* one a *C,* and one an *F.* Can you determine which is which? Why?

Question: The fifteenth- and sixteenth-century voyages of exploration produced lasting changes in the political and social structures of western Europe. Would you say that these voyages tended to hasten or delay the growth of national states? Explain.

Student I

Grade ____

I don't think one can make a decision about whether these voyages were positive or negative. I mean they caused competition sometimes because people wanted to raise cattle and stuff like that but that doesn't mean that they helped or hurt.

Personally, I think it hurt because people probably went to war to fight over cattle and corn and stuff. And besides, explorers had a hard time getting around. They certainly didn't have airplanes like we have today, but their maps were kinda good because some guy whose name was Harry (or Henry—something like that) made an important contribution. It seems like they sure didn't know very much in the old days cause some things happened that weren't planned.

In sum, I guess that the trips hastened the growth for the things I said in this essay.

Student 2

Grade ____

The explorations of the fifteenth and sixteenth centuries hastened the growth of the national states. The reasons have to do with danger, wealth, trade, and pride.

One of the prime reasons for the beginning of national states was a common danger from outside. Because countries went to war over the right to control certain colonies and trade routes, they had to unite within in order to fight off an aggressor.

Other forms of competition between one country and another contributed to the growth of national states. Competition was fierce for land. The resources of the new lands (such as coffee, spices, minerals) were considered valuable.

The voyages of exploration is a rather ambiguous term because actually there was no sudden burst of interest in exploring the world around them—they just were looking for easier trade routes to the Orient. This so-called age of exploration, if it was indeed exploring, was quite by accident.

When the first countries colonized the "New World" every other country now wanted to get in on it. However, to make voyages in the first place, knowledge was needed in ship-building and navigation. Henry the Navigator bettered the conditions of European states by contributing to navigation, maps, etc. It is, therefore, easy to see that without fifteenth- and sixteenth-century exploration the national states would have grown more slowly.

Student 3

Grade ____

There are three reasons why the explorations of the fifteenth and sixteenth centuries hastened the growth of the national states.

The first reason was trade because people wanted coffee, tea, and spices, since they were considered valuable products.

The second reason was greed. Many countries wanted to control certain colonies because of the wealth they possessed. Because of this greed there were wars that led to much killing and bloodshed.

Finally, the key reason was money (of sorts). Those who controlled the colonies also controlled the wealth because of the fact that the colonies usually had resources that were worth a lot.

All of these students answered the same question, yet their answers varied considerably. Think about the content of each answer. Think about the grade you would assign each. Write your reasons for assigning the grades you did to each essay. Now discuss your reasons with a classmate. Together, analyze the differences in the *structure* and the *content* of each response.

Using Key Words in Essays and Papers

Students often fail to answer essay questions adequately because they don't fully understand the terminology used in the questions. For example, if you are asked to *compare* two theories and instead you *contrast* them, you will probably receive very few points. The list that follows is included simply to familiarize you with key words that frequently appear in essay questions. These key words are also used when professors assign papers for class. Although you may already know many of these words, you should still learn those that you don't know and review those that you do know. Many times, more than one key word appears in a question (for example, "*List* the most important causes of the Korean War, and *justify* your answer"). Make sure that you read questions carefully and answer all parts.

The following list is organized into the two categories of questions discussed earlier in this text: memory- and higher-level or critical-thinking questions. The categories are only rough guidelines, however; some of the memory questions, for example, also require you to do some interpretation, a critical-thinking skill.

Memory-Level Key Words

1. *Define*   Definitions call for concise, clear meanings. Your definition should be the one used for that subject matter. The definition should sound authoritative, as if written by the textbook author. Details are usually not required, but the definition should include: the class to which the term belongs; the usual context in which it is used; limitations to the use of the term; and whatever differentiates it from other items in the same class.

2. *Describe*   All four of these key words ask for an organized description.
   Outline   Give main points and important supporting information.
   State   Leave out minor details. Present the information in an orga-
   Summarize   nized fashion, clearly stating the main points first and following with supporting information.

3. *List*   These key words ask you to prepare a list or an outline. Write
   Enumerate   out, point by point (with numbers, if possible), the answer. These questions also require you to be brief, so don't go into much detail.

4. *Diagram*   These key words require you to explain something or to clar-
   Illustrate   ify another answer with concrete examples, figures, or diagrams. To *illustrate* usually means to give concrete examples; to *diagram* means to give a graphic presentation, with labels to identify parts.

5. *Trace*   To *trace* means to follow the development of something, from its beginning to some other point. You might trace the histori-

cal events that led to some conflict, or trace a series of scientific discoveries that led to a major breakthrough. In any case, begin at the point of origin and proceed, step by step, to the culmination.

Higher-Level or Critical-Thinking Key Words

1. *Compare*
   Contrast
   Relate

   These key words ask you to examine two or more ideas, issues, results in a critical way. To *compare* usually means to state the *similarities*. To *contrast* means to state the *differences*. To *relate* means to emphasize whatever connections or associations might exist. A good strategy for these questions is first to describe or define the things individually, and then to discuss the similarities, differences, or associations.

2. *Discuss*
   Explain
   Interpret
   Review

   These key words all call for complete and detailed answers. You are being asked first to define a term, event, quality, concept, or problem. Then you must state the "how" or "why"— to interpret the definition or to elaborate on it. To *discuss* usually means to state the events or conditions that give rise to the issue or results. To *review* requires a critical examination with comments that elaborate. Sometimes, however, to *review* simply asks for a list.

3. *Criticize*

   To *criticize* means to express your judgment about the correctness or the merit of factors under consideration, to describe the factors, and to give the results of your own analysis. Discuss limitations and good points.

4. *Evaluate*

   To *evaluate* also means to express judgment, but from more of an authoritative than a personal point of view. Follow the same format as for *criticize* questions.

5. *Justify*
   Prove

   These key words ask you to prove or give evidence in support of some conclusions, events, or decisions. Your task is to convince the reader that the evidence supports the conclusions. To *justify* usually means to give evidence or arguments in favor of the conclusion; your personal arguments may be included. To *prove* also means to give evidence, but you need to use authoritative evidence and make a stronger case. Both terms are usually used as the second part of two-part questions ("Explain . . . and justify your answer").

Writing Class Papers

Many college courses require you to write papers outside of class. The critical-thinking questions just listed are often used in these assignments. Because these papers are assigned outside of class and allow you to use reference materials, they are not designed to test your knowledge. Rather, papers are usually designed to get you to do additional research and to think critically. In your papers, you are sometimes asked to draw conclusions from information you have gathered ("compare," "contrast," "relate," "interpret," "criticize," "synthesize," "evaluate" are key words). Other times, you are asked to take a position and write persuasively about that position ("justify," "prove," "support" are key words). Remember that, like in an essay test, your task is twofold: Show the professor that you have researched and know the important information (therefore, include main ideas and details) and show that you can critically think about that information and can reach conclusions that you can defend. Detailed suggestions for writing research papers are beyond the scope of this book; we recommend that you take a writing course at your college, if you feel your writing skills are weak.

Application Exercises (DTT)

1. Read the following essay questions from "Great Promises, Bitter Disappointments, 1960–1968." Select one, and construct a well-written answer according to the guidelines discussed in this section.

   (a) Historians say that the televised debates of the 1960 presidential elections changed the media's role in American politics. What happened in those debates? Analyze their importance in changing how candidates used the media.

   (b) What expectations and constraints did Kennedy face in establishing his domestic New Frontier? (Note that this and other possible essay questions are given by the author of "Great Promises, Bitter Disappointments, 1960–1968" at the beginning of the chapter and at the beginning of sections.)

   (c) Compare and contrast the successes of John F. Kennedy and Lyndon B. Johnson in establishing civil rights and human service programs.

   (d) The civil rights struggle was carried out both by nonviolent resistance and by more militant strategies. Which strategies, in your opinion, were more successful? Justify your answer.

2. Predict two additional essay questions for "Great Promises, Bitter Disappointments, 1960–1968." Using one of your questions,

   (a) prepare an outline, map, or jot list (as discussed in the section on **PORPE**).

   (b) go through the **R**ehearse step of **PORPE** until you feel you know the material without looking.

   (c) write a **P**ractice essay.

   (d) **E**valuate your essay, using the checklist in this chapter.

Application Exercises (Your Courses)

1. Predict two essay questions for one of your courses. Use a course that is likely to have essay questions on an exam. For both of these questions,

    (a) prepare an outline, map, or jot list (as discussed in the section on **PORPE**).

    (b) go through the **R**ehearse step of **PORPE** until you feel you know the material without looking.

    (c) write a **P**ractice essay.

    (d) **E**valuate your essay, using the checklist in this chapter.

Test Anxiety

A great number of students experience such extreme anxiety in a testing situation that it sabotages their performance. To learn your test-anxiety level, rate yourself from 1 to 5 on each of the following items. If the statement is *always* true for you, give yourself a 5. If it is *never* true for you, give yourself a 1. If you are not at either extreme, give yourself a 2 for *rarely,* a 3 for *sometimes,* or a 4 for *often.*

1. I have visible signs of nervousness, such as sweaty palms, shaky hands, and so on, right before a test.

    ___   ___   ___   ___   ___
     1   2   3   4   5

2. I have "butterflies" in my stomach.

    ___   ___   ___   ___   ___
     1   2   3   4   5

3. I feel nauseated.

    ___   ___   ___   ___   ___
     1   2   3   4   5

4. I read through the test and feel that I don't know any of the answers.

    ___   ___   ___   ___   ___
     1   2   3   4   5

5. I panic.

    ___   ___   ___   ___   ___
     1   2   3   4   5

6. My mind goes blank.

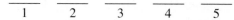

   1   2   3   4   5

7. I remember the information that I blanked out on once I get out of the testing situation.

   1   2   3   4   5

8. I have trouble sleeping the night before a test.

   1   2   3   4   5

9. I make mistakes on easy questions or put answers in the wrong places.

   1   2   3   4   5

10. I have difficulty choosing answers.

   1   2   3   4   5

If you gave yourself 4s or 5s on several of these questions, you may suffer from test anxiety. Although no medication can cure the suffering, understanding what test anxiety is and what causes it will go a long way toward controlling it.

Many students experience text anxiety because they haven't prepared well; it becomes a defense against taking the blame for poor preparation. If you prepare well and feel confident that you know the material, your test anxiety should be greatly reduced. There is a difference between feeling anxiety when you are not prepared and feeling anxiety when you are. If you are well prepared and still experience extreme nervousness in a testing situation, consider these suggestions:

- *Allow yourself plenty of time to get to the test;* don't rush. If you are anxious before the test, you will be anxious during it.

- *Deliberately relax before a test.* Don't look through your notes right before a test; you probably won't learn any more information, anyway. A last-minute cramming session may only tense you up even more.

- *Do not talk to others before the test,* because anxiety is contagious. If someone asks you a question on the test material and you're not sure of the answer, you might become anxious. To avoid this problem, just sit quietly thinking about the material you studied.

- *Have a plan of attack.* Those who do not know their plan of attack are the ones who panic. Decide ahead of time how you are going to approach the test. For example, remember to do the easy items first; this strategy will increase your confidence and probably reduce your anxiety. Some students feel most comfortable doing essay questions first; others do multiple-choice questions first. You don't have to work through the test in the order in which the questions are presented.

- *Relax during the test.* Some tension is normal and is actually good for you; accept it. Use the tension constructively to help you to concentrate. But if you are too anxious—if you panic—it spirals you down, as illustrated in Figure 12.1. Learn how to handle your tension and anxiety through desensitization. Anxiety cannot exist if the body is relaxed. Try the following brief exercise immediately preceding the exam; it may help relieve excess tension.

  1. Take several deep breaths, exhaling slowly while you let your shoulders drop in a relaxed manner. Inhale deeply (count: one, two, three, four, five); then exhale slowly (six, seven, eight, nine, ten). Do this several times.

  2. Roll your head slowly—right ear to right shoulder (count: one, two, three), head back (four, five, six), left ear to left shoulder (seven, eight, nine), head forward (ten, eleven, twelve). Do this twice clockwise and then twice counterclockwise.

  3. Make a fist with both hands and deliberately hold them for five counts. Now slowly extend the fingers, releasing the tension in your arms. Do this several times. This exercise helps you to feel the difference between tension and relaxation.

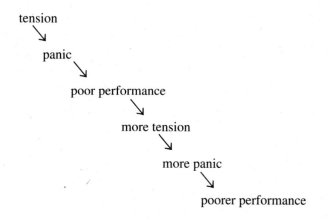

Figure 12.1 The Downward Spiral of Test Anxiety

- *Avoid superstitions.* Students often get into trouble because they begin to watch the responses. When they start running a succession of *true*'s or *b*'s, they think they should not be making the same responses so many times in a row. This is not necessarily true. Most instructors have not set up any kind of pattern.

If you follow the suggestions in this chapter for taking objective and essay exams and reducing test anxiety, chances are that your performance will improve. But reading the suggestions and putting them into practice are two different things. As with the other suggestions in this book, you must practice to become proficient.

Key Ideas

1. Knowing the academic tasks in your classes will guide you in successful preparation for tests.
2. Doing well on exams requires applying the strategies discussed in this text.
3. Careful planning and daily reviewing are two key components of scoring high on exams.
4. Preparing for objective tests differs considerably from preparing for essay tests.
5. Approach all tests systematically.
6. Excessive anxiety can hamper your test performance.

Two Scenarios to Think About and Discuss

We have included two final scenarios for you to think about and discuss. Both of these scenarios should challenge you to think about all of the strategies you have learned in *Developing Textbook Thinking*. In each case, think about your strengths and weaknesses and what you should do in order to be a self-regulated learner and to perform well in the class.

Scenario 1: Chris

Scenario: In the third week of the quarter, Chris had her first psychology 101 exam. The test, which was worth 25 percent of her grade (she would have two other tests and a cumulative final exam, each worth 25 percent), consisted of 40 multiple-choice items and 5 identification items. All items were worth 2 points each. Chris was responsible for learning 5 text chapters as well as her lecture notes for the first 3 weeks of class. It should be noted that her professor's lectures tended to cover the same concepts that were presented in the text and that the majority of the information was theoretical in nature, thus requiring her to conceptualize rather than simply memorize. Chris's professor had exams from the past 2 years on file in the library and available for students.

Chris's approach to getting ready: To her credit, Chris likes to learn new things and is actually considering psychology as her major. For the most part, she found the information interesting. She knows the importance of interacting with the material every day and initially made an effort to do this. She made a schedule that outlined when and how she would prepare, but stuck with it only part of the time. She had most of the reading completed by the beginning of Week 3 and had annotated sporadically and inconsistently throughout her reading. Three days before the test, she decided to go back and reread so that she could do a better job of annotation. She abruptly changed her mind, however, and decided that making a set of concept cards might be helpful for memorizing the different theories, experiments, and important people. She finished her concept cards the day before the test. Chris got together with two classmates the night before the test. She sat in the study group and listened as the others discussed the important information and predicted and answered potential test questions. She spent most of her study time memorizing the key terms on her concept cards.

How could Chris improve her studying? Using all of what you have learned about what it takes to be a successful student, write down a critique of Chris's study habits; then list suggestions for her to improve. Discuss your ideas with a group of classmates. Compare your critiques and your suggestions and discuss the reasons you chose the suggestions you did.

Scenario 2: Michael

The Setting: Michael has enrolled in an introductory political science course to satisfy core requirements. The class takes place in a large auditorium, and there are almost 100 other students taking this class with him. The professor lectures for four days, and there is a discussion group of about 20 students led by a discussion leader that meets one day per week. Although Michael doesn't particularly like political science, the professor's lectures tend to be interesting, because she often uses "stories" as examples of some of the points she is trying to make. But mostly, she presents the information in a systematic way that is relatively easy to follow. His discussion leader, on the other hand, has obviously never led any kind of a discussion before. Most of the discussion sessions are boring and offer very little in the way of additional information, although they are supposed to help prepare him for the essay portion of the test. They are supposed to focus primarily on the book of original source readings. To make matters worse, it is the discussion leader, not the professor who will grade his exam. On a positive note, the discussion leader encourages him to "come talk to him if you are having problems."

Texts for this class include a traditional political science textbook; a book of readings, most of which are original sources; current newspaper readings from the *New York Times*; and, of course, class lectures and discussion group notes.

The Course Task: Michael has a weekly quiz on the *New York Times* readings; each question is worth 10 points. He can drop his two lowest quiz scores. Additionally, he has three quizzes and two major exams. The quizzes (given approximately every three weeks) consist of 25 multiple-choice questions covering primarily the text and lectures. The two exams, one midterm and one final, consist of essay questions. For the midterm, the professor will give six possible questions the Friday before the exam; two of the questions will be selected for Monday's midterm. For the final, the same procedure will be followed except that the questions will be given out on the last day of class and the exam will consist of three rather than two essay questions.

The professor has said the following things in class about the quizzes and tests:

- Weekly *New York Times* quizzes will cover assigned readings from the newspaper only. The items will cover general ideas presented, not "picky details." Generally these articles will not be discussed in class.

- The three 25-point quizzes will cover primarily the textbook and lectures. There is some overlap between these two sources, but the class will be expected to read on their own as everything cannot be covered in class. These questions will also tap "important" information rather than minor details.

- The two essay exams (each consisting of 5 essay questions, each essay worth 20 points) will expect students to integrate and synthesize the information from all sources, with an emphasis on the readings discussed in the weekly discussion groups. Students are expected to show that they can analyze and think critically. They will also be expected to write in a coherent and cohesive fashion. Although, technically, points are not taken off for mechanics, grammar, and usage, the discussion leader should be able to understand and follow the points students are trying to make.

What are the right things to do in this class? Michael's goal is to make an *A* or a *B*. Using all of what you have learned about what it takes to be a successful student (even in courses you may not like), what would you advise Michael to do to succeed in the class?

Write down the suggestions you would make to Michael; then discuss your ideas with a group of classmates. Compare your ideas and discuss why each person selected the suggestions he or she did.

Application Exercise (DTT)

1. For most of the applications in this chapter, we have used, "Great Promises, Bitter Disappointments, 1960–1968" as an example. For this exercise, use one of the other selections from the appendix. The selections have tests that go with them.

   (a) Read, annotate, and study the selection.

   (b) Use the study strategies and test-preparation strategies we have discussed in this chapter.

   (c) Take the test that goes with the selection.

   (d) Write an essay that discusses

   - how well I did on the test.
   - what study strategies I used and how well they worked in preparing for the test.
   - what test-preparation strategies I used and how well they worked.
   - what I would do differently in preparing for this test again.

Application Exercise (Your Courses)

1. As you prepare for tests in your courses, use the study and test-preparation strategies we have discussed in this textbook. After you get the results back from one of your tests, write an essay that discusses

   (a) how well I did on the test.

   (b) what study strategies I used and how well they worked in preparing for the test.

   (c) what test-preparation strategies I used and how well they worked.

   (d) what I would do differently in preparing for this test again.

Notes

1. M. L. Simpson, "PORPE: A Writing Strategy for Studying and Learning," *Journal of Reading,* 29(5), 1986, pp. 407–14.

Appendix: Selections from a Variety of Texts

The Psychology of Memory

Key Questions

1. How do you remember?

2. Where in the brain are memories located?

3. Why do you forget?

4. How can you improve your memory?

From *Introductory Psychology* by Morris K. Holland. Copyright © 1981 by D.C. Heath and Company. Used by permission of Houghton Mifflin Company.

And there was the man who couldn't remember three things: names, faces, and—he forgot what the third was. His wife, however, had the worst memory in the world: She remembered everything.

Memory is often taken for granted, but it is central to the ability to grow. In order to learn from the past, you must be able to remember it.

What would you be like without memory? Even the simplest task would be impossible. For example, you could not repeat your name or find your way home. You could not read this sentence. You would have no knowledge of the beginning of the sentence by the time your eyes reached the end of the sentence. Without memory you would not learn from experience. Without the ability to learn from the past you would begin anew at every moment. In effect, you would remain an infant throughout your life.

Memory Processes

How are you able to remember past experiences and events? Since you do not have a camera in your mind, how can you remember a picture? Since you do not record music with your brain, how can you remember a song once heard? Human memory is still a mysterious process that we know relatively little about. Logically, however, we know that remembering requires at least three processes: getting information in the mind, retaining it, and then getting it out. These processes are called encoding, storage, and retrieval.

Encoding

Memories are not the same as real events: I do not have actual music in my mind; my house is not actually in my head. Memories can be thought of as consisting of information, rather than of physical objects such as houses. **Encoding** is the process of changing physical scenes and events into the form of information that can be stored in memory. This "form" of information used in recording memories is the memory code. Thus the process of encoding consists of changing the physical energy in the environment (for example, a sound) into memory codes.

What is this code? Evidence shows that memories of recent letters or words are often encoded into labels or sounds. In a complex experiment designed to test the capacity of memory, the participants were allowed one very brief glance at a group of twelve letters printed on a card; then asked them to name as many letters as they could remember. On the average, they were able to name only four or five letters. But the errors that they made were very interesting. Although the letters were presented visually, the participants tended to confuse letters that *sounded* alike; for example, they would mix up D and E or B and C. This finding indicates something about the nature of the memory code in this task: People must be encoding what the letters sound like, and then storing the sound codes. If people encoded what the letters looked like, they would have made more confusions among letters that looked alike than among letters that sounded alike. Other experimenters have confirmed that errors made in recalling visually presented items tend to be acoustically related (related by sound) to the missed item. That is, people are more likely to confuse E with C (an acoustic confusion) than they are to confuse E with F (a visual confusion). These brief memories of recent events are sometimes encoded into the spoken sounds of letters or words.

More permanent memories are not influenced so much by sound similarity. The memory for material that is highly practiced tends to be influenced more by semantic similarity—similarity in meaning. Apparently, material that is more permanently stored in memory is encoded into meanings rather than into sounds. Since you can remember pictures of all sorts—even abstract designs— it is clear that the sound code and the meaning code are not the only memory codes we have available. An image code is also used.

Storage

After an event is encoded, the information must be retained. How is it stored? We know that memory **storage** is not a random filing away of information; the information is systematically organized or structured. Things that are related to each other tend to be stored together. This can be shown by the fact that you tend to remember things in clusters. If you put a random list of words into memory, an organized list tends to come out. If you were to read the words: green, north, red, blue, south, yellow, east, you would later tend to recall the directional words in one group and all the color words in another group. Apparently memory storage is organized around units of meaning.

Another type of organization depends not upon meaning but upon the order of occurrence. Events that occur at about the same time tend to be clustered or grouped together. Memorize these numbers:

$$6 \quad 4 \quad 9 \quad 5 \quad 1 \quad 7 \quad 8 \quad 2 \quad 3$$

Chances are, you learned the numbers not as nine individual digits, but as two or three groups of digits, like this:

$$649 \qquad 517 \qquad 823$$

Memorizing numbers like these is easier when you group them in clusters of three or four. These clusters or groups are called *chunks,* and the process of grouping items into such units is called **chunking.**

Research has shown that our ability to recall material that is presented only once is quite limited, and that our capacity depends upon the number of chunks involved, not the number of individual items of information. On the average, the limit to the amount of material seen once that we can recall seems to be about five to seven chunks. You can increase the amount of information you can recall by increasing the number of items in each chunk. In the example using digits, if you have one digit per chunk you would be able to recall only five to seven digits; if you increased the number of digits per chunk to three, you would be able to recall fifteen to twenty-one digits.

This limitation on storage capacity does not hold for all types of learning situations. With adequate time for rehearsal, study, and review, human memory has an essentially unlimited storage capacity.

Retrieval

In order to remember an event, you must first get the information about the event into usable form in memory; this is the encoding process. Then you must retain the information for some period of time until you need it; this is the storage process. The third essential feature of the memory process is **retrieval:** finding and using the stored information. How do you retrieve your memory of the meaning of the word chunk? In a sense you have the word and its meaning "on file" and you "look it up"; but your mind is not a dictionary and memory retrieval is not the same as looking something up in a book.

Your Mental Library If your "filing system" were completely random and mixed up, you would never be able to find what you need. You can retrieve memories because memory storage is organized. It can be compared to a library. Libraries use complex filing systems, typically grouping together the books that are meaningfully related. Different books concerning psychology would be filed in the same general area, for example. Sometimes libraries keep "recent arrivals" separate, so that you can quickly find the newest books in print. Your memory storage and retrieval system in certain ways resembles a library. Your memory is a library of information, organized so that those items are grouped together that are meaningfully related. In addition, the "recent arrivals" (the most recent events) are kept separate, so as to be quickly accessible.

On the Tip of Your Tongue Sometimes when you try to retrieve from your memory the name of a person, you fail. You know that you have it in memory, but you can't quite locate it. You describe what happened to you by saying that the person's name was "on the tip of your tongue." This frustrating experience has been called the **tip-of-the-tongue phenomenon.** The remarkable thing about the experience is that you often know about how long the word is, you may even know the number of syllables, you may even know the beginning letter of the word, but you cannot recall the word. It is as if you know part of the library "call number" for the book, but not the remainder and therefore cannot find the book. If your memory filing system uses the first letter of words in its indexing system, you would expect that it would be easier to recall a word if you were provided with its first letter, and this has been demonstrated to be the case.

Photographic Memory

Photographic memory is the rare ability to remember in great detail whole scenes or pages from books that were looked at once. Incredibly, such persons are able to retain visual information in memory in a form similar to a photograph. A more technical name for photographic memory is **eidetic imagery.** Children seem to have this ability more often than adults. In one study, 151 children were tested for eidetic imagery, and 12 children were found who showed this remarkable memory ability. Although 5 to 10 percent of children have some eidetic ability, almost no adults have been found to have this ability. It is not known why the ability disappears with age, but one possibility is that the culture and the educational system destroy it. This is a "brass-tacks" culture; it is factually oriented, verbally oriented, and distrustful of the visual imagination.

Elizabeth Rarely is an adult found who possesses this remarkable ability. One of the few documented cases is that of a woman named Elizabeth. Elizabeth showed an amazing talent for remembering visual information in great detail. A demonstration of her memory capacity was her ability to look at one picture of thousands of random dots with her right eye, then, *weeks later,* look at another similar but slightly different picture with her left eye and combine them into a single pattern. Apparently she could take the information given separately to each of her eyes and put together the picture she would have seen if the information had been originally presented to both her eyes simultaneously. She "saw," using her memory, although she had never actually seen with her eyes this complete pattern.

The Case of S. One of the most carefully documented cases of photographic memory was investigated by A. R. Luria, a famous Russian psychologist. Luria had the opportunity to study the mind of the man he called S. for thirty years. Luria set out to test the limits of S.'s memory.

> When I began my study of S. it was with much the same degree of curiosity psychologists generally have at the outset of research, hardly with the hope that the experiments would offer anything of particular note. However, the results of the first tests were enough to change my attitude and to leave me, the experimenter, rather than my subject, both embarrassed and perplexed.
>
> I gave S. a series of words, then numbers, then letters, reading them to him slowly or presenting them in a written form. He read or listened attentively and then repeated the material exactly as it had been presented. I increased the number of elements in each series, giving him as many as thirty, fifty, or even seventy words or numbers, but this, too, presented no problem for him. . . .
>
> As the experimenter, I soon found myself in a state verging on utter confusion. An increase in the length of a series led to no noticeable increase in the difficulty for S., and I simply had to admit that the capacity of his memory *had no distinct limits.* . . . Experiments indicated that he had no difficulty reproducing

any lengthy series of words whatever, even though these had originally been presented to him a week, a month, or even many years earlier.

How was S. able to remember so much? When S. was asked how he did it, he described the process as reading off the words or numbers from the paper on which they were originally written; it was as if he continued to see the list. If words were read out loud to him, the sound of each word would produce a visual image; the sounds were changed into colored splotches, lines, or splashes. S.'s visual imagery was very vivid and sometimes bothersome. As S. described it:

> To this day, I can't escape from seeing colors when I hear sounds. What first strikes me is the color of someone's voice. Then it fades off . . . for it does interfere. If, say, a person says something, I see the word; but should another person's voice break in, blurs appear. These creep into the syllables of the words, and I can't make out what is being said.

For S. all sounds seemed to be encoded into colored visual images, and it was the images that were remembered.

Interim Summary

Remembering requires three basic processes: encoding, storage, and retrieval. Encoding involves putting information into memory by changing the physical energies in the world into memory codes that can be retained. Verbal items like letters and words are initially encoded acoustically; that is, they are changed into labels or sounds. Storage is the process of retaining information over time. Memory storage is organized, with similar items linked together by associations; sometimes items are clustered, or chunked. Retrieval refers to the process of getting at the stored information so that it can be used. The "tip-of-the-tongue" phenomenon is an example of a failure of retrieval. Photographic memory, or eidetic imagery, is the rare ability to encode, store, and retrieve whole scenes or pages of information.

Memories in the Brain

Thinking and remembering are activities of the brain, a complicated structure that is composed of billions of nerve cells. If you were to look at a human brain, what you would see is the outer surface of the brain, the cerebral cortex, a gray wrinkled covering in which many of the most important brain processes occur. Among other things, the brain is a storehouse of memories.

The Search for the Engram

Where is memory in the brain? Is there a *place* in the brain where the memory of your name might be located? Your body has the ability to retain past experience, but where is it kept? In a series of experiments with rats many years ago, Karl Lashley searched the brain for the physical location of memory. He believed that memories stored in the brain must have a physical form, something he called the **engram.** He reasoned that if he could cut out different parts of the brain he might find where memories are kept. If the memory were cut out with the piece of brain, the animals would not be able to remember. Lashley began by teaching rats to solve a maze, then cutting out particular parts of their brains. He would then test them to see if they remembered how to solve the maze. Surprisingly, Lashley found that in rats memory does not seem to be located in a particular place in the brain; instead, widespread areas of the surface of the brain are involved in each memory. We know today that memory seems to be spread out all through the cortex, but that there are particular brain structures which are essential in order to memorize anything; these structures lie hidden beneath the cortex on each side of the brain.

The Man with Half a Brain

Along the midline of the brain from the front to the back is a deep fold, dividing the brain into two halves called cerebral hemispheres. The left hemisphere controls most of the right side of the body and the right hemisphere controls most of the left side of the body. What do you suppose would happen to you if you lost half your brain?

Small injuries to the brain sometimes produce rapid death; extensive damage to the brain sometimes has little effect. The important factor, of course, is what part of the brain is damaged. You might expect that if you could survive the loss of half your brain, you would wind up with only half a mind. The following case describes what actually happened to one man.

A forty-seven-year-old right-handed man came to the hospital with complaints of being speechless and having seizures in the right arm and face. Five months later a brain operation was performed and a tumor was removed from his left hemisphere. The tumor recurred, so a year later the entire left hemisphere was removed in one piece. Because the left hemisphere was removed and it controls the right side of the body, the operation resulted in paralysis on the right side. The man could not move his right arm and right leg. Remarkably, however, the man's hearing, personality, intelligence, and memory were essentially unaffected by the operation. In this case, half a brain was almost as good as a whole brain. Apparently removing half the brain had little effect on the mind itself.

Brain Chemistry

Recently scientists have proposed that memory may be based on chemical changes in the brain. The search for the physical basis of memory (the engram) has focused on certain kinds of brain chemicals called "protein molecules." Brain cells continuously manufacture protein molecules, a process guided by a substance called **RNA** (*ribonucleic acid*). The physical basis of memory may involve these protein molecules. Interfering with the manufacture of these protein molecules has been shown to produce memory loss in animals. Furthermore, the amount of RNA in the brain seems to increase after learning.

Remembering with the Help of Electricity

A famous brain surgeon, Wilder Penfield, investigated the function of the brain by stimulating the cerebral cortex at different points with a weak electrical current. The current was applied by gently touching the brain surface with a fine wire electrode during a brain operation in which the patient was awake. The operation can be carried out under local anesthesia because the brain itself has no pain receptors and is quite insensitive to pain. Penfield found that electrically stimulating the brain in certain areas occasionally causes past sensory experiences to recur. Old memories are suddenly brought to life again. Penfield described this procedure and the experiences of two of his patients.

> Occasionally during the course of a neurological operation under local anesthesia, gentle electrical stimulation in this temporal area, right or left, has caused the conscious patient to be aware of some previous experience. The experience seems to be picked out at random from his own past. It comes back to him in great detail. . . .
>
> A woman heard an orchestra playing an air while the electrode was held in place. The music stopped when the electrode was removed. It came again when the electrode was reapplied. On request, she hummed the tune, while the electrode was held in place, accompanying the orchestra. It was a popular song. Over and over again, restimulation of the same spot produced the same song. The music seemed always to begin at the same place and to progress at the normally expected tempo. All efforts to mislead her failed. She believed that a Gramophone was being turned on in the operating room on each occasion, and she asserted her belief stoutly in a conversation some days after the operation.
>
> A boy heard his mother talking to someone on the telephone when an electrode was applied to his right temporal cortex. When the stimulus was repeated without warning, he heard his mother again in the same conversation. When the stimulus was repeated after a lapse of time, he said, "My mother is telling my brother he has got his coat on backwards. I can just hear them. "The surgeon then asked the boy whether he remembered this happening. "O yes," he said, "just before I came here."

The fact that stimulating specific spots on the brain activated specific memories in Penfield's patients does not prove that these memories were located only in these brain areas. To be sure, this is one possibility. Other possibilities are that the electrical stimulation activated not a memory but a retrieval mechanism or that it activated merely one of numerous brain locations involved with each memory.

Interim Summary

A particular memory is apparently not located in a particular place in the brain. Instead, as Lashley discovered, widespread areas of the brain may be involved in each memory. Some researchers now believe that certain complex chemicals are produced when learning occurs and that these are the key to the physical basis of memory. The electrical activity of the brain is important also. It has been found that electrical stimulation of certain parts of the brain can bring old memories back to life.

Theories of Memory

A theory of the memory system is an attempt to account for the various facts of human memory that have been discovered. Psychologists have proposed different types of theories of memory. Some focus on a description of hypothetical memory structures, and others focus on the processes that are assumed to take place when material is encoded, stored, or retrieved from memory.

The Duplex Theory of Memory

According to the **duplex theory of memory,** we have two memory systems for storing information—one for remembering something for a short time and a second for remembering something for a long time. (The term *duplex* means having two parts.) **Short-term memory (STM)** is the system for storing information for just a few seconds, and **long-term memory (LTM)** is the system for storing information for much longer periods.

Short-Term Memory Short-term memory appears to be able to hold information for up to thirty seconds or so, but the duration of short-term memory varies under different conditions. By rehearsing the information in short-term memory (repeating it over and over), the items can be retained over long periods of time. The reason is that each time you rehearse an item you give it new life in short-term memory. In effect, each rehearsal puts the information back into short-term memory anew. When you try to remember a telephone number, you are using your short-term memory system, and you probably rehearse the number by saying it to yourself again and again. Short-term memory also has a *limited capacity.* That is, not only does it not hold information for very long, but it cannot hold very much information at one time. You cannot keep fourteen telephone numbers in your short-term memory at one time. Various studies have shown that the capacity of short-term memory is limited to about five to seven new and unrelated items, or five to seven *chunks* of information.

Long-Term Memory Long-term memory has neither the time limit nor the capacity limit of short-term memory. Information in long-term memory may last for months or decades. Your childhood memories are stored in your long-term memory system. There appears to be no limit to the number of memories that can be kept in the long-term memory system. You already have thousands of different memories in this system. Information enters the short-term memory system and then is either lost or transferred to the long-term memory system. A process that facilitates this transfer is rehearsal. Unlike short-term memory, long-term memory suffers from retrieval problems. That is, as you may have experienced fairly often, you know that a particular piece of information is in your long-term memory system, but you are unable to locate it when you need it. In fact, you probably had this experience on your last exam.

The Levels-of-Processing Theory

An alternative to the duplex theory of memory, with its STM and LTM, is the **levels-of-processing theory of memory.** This theory denies that there are different parts or systems of memory and emphasizes instead different memory processes. According to this view, we do not have a short-term memory system with a limited capacity for retaining information; instead, our memory is limited because of the way we process and store information. The central assumption of this theory is that we process information at different levels and that this determines how well we remember it. The first level is that of simple perception: We see or hear or feel the stimulus. A deeper level of analysis occurs when we process the shape of the letters of a word or the sound of a word. A still deeper level of processing occurs when we determine the meaning of the word or sentence. The level of processing is even deeper when we not only think of the meaning of the item, but also form a mental image of it. The deepest level of processing occurs when we think of the meaning of the item within a context of interrelated items. For example, instead of trying to remember the word *fork* out of context, we could try to remember it by making up a story involving it or by thinking of it in relationship to other similar words (*spoon, knife,* and so on).

Research shows that retention of material processed at "shallow" levels is very poor, but retention of material processed at "deep" levels is good. A way to assure deeper levels of processing is by means of the rehearsal technique. One way to rehearse something you are trying to remember is to say it to yourself over and over. For example, if you are trying to remember a telephone number that you looked up, you will repeat the number to yourself on your way to the telephone. This type of rehearsal does not involve a very deep level of processing, since the number is not placed within a context of meaning. Rote repetition as a method of rehearsal is called **maintenance rehearsal,** because it is effective only in maintaining the item in memory for as long as the rehearsal continues. When you stop saying the telephone number to yourself, you tend to forget it quickly. If you want to remember the number for a longer period, you will need to try a different rehearsal technique. Associating the number with something meaningful and thinking of the number within this context is called **elaborative rehearsal.** For example, how could you remember the telephone number 245-1491 using elaborative rehearsal? The first step would involve thinking of some connections between the number and something meaningful. For example, you might think that the first part (245) is 100 more than your weight and the second part (1491) is the year before Columbus was supposed to have discovered America. These sorts of connections are examples of elaborative rehearsal.

The Duplicative and Reconstructive Theories

Test your memory for the following sentences. Follow these instructions carefully: Read each sentence, count to five, answer the question on the right, then go on to the next sentence; continue until you have read all of the sentences and answered all of the questions on the right.

Sentence	(Count to Five)	Question
The hill was steep		What was?
The cat, running from the barking dog, jumped on the table.		From what?
The old car climbed the hill.		What did?
The cat, running from the dog, jumped on the table.		Where?
The car pulled the trailer.		Did what?
The scared cat was running from the barking dog.		What was?
The scared cat jumped on the table.		Did what?
The old car climbed the steep hill.		What did?
The large window was on the porch.		Where?
The car pulling the trailer climbed the steep hill.		Did what?
The cat jumped on the table.		Where?
The car pulling the trailer climbed the hill.		What did?
The dog was barking?		Was what?
The window was large.		What was?

STOP. Cover the preceding sentences so you cannot see them. Now read the sentences below and mark each as "old" (in the list above) or "new" (not in the list above).

The car climbed the hill.	Old ____	New ____
The scared cat, running from the barking dog, jumped on the table.	Old ____	New ____
The window was on the porch.	Old ____	New ____
The barking dog jumped on the table.	Old ____	New ____
The scared cat was running from the dog.	Old ____	New ____
The old car pulled the trailer.	Old ____	New ____
The cat was running from the barking dog.	Old ____	New ____
The old car, pulling the trailer, climbed the hill.	Old ____	New ____

The cat was running from the dog.	Old ____ New ____
The scared cat, running from the dog, jumped on the table.	Old ____ New ____
The old car pulling the trailer climbed the steep hill.	Old ____ New ____
The car climbed the steep hill.	Old ____ New ____

STOP. Count the number of sentences you judged "old," then read the explanation that follows in order to understand what this means about your memory.

Which sentences did you remember from the first list and mark as "old"? Check the ones you marked as "old" to determine whether they were in fact in the first list. You will find that none of the sentences were actually repeated; every one of them was "new." How can you explain the fact that you "remembered" sentences that you had not read before?

Sometimes your memory plays tricks on you. You think you remember seeing something that you have never seen before. The face of a stranger in a crowd somehow seems familiar.

Memory mistakes are sometimes useful. They help to show how memory works. Theories of memory are concerned with how past experiences are used in remembering and how they are retained over time. One theory, the **duplicative theory of memory,** proposes a relatively exact storage system, in which the details of past experience are "filed away" and copies later retrieved. From this point of view, memory mistakes might come from misfiling information or failing to retrieve it properly.

A second theory, **the reconstructive theory of memory,** proposes that memory is creative and that duplications or copies of experience are not retained. Instead, what is stored is the meaning and basic facts of experience. According to this theory, remembering involves an imaginative reconstruction made from past experience as a whole. The memory test you have just taken shows that this reconstructive theory has some merit. If you can "remember" things you have never seen before, remembering must involve a creative, or reconstructive, process. Remembering must be more like creating a painting of a past scene than like pulling a photo out of a file. One study of memory used sentences like the ones in the preceding memory tests and found that people were quite sure they had seen sentences before that were completely new. When a new, complex sentence combined several parts of old sentences, people were especially sure that they had seen it before.

Interim Summary

The duplex theory of memory proposes that we have two memory structures or systems: a short-term memory and a long-term memory. The levels of processing theory focuses on *processes* rather than *structures.* It proposes that our memory for information depends upon how we process it. Information processed at a deeper level, through elaborative rehearsal, is retained better than information processed at a shallow level, through maintenance rehearsal. Finally, two theories address how information is stored and retrieved. The duplicative theory proposes a relatively exact storage system, from which information is retrieved intact. By contrast, the reconstructive theory proposes that only the basic *meaning* of experience is stored and that "retrieval" involves a reconstruction of past experience.

Measures of Forgetting

How much do you remember of what you have read in this book? Do you remember more, or less, than the average?

These questions could be answered only if your memory could be measured in some way. Scientists studying memory have devised a number of ways to measure forgetting. Each measure gives a slightly different answer to the question of how much you have forgotten.

The Recall Method

One method that provides a measure of forgetting is the **recall method**. In the recall method you are asked to reproduce exactly what you have read or seen. Can you recall the first sentence of this chapter? If so, you would be able to write it down exactly, word for word. Can you recall the names of all the presidents of the United States? If so, you would be able to write them down.

A pioneer in the study of human memory, the German scientist Hermann Ebbinghaus used the recall method in his experiments in the late 1800s. Ebbinghaus wrote lists of meaningless groups of letters called **nonsense syllables**—for example, FUB, ZID, SEB, HOK, and so on. His procedure was to read through the list of nonsense syllables at a uniform rate and then, after varying delays, stop to test himself by trying to recall as many items from the list as he could. One of Ebbinghaus's discoveries was that the first and last syllables on the list were typically recalled more easily than the ones in the middle. In a long list, he found that he was more likely to be able to recall the first one or two and the last one or two but was more likely to forget the items in the middle of the list. This effect has been called the **serial-position effect.** Because of the serial-position effect, if you went to the store after memorizing a long grocery list you would be more likely to forget to buy items in the middle of the list than items at the beginning or end.

The Recognition Method

A second method used to measure forgetting is the **recognition method.** In the recognition method you are shown an item and asked whether you have seen it before. Consider this sentence: "Ask not what you country can do for you, ask what you can do for your country." Do you recognize this sentence? Have you experienced it before? You may very well have heard it before or read it somewhere, since it is a famous quotation from President John Kennedy. Have you ever taken a multiple-choice examination? Multiple-choice examinations are recognition tests, since they present the alternatives and ask you to recognize the correct one.

Your ability to recognize what you have experienced before is extremely large. Faces from the past, scenes from your childhood, phrases from songs or poems—all in varying degrees—are recognized as familiar. In one study, students were presented with 612 different colored pictures; later, they were shown a mixture of these pictures and many new ones. The students correctly recognized an average of 97 percent of the pictures as being those they had seen earlier. The same psychologist showed other people 1,224 sentences, then later tested their ability to recognize them. They were able to recognize correctly 88 percent of the sentences.

The Relearning Method

In the **relearning method** you are first given some new material to learn, and a measure is taken of how long this takes; later you are asked to learn it again (relearn it), and a measure is again taken of how long this takes. Relearning material is usually easier than learning it the first time, because you have not completely forgotten it. If you were to retake a course that you took last year, it would be easier for you the second time around because you have retained some of the material presented in the course. By measuring how much easier it is the second time around, the relearning method obtains a measure of how much you have retained.

Interim Summary

Three measures of forgetting are the recall method, the recognition method, and the relearning method. The recall method involves reproducing your past experiences. The recognition method requires only that you indicate whether you have experienced something before. The relearning method yields a measure based on how much easier it is to learn a body of material the second time as compared to the first time.

Why You Forget

Often memory fails and you forget. Why do you forget? Can you remember the exact wording of the first sentence of this chapter? You most likely have forgotten. There are two general possible explanations for the fact that you have forgotten the sentence: First, a certain amount of time has passed, and second, other sentences you have read more recently may have disrupted the memory of the first sentence. These two general explanations are the basis for prominent theories of forgetting, the decay theory and the interference theory.

Decay

The **decay theory** states that memories weaken spontaneously as time passes; that is, they "decay." According to this theory, you have forgotten the first sentence of this chapter because you read it some time ago; the memory of the sentence decayed or weakened more and more as time passed until the memory was too faint or weak to remember. One way memory decay has been studied is with memories over very short intervals. Evidence shows, for example, that there are brief sensory memories that fade rapidly with time, for both visual events and auditory events. It is difficult to prove that decay occurs, however, in the forgetting of complex material. The problem is the difficulty of deciding where forgetting was due simply to the passage of time or to interference from activities that occurred in that time period.

Interference

The **interference theory** states that memories weaken because of the action of other memories interfering with them. Learning the name of one new friend is a lot easier than learning the names of ten new friends; the memory of each name may suffer from interference due to the other memories. According to the interference theory, you have forgotten the first sentence of this chapter because you have read many other sentences before it and after it, and the memories of these other sentences create interference.

Two kinds of interference have been identified: proactive interference and retroactive interference. **Proactive interference** occurs when your memory for something you learned recently is interfered with by some previously learned material. In preparing for exams, if you study sociology and then psychology, your memory for the psychology material may be interfered with by the sociology material you learned first, because of proactive interference. Your memory for material in this chapter may be interfered with by material you learned in the previous chapter, because of proactive interference.

A second type of interference, **retroactive interference,** occurs when your memory for something you learned at one time is interfered with by something you learned later. In preparing for exams, if you study sociology first and then psychology, your memory for the sociology may be interfered with by the psychology material you learned later, because of retroactive interference (see the diagram following). Your memory for material in the previous chapter may be interfered with by your learning of the material in this chapter, because of retroactive interference. When you read Chapters 4, 5, and 6, your memory for Chapter 5 may be interfered with by the material in Chapter 4 (proactive interference) and by the material in Chapter 6 (retroactive interference).

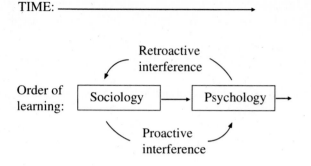

TIME: —————————————————————→

Order of learning:

Retroactive interference

Sociology → Psychology →

Proactive interference

It has proved very difficult to establish which one of the two theories of forgetting, the decay theory or the interference theory, is the better explanation of why we forget. Probably both theories are right, and some forgetting is due to decay and some to interference.

Repression

When you repress a memory, you block it from consciousness. It is possible that certain memories are too painful to relive and so are forgotten. According to Freud, **repression** is a major psychological defense we all use against anxiety; we repress painful experiences in order not to feel the anxiety that would accompany their memories. A victim of child abuse may repress the painful memories as a means of coping with the traumatic incidents. Our everyday failures of memory are sometimes due to repression. Freud cites the case of a man who repeatedly forgot the name of an acquaintance, and he shows how the forgetting may be explained as repression; it seems that the acquaintance had married a woman whom the man had hoped to marry himself. His forgetting was a way of dealing with the anxiety of this painful experience.

Amnesia

Amnesia is a loss of memory due to shock or injury. Sometimes the loss of memory is for the immediate past and at other times it is for events in the remote past. Persons with amnesia cannot remember certain facts of their histories; sometimes they cannot even remember their own names. What is it like to experience amnesia? One person described it this way:

> With an assurance to my wife that I would be back in a minute or two, I went out and failed to return. The next thing that I remember is a sound of rifle shots and some short bursts of machine-gun fire coming from the other side of a hill on the right of a road on which I was walking. I was conscious of being dirty, unshaven, and footsore. I did not seem to be particularly hungry or thirsty. I had a feeling of puzzlement upon my mind, not unlike that which one may experience on waking from a deep sleep in a strange place. Where was I? Who was I?

Something was wrong, but what was it? I knew my own name and recognized my own writing when I jotted it down on a bit of paper, but everything else seemed uncertain and unstable. . . . It was some few minutes before I realized fully that I had absolutely no recollection of any course of events which could have brought me to the existing position. The immediate past seemed to be "a perfect and absolute blank."

Shortly afterward the man went to the police, who located his wife and family. He still could not remember the events of the past twenty years of his life. Gradually his memory returned, and he wrote a book about his experiences, but he never learned what caused the amnesia.

Brain Injury   Sometimes amnesia results from a blow to the head or an injury to the brain. Often when people are knocked unconscious, they fail to remember the blow that did it and also the events occurring just before the blow. Memory for these prior events usually recovers fairly quickly following the return of consciousness, but a memory failure for the events of the few seconds preceding the loss of consciousness may last even after recovery from the head injury. One patient suffered severe memory loss following a brain operation.

He could no longer recognize the hospital staff, apart from Dr. Scovill himself, whom he had known for many years; he did not remember and could not re-learn the way to the bathroom, and he seemed to retain nothing of the day-to-day happenings in the hospital. . . . The same forgetfulness applies to people he has met since the operation, even to those neighbors who have been visiting the house regularly for the past six years. He has not learned their names, and he does not recognize any of them if he meets them in the street.

This patient experienced amnesia for events preceding the operation and in addition was unable to retain new information in memory after the operation.

The Case of the Anxious College Student   Occasionally amnesia has an emotional origin. To experience severe loss of memory can be a defense against unbearable anxiety. If you lose all memory of your identity, you start anew, with no painful conflicts. The case of G. R. is an example of amnesia with a psychological origin:

Mr. G. R. was a twenty-four-year-old college student. He was the only son of an extremely ambitious father who was a very successful engineer. His mother was perfectionistic, obsessional, and domineering. The young man was in his third year of university study, struggling to get through a pre-engineering course, in which he was not in the slightest bit interested. However, he felt he had to continue, largely as a result of irresistible parental pressure. He had already failed one year in this course.

His third year was further complicated by the fact that he had made a marriage which had been kept secret, in as far as his parents were concerned. . . .

The marriage had involved emotional and time demands, which had still further interfered with his college performance. He had become extremely anxious about the probable results of examinations, which were due to begin in a few weeks' time. One Friday afternoon, after classes, he took part in a "bull session" in the college dormitory. This left him thoroughly convinced that he would not be able to pass his examinations. This served as the precipitating event.

He started for home, but did not arrive there. Late that evening he was found wandering in the streets of a city some two hundred miles away from the site of his college.

The loss of personal identity is a terrible price to pay for the relief from anxiety. People suffering from anxiety-induced amnesia typically recover from their amnesia and are able to develop less destructive solutions to their conflicts. A trained psychotherapist can sometimes help with this transition.

Interim Summary

Two theories that explain forgetting are the decay theory and the interference theory. According to the decay theory, people forget because memories fade or decay over time. According to the interference theory, people forget because one memory has been interfered with by other memories. This interference can be either proactive (from older memories) or retroactive (from newer memories). Forgetting can also be due to repression, a defensive process in which painful memories are blocked from consciousness. Amnesia is a loss of memory for past events or personal identity resulting from a brain injury or from emotional distress.

Improving Your Memory

The challenge of how to improve your memory is an old one. The Greeks invented the "art of memory," creating memory systems by which memory could be improved. Since that time innumerable systems have been invented, most of which depend upon the **principle of orderly association:** Items to be remembered are paired with concrete and orderly images. This is a technique for producing a greater depth of processing through elaborative rehearsal. New items to be remembered are matched up with old images already familiar. The set of old images serves as a retrieval aid for the new material:

For one system, you must learn the following rhyme:

> One is a bun,
> Two is a shoe,
> Three is a tree,
> Four is a door,
> Five is a hive,
> Six is sticks,

Seven is heaven,
Eight is a gate,
Nine is wine, and
Ten is a hen.

The rhyme matches a specific image of an object with each number. When you have learned this system, you are able to remember a list of words by combining and associating the words to be remembered with the image from the rhyme. For example, if the first word to be remembered is "wheel," you might imagine a bun with wheels on it speeding around a track. If the second word is "flower," you might imagine a flower growing out of a shoe. The system has been shown to improve memory dramatically. Why don't you try it?

Another popular memory system, using the principle of orderly association, involves imagining items to be remembered in different places. The Russian psychologist Luria studied a man, S., with a photographic memory (mentioned earlier) who went on to become a professional entertainer specializing in feats of memory. One of his techniques for remembering lists of words was to distribute images of them along some roadway or street he visualized in his mind. When it came time to remember the words, he would imagine himself walking along the roadway looking for words. On the rare occasion when S. made an error, it was often attributable to some difficulty in the placement of the word.

> I put the image of the *pencil* near a fence . . . the one down the street, you know. But what happened was that the image fused with that of the fence and I walked right on past without noticing it. The same thing happened with the word *egg*. I had put it up against a white wall and it blended in with the background. How could I possibly spot a white egg up against a white wall?

You will not develop the fantastic ability of S. for memorizing material, but your memory can be improved by using the principle of orderly association.

Summary

1. Memory requires three important processes: encoding, storage, and retrieval.

2. Encoding involves putting information into memory by changing the physical energies in the world into memory codes that can be retained.

3. Storage is the process of retaining information over time. Memory storage is organized, with similar items linked by association.

4. Retrieval refers to the process of getting at the stored information so that it can be used.

Source: From *Introductory Psychology* by Morris K. Holland. Copyright © 1981 by D. C. Heath and Company. Used by permission of Houghton Mifflin Company.

5. Photographic memory—or eidetic imagery—is a rare ability to remember in great detail whole scenes or pages from books that were seen once.

6. Memories appear not to be located in one spot in the brain but instead to be widespread throughout the cortex.

7. According to the duplex theory of memory, there are two memory systems for storing information—short-term memory and long-term memory.

8. Short-term memory appears to hold information for just a brief time—up to about thirty seconds—and has a very limited capacity. Long-term memory holds material for much longer periods—sometimes for a lifetime—and has an essentially unlimited storage capacity.

9. According to the levels-of-processing theory of memory, memory is limited because of the fact that some information is processed at only a "shallow" level, perhaps through rote rehearsal. Retention is much better for material processed at deeper levels, through elaborative rehearsal.

10. The duplicative theory of memory proposes a relatively exact storage system, while the reconstructive theory of memory proposes that remembering involves imaginative reconstructions of past experience.

11. Three measures of forgetting are the recall method, the recognition method, and the relearning method.

12. Two general explanations have been proposed to account for why people forget: the decay theory and the interference theory.

Vocabulary Exercises

Part I

Directions: The lists that follow contain words used in the preceding selection. Make vocabulary cards for each unfamiliar word using the procedures outlined in Chapter 6. For the content-specific terms, you might also want to refresh your memory about how to do concept cards, which will prove very helpful as you study for the exam on this selection. The procedure for making concept cards is in Chapter 10.

Content-Specific Terms

encoding   274
storage   275
chunking   275
retrieval   276
tip-of-the-tongue phenomenon   276
eidetic imagery   277
engram   279
RNA   280

duplex theory of memory   281
short-term memory   281
long-term memory   281
levels-of-processing theory   282
"shallow" levels   282
"deep" levels   282
maintenance rehearsal   282
elaborative rehearsal   283

General Words

Part II

Directions: After you have completed your vocabulary cards, use an organizational activity to group similar words together. For example, you could group together all terms that are associated with the *duplex theory of memory* or all words that are in some way associated with *forgetting*. Once you group the words together, they will be much easier to learn as one *chunk* of information rather than as disconnected pieces.

Part III

Directions: After you have rehearsed the words using the methods outlined in Chapters 6 and 10, do the following application exercise. If you do well on this activity, you should have learned many of the key concepts presented in "The Psychology of Memory."

Application Exercise

1. When you engage in **elaborative rehearsal** you _____

   _____.

2. An example of a **nonsense syllable** would be _____

   _____.

3. An example of **chunking** would be _____

   _____.

4. You would want to process information **deeply** when _____

   _____.

5. It would be okay to process information at a **shallow** level when _____

   _____.

6. An example of the **principle of orderly association** would be _____

   _____.

7. **Proactive interference** might occur if _____

   _____.

8. **Retroactive interference** might occur if _____

   _____.

9. The major difference between the **duplex theory of memory** and the **levels-of-processing theory of memory** is _____

   _____.

10. **Short-term memory** is useful when _____

    _____.

11. **Long-term memory** must be used when you _____

    _____.

12. If you could form **eidetic images,** you could _____

    _____.

13. When you can't **retrieve** something _____

    _____.

14. An example of a **recognition** task would be _____

    _____.

15. An example of a **recall** task would be _____

    _____.

16. When you **encode** information you _____

    _____.

17. When memories **decay** they _____

    _____.

18. The major difference between the **duplicative theory of memory** and the **reconstructive theory of memory** is that _____

    _____.

19. The **serial-position effect** occurs when _____

_____.

20. Researchers have searched for an **engram** because _____

_____.

21. **Storage** is important to the memory process because _____

_____.

22. **Amnesia** occurs when _____

_____.

23. You might **repress** a memory because _____

_____.

24. You might use **maintenance rehearsal** if _____

_____.

Application Exercises
for "The Psychology of Memory"

1. Engage in Before-reading strategies. Activate your prior knowledge on memory by asking yourself questions. Then preview the selection. What is the overall focus? Use the headings and subheadings, the questions at the beginning of the chapter, and the interim summaries to guide your previewing.

2. Make a skeletal map of the selection's major concepts. Then formulate several questions (be sure to formulate some higher-level questions) to help guide your reading.

3. Read and annotate the selection. Make sure that your annotations show relationships among ideas and that you annotate examples when appropriate.

4. Construct concept cards (see the vocabulary exercise) for the key terms. Include examples on your concept cards.

5. Construct a map that focuses on the memory processes. (*Hint:* There are three memory processes—encoding, storage, and retrieval.)

6. Make a chart that contrasts the three different measures of forgetting.

7. On a 3×5 card, list all of the key concepts that you need to know for this selection. Do several talk-throughs, either alone or with a study partner.

8. Use **PLAE** to devise a study plan for the selection. Be specific in your planning, and allow enough time to review and to complete several talk-throughs.

9. Using the **PORPE** procedure, predict and answer two essay questions. Practice writing out the answers without looking at your rehearsal strategies.

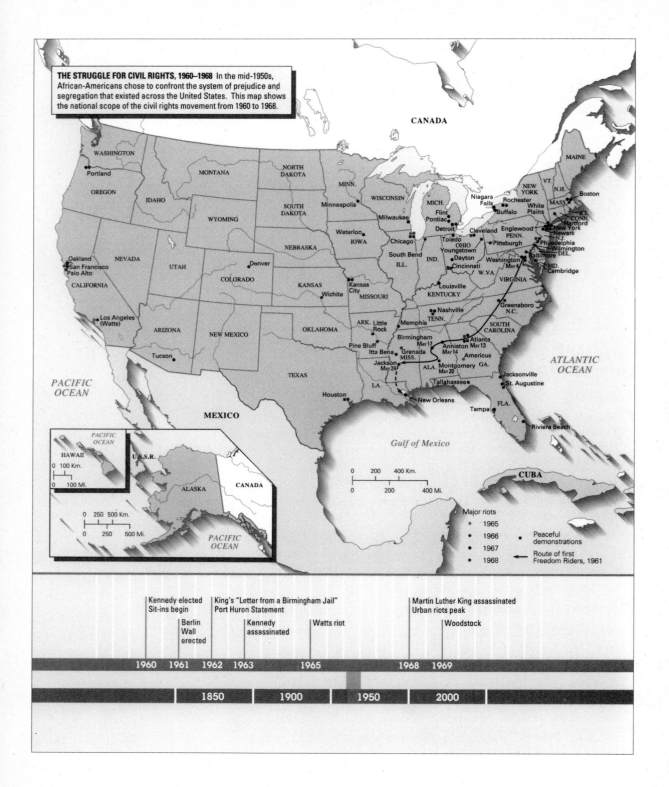

THE STRUGGLE FOR CIVIL RIGHTS, 1960–1968 In the mid-1950s, African-Americans chose to confront the system of prejudice and segregation that existed across the United States. This map shows the national scope of the civil rights movement from 1960 to 1968.

CANADA

WASHINGTON

OREGON

Portland

IDAHO

MONTANA

NORTH DAKOTA

SOUTH DAKOTA

WYOMING

NEBRASKA

MINN.

Minneapolis

WISCONSIN

MICH.

MAINE

N.H.

VT.

NEW YORK

Niagara Falls

Rochester

Buffalo

White Plains

MASS.

Boston

CONN.

Hartford

R.I.

Milwaukee

Flint

Pontiac

Detroit

Cleveland

Englewood

New York

Newark

N.J.

PENN.

NEVADA

UTAH

COLORADO

KANSAS

Denver

Oakland
San Francisco
Palo Alto

CALIFORNIA

Los Angeles (Watts)

ARIZONA

NEW MEXICO

Tucson

Waterloo

IOWA

Chicago

South Bend

IND.

ILL.

OHIO

Toledo

Youngstown

Dayton

Cincinnati

Pittsburgh

Philadelphia

Wilmington

DEL.

Baltimore

MD.

Washington
MAY 4

Cambridge

W.VA.

VIRGINIA

Louisville

KENTUCKY

Kansas City

Wichita

MISSOURI

OKLAHOMA

ARK.

Little Rock

Memphis

TENN.

Nashville

Greensboro N.C.

SOUTH CAROLINA

Birmingham
MAY 17

Pine Bluff

Itta Bena

Grenada
MISS.

Jackson
MAY 24

ALA.

Anniston MAY 13

Montgomery
MAY 20

Atlanta

MAY 14

Americus

GA.

Jacksonville

St. Augustine

Tallahassee

ATLANTIC OCEAN

TEXAS

LA.

Houston

New Orleans

Tampa

FLA.

Riviera Beach

PACIFIC OCEAN

MEXICO

Gulf of Mexico

CUBA

0   200   400 Km.

0   200   400 Mi.

PACIFIC OCEAN

HAWAII

0   100 Km.

0   100 Mi.

U.S.S.R.

ALASKA

CANADA

0   250   500 Km.

0   250   500 Mi.

PACIFIC OCEAN

Major riots

• 1965

• 1966

• 1967

• 1968

■ Peaceful demonstrations

← Route of first Freedom Riders, 1961

Kennedy elected
Sit-ins begin

Berlin Wall erected

King's "Letter from a Birmingham Jail"
Port Huron Statement

Kennedy assassinated

Watts riot

Martin Luther King assassinated
Urban riots peak

Woodstock

| 1960 | 1961 | 1962 | 1963 | 1965 | 1968 | 1969 |

| 1850 | 1900 | 1950 | 2000 |

Great Promises, Bitter Disappointments, 1960–1968

JFK and the New Frontier

- What expectations and constraints did Kennedy face in establishing his domestic New Frontier?
- How did Kennedy's approach to civil rights differ from Eisenhower's?

Flexible Response

- What choices and expectations shaped Kennedy's Cold War foreign policies?
- How did his policies contribute to the Cuban missile crisis?

Beyond the New Frontier

- How did Johnson's Great Society expand on the New Deal?
- How did the outcome of the Great Society's programs contribute to increased disillusionment and social tensions?

Confronting America

- How did the expectations of African-Americans change as the civil rights movement changed from a primarily southern movement confronting legal discrimination to a national movement combating poverty and social prejudice?

Introduction

Expectations
Constraints
Choices
Outcomes

Running for the presidency, John F. Kennedy symbolized a new beginning and promised an interventionist government that many *expected* would provide a better society for all Americans. He energized the nation, raising expectations especially among the poor and minorities that he would press for solutions to end poverty and discrimination. But Kennedy faced political *constraints* in the form of conservatives in Congress who objected to an expansion of liberal programs and civil rights legislation. As a result, during his three years in office

Kennedy achieved only part of his goals. Constrained by Republican and southern Democratic opposition, Kennedy *chose* to delay civil rights legislation and not to press forward with aid to education and health care. The *outcome* was a domestic record of legislation that expanded on existing programs but did not chart new paths of social policy.

Kennedy also vowed to intensify the global struggle against communism, especially in developing nations. To defeat communism, Kennedy *chose* to loosen past military budget constraints, funding both an arms race and a space race with the Soviet Union. Yet, despite Kennedy's vigor and emphasis on winning the Cold War, the *outcome* was not a safer and less divided world. The erection of the Berlin Wall, the Cuban missile crisis, and events in Vietnam symbolized heightened tension.

Building on Kennedy's legacy, Lyndon Johnson *chose* to create the largest expansion of New Deal–style legislation since the Depression. Johnson's Great Society waged a war on poverty and discrimination, promoted education, and created a national system of health care for the aged and poor. But Johnson also faced *constraints*. Conservatives opposed the Great Society's social and political goals, while some moderates and even a few liberals objected to its cost and the ineffectiveness of many programs. An expanding and increasingly unpopular war in Vietnam also added *constraints* to Johnson's domestic program and power as president.

By 1968, growing social and political turmoil was contributing to the rejection of liberal policies. The optimistic *expectations* Kennedy had inspired were declining amid the apparent divisions and excesses of American society. Within the civil rights movement, Black Power leaders *chose* confrontation over compromise. Urban riots and violence drove wedges between African-American leaders and some white supporters. The emergence of a youth-centered counterculture that *chose* to reject traditional social and moral values and stressed personal freedoms also worked to fragment American society. The *outcome* was that a decade that began with great optimism ended much differently. By 1968, few Americans *expected* that the federal government could ensure a positive future.

JFK and the New Frontier

- What expectations and constraints did Kennedy face in establishing his domestic New Frontier?
- How did Kennedy's approach to civil rights differ from Eisenhower's?

Republicans had every reason to worry as the 1960 presidential campaign neared. The last years of the 1950s had not been kind to the Republican party. The Cold War seemed to be going badly as the Soviets downed an American spy plane over the Soviet Union, launched *Sputnik* into space, and supported Castro in Cuba. Domestically, there seemed little or no direction from the White House or from Republicans in Congress to deal with the problems of

New Frontiers

1960 Kennedy elected president
Sit-ins begin
Boynton v. Virginia
Birth-control pill marketed

1961 Bay of Pigs invasion
Alliance for Progress
Peace Corps formed
Berlin Wall erected
Vienna summit
Shepard rides *Mercury*
    capsule into space
Freedom rides begin
SNCC formed

1962 *Baker v. Carr*
Engle v. Vitale
Glenn orbits Earth
Cuban missile crisis
Meredith enrolls at the
    University of Mississippi
King's "Letter from a
    Birmingham Jail"
SDS's Port Huron
    Statement
Harrington's *The Other
    America*

1963 Limited Test Ban Treaty
Kennedy assassinated;
    Johnson becomes
    president
Gideon v. Wainright
March on Washington
Equal Pay Act
Diem assassinated

1964 Civil Rights Act
Freedom Summer in
    Mississippi
War on Poverty begins
Economic Opportunity Act
Johnson elected president
Escobedo v. Illinois
Griswold v. Connecticut
Berkeley Free Speech
    Movement

1965 Malcom X assassinated
Watts riot
Selma march
Voting Rights Act
Medicaid and Medicare
Elementary and Secondary
    Education Act
Immigration Act

1966 Carmichael announces
    Black Power
Black Panther party formed
Model Cities Act
Miranda v. Arizona

1967 Ginsberg organizes first
    "be-in"
Urban riots in one hundred
    twenty-seven cities

1968 Martin Luther King, Jr.,
    assassinated
Urban riots in one hundred
    sixty-eight cities
Kerner Commission Report
Vietnam peace talks begin
    in Paris
Fair Housing Act

the country: civil rights, a weak economy that in 1960 tumbled into another recession, and a soaring national debt that had reached $488 billion by 1960. Democratic victories in the congressional elections of 1958 signaled that Democrats were again the majority, if not the dominant, party. Vice President Richard Nixon speculated that for a Republican presidential victory to occur, the "candidate would have to get practically all Republican votes, more than half of the independents—and, in addition, the votes of 5 to 6 million Democrats." A Republican victory would have been difficult even for Eisenhower, whose health and age, and the **Twenty-second Amendment,** prevented him from running for a third term.

On the Democratic side loomed **John Fitzgerald Kennedy,** a youthful, vigorous senator from Massachusetts who had run a successful primary campaign—beating Hubert Humphrey and Lyndon B. Johnson—and gained a first ballot nomination. Kennedy, a Harvard graduate, came from a wealthy, Catholic, Massachusetts family. Some worried about his young age (43) and lack of experience, and others worried about his religion—no Catholic had ever been elected president. To lessen these possible liabilities, Kennedy had astutely added the politically savvy Senate majority leader **Lyndon Baines Johnson** of Texas to the ticket, called for a new generation of leadership, and emphasized that those who were making religion an issue were bigots. Drawing on the legacy of Franklin Roosevelt, he challenged the nation to enter a **New Frontier,** to improve the overall quality of life of all Americans, and to reenergize American foreign policy to stand fast against the Communist threat.

Facing Kennedy was Eisenhower's vice president, Richard M. Nixon. Trying to distance himself from the image of Eisenhower's elderly leadership, Nixon promised a forceful, energetic presidency and emphasized his executive experience and history of anticommunism. He, too, promised to improve the quality of life, support civil rights, and defeat international communism. Several political commentators called the candidates "two peas in a pod" and speculated that the election would probably hinge on appearances more than issues.

Trailing in the opinion polls and hoping to give his campaign a boost, Nixon agreed to televised debates with Kennedy. He was proud of his debating skills and thought he could adapt them successfully to radio and television. Kennedy seized the opportunity, recognizing that the candidate who appeared more calm and knowledgeable—more "presidential"—would "win" the debate. Before the camera's eye, in the war of images, Nixon made a poor impression. Having been ill, he appeared tired and haggard. He looked at Kennedy and not the camera whenever answering questions—a good debating technique but a disastrous television tactic. Worst of all, he seemed to sweat. In contrast, Kennedy

Twenty-second Amendment   Amendment to the Constitution in 1951 that limited presidents to two terms in office.

John Fitzgerald Kennedy   Massachusetts senator elected president in 1960, who established the Peace Corps and forced Khrushchev to remove Soviet missiles from Cuba; he was assassinated in 1963.

Lyndon Baines Johnson   Senate majority leader who became Kennedy's vice president in 1961, and president when Kennedy was assassinated in 1963.

New Frontier   Program for social and educational reform put forward by John F. Kennedy; though charismatically presented, it was resisted by Congress.

appeared fresh and confident, facing the television camera and the television audience while speaking. The differences in appearance were critical. Unable to see Nixon, the radio audience believed he won the debates, but to the 70 million television viewers the winner was the self-assured and sweat-free Kennedy.

The televised debates helped Kennedy, but victory rested in his ability to hold the Democratic coalition together, maintaining southern Democratic support while wooing African-American and liberal voters. The Texan Johnson used his political clout to keep the South largely loyal even as Kennedy blasted the lack of Republican leadership on civil rights. Martin Luther King, Jr., had been arrested for civil rights activities in Atlanta, and in a grand gesture, Kennedy telephoned Coretta Scott King to express his concern about her husband's jailing. Kennedy's brother Robert used his influence to get King freed, convincing even the staunchest Protestant black ministers, including Martin Luther King, Sr., to overlook Kennedy's religion and endorse him—and every vote was critical. When the ballots were counted, Kennedy had scored the narrowest of victories. Nixon had carried more states, 25 to 21, but Kennedy had a narrow margin over Nixon in popular votes and had won the electoral count, 303 to 219. (The independent southern candidate Harry Byrd earned 15 electoral votes.) Despite voting irregularities in Chicago, Illinois, and Texas, Nixon did not contest the election (see Map 29.1).

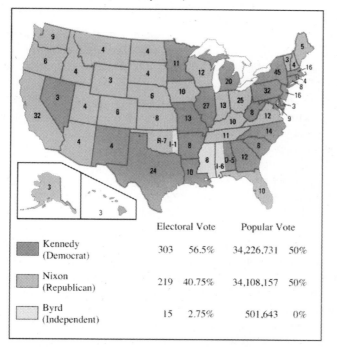

		Electoral Vote		Popular Vote	
Kennedy (Democrat)		303	56.5%	34,226,731	50%
Nixon (Republican)		219	40.75%	34,108,157	50%
Byrd (Independent)		15	2.75%	501,643	0%

MAP 29.1 Election of 1960 Although Richard Nixon won in more states than John F. Kennedy in the closest presidential election in the twentieth century, Kennedy defeated his Republican opponent by a slim eighty-four electoral votes and fewer than nineteen thousand popular votes.

The New Frontier

The weather in Washington was frigid when Kennedy gave his inaugural address, but his speech fired the imagination of the nation. Speaking in idealistic terms, avoiding any mention of specific programs, he promised to march against "the common enemies of man: tyranny, poverty, disease, and war itself." He asked all Americans to participate, exhorting them to "ask not what your country can do for you—ask what you can do for your country."

Kennedy's staff and cabinet kept up the image of change and activism. Recruiting from businesses and universities, he appointed men and women whom one reporter dubbed the "best and the brightest." Rhodes scholars and Harvard professors were prominent, including historian Arthur Schlesinger, economist John Kenneth Galbraith (both personal advisers), McGeorge Bundy (national security director), and Dean Rusk (secretary of state). Ford Motor Company's president, Robert McNamara, was tapped for secretary of defense. In a controversial move, Kennedy gave the position of attorney general to his younger brother Robert. John Kennedy praised his choices as men with "know-how," experienced in solving problems. Not everyone, however, was convinced. Referring to the lack of political background among appointees, Speaker of the House Sam Rayburn remarked that he would "feel a whole lot better . . . if just one of them had run for sheriff once."

Rayburn had noted a critical point. Kennedy and his staff wanted to be activists, leading the nation along new paths of liberalism, but Congress was likely to be an obstacle. Democrats had lost twenty-one seats in the House in the 1960 election and since 1937 many congressional Democrats had voted with Republicans to prevent any notable expansion of the New Deal. It would be "very difficult" to pass controversial legislation, Kennedy told his staff, and so he decided to delay civil rights and social legislation and instead concentrate on shaping foreign policy and improving the economy.

To spur economic recovery, Kennedy turned to "new economics" as advocated by Walter Heller, his chairman of the Council of Economic Advisers, and called for more government spending and business and income-tax cuts. The defense budget was the first beneficiary, growing by almost 20 percent ($6 billion). Kennedy also asked Congress for a modest domestic program that included increases in social security coverage and benefits and in the minimum wage, an extension of unemployment insurance, a housing and **urban renewal** bill, and aid to education. By the autumn of 1961, Congress had passed all but the education bill and tax cuts. Meanwhile, the economy was also rebounding from the "Eisenhower recession" as unemployment fell by 2 percent from a 1960 high of 7 percent.

The booming economy, however, created a new problem: inflation. Fearful of slowing economic growth, Kennedy established informal price and wage guidelines for businesses and labor unions. Most accepted the president's for-

---

urban renewal   Effort to revitalize rundown city centers by providing federal funding for the construction of apartment houses, office buildings, and public facilities.

mulas, but in early 1962 United States Steel and a few other steel makers raised their prices above Kennedy's ceiling. He took it as a personal insult and lashed out at U.S. Steel. Announcing that the new price was not in the public interest, he told the Federal Trade Commission and FBI to investigate the steel maker for possible **price fixing** and other fraudulent business practices, and he threatened to reduce its government contracts. Facing an angry president and being undersold by other steel companies, Roger Blough, president of U.S. Steel, retreated and lowered prices. Kennedy gloried in the victory but allowed steel prices to rise the following year. As 1962 ended, the White House boasted that the economy was strong and that forty of fifty-four bills had been passed in the first 170 days of Kennedy's administration. When liberals complained about the lack of civil rights legislation and new social programs, Kennedy hid behind the Republican–southern/conservative Democratic coalition. "There is no sense in raising hell and then not being successful," he told them. He promised a liberal package for 1963 and 1964, including a civil rights bill and programs to attack poverty.

Civil Rights and the Kennedys

During the campaign, Kennedy had promised a "moral leadership" and executive action in support of civil rights, and African-American leaders looked forward to a more interventionist federal government. But once in office, Kennedy moved cautiously. He did appoint several blacks to high office and district courts, including Thurgood Marshall to the United States Circuit Court, but civil rights advocates were far from satisfied. They noted that several of his judicial appointments went to recognized segregationists, including Harold Cox of Mississippi, who once, in court, had referred to African-Americans as "niggers" and "chimpanzees," and that there was no immediate civil rights legislation. Despite his campaign pledge to do so immediately, Kennedy did not lift his pen to ban segregation in federal housing until November 1962, and a civil rights bill was not forthcoming until 1963. But civil rights activism was a grass roots movement, not a product of federal action, and activists continued to confront segregation. They resolved, if necessary, to force governmental action.

Even as Kennedy assumed office, a new wave of black activism was striking at segregation in the South in the form of **sit-ins** and boycotts. The sit-ins began when four freshmen at Carolina A&T in Greensboro, North Carolina, decided to integrate the public lunch counter at the local Woolworth's store. On February 1, 1960, they entered the store, sat down at the counter, and ordered a meal. A black waitress told them she could not serve them, but still they sat and waited for service. Soon, people were passing by, hurling insults or giving

price fixing   Illegal mutual agreements among competing firms to hold prices at a certain level; the price is usually somewhat inflated so that all firms will make larger profits.

sit-in   The act of occupying the seats or an area of a segregated establishment to protest racial discrimination.

encouragement, but no one tried to remove or arrest them. When the store closed, they were unserved but energized by their confrontation with segregation. They returned to campus as heroes and the next day twenty A&T students sat at the lunchcounter demanding service. By the end of the week, similar sit-ins had spread throughout the South.

Begun by students, the sit-ins remained largely a student movement supported by the more established civil rights groups, especially the Congress of Racial Equality (CORE) and King's Southern Christian Leadership Conference (SCLC). In April 1961, the **Student Nonviolent Coordinating Committee (SNCC, "snick")** was formed to coordinate the dramatically increasing sit-in activities as the number of sit-ins and boycotts of stores, recreational facilities, libraries, bus and train stations, and lunchrooms that segregated or refused to serve African-Americans increased. Over seventy thousand people protested for integrated public facilities in more than one hundred forty cities, including some outside the South, in Nevada, Illinois, and Ohio. Many of those participating in demonstrations were like [author] Alice Walker, young college students. In some cities, including Greensboro, equal service was achieved with a minimum of resistance, but particularly in the deep South, whites resisted violently to protect segregation. In Orangeburg, South Carolina, protesters were blasted with high-pressure fire hoses and arrested. Overall, thousands of "sit-in-ers" were beaten and jailed, but many saw jail as just another place to protest. CORE leader Thomas Gaither called for a "jail-in."

Sharing headlines with those "sitting-in" were the **freedom riders.** Prior to Kennedy taking office, the Supreme Court had ruled in *Boynton v. Virginia* that all interstate buses, trains, and terminals be desegregated. CORE's James Farmer planned a series of "freedom rides" to force integration on southern bus lines and stations. Farmer knew that riders would meet with opposition, creating a crisis and putting pressure on the executive branch to uphold the Court's decision. The first buses of freedom riders left Washington, D.C., in May 1961, headed toward Alabama and Mississippi. The freedom riders expected trouble. Governor John Patterson of Alabama had announced that integration would come only over his "dead body." In Anniston, Alabama, a mob of angry whites attacked the buses, smashing their windows and setting them on fire and severely beating several freedom riders. The savagery continued at Birmingham, with one freedom rider needing 53 stitches to close his head wound. When asked why no police were at the station to protect the riders, the Birmingham public safety commissioner Eugene "Bull" Connor explained that it was a holiday—Mother's Day.

As Farmer had predicted, the violence forced the federal government to respond. Hoping to avoid further bloodshed, Justice Department official John

Student Nonviolent Coordinating Committee   Organization formed to give young blacks a greater voice in the civil rights movement; it initiated black voter registration drives and freedom rides.

freedom riders   Civil rights protesters who rode buses throughout the South in 1961 to press for integration in bus terminals.

Seigenthaler obtained state and local protection for the riders through Alabama. But as the buses approached Montgomery, the police and National Guard escorts mysteriously vanished, leaving the freedom riders to face a large and violent crowd alone. "There are no cops," John Doar of the Justice Department phoned Robert Kennedy. "It's terrible." The brutal attack left many freedom riders injured, including federal agent Seigenthaler, who was beaten unconscious when he rushed to help a female rider. After an hour of terror, the police finally arrived and restored order.

A livid attorney general deputized local federal officials as marshals and ordered them to escort the freedom riders to the state line, where Mississippi forces would take over. Battered and bloodied, the riders continued to the state capital, Jackson. There they were peacefully arrested for violating Mississippi's recently passed **public order laws.** The jails quickly filled as more freedom riders arrived and were arrested. The nation waited for the administration to act. Finally, in September 1961, the Interstate Commerce Commission declared it would uphold the Court's decision prohibiting segregation. Faced with direct federal involvement, most state and local authorities grudgingly accepted the desegregation of bus and train terminals.

A year later **James Meredith** integrated the University of Mississippi. Meredith, an air force veteran and student at a black college, heard Kennedy's inaugural speech and decided to transfer to Mississippi, knowing that Governor Ross Barnett had vowed to go to jail before allowing blacks to enroll. Robert Kennedy sent five hundred federal marshals to guard Meredith, hoping a show of force would prevent violence. The tactic did not work. Thousands of white students and nonstudents attacked Meredith and the marshals. Two people were killed and 166 marshals were wounded before 5,000 army troops arrived and restored order. Protected by federal forces, Meredith finished the year, and in May, the University of Mississippi had its first African-American graduate.

"Old Miss" was but one victory as the sit-ins and boycotts continued. Martin Luther King, Jr., and the SCLC focused their attention on overturning segregation in Birmingham, Alabama. The civil rights movement must go forward or die, King told reporters, and Birmingham was the "point of no return." Organizers pushed an economic boycott of stores and planned a series of protest marches demanding the integration of Birmingham's businesses. King also expected a violent white reaction to force federal intervention and raise national support. On Good Friday, 1963, he led the first march and along with others was quickly arrested. From his cell, using smuggled paper and pen, he wrote a nineteen-page "letter" defending his confrontational tactics and aimed at those who denounced his activism in favor of patience. The "Letter from a

public order laws   Laws passed by many southern communities to discourage civil rights protests; they allowed the police to arrest anyone suspected of intending to disrupt public order.

James Meredith   Black student admitted to University of Mississippi under federal court order in 1962; in spite of rioting by racist mobs, he finished the year and graduated in 1963.

Birmingham Jail" called for immediate and continuous, peaceful civil disobedience. Freedom was "never given voluntarily by the oppressor," King asserted, but "must be demanded by the oppressed." Smuggled out of jail and read aloud in churches and printed in newspapers across the nation, the letter rallied support for King's efforts in Birmingham.

On May 3, young and old alike filled the streets of Birmingham and confronted "Bull" Connor's police, who attacked the marchers with nightsticks, attack dogs, and high-pressure fire hoses. Television caught it all, including the arrest of over 1,300 battered and bruised children. Connor's brutality not only horrified much of the American public but caused many Birmingham blacks to reject the tactic of **nonviolence.** To many it appeared that the South was teetering on the verge of a race war, as on the following day, many African-Americans fought the police with stones and clubs. Fearing more violence, King and Birmingham's business element met on May 10, 1963, and white business owners agreed to hire black salespeople. Neither the agreement nor King's pleading, however, halted the violence, and two days later President Kennedy ordered three thousand troops to Birmingham to maintain order and to uphold the integration agreement. Reflecting on the outcomes, King observed, "The sound of the explosion in Birmingham reached all the way to Washington."

Indeed, the sound had reached the White House and helped Kennedy conclude that the time had come to fulfill his campaign promise to make civil rights a priority. In June 1963, speaking to Congress and the nation, he made civil rights an immediate moral issue. In strong words, he announced that America could not be truly free "until all its citizens were free" and that he would send Congress civil rights legislation that would mandate integration in places of public accommodation. The speech did little to convince Congress to pass the civil rights bill, however. To pressure Congress to act on the bill, King and other civil rights leaders organized a march on Washington.

The August 28 **March on Washington** exceeded all expectations. It was the largest crowd to assemble in American history, with over 250,000 people. King capped the day with an address that electrified the throng. He promised to continue the struggle until justice flowed "like a mighty stream," and he warned about a "whirlwind of revolt" if black rights were denied. "I have a dream," he offered, "that even Mississippi could become an oasis of freedom and justice" and that "all of God's children, black men and white men, Jews and Gentiles, Protestants and Catholics, will be able to join hands and sing . . . 'Free at last! Free at last! Thank God almighty, we are free at last!'"

Nationally, the march and reactions to white violence against African-Americans worked in favor of civil rights legislation. The civil rights bill cleared the House Judiciary Committee with bipartisan support and by No-

nonviolence   Doctrine of rejecting violence in favor of peaceful tactics as a means of gaining political objectives.

March on Washington   Meeting of a quarter of a million civil rights supporters in Washington in 1963, at which Martin Luther King, Jr., delivered his "I Have a Dream" speech.

vember, as Kennedy left for a campaign trip to Dallas, it was near passage in the House of Representatives. But the massive outpouring of support for civil rights did not translate into a better climate in the South. Within weeks of King's "I Have a Dream" speech, four young girls attending Sunday School died when their Birmingham church was bombed. Civil rights advocates had few illusions. Civil rights laws would help give African-Americans legal protection on paper, but it would not shield them from racial hatred and violence.

Flexible Response

- What choices and expectations shaped Kennedy's Cold War foreign policies?
- How did his policies contribute to the Cuban missile crisis?

If Kennedy was slow to bring federal power to bear on civil rights, he, like Eisenhower, had no reluctance to use executive power when it came to foreign policy—and like Franklin Roosevelt, he intended to direct foreign policy from the White House. He wanted to make a difference and do it quickly. "Let's not worry about four years from now," he told his advisers. "What do we do tomorrow?" To accomplish his activist goals, Kennedy relied on a circle of close advisers, principally Robert Kennedy, McGeorge Bundy, Robert McNamara, and Walter Rostow—"action intellectuals" who were willing to take risks to meet whatever challenges the United States faced, from the arms race, to the space race, to winning the allegiance of Third World countries.

To back up his foreign policies, Kennedy released the military from budget constraints imposed by Eisenhower. Military spending should not be "bound by arbitrary budget ceilings," Kennedy told Congress. Quickly, the Pentagon began a build-up of both nuclear and conventional forces. Space exploration also received a new priority. The United States seemed to have fallen alarmingly behind in the so-called **space race** when, in April 1961, the Soviets hurled the first human being, **cosmonaut** Yuri Gagarin, into space. The American Mercury program, also designed to send an astronaut into space, had suffered several setbacks. Therefore, Kennedy informed Congress, immediate funding was needed not only to catch up with the Soviets but to beat them to the moon by the end of the decade. Congress agreed and funded the Apollo project, which reached its goal in 1969.

But the country's Cold War challenges were not limited to racing against Soviet arms development and space exploration. An equally important confrontation had been shaping up in the developing regions of the globe. In the

space race Competition between the United States and the USSR to develop space technology; the Soviets launched the first manned space flight in 1961, but in 1969 the United States put the first man on the moon.

cosmonaut A Soviet astronaut.

Third World, the key problems remained economic inequalities, nationalism, and revolution. Kennedy focused on two strategies, military and economic, to win the "hearts and minds" of emerging nations. Special military units, like the Green Berets, were trained to deal with insurgency, able to live off the countryside while gaining the people's trust. Working with friendly governmental forces, they would help defeat the anti-American foes and provide stability. A multifaceted economic approach was to include direct governmental aid and increased private investment, along with the personal involvement of American volunteers in the **Peace Corps,** composed mostly of idealistic college-age men and women who were eager to help the people of developing nations.

Latin America posed a special problem. The inability of this region of dominant American influence to develop economically, socially, and politically, and the presence of a Communist regime in Cuba, seemed to many in the world to expose a weakness in the American system. Kennedy intended to deal with both issues. First he would remove Fidel Castro by proceeding with the Eisenhower administration's plans to topple the Cuban leader. In March 1960, the Central Intelligence Agency had begun training Cuban exiles and mercenaries for an invasion of Cuba—Operation Pluto. In January 1961, the newly elected president gave the operation his approval—although there was growing concern that such a raid would not be strong enough to remove Castro.

The invasion of Cuba began on April 17, 1961. Over 1,400 Cuban exiles landed at the **Bay of Pigs,** a swampy area nearly 80 miles from the mountains that were to be their refuge if the attack did not go smoothly. It did not. The predicted uprisings in support of the invaders did not occur, and within three days, Castro's forces had captured or killed most of the invading force. Kennedy took responsibility for the fiasco but indicated no regrets for his aggressive policy and the violation of Cuban territory, vowing to continue the "relentless struggle" against Castro and communism.

To blunt the growing appeal of Castroism, and to show Latin Americans that the United States was still their best and most powerful friend and neighbor, Kennedy announced a sweeping foreign aid package, the **Alliance for Progress.** He proposed over $20 billion in aid to show that "liberty and progress walk hand in hand." In return, Latin American nations were to introduce land and tax reforms and commit themselves to improving education and their overall standard of living. Action fell short of promises. The United States granted far less than proposed, and Latin American governments implemented few reforms and frequently squandered the aid, much of which ended up in the

Peace Corps   Program established by President Kennedy in 1961 to send young American volunteers to other nations as educators, health workers, and technicians.

Bay of Pigs   Site of an invasion of Cuba in 1961 by Cuban exiles and mercenaries sponsored by the CIA, which was crushed within three days and which embarrassed the United States.

Alliance for Progress   Program proposed by Kennedy in 1961, through which the United States provided aid for social and economic programs in Latin American countries.

pockets of government officials. Throughout the 1960s in Latin America, the gap between rich and poor widened as did the number of military dictatorships.

To try to recapture some of the "can-do" image deflated by the Bay of Pigs disaster, Kennedy sought an opportunity to stand toe to toe with the Soviets. Soviet leader Nikita Khrushchev and Kennedy, wanting to test each other's mettle, agreed to meet in Vienna in early June 1961 to discuss Berlin, Laos, and a nuclear test ban treaty. The results of their talks were mixed. After his first private meeting with the Soviet leader, Kennedy was shaken and angry. He thought that Khrushchev had bullied him and that his response had been feeble. In following meetings, Kennedy stood his ground more firmly, stressing that the United States would remain true to its international commitments, especially in Berlin. Khrushchev was unmoved and maintained a December deadline for Allied withdrawal from Berlin.

Returning home, determined not to appear weak under increasing Soviet pressure against Berlin, Kennedy asked for large increases in military spending and called 51,000 reservists to active duty. Some within the administration advocated the use of force if the East Germans or the Soviets interfered with Western access to or control of West Berlin. Meanwhile Khrushchev, appearing in military uniform, bellicosely reaffirmed Moscow's commitment to wars of national liberation, and he renewed atmospheric atomic bomb testing. American testing started shortly thereafter. To some it appeared that Kennedy and Khrushchev were moving to the brink of war over Berlin.

In August, the Soviets and East Germans added a new point of confrontation by erecting a wall between West and East Berlin to choke off the flow of refugees fleeing East Germany and Eastern Europe. Although the Wall challenged Western ideals of freedom, it did not directly threaten the West's presence in West Berlin and so required no military response by the United States. When Khrushchev announced that he no longer cared about the December deadline, the crisis faded, leaving only the Wall—and those who died trying to cross it—as a stark reminder of where Soviet and American interests collided.

Far more serious than the Berlin crisis was the possibility of nuclear confrontation over Cuba in October of 1962. On October 14, an American U-2 spy plane flying over the island discovered that medium-range nuclear missile sites were being built there. Launched from Cuba, such missiles would drastically reduce the time the United States had to launch a counterattack on the Soviet Union. Clearly, the missiles in Cuba were unacceptable to Kennedy, who decided on a showdown with the Soviets and organized a small crisis staff.

Negotiations were out of the question until the missiles were removed or destroyed. The military offered a series of recommendations ranging from a military invasion to a "surgical" air strike to destroy the missiles. All were rejected as too dangerous, possibly inviting a Soviet attack on West Berlin or American nuclear missile sites in Turkey. President Kennedy, supported by his brother, decided to blockade Cuba until Khrushchev met the U.S. demand to remove the missiles. On Monday, October 22, Kennedy went on television and radio to inform the public of the missiles and his decision to quarantine Cuba. With one hundred eighty American warships ready to stop Soviet ships carrying supplies for the missiles, army units converged on Florida. The **Strategic Air Command** kept a fleet of nuclear-bomb-carrying B-52s in the air at all times. On Wednesday, confrontation, and perhaps war, seemed imminent as two Soviet freighters and a Russian submarine approached the quarantine line. Robert Kennedy recalled, "We were on the edge of a precipice with no way off." His anxiety was echoed around the world.

The Soviet vessels, however, stopped short of the blockade. Khrushchev had decided not to test Kennedy's will. On October 26, he sent a message through NBC's John Scali that the Soviet Union was ready to remove the missiles from Cuba if the United States publicly announced it would not invade the island. Relieved, Robert Kennedy told Scali that the United States and the Soviet Union had stood "eyeball to eyeball" and that the Soviets "had blinked first." More diplomatic maneuvering followed, but the basis of a solution had been found. The United States publicly pledged not to invade Cuba, and Khrushchev ordered the removal of the missiles. In a nonpublicized, separate agreement, the United States also agreed to remove its missiles from Turkey.

Kennedy basked in the victory. In a contest of wills he had bested Khrushchev. But he also recognized how near the world had come to nuclear war and that it was time to improve Soviet-American relations. A "hot line" telephone link was established between Moscow and Washington to allow direct talks in case of another East-West crisis. In a major foreign policy speech in June 1963, Kennedy suggested an end to the Cold War and offered that the United States, as a first step toward improving relations, would halt its nuclear testing. By July, American-Soviet negotiations produced the **Limited Test Ban Treaty,** which forbade those who signed to conduct nuclear tests in the atmosphere, in space, and under the seas. Underground testing, with its verification problems, was still allowed. By October 1963, one hundred nations had signed the treaty, although the two newest atomic powers, France and China, refused to participate and continued to test in the atmosphere.

Vietnam

Berlin, Cuba, and nuclear weapons were not the only hot points. Southeast Asia represented one of the most significant challenges that faced the United States. In early 1961, the major Indochina crisis involved Laos, a small land-locked nation to the west of Vietnam. Communist insurgents, the Pathet Lao, were winning a civil war. Dissuaded by Eisenhower from involving American

Strategic Air Command   Air force agency formed in 1946 to control America's long-range nuclear strike force.

Limited Test Ban Treaty   Treaty signed by the United States, the USSR, and nearly one hundred other nations in 1963, banning nuclear weapons tests in the atmosphere, in outer space, or under water.

troops, Kennedy sought and achieved a diplomatic solution. With Soviet approval, by July 1962, a neutral government was installed in Laos.

Almost immediately Laos was replaced as a trouble spot by South Vietnam. South Vietnamese president **Ngo Dinh Diem** was losing control of his nation. In the countryside, South Vietnamese Communist rebels, the **Viet Cong,** controlled a large portion of both land and people, having battled Diem's troops (the Army of the Republic of Vietnam, or ARVN) to a standstill. Military advisers argued that the use of American troops was necessary to turn the tide. Kennedy was more cautious. "The troops will march in, the bands will play," he said privately, "the crowds will cheer; and in four days everyone will have forgotten. Then we will be told we have to send in more troops. It's like taking a drink. The effect wears off, and you have to take another." The South Vietnamese forces would have to continue to do the fighting, but the president agreed to send more "advisers." By November 1963, the United States had sent $185 million in military aid and had committed 16,000 advisers to Vietnam—compared with only a few hundred in 1961.

The Viet Cong were only part of the problem. Diem's administration was unpopular and out of touch with the majority of South Vietnamese. A Roman Catholic whose family had lived in the north and had been French officials and minor landholders, Diem was no believer in republican forms of government or society. He ruled through a handpicked, largely Catholic, bureaucracy whose loyalty to Diem was the key to advancement. Everywhere there appeared political opposition to his rule, from Buddhists, crime bosses, political reformers, and his own military. With American support and direction, Diem cracked down on his opponents. Reformers, rival officers, and protesting Buddhists were jailed, tortured, and killed. Protesting Diem's rule, on June 10, 1963 a Buddhist monk set himself on fire. Other **self-immolations** followed. To the shock of many Americans, Diem's sister-in-law, Madame Nhu referred to the protests as "Buddhist barbecues" and "the barbecue show." To Kennedy and his advisers, Diem and his inner circle had become liabilities, and the administration secretly informed several Vietnamese generals that it would approve of a change of government. The army acted on November 1, killing Diem and creating a new military government. However, the change of government brought neither political stability nor improvement in the South Vietnamese army's capacity to fight the Viet Cong.

Death in Dallas

In late 1963, with his civil rights bill and $13.5 billion tax cut in limbo in Congress, a mushrooming military commitment in Vietnam, and an economy that

Ngo Dinh Diem   President of South Vietnam in 1954 who jailed and tortured opponents of his rule and who was assassinated in a coup in 1963.

Viet Cong   Vietnamese Communist rebels in South Vietnam.

self-immolation   Suicide by fire as an act of sacrifice to a cause.

had turned sluggish, Kennedy began to prepare for the 1964 presidential race. Watching his popularity drop to under 60 percent by September, he decided to visit Texas in November to try and heal divisions within the Texas Democratic party. There he was assassinated on November 22, 1963. Strong evidence suggested that Lee Harvey Oswald fired the fatal shots. Oswald was captured quickly by police, but the next day a local nightclub owner and gambler, Jack Ruby, stepped out of a crowd, and shot him to death in the basement of the police station. Many wondered if Kennedy's assassination was the work of Oswald alone or part of a larger conspiracy. To dispel rumors, the government hastily formed a commission headed reluctantly by Chief Justice Earl Warren to investigate the assassination and determine if others were involved. The commission hurriedly examined most, but not all, of the available evidence and announced that Oswald was a psychologically disturbed individual who had acted alone—that there were no other gunmen nor any conspiracy. Most Americans willingly accepted the findings.

Kennedy's assassination traumatized the nation. Many people, in their anguish, soon canonized the fallen president as a brilliant, innovative chief executive who combined vitality, youth, and good looks with forceful leadership and good judgment. Lyndon B. Johnson, sworn in as president as he flew back to Washington on the plane carrying Kennedy's body, did not appear to be cut from the same cloth. Kennedy had attended the best eastern schools, enjoyed the cultural and social life associated with wealth, and liked to surround himself with intellectuals. Johnson, a product of public schools and a state college of education, distrusted intellectuals. Raised in the hill country of Texas, his passion was politics. He entered the national scene as a New Deal Democrat and soon became a political force in Washington. By 1960, his congressional experiences were unrivaled: He had served from 1937 to 1948 in the House of Representatives, and from 1949 to 1961 in the Senate, where he had been Senate majority leader. Johnson knew how to wield political power and get things done in Washington. He was famous for his "treatment," in which he would overpower people by putting his face inches from theirs, sometimes grabbing their lapels, and overwhelming them with a barrage of facts, fictions, humor, and threats. Political columnists Roland Evans and Robert Novak wrote that it was "an almost hypnotic experience and rendered the target stunned and helpless."

Beyond the New Frontier

- How did Johnson's Great Society expand on the New Deal?
- How did the outcome of the Great Society's programs contribute to increased disillusionment and social tensions?

Five days after Kennedy's death, Johnson asked Congress for "no memorial oration or eulogy," other than the passage of Kennedy's civil rights bill. At the same time, Johnson applied the "treatment" to several politicians and, in February, Kennedy's tax cut was approved. The civil rights bill moved more slowly, especially in the Senate, where it faced a stubborn southern filibuster. Johnson traded political favors for Republican backing to silence the fifty-seven-day filibuster, and the **Civil Rights Act of 1964** became law on July 2. The law made it illegal to discriminate for reasons of race, religion, or gender in places and businesses that served the public. Putting force behind the law, Congress established a federal Fair Employment Practices Committee (FEPC) and empowered the executive branch to withhold federal funds from institutions that violated the act.

Johnson had passed two major landmarks of the New Frontier, but he was unwilling merely to reflect Kennedy's image. He intended to have a domestic program as ambitious as his political passion. A Johnson-led **Great Society** would declare war on racial injustice and poverty. In 1962, Michael Harrington had alerted the public to wide-scale poverty in America with his book *The Other America.* Harrington's study projected that one-fifth of the population, 35 million people, lived in poverty. A government study established the poverty line for an urban household of four at $3,130, and $1,925 for a rural family. Using those figures, nearly 34.6 million Americans lived in poverty, with almost 40 percent (15.6 million) under the age of 18.

Johnson's assault against poverty was to be fought on two fronts: expanding opportunities and improving the social environment. He believed that state and local governments were unable or politically unwilling to take the action necessary to break the cycle of poverty. Therefore, he projected a huge expansion of federal responsibility, funds, and power in the area of social welfare. Special efforts would be made to provide education and job training, especially for the young. "Our chief weapons will be better schools, . . . better training, and better job opportunities to help more Americans, especially young Americans, to escape from squalor and misery." The Manpower and Development Training Act, Job Corps, Head Start, and the Work Incentive Program all aimed at providing new educational and economic opportunities for the disadvantaged. In 1964, the Job Corps enrolled unemployed teens and young adults (16 to 21) needing job skills, while the Volunteers in Service to America (VISTA) served as a Peace Corps for the United States, sending young, service-minded, mostly middle-class men and women to work in regions of poverty. In 1965, Head Start reached out to prekindergarten children to provide disadvantaged preschoolers an opportunity to gain important thinking and social skills. The Office of Economic Opportunity (OEO) was created in 1964 to coordinate much of the War on Poverty, including ambitious and innovative Community Action Programs (CAP). CAP allowed the disadvantaged to deal with their local problems, especially those involving housing and jobs. Although many

Civil Rights Act of 1964   Law that barred segregation in public facilities and forbade employers to discriminate on the basis of race, religion, sex, or national origin.

Great Society   Program called for by Lyndon Johnson in 1965, which included plans to reduce poverty, protect civil rights, and fund education.

community groups were mobilized under CAP, the program was never as effective as projected. Poor local leadership and rivalries with other agencies over funds and turf frequently disabled its efforts. CAP did, however, energize many communities, generate local agencies like Legal Aid, and breed new community leaders who took their place in the political structure.

Conservative Response

Johnson's Great Society offered a tempting political target to the Republicans and **Barry Goldwater,** the Republican presidential nominee in 1964. Senator Goldwater of Arizona had risen on a wave of conservative and ultraconservative ideology, the **New Right,** that was cresting through the Republican party. Intellectually led by William F. Buckley and the *National Review,* the New Right decried many of the political and social changes taking place in society. According to these conservatives, traditional American values of localism, self-help, and individualism were being destroyed by a New Deal–style, national welfare state. Rabidly anti-Communist groups like the John Birch Society made McCarthy-like denouncements of liberal American politicians and programs. But Democrats were not the only target of conservatives. The Supreme Court, they argued, had violated its constitutional role and actively promoted liberal political and social causes. The John Birch Society went so far as to demand the impeachment of Chief Justice Earl Warren.

From the mid-1950s through the 1960s, the Supreme Court under Warren handed down one decision after another that angered conservatives. To them, the Court seemed to be forcing the liberal agenda of individual rights, social justice, and equality down society's throat. The high Court not only had promoted civil rights but had also expanded the rights of individuals, often at the expense of state authority. In *Yates v. US* (1957), the Court's decision released fourteen officials of the American Communist party who had been imprisoned for publicly advocating the overthrow of the American government. The Court decided that verbal statements, unless accompanied by actions, did not constitute a crime. In *Gideon v. Wainright* (1963), *Escobedo v. Illinois* (1964), and *Miranda v. Arizona* (1966), the Court's rulings declared that all defendants had a right to an attorney, even if the state had to provide one, and that anyone who was arrested had to be informed of the right to remain silent and to have an attorney present during questioning (the *Miranda* warning). The New Right argued that these and other decisions tipped the scale of justice too much in favor of the criminal at the expense of society. Conservatives believed that the Warren Court's actions also threatened traditional values by allowing the publication and distribution of sexually explicit materials (in *Jacobvellis v. Ohio,*

Barry Goldwater   Conservative Republican and senator from Arizona who ran unsuccessfully for president in 1964.

New Right   Conservative movement that opposed the political and social reforms of the 1960s, demanding less government intervention in the economy and a return to traditional values.

1963) and by forbidding prayers (*Engel v. Vitale,* 1962) and the reading of the Bible (*Abington v. Schempp,* 1963) in public schools. Disturbing to many, including a minority on the Court, was the 1964 *Griswold v. Connecticut* decision that overturned Connecticut's laws forbidding the sale of contraceptives, arguing that individuals have a right to privacy that the state cannot abridge. Much less controversial was the *Baker v. Carr* ruling in 1962 that established the goal of making congressional districts "as nearly as practicable" equal in population—"one person, one vote."

Shaping the Great Society

To the New Right, Johnson's Great Society programs and the Warren Court's judicial activism fit the same mold. Both advocated social legislation and values that rewarded people the conservatives characterized as lazy and immoral at the expense of hard-working, solid American families. Plain-spoken and direct, Goldwater offered most conservatives a chance to reassert their brand of traditional values and patriotic ideals. He had voted against the Civil Rights Act and against censuring McCarthy. He opposed "Big Government" and New Deal–style programs. On the world stage, Goldwater promised a more intense anti-Communist crusade. Where Johnson promised not to Americanize the war in Vietnam—"American boys," Johnson swore, would not "do the fighting for Asian boys"—Goldwater stood for "victory over communism" and was willing to commit American troops in Vietnam and even use nuclear weapons against Communist nations, including Cuba and North Vietnam, if necessary.

In the war of slogans and television spots, Johnson's ads scored more points. One memorable Goldwater slogan, "In your heart you know he's right," was modified by Democrats who added, "Yeah, far right!" and "In your guts you know he's nuts." Another Johnson ad suggested that a trigger-happy Goldwater would lead the nation into a nuclear holocaust. In a lopsided election, American voters supported liberalism over conservatism and chose containment over incinerating Communists. Although Goldwater did well in the deep South, he received less than 10 percent of the electoral vote and only 38.4 percent of the popular vote. Over forty new Democratic legislators followed Johnson to Washington, D.C., swelling the Democratic majority in the House of Representatives.

Having beaten Goldwater, Johnson pushed forward legislation to enact his Great Society. Between 1965 and 1968, over sixty programs were put in place. Most of these sought to provide better economic and social opportunities by removing social and economic barriers thrown up by health, education, region, and race. The Appalachian Regional Development Act (1965), Public Works and Development Act (1965), and Model Cities Act (1966) focused on developing economic growth in cities and long-depressed regional areas. An Omnibus Housing Bill (1965) provided $8 billion for constructing low- and middle-income housing and supplementing low-income rent programs. In a related move, the cabinet position of Secretary of Housing and Urban Development (HUD) was created. Mass transit laws (1964 and 1966) provided needed funds for the nation's bus and rail systems, and consumer protection legislation established new and higher standards for product safety and truth in advertising. First Lady "Ladybird" Johnson's beautification program turned national attention to the environment, while the National Wildlife Preservation Act (1964) and the Clean Water Restoration Act (1966) were among the first conservation projects since Theodore Roosevelt. Immigration laws also underwent major modification, dropping the racial and ethnic discrimination that had been established in the 1920s, by setting a uniform yearly limit on immigration from any one nation.

At the top of Johnson's priorities, however, were health and education. Above all, he wanted those two "coonskins on the wall." The Elementary and Secondary Education Act (1965) was the first general educational funding act by the federal government. It granted more than a billion dollars to public and parochial schools for textbooks, library materials, and special education programs. Poorer and rural school districts were supposed to receive the highest percentage of federal support. But, as with many of the Great Society's programs, application fell short of intention, and much of the money went to more affluent suburban school districts. Johnson's biggest "coonskin" was the Medical Care Act (1965) which established **Medicaid** and **Medicare.** Administered within the social security structure, Medicare helped the elderly cover their medical costs. For those on welfare, Medicaid provided funds to states to provide free health care.

Despite the flood of legislation, by the end of 1965 many Great Society programs were underfunded and diminishing in popularity. Antipoverty reformers and black leaders asked for more funds—a domestic Marshall Plan—but the dollars never came. An expanding American war in Vietnam, white backlash to urban riots, and partisan politics were forcing reductions in the budget of the **War on Poverty** and changing the administration's priorities. Still, by 1970 the Great Society had contributed to an almost 10 percent decrease in the number of people living below the poverty line and a one-third drop in the infant mortality rate. Between 1963 and 1968, African-American unemployment fell nearly 42 percent while average family income rose 53 percent.

Medicaid   Program of health insurance for the poor, which was established in 1965 and which provided states with funding to buy health care for people on welfare.

Medicare   Program of health insurance for the elderly and disabled, which was established in 1965 and under which the government paid the bills for health care supplied by private doctors and hospitals.

War on Poverty   Program proposed by Lyndon Johnson in 1964, which aimed to help Americans escape poverty through education, job training, and community development.

Confronting America

- How did the expectations of African-Americans change as the Civil Rights movement changed from a primarily southern movement confronting legal discrimination to a national movement combating poverty and social prejudice.

The decade of the 1950s created a powerful image of a suburban, affluent, and stable American society, a pretty picture that was reflected in popular magazines, movies, and in the minds of those who classified themselves as part of the middle class. Although that image mirrored part of the American reality, it was an incomplete and flawed picture. Throughout the decade, it was clear that there were many Americans who neither matched the popular image nor accepted it. African-Americans and other minorities called for equality and the end of second-class citizenship, many women were disillusioned with their roles as mother and housewife, and an increasing number of young people faulted society's emphasis on materialism and tradition. These and other groups saw the election of John F. Kennedy and his call for change and social activism as providing a new set of social choices. With Kennedy and Johnson in the White House, there was the expectation among many activists that government would no longer stand on the sideline or oppose social change but would support it. Activists were also realistic: Without a grassroots demand for change, they knew, even a socially liberal government was unlikely to act. Nowhere was this more clearly evident than in the continuing quest by African-Americans for civil and political rights. During Kennedy's administration, African-Americans had continued to rely on their own efforts to combat segregation and discrimination, while begging, encouraging, prodding, and even forcing the federal government to act. They were determined to keep the same pressure on Johnson.

Freedom Now

Reflecting Johnson's own desires and responding to African-American and liberal desires, early in the new administration (1965), the president advanced on the issue of civil rights by signing an Executive Order that required government contractors to ensure nondiscrimination in jobs. He also appointed the first African-American cabinet member, Secretary of Housing and Urban Development Robert Weaver; the first African-American woman federal justice, Constance Baker Motley; and the first black on the Supreme Court, Thurgood Marshall. Blacks applauded the president's actions but realized that large pockets of active opposition to civil rights continued to infect government and society. Civil rights leaders therefore wanted to push voting rights as the next step in achieving equality. For nearly one hundred years, most southern whites had viewed voting as a function for whites only, and through their control of the ballot had maintained their political power and a segregated society. Hoping to pull the federal government behind their efforts to expand black political and social rights, civil rights leaders targeted Alabama and Mississippi.

The result was "the **Freedom Summer** of 1964." Led by SNCC's Bob Moses, whites and blacks went to Mississippi to open "Freedom Schools" and to encourage African-Americans to register to vote. The Freedom Schools taught basic literacy and black history, stressed black pride and achievements. They also tutored African-Americans on the Mississippi voter literacy test. As in several southern states, all answers, including "a reasonable interpretation" of a section of the state constitution and a description of "the duties and obligations of citizenship," had to satisfy a white registrar. Confronting this obstacle took a massive effort, and white hostility made the work dangerous. "You talk about fear," one Freedom Summer organizer told recruits. "It's like the heat down there, it's continually oppressive. You think they're rational. But, you know, you suddenly realize, they want to kill you." Civil rights violence in Mississippi occurred almost daily from June through August of 1964. There were over thirty-five shooting incidents; thirty buildings, many of them churches, were bombed; and six Freedom Summer workers were murdered while hundreds were beaten and arrested. But the crusade registered nearly sixty-thousand new African-American voters.

Although the 1964 Civil Rights Act had made discrimination illegal; clearly it was still practiced throughout much of the South, and civil rights leaders were just as clearly determined to eliminate it. Change would occur, Martin Luther King told reporters, because nonviolent demonstrators would go into the streets to exercise their constitutional rights and be attacked by racists, "unleashing violence against them." Seeing the violence, King explained, "Americans of conscience in the name of decency" would demand federal intervention and legislation, and under public pressure, the administration would intervene and initiate "remedial legislation." King and other civil rights leaders selected Selma, Alabama, as their target, because the white community there, and its sheriff Jim Clark, vehemently opposed integration. Clark could not have fit the negative image of the southern segregationist better. Pot-bellied, he wore mirrored sunglasses and a helmet and carried a swagger stick. His temper was short, and he had sworn never to integrate.

As expected, Sheriff Clark confronted protesters, arresting nearly two thousand before King called for a **freedom march** from Selma to Montgomery to increase the pressure. On March 7, 1965, hundreds of freedom marchers faced fifty Alabama state troopers and Clark's mounted officers at Pettus Bridge. After ordering the marchers to halt, the state troopers fired tear gas and charged. As marchers fled back to Selma, Clark's men chased them down, wielding rubber tubing wrapped with barbed wire. Television coverage of the onslaught

Freedom Summer   Effort by civil rights groups in Mississippi in the summer of 1964 to register black voters and cultivate black pride.

freedom march   Civil rights march from Selma to Montgomery, Alabama, in March 1965; the violent treatment of protesters by local authorities helped stir national opinion in favor of the civil rights.

stirred nationwide condemnation of Clark's tactics and support for King and the marchers. Johnson told Governor George Wallace that he would not tolerate any further interference with the march. When 25,000 resumed the march on March 25, they were escorted by the National Guard.

Johnson also used the violence in Selma to pressure Congress to pass his voting rights bill, which he had proposed during his 1965 State of the Union address. Approved in August, the 1965 **Voting Rights Act** banned a variety of methods that states used to deny blacks the right to vote, including Mississippi's literacy test (See Map 29.2). In Selma, 60 percent of qualified African-American voters registered, voted, and stopped Sheriff Clark's bid for reelection.

By the end of 1965, federal legislation had confirmed what the Supreme Court had implied in the *Brown* decision: Official, *de jure* segregation was illegal in the United States. But equality depended on more than laws. Many other ways remained to deny minorities an equal place in America. Neither the 1964 Civil Rights Act nor the 1965 Voting Rights Act guaranteed justice, removed oppressive poverty, provided jobs, or ensured a higher standard of living. *De facto* discrimination and prejudice remained, and African-American frustrations—born of raised expectations, poverty, prejudice, violence—soon changed the nature of civil rights protest and ignited northern cities.

By 1964, more than half of the nation's black population lived in northern cities. More were arriving every year—over 1 million in the 1960s. Nearly all were poor and unskilled. They entered a society with shrinking job opportunities and growing problems. Unskilled jobs were declining and urban black unemployment was high, while social services, despite Great Society programs, were too meager and often too mean-spirited to provide adequate support. In New York City, a protester's sign spelled out the reality of civil rights for northern blacks: "I'd eat at your lunch counter—if only I had a job." Poverty and false hopes led to increased violence and crime while largely white police forces were seen by African-Americans as suppressors rather than protectors. James Baldwin observed that the police were "the force of the white world" and moved through black neighborhoods "like occupying soldiers in a bitterly hostile country." By the mid-1960s, the nation's cities were primed for racial violence. Minor race riots occurred in Harlem and Rochester, New York, during the summer of 1964, but it was the 1965 Watts riot that shook the nation.

Watts did not look like most ghettoes. It was a community of largely single-family homes and duplexes, many with garages that housed family cars. The fairly new buildings were usually well maintained. There was little open discrimination in Los Angeles, no restrictions on voting, public transportation, or eating at lunch counters. Los Angeles was among the nation's leaders in public

Voting Rights Act   1965 law that suspended literacy and other voter tests and authorized federal supervision of registration in places where tests had been used.

Watts   Predominantly black neighborhood of Los Angeles where race riots in August 1965 did $200 million in damages and took the lives of 28 blacks.

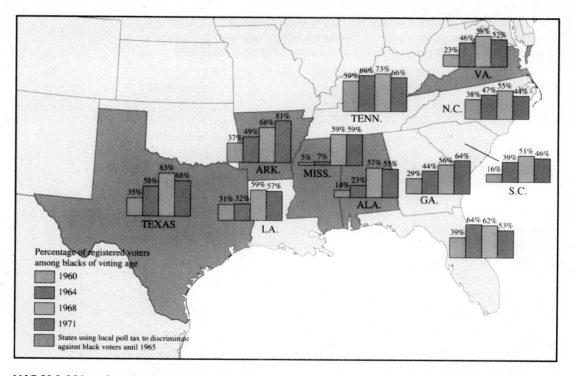

MAP 29.2 African-Americans and the Southern Vote, 1960–1971 An important part of the civil rights movement was to reestablish the African-American vote that had been stripped away in the South following Reconstruction. Between 1960 and 1971, with the outlawing of the poll tax and other voter restrictions, African-American voter participation rose significantly across the South.

assistance programs, spending more than $500 million a year. But outward appearances were deceptive. The 50-square-mile area called Watts was home to more than 250,000 African-Americans, more than four times the people per block than in the rest of the city. Male unemployment was 34 percent and almost two-thirds of the residents were on public assistance. Schools were overcrowded and a bureaucratic maze choked city services. The mayor of Los Angeles, Sam Yorty, disapproved of federal anti-poverty programs that interfered with his control and had prevented $20 million of federal aid from being used. The nearly all-white L.A. police force (of 205 officers assigned to Watts, only 5 were black) had earned a reputation for racism and brutality. Police Chief William Parker disliked "Communists" and civil rights leaders because he felt that, like criminals, they undermined respect for law and order. In this climate, Officer Lee Minikus stopped Marquette Frye for drunk driving on August 11, 1965. What started as a simple arrest soon mushroomed into a major riot. A crowd of onlookers gathered as more police arrived and as Frye and Minikus began to scuffle. The police charged through the crowd of about 150 bystanders using nightsticks, and word quickly rushed through Watts that the police were attacking innocent people. The Watts riot followed, as many residents pelted the police with stones and bottles and vented their frustrations and anger by looting and setting fire to cars and stores. When firemen and police arrived to restore order and put out the flames, they had to dodge snipers' bullets and **Molotov cocktails.** Thirty-six hours later, Los Angeles authorities called for the California National Guard. It took 14,000 ill-equipped guardsmen, with no riot training, together with over 1,000 police and 800 sheriff's deputies to calm the storm. The costs were high: 34 dead, including 28 African-Americans, more than 900 injured, and over $45 million in property destroyed. The police arrested 4,000 rioters and convicted 350 of felonies and nearly 1,500 others for various misdemeanors. The rest were released.

The Watts riot shattered the complacency of many northern whites who had supported civil rights in the South while ignoring the plight of the inner cities. It also demonstrated a gap between the attitudes of northern blacks and those of many civil rights leaders. In 1964, King had received the Nobel Peace Prize, but in 1965, when he spoke to the people of Watts after the rioting, he discovered they had little use for his "dreams." He was shouted down and jeered. "Hell, we don't need no damn dreams," one skeptic remarked. "We want jobs." Watts was only the beginning. More deadly urban riots followed, and a new, militant approach to racial and economic injustices erupted: the **Black Power** movement.

The new voices of Black Power called on blacks to seek power through solidarity, independence, and, if necessary, violence. African-Americans needed to use the same means as whites, argued one veteran of the battle to integrate Mississippi: "If he pose with a smile, meet him with a smile, and if he pose with a gun, meet him with a gun." Many in SNCC and CORE agreed. SNCC's leader, Bob Moses, by the winter of 1965, had had too much of clubs, dogs, threats, and jails. Emotionally spent, he resigned, changed his name, and moved north. The new leadership led by **Stokely Carmichael** exalted Black Power: "I'm not going to beg the white man for anything I deserve," he announced. "I'm going to take it." SNCC and CORE quickly changed from biracial, nonviolent organizations to Black Power resistance movements.

The cry of "Black Power!" had established roots in inner cities across the nation. Among those receptive to a more militant approach were the **Black Muslims** (the Nation of Islam) founded by Elijah Muhammad in the 1930s. The Black Muslim movement attracted mostly young males and demanded adherence to a strict moral code that prohibited the use of drugs and alcohol.

Molotov cocktail   Makeshift bomb made of a bottle filled with gasoline.

Black Power   Movement beginning in 1966 that rejected the nonviolent, coalition-building approach of traditional civil rights groups and advocated black control of black organizations.

Stokely Carmichael   Civil rights activist who led SNCC and who coined the term "black power" to describe the need for blacks to use militant tactics to force whites to accept political change.

Black Muslims   Popular name for the Nation of Islam, an African-American religious group founded by Elijah Muhammad, which professed Islamic religious beliefs and emphasized black separatism.

Preaching black superiority and independence from an evil white world, Black Muslims looked to the black community for regeneration and improvement. With little understanding of Black Muslim goals of self-improvement, most whites focused solely on the group's hostility toward whites and considered the movement a threat to peace and order. By the early 1960s, there were nearly a hundred thousand Black Muslims, but most whites were concerned with only one: **Malcolm X.**

By the age of 20, Malcolm Little's life of hard drugs, pimping, and burglary had put him in prison. Behind bars, his intellectual abilities blossomed. He devoured the prison library, took correspondence courses, and converted to the Nation of Islam—becoming Malcolm X. On his release in 1952, he quickly became one of the Black Muslims' most powerful and respected leaders. A mesmerizing speaker, he proclaimed the ideals of black nationalism and separatism. He rejected integration with a white society that, he said, emasculated blacks by denying them power and personal identity. "Our enemy is the white man!" he roared. But in 1964, he reevaluated the policy of rejecting cooperation with whites and other civil rights groups. Although still a black nationalist, he admitted that to achieve their goals Black Muslims needed to cooperate with other groups, including some whites. He broke with Elijah Muhammad and the defection cost him his life. On February 21, 1965, three Black Muslims assassinated him in Harlem. After his death, Malcolm X's *Autobiography,* chronicling his personal triumph over white oppression, became a revered guide for many blacks.

Malcolm X represented only one model for urban blacks. Others pursued direct action against white power and advocated violence, nearly drowning out the nonviolent voice of King. Huey P. Newton and Bobby Seale, in October 1966, organized the **Black Panthers** in Oakland, California. Although they pursued community action, like developing school lunch programs, they were more noticeable for adopting Mao Zedong's adage that "power flows from the barrel of a gun." The Black Panthers were well armed. Their willingness to use violence frightened many, but some applauded the militance and urged others to follow suit. New SNCC leader H. Rap Brown told listeners to grab their guns, burn the town down, and shoot the "honky." The summer of 1967 seemed to bring Brown's words to life. Over seventy-five major riots took place, the deadliest occurring in Detroit and Newark, resulting in a nationwide total of eighty-seven dead and over 16,300 arrested.

Finally, after a third year of urban riots, Johnson created a special commission chaired by Governor Otto Kerner of Illinois to investigate their causes.

Malcolm X   Black activist who advocated black separatism as a member of the Nation of Islam; in 1963 he converted to orthodox Islam and two years later he was assassinated.

Black Panthers   Black revolutionary party founded in 1966, which accepted violence as a means of social change; many of their leaders were killed in confrontations with police or sent to prison.

The committee's report, issued in March 1968, put the primary blame on the racist attitudes of white America. The study described two Americas, one white and one black, and concluded:

> Pervasive discrimination and segregation in employment, education, and housing have resulted in the continuing exclusion of great numbers of Negroes from the benefits of economic progress.

The Kerner Commission believed the solution to the riots and America's racial problem was a "compassionate, massive and sustained" commitment "backed by the resources of the most powerful and richest nation on this earth."

Just a month later, a new wave of riots spread across the United States following the assassination of Martin Luther King, Jr., by a white racist. King had worked hard to regain his leadership of the civil rights movement since the Watts riot and the emergence of Black Power. Shifting from legal rights to economic rights, he had become a champion of the black urban **underclass,** criticizing the capitalistic system that relegated millions to poverty. Still an advocate of nonviolence, King called for mass demonstrations to compel economic and social justice. King was in Memphis supporting striking black sanitation workers when, on April 4, 1968, he was gunned down by James Earl Ray. Spontaneously, African-Americans took to the streets in over 125 cities. Sections of Washington, D.C., itself were engulfed in flames.

As American cities burned and cries of "Burn, Baby, Burn," and "Black Power!" emerged from the smoke, a white backlash occurred. Many Americans, fearful of Black Power advocates and increased urban violence, backed away from supporting civil rights. Republican politicians were especially vocal. Governor of California Ronald Reagan argued the "riff-raff" theory of urban problems: "Mad dogs" and "lawbreakers" were the sole cause of the trouble. Governor Spiro Agnew of Maryland blamed activists like H. Rap Brown and urged that he be jailed. Senator Everett Dirksen and House leader Gerald Ford suspected a Red conspiracy. Most Americans applauded as police cracked down on the Black Panthers, arresting or killing its membership. As the 1968 political campaign began, law and order replaced the Great Society and the War on Poverty as the main issue. The backlash was in part a result of white dread of Black Power and a reaction to the violence of the urban riots, but it was also a reaction to fears that traditional American society was being torn apart at the seams. As alarming to many Americans as the revolution that was reshaping African-American attitudes was the growing tendency of the nation's youth—including white, middle-class young people—to confront and reject traditional social and political values.

underclass   Term identifying the lowest economic class, with the implication that its members are so disadvantaged by poverty that they have little or no chance to move upward economically.

The Challenge of Youth

High school and college-aged students were among the most active social groups during the decade of the sixties. The first wave of "baby boomers" were now young adults, and they were going to college in record numbers. In 1965, over 40 percent of the nation's high school graduates were attending college, a leap of 13 percent from 1955 and of nearly 30 percent since World War II. Graduate schools, too, swelled in size and churned out Ph.D.s—over half of all doctorates awarded from the Civil War until 1970 were conferred during the 1960s. Although the majority of young adults maintained the typical quest for family, a good-paying job, and a house in the suburbs, as the decade progressed, some took up social concerns and personal fulfillment as alternative values. The civil rights movement, the fear of nuclear destruction, and Kennedy's idealistic imagery inspired many youths to think first of improving the human community. By the middle of the decade, the image of America's young adults had changed: they were active and would be heard, no longer apathetic or self-absorbed, merely seeking jobs, homes, and the suburban lifestyle. The transformation was especially true among those attending colleges and universities.

On college campuses across the nation, many students—often encouraged by professors—began to question the role of the university and the goal of education. Particularly at huge institutions like the University of California at Berkeley and at Los Angeles and the University of Michigan, students complained that humanism and concern for individuals were missing from education. Known by matriculation numbers instead of names, students were stuffed into courses based on impersonal evaluation tests and taught by professors or teaching assistants who preferred to be in the lab or library. Education seemed sterile, more like an assembly line producing a standardized product than an effort to create an independent, thinking individual. Paul Goodman, in *Growing Up Absurd,* argued that schools destroyed natural creativity and replaced it with a highly structured system that stressed order and conformity. Education was designed to meet the needs of administrators and teachers, not students. Reflecting Goodman's view, many students demanded freedom of expression and a new, more flexible attitude from college administrators and faculty.

Campus activists confronted a broad spectrum of issues, from those directly related to campus life to those dealing with the nation and the world. Denouncing course requirements and restrictions on dress, behavior, and living arrangements, students insisted on more personal choices in selecting courses and pursuing lifestyles. By the end of the decade, many colleges and schools had relaxed or eliminated dress codes. Long hair was accepted for males, and casual clothes like faded blue jeans and shorts were common dress for both sexes on most college campuses. Colleges also lifted dorm curfews and other residence requirements. Some dorms became co-ed. Academic departments reduced the number of mandatory courses, allowing students more options in their educational program, and pass/fail grades were instituted. The "open" and liberal arts major, students argued, had as much value as the pre-med or business major. Learning for its own sake was as important as "arbitrarily given" grades or **vocational** or professional training. By the beginning of the 1970s, many colleges and even some high schools had introduced programs in nontraditional fields like African-American, Native American, and women's studies. Although it remained popular, the "Greek system" of fraternities and sororities declined in reputation and importance on many campuses.

Setting their sights beyond the campus community, some student activists urged that the campus should be a haven for free thought and a marshaling ground for efforts to change society significantly. At the University of Michigan in the early 1960s, Tom Hayden and Al Haber broke new ground in campus consciousness when they organized **Students for a Democratic Society (SDS).** Hayden wanted to throw off the "silent generation" label and harness student energy to attack complacency and indifference in American society. SDS members insisted that Americans recognize that their affluent nation was also a land of poverty and want, that the **military-industrial complex** dominated the economy and society, and that business and government chose to ignore social inequalities. In 1962, SDS issued its Port Huron Statement, which maintained,

> The search for truly democratic alternatives to the present, and a commitment
> to social experimentation with them, is a worthy and fulfilling human enter-
> prise, one which moves us and, we hope, others today.

Hayden argued that the country should allocate its resources according to social need and strive to build "an environment for people to live in with dignity and creativeness."

SDS and other activist groups believed that most college administrators and faculty members opposed the idea of the campus as a base for social criticism and activism. Throughout the decade, students clashed with college authorities in struggles over what kind of forum the college should represent. The earliest major confrontation occurred at Berkeley in 1964 and became a model for those that followed.

At Berkeley, activists led by Mario Savio protested **Establishment** repression when the administration tried to prevent students from using a plaza on campus to recruit supporters and solicit funds for various social and political causes, including the civil rights movement. Fresh from the Freedom Summer,

vocational   Providing training in a special skill to be pursued in a trade.

Students for a Democratic Society   Left-wing student organization founded in 1960 to criticize American materialism and call for social justice.

military-industrial complex   Term first used by Eisenhower to describe the arms industry; in the 1960s it was used by radicals to describe all those in power who benefited from U.S. militarism.

Establishment   The established social order, or the group that holds most of the power and influence in a society.

Savio demanded freedom of speech and political activism on campus. Claiming that the university was not fulfilling its moral obligation to provide an open forum for education and free thought, Savio asked students and faculty to disrupt the university's activities: to jam the gears, to bring the machine to its knees, so that students could be unleashed. Over six thousand students responded, seizing campus sites, including the administration building, boycotting classes, and yelling and chanting what many consider vulgar four-letter words. Savio and two other organizers were arrested, expelled, tried for inciting a riot, and sentenced to four months in jail—but Chancellor Clark Kerr and the administration agreed to allow freedom of expression, including political literature, on campus.

The Berkeley Free Speech Movement encouraged other campus organizers to assert their right to address social and political issues. Student activists in growing numbers focused their attention on civil rights, the environment, and social and sexual norms. By the late sixties, though, their loudest protests opposed American foreign policy, the military-industrial complex, and the war in Vietnam. As the next chapter will show, opposition to the war in Vietnam and the draft would further expand the number of student activists and increase pressure on the Johnson administration to modify its policies.

Aside from politics, the youth movement's discontent with social and cultural norms found expression in what was labeled the **counterculture.** As the New Left rejected political standards and values, so also many young people spurned the traditional moral and social values of their parents and the fifties. "Don't trust anyone over 30," was the motto of the young generation. Counterculture thinking rejected conformity and glorified freedom of the spirit and self-knowledge. A large number of teens and young adults began to accuse American society of being "plastic" in its materialism and disregard for change, and they sought ways to express their dissatisfaction. Music was one of the most prominent forms of defiance. Some musicians, like Bob Dylan and Joan Baez, challenged society with protest and antiwar songs aimed at specific problems. Folk music and protest rock, however, were only a small part of the music challenge. For the majority, rock 'n' roll, which took a variety of forms, remained dominant. Performers like the **Beatles,** an English group that exploded on the American music scene in 1964, were among the most popular, sharing the stage with such other British imports as the Rolling Stones and the Animals, whose behavior and songs depicted a life of pleasure and lack of social restraints. Other musicians, like the Grateful Dead and Jimi Hendrix, turned rock 'n' roll into a new form of music, psychedelic **acid rock,** whose

counterculture   A culture with values or lifestyles in opposition to those of the established culture.

Beatles   English rock group that gained international fame in 1962 and disbanded in 1970; they were known for the intelligence of their lyrics and their sophisticated instrumentation.

acid rock   Rock music having a driving, repetitive beat and lyrics that suggest psychedelic drug experiences.

swirls of sound and lyrics acclaimed a drug culture and attacked social conventions.

The message of much music of the sixties was wrapped up in drug use—"get high" or "stoned"—reflecting a view that drugs offered another way to be free of the older generation's values. Todd Gitlin, president of SDS, thought that "to get access to youth culture," a person "had to get high." For many in the sixties generation, marijuana, or "pot," was the primary means to get high. Marijuana advocates claimed that it was nonaddictive and that, unlike the nation's traditional drug—alcohol—it reduced aggression and heightened perception. Thus, they argued, marijuana contributed to the counterculture's ideals of peace, serenity, and self-awareness. A more dangerous and unpredictable drug also popular with some of the counterculture was LSD, lysergic acid diethylamide. LSD, or "acid," was a hallucinogenic drug that altered the user's perceptions of reality and had originally been developed for interrogation purposes by government agencies like the CIA. Harvard psychology professor **Timothy Leary** used the drug and argued for its widespread consumption. He believed that by "tripping" on LSD people could free themselves—"blow their minds," "turn on, tune in, and drop out"—of the rat race that was American society. Although most youths did not use them, drugs offered some within the counterculture and the nation a new experience that many believed was liberating. Drugs also proved to be self-destructive and deadly, contributing to the deaths of several counterculture figures, including musicians Jimi Hendrix, Jim Morrison, and Janis Joplin.

Another realm of traditional American values the counterculture overturned was sex. Some young people appalled their parents and society by questioning and rejecting the values that placed restrictions on sexual activities. Sex was a form of human expression, they argued, and if it felt good, why stifle it? A new openness about sexuality and a relaxation of the stigma on extramarital sex turned out to be a significant legacy of the sixties. But the philosophy of **free love** also had a negative side as increased sexual activity contributed to a rapid rise in cases of venereal disease. The notion of free love also exposed women to increased sexual assault as some men chose to assume that all "liberated" women desired sexual relations.

Perhaps the most colorful and best-known advocates of the counterculture and its ideals were the **Hippies.** Seeking a life of peace, love, and self-awareness—governed by the law of "what feels good" instead of by the rules of traditional behavior—Hippies tried to distance themselves from society. They flocked in large numbers to northern California, congregating especially

Timothy Leary   Harvard professor and counterculture figure who advocated the expansion of consciousness through the use of drugs such as LSD.

free love   Popular belief among members of the counterculture in the 1960s in having sexual activity with as many partners as they liked.

Hippies   Members of the counterculture in the 1960s who rejected the competitiveness and materialism of American society and searched for peace, love, and individual autonomy.

in the Haight-Ashbury neighborhood of San Francisco, where they frequently carried drug abuse and free love to excess. Elsewhere, some Hippie groups abandoned the "old-fashioned" nuclear family and lived together as extended families on communes. Hippies expressed their nonconformism in their appearance, favoring long unkempt hair and ratty blue jeans or long flowered dresses. Although the number of true Hippie dropouts was small, their style of dress and grooming greatly influenced young Americans.

The influence of the counterculture peaked, at least in one sense, in the summer of 1969, when an army of teens and young adults converged on **Woodstock,** New York for the largest free rock concert in history. For three days, through summer rains and deepening mud, more than four hundred thousand came together in a temporary open-air community, while many of the most popular rock 'n' roll bands performed day and night. Touted as three days of peace and love, sex, drugs, and rock 'n' roll, Woodstock symbolized the power of counterculture values to promote cooperation and happiness.

The spirit of Woodstock was fleeting. For most people, at home and on campus, the communal ideal was impractical, if not unworkable. Nor did the vast majority of young people who took up some counterculture notions completely reject their parents' society. Most stayed in school and continued to participate in the society they were criticizing. To be sure, the counterculture had a lasting impact on American society—on dress, sexual attitudes, music, and even personal values—but it did not reshape America in its image.

Summary

Expectations
Constraints
Choices
Outcomes

The *outcome* of Kennedy's election was a wave of renewed optimism and liberalism. Kennedy's call for a more responsible society and government was at the heart of his New Frontier and of Johnson's Great Society as well. Kennedy raised *expectations,* but faced political *constraints,* and it was Johnson's Great Society that greatly expanded the role of government in social affairs. Heightened *expectations* were clearly visible among the African-Americans who looked to Kennedy, and later to Johnson, for legislation to end segregation and discrimination. As Kennedy took office, African-American leaders *chose* to launch a series of sit-ins and freedom marches designed to keep the pressure on American society and the government. Kennedy responded by introducing a civil rights act in 1963 that was finally passed in 1964—after his assassination.

Woodstock   Free rock concert in Woodstock, New York, in August 1969, which attracted 400,000 people and was remembered as the classic expression of the counterculture.

In foreign policy, Kennedy *chose* to expand the international struggle against communism. Confrontations over Berlin and Cuba, a heightened arms race, and an expanded commitment to Vietnam were *outcomes* accepted as part of the United States' global role and passed intact to Johnson.

As president, Johnson *chose* to expand on the slain president's New Frontier. The 1964 Civil Rights Act, the 1965 Voting Rights Act, and Great Society legislation, were designed to wage war on poverty and discrimination, while providing federal aid to education and creating a national system of health insurance for the poor and elderly. But by 1968, the growing societal and political divisions constrained liberalism. Despite legal and political gains, many African-American activists *chose* to become more militant in their demands for social and economic equality. The nation's youth too seemed unwilling to accept the traditional values of society, and they demanded change. Disturbed by the turmoil, conservatives and many moderate Americans chose to oppose government programs that appeared to favor the poor and minorities at their expense. The *outcome* was that a decade that had begun with great promise produced for many, disappointment and disillusionment.

Selected Readings

Bernstein, Irving. *Promises Kept: John F. Kennedy's New Frontier* (1991).

A brief and balanced account of Kennedy's presidency that nonetheless presents a favorable report of the accomplishments and legacy of the New Frontier.

Berschloss, Michael. *The Crisis Years: Kennedy and Khrushchev, 1960–1963* (1991).

A strong narrative account of the Cold War during the Kennedy administration and the personal duel between the leaders of the two superpowers.

Carson, Clayton. *In Struggle: SNCC and the Black Awakening of the 1960s* (1981).

A useful study that uses the development of SNCC to examine the changing patterns of the civil rights movement and the emergence of black nationalism.

Gitlin, Todd. *The Sixties: Years of Hope, Days of Rage* (1987).

A readable and impressionistic examination of the political and cultural changes that occurred throughout the 1960s.

Kearns, Doris. *Lyndon Johnson and the American Dream* (1977).

An effective study of how Johnson's background and values shaped his career and the Great Society.

Wolfe, Tom. *The Electric Kool-Aid Acid Test* (1968).

A classic account of the dimensions of the counterculture.

Easy Rider (1969) and *The Graduate* (1967) are two period films that critique traditional social and cultural norms and provide a glimpse of the "values" of the 1960s.

Vocabulary Exercises

Context

The vocabulary used in "Great Promises, Bitter Disappointments, 1960–1968" can be difficult for three reasons. First, there may be many general vocabulary words with which you are unfamiliar. Second, there are many content-specific terms in this chapter that you may have heard of but do not really know or understand. Finally, on numerous occasions this chapter uses figures of speech that may also give you problems. Thus it is important to be aware that all of these difficulties are present as you proceed to understand this chapter.

To make the task a bit easier, we have identified some of these difficult words. First go through the list of general words. For the words you do not know, find them in the chapter (the page number is provided for you), read how the word is used in context, and then look the word up in the dictionary and write down the dictionary definition that best reflects how the word is used in context. Finally, a space has been left at the bottom of the list for you to add additional words that are unfamiliar to you that you might come across in the chapter. Be sure to make cards for these words also.

Now look at the list of content-specific words. There are 52 content-specific words that have been defined for you in the text and probably others that have not. Remember that words such as these are much more likely to be found in history texts than in any other type of text. Although all of the words on this list have been defined for you using bold face within the chapter, there may be others that also give you trouble. Such terms would be those that the authors feel that you might already know. Be careful of these words as you read and annotate the chapter. If the given definition is not clear to you or there are other terms that are totally unfamiliar to you, be sure to get some assistance. How might you get some help in figuring out what these words mean?

For the concept-specific words, you may first want to go through the list and check any words that you have no idea of what they mean. You would certainly want to make concept cards for these terms. This strategy was outlined in Chapter 10. Be sure to group terms dealing with the same topic together for easier learning.

Finally there is the problem with the use of figurative language. In this particular chapter, much of the figurative language comes from quotes that were made by politicians or activists. Be aware that some figurative language may occur when you see quotes in this chapter—sometimes but not always. Following the content-specific terms we have listed some instances, but there may be other expressions that you do not understand. If so, list them as you encounter them so that you can get clarification if necessary.

General Words

Content-Specific Terms

Are there other content-specific words in this chapter with which you are unfamiliar? If so, list them below.

53.

54.

55.

56.

57.

Figurative Language

1. Several political commentators called the candidates "two peas in a pod"...

2. Kennedy seized the opportunity, recognizing that the candidate who appeared more calm and knowledgeable—more "presidential"—would "win" the debate.

3. "Eisenhower recession"

4. "action intellectuals"

5. "can-do" image

6. a "surgical" airstrike

7. ... the United States and the Soviet Union had stood "eyeball to eyeball" and that the Soviets "had blinked first."

8. A "hot line" telephone link was established ...

Application Exercises

1. Preview the selection. Try to see the "big picture." Although this selection has numerous headings, it basically focuses on the Kennedy and Johnson eras. Keep this idea in mind as you preview. Also note the title of the selection, "Great Promises, Bitter Disappointments, 1960–1968." Think about this title as you preview. Finally, as you are previewing notice that the selection is organized around **expectations, constraints, choices,** and **outcomes.** These four factors are also used to summarize the selection. It may help to organize your thinking in this way as well.

2. Formulate ten memory-level and five higher-level questions from your previewing.

3. Read and annotate the selection, keeping the information organized around the key ideas.

4. Using the following labels, organize the information from the selection.

Note that there might be some overlap. For example, "Bay of Pigs" is a place, but there was also a "Bay of Pigs" incident (event).

people
places
events
LBJ
JFK
domestic policies
foreign policies

You could also organize this selection around the four factors in the introduction—expectations, constraints, choices, and outcomes. Think about these factors for both Kennedy and Johnson or for a key event such as the civil rights movement or the Vietnam War.

5. Make a time line on the civil rights movement that spans the Kennedy and Johnson years.

6. Modify the questions you posed in Application Exercise 2 above. Add more questions if necessary. Use the question/answer format.

7. Using PORPE, predict and answer two essay questions that might be asked about this selection. Remember to follow the instructions in Chapter 12 about how to write good answers for essay questions.

8. Make a talk-through card that shows how you have organized the ideas in the selection for studying.

9. **EVALUATION:** Which strategies best helped you learn the material in this selection? Why were they helpful? Remember in history classes that you take, you will want to remember these strategies to help you be a more efficient and effective learner. Note that these strategies probably differ quite a bit from those you might choose to use in biology or physics.

Selection from a Physical Science Text

Weather Forecasting

Humans have long desired to control the weather. However, little progress has been made toward achieving this desire; and as the next best thing, the preoccupation of observing and attempting to predict the weather developed. The influence of the weather on everyday activity has grown to the extent that this preoccupation has become the sole occupation of many modern meteorologists, who are known as weather forecasters.

Weather forecasters are much maligned. When the weather fails to follow the forecast, they are the targets of many unflattering remarks. Bad weather that spoils a planned outing is blamed on the forecaster's shortsightedness, if not on the forecaster. Although meteorologists are scapegoats, they do a commendable job and on the average are correct about 80 percent of the time.

Accurately predicting atmospheric behavior is a difficult task. Changes in the weather are governed by scientific principles. However, the atmosphere is complex and contains so many variables that meteorologists must combine empirical and scientific knowledge in making reasonable forecasts. Weather data are collected and processed by the most modern means. From the current weather conditions, future conditions are projected, according to established behavior patterns. This selection deals with a few of the many aspects of weather forecasting.

The National Weather Service

The United States **National Weather Service** (formerly the Weather Bureau) is the federal organization that provides national weather information. It forms part of the National Oceanic and Atmospheric Administration (**NOAA**—pronounced "Noah"), which was created within the U.S. Department of Commerce in 1970.*

The original U.S. Weather Bureau grew out of the Army Signal Corps, which maintained an early telegraph system that was used for weather reporting. It became a part of the Department of Agriculture in 1891 and then part of the Department of Commerce in 1940. The Bureau's early activities were primarily directed toward weather forecasting as an aid to agriculture. However,

---

Source: From *Introduction to Physical Science,* Seventh Edition by Shipman, Wilson, and Todd. Copyright © 1993 by D.C. Heath and Company. Used by permission of Houghton Mifflin Company.

*Because the National Weather Service issues its surface weather reports using British units, this chapter presents weather statistics in British units first, followed by SI units, where appropriate, in parentheses.

the greatest impetus for its growth came with the development of aviation, for which up-to-date weather reports are vital. Today, the Weather Bureau is known as the National Weather Service, and its activities are concerned with every phase of the weather.

The nerve center of the National Weather Service is the **National Meteorological Center** (NMC) located just outside Washington, D.C., in Suitland, Maryland. It is the NMC that receives and processes raw data taken at numerous weather stations. Currently, complete weather observations are collected at 260 National Weather Service facilities by some 1,200 people. Also available are aircraft and radar reports, upper-air monitoring, and data from weather satellites.

The NMC analyzes and makes forecasts from the received data. Other central National Weather Service organizations deal with specialized conditions such as hurricanes, tornadoes, and severe storms. From these central organizations, data go to Forecast Offices, which have the responsibility for warnings and forecasts for states, or large portions of states, and assigned zones. State forecasts are issued twice daily for a time period up to 48 hours. An extended outlook, up to five days, is issued daily for these same areas. The forecast organizational structure is shown in Figure 23.1.

Weather Service Offices represent the third echelon of the forecast system. Local forecasts are adoptions of state forecasts. They are issued to meet local requirements and to provide general weather information to the public. The

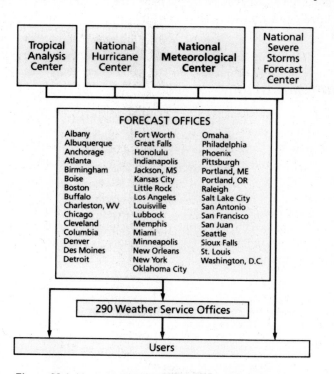

Figure 23.1 National Weather Service forecast organization

local forecasts are distributed by telephone services, and by radio and television broadcasts, including VHF–FM (very high frequency—frequency-modulated) radio stations near major population centers that transmit weather information continuously 24 hours a day, 365 days a year.

Let's take a closer look at how forecasts are made and distributed. The operations of the NMC are almost completely automated, and data are handled by high-speed computers, printers, and communication systems. Analyses are made twice daily at 0000 hours and 1200 hours Greenwich Mean Time (7 A.M. and 7 P.M. EST). A preliminary analysis is made after 1.5 hours of data reception. An operational analysis is made after 3.5 hours, when 80 percent of all incoming data have been received. The computer takes a half hour to analyze the information, and the analysis is completed before the data are 4 hours old. The NMC estimates the same analysis would take five people working 8 hours to complete. Manual analyses are made on certain portions of the data as a check on the computer.

Once the analyses are completed, three somewhat different simulations of the weather begin. The simulations use the basic laws of physics and some statistics to calculate values of temperature, wind, humidity, and rain at equally spaced locations over the entire globe and at a number of different altitudes. The results are sent out, almost untouched by human hands, to National Weather Service field offices and other users for guidance in making forecasts. Quality control is done in the field. The forecaster must estimate possible errors and use the results that appear to be best for his or her purpose, together with other knowledge, to make forecasts.

The distribution phase was once done by the teletype circuits that brought in the data. Facsimile circuits transmitted charts and 2,500 weather maps. However, the National Weather Service now uses a data-handling system known as AFOS (*A*utomation of *F*ield *O*perations and *S*ervices). The AFOS system uses minicomputers and TV-type displays in a network of more than 200 automated weather offices. The network has four loop circuits in different regions of the country and is centrally linked to the NMC.

The AFOS has done away with the older system of teletypewriters and facsimile machines and the enormous quantities of paper they generated. Instead, weather information from the minicomputer systems is displayed on video screens. However, the AFOS system is outdated and will be obsolete in a short time. It was not designed to take advantage of data from satellites and the relatively new Doppler radar, which is discussed later.

The National Weather Service will replace the AFOS system with specialized computer workstations called Automated Weather Information Processing Systems (AWIPS) in the 1990s. This computer system will allow forecasters to analyze quickly the most meaningful information from a diverse set of observations. Unlike AFOS, it will integrate large-scale weather data from the NMC satellite imagery and local radar coverage.

As a rule, the National Weather Service is dedicated to getting the weather information to the public by the fastest means available; however, there is an exception. In wartime, weather data are of great military value and become classified information. During Word War II, weather reports were not made public except in cases of severe weather, in which warnings were necessary to prevent property damage and loss of life. The news media were prohibited from mentioning anything that pertained to the weather. Farmers were simply told it would be a good day to make hay, or sports fans learned a rained-out ball game was called off due to conditions beyond control. As one sportscaster put it, "Well, folks, I can't say anything about the weather, but that isn't perspiration on the pitcher's face."

As technology increases and facilities expand, better weather forecasts become available. The predictions of the National Weather Service meteorologists are estimated to be about 80 percent accurate. This accuracy, of course, depends on the weather element and location. For example, predictions of no rain in parts of Arizona during the summer are almost 100 percent correct.

The method of reporting the weather has also changed over the years. In the past, forecasts of precipitation used terms such as *probable, likely,* and *occasional.* Precipitation forecasts are now expressed in "percentage probabilities," such as a 70 percent chance of rain. The percentage probability given in such a forecast results from a consideration of two quantities: (1) the probability that a precipitation-producing storm will develop in, or move into, the forecast area; and (2) the percentage of the area that the storm is expected to cover. Thus in summer when storms (because they are convectional) tend to be more isolated, or scattered, the probability that your immediate area will get rain tends to be less than in the winter when frontal storms are more prevalent. The percentage probabilities give the public a better indication of what the weather might be.

Although many hours of work go into making the daily weather forecasts as accurate as possible, they sometimes fail to hold true. But after all, if the forecasts were always correct, wouldn't it take a bit of the excitement out of life?

Data Collection and Weather Observation

In 1870 weather data in the United States were taken by the Army Signal Corps at 24 stations. Today, weather observations are collected from approximately 1,000 land stations, 6 fixed ocean stations, and several hundred merchant vessels of all nationalities. Many of the land stations are associated with airport operations. Volunteer observers also supply climatology data from about 12,000 substations around the country.

Weather stations are concerned with the basic meteorological measurements of temperature, pressure, humidity, precipitation, and wind direction and speed. The instruments used are also basically the same but have official specifications and, in some cases, may be automated to supply continuous readings.

A typical installation for data collection may include a hut used as an **instrument shelter** with louvered sides, a ventilated floor, and a double roof with an air space between. This construction permits air measurements to be taken free from insolation influences. The instrument shelter may contain a maximum-minimum thermometer, a psychrometer, and a thermograph, which is an automatic temperature-recording device. Quite often these automated instruments are connected electronically to nearby offices.

A hydrothermograph is sometimes available and records the temperature as well as the relative humidity by hygrometric means, thus eliminating the need for the psychrometer. The relative humidity and temperature measurements are taken 6 ft above ground level. The maximum and minimum daily temperatures are important weather observations. They may be measured with a set of maximum-minimum thermometers.

The **maximum thermometer** is a mercury thermometer with a constriction in the lower part of its capillary bore (Figure 23.5a). The pressure of the expanding mercury in the bulb causes the mercury to pass through the constriction as the temperature increases. When the temperature decreases, the mercury is unable to pass back through the narrow constriction. Thus the column of mercury above the constriction indicates the highest temperature reached.

The maximum thermometer is reset by shaking. Shaking forces the mercury back into the bulb and readies the thermometer for a new reading. (Clinical thermometers are of similar construction and are maximum thermometers. A common error in taking one's temperature at home is forgetting to reset the thermometer.)

The **minimum thermometer** (Figure 23.5b) is an alcohol thermometer that contains a thin, colored-glass, dumbbell-shaped rod in its bore called the *index*. The surface tension of the alcohol surface draws the index with it to the lowest point of descent of the liquid column surface. When the temperature increases

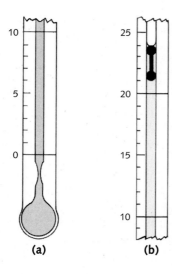

Figure 23.5 Maximum and minimum thermometers
(a) A constriction of the capillary bore prevents the mercury from returning to the bulb when the temperature decreases, so the thermometer retains its highest (maximum) reading. (b) Surface tension draws the index rod (black) to the lowest descent of the liquid column surface. When the temperature increases, the alcohol expands, and the liquid flows around the index, leaving it at the lowest (minimum) temperature.

and the alcohol expands, the liquid flows around the index, leaving it at the lowest position. Thus the upper end of the index marks the lowest or minimum temperature reached. In operation, the minimum thermometer is positioned horizontally. Positioned vertically, the glass index would fall through the liquid to the bottom of the tube. The thermometer is reset by tilting it downward.

Another type of maximum-minimum thermometer that gives both readings uses a U-tube with two liquids. The U-tube contains mercury in the bottom and a clear, expanding liquid above. There is a reservoir of this liquid at the top of the left side of the U-tube. As the temperature increases, the liquid inside expands and forces the mercury column *down* on the left side, and *up* on the right side, carrying with it the maximum index.

As the temperature decreases, the liquid contracts, causing the mercury column on the left side of the U-tube to rise and carry the minimum index with it. The maximum index remains at its highest graduation or maximum temperature, and the minimum index is carried to its lowest graduation or minimum temperature. The indexes, which are magnetic, are reset with a small ceramic magnet.

A **rain gauge** is an open container that automatically weighs and records the accumulated precipitation. The collection bucket of the rain gauge is mounted on a weighing mechanism having a scale that converts the weight of the rain to equivalent inches. The rain gauge is also used for snow measurements. The collection bucket is sprayed with special chemicals that melt the snow so its water equivalent can be measured.

Open exposure and immediate locale are not critical for barometric readings, as they are for the rain gauge, and barometers are usually kept indoors because of their intricate construction.

The National Weather Service has begun work on a new system of data collection. The Automatic Surface Observations Systems (ASOS) program is developing modular units that will be used to monitor weather conditions automatically. Modern technology will be used to acquire, process, and distribute the surface observations to various forecasting systems. Plans call for over 200 units to be deployed across the country in the 1990s.

Radar (*ra*dio *d*etecting *a*nd *r*anging) is used to detect and monitor precipitation, especially that of severe storms. Radar operates by sending out electromagnetic waves and monitoring the returning waves that have been reflected back from some object. In this manner the location of the object may be determined. The objects of interest in weather observations are storms and precipitation. Continuous radar scans are now commonly seen on TV weather reports.

There are 230 conventional weather radars deployed across the United States. Installations are located mainly in the tornado belt of the midwestern United States and along the Atlantic and Gulf coasts where hurricanes are probable. Additional radar information is obtained from air traffic control systems at various airports. The NMC is linked to radar stations by telephone circuits, and its meteorologists can view the current radar scans across the country on television screens.

Following is a discussion of a relatively new type of radar now in use that helps forecasters to detect storms earlier than conventional radar. [Doppler Radar]

Upper-air observations are important in the collection of meteorological data. These observations are made chiefly with radiosondes (radio sounding equipment). A **radiosonde** is a small package of meteorological instruments combined with a radio transmitter. It is carried aloft by balloons, and data are transmitted to ground receiving stations. The wind direction and speed may also be obtained by tracking the flight of the radiosonde.

The carrier balloon eventually bursts, and the radiosonde descends slowly by means of a small parachute. Parachute descent prevents damage to the instruments and anything in the radiosonde's path on landing. Directions on the radiosonde request the finder to return the instruments to the National Weather Service, where they are reconditioned and flown again. Approximately 150 National Weather Service offices engage in radiosonde observations.

To get better wind information, a special-purpose Doppler radar called a wind profiler was developed. The profiler senses winds from about 1,600 ft to 55,000 ft (about 500 to 17,000 m) in altitude. By a comparison of radar beams, the profiler "profiles," or measures, upper-air wind directions and speeds. A demonstration network with 30 wind profilers is being installed in several Midwestern states.

Rockets are used in upper-atmosphere data collection, but probably the greatest progress in general weather observation has come with the advent of weather satellites. Before satellites, weather observations were unavailable for more than 80 percent of the globe. The first weather picture was sent back from space on April 1, 1960, from the 118-kg (260-lb) TIROS-1 (*T*elevision *I*nfrared *O*bservation *S*atellite). The first fully operational weather satellite system was in place by 1966. These early satellites traveled from pole to pole at altitudes of several hundred miles and monitored only a limited area below the orbital path. It took almost three orbits to photograph the entire conterminous United States.

Today, a fleet of GOESs (*G*eostationary *O*rbiting *E*nvironmental *S*atellite), which orbit at fixed points above the equator, and polar-orbiting satellites including a more recent 1040-kg TIROS, provide an almost continuous picture of weather patterns all over the globe. At an altitude of about 22,800 mi (36,800 km), the GOES orbiters have the same orbital period as that of Earth's rotation and hence are "stationary" over a particular location. At this altitude the GOESs can send back pictures of large portions of Earth's surface.

Geographic boundaries and longitude and latitude grids are prepared by a computer and electronically combined with the picture signal so the areas of particular weather disturbances can be easily identified.

With satellite photographs meteorologists have a panoramic view of the weather conditions. The dominant feature of the photograph is, of course, the cloud cover. However, with the aid of radar, which uses a wavelength that picks up only precipitation, the storm areas are easily differentiated from regular cloud cover. Successive photographs of these storm centers give an indication of their movement, growth, and behavior, thus aiding weather forecasting.

Several improved GOES satellites (called GOES-NEXT) are planned to be put into orbit in the 1990s. Higher-resolution night sensors on board the GOES-NEXT satellites will aid forecasters in tracking dangerous storms not easily recognizable with current GOES imagery.

Another important feature of the satellite is **infrared measurements.** The energy and wavelength of emitted radiation depend on the temperature of the radiator. Objects with normal temperatures emit radiation energy in the infrared region of the spectrum. Hence using a spectrometer to determine the wavelength in this region provides a method of determining the temperature.

Normally, temperature measurements versus altitude are taken by conventional methods using radiosondes. However, infrared spectrometers now permit these measurements to be taken from lower-altitude, polar-orbiting satellites. This method offers a great advantage, because satellites can cover all areas of Earth, some of which have never been monitored by radiosonde because of their inaccessibility. This represents a major step in making the meteorologists' global weather picture more complete.

Developmental work is being done on a thermodynamic profiler called a *Radio Acoustic Sounding System* (RASS). This system uses sound waves to measure air temperature to a height of about 19,000 ft (5,800 m). The speed of sound in air depends on the air temperature. The RASS is to be used in conjunction with the Doppler radar wind profiler. The enhanced radar picks up the sound reflections while measuring wind speed and direction.

One of the more recent down-to-earth atmospheric observations is the **air pollution potential.** The pollution problem becomes severe when certain atmospheric conditions prohibit the dispersal of pollutants. Using upper-air observations, the NMC prepares wind and air-current data that are analyzed for potential pollution conditions. Advisory forecasts are issued to areas in which stagnation conditions are expected to persist for at least 36 hours. The air pollution potential provides an opportunity for pollution control and research, particularly in studying the influence of meteorological factors on the pollution conditions observed.

Another increasingly common atmospheric observation not related to weather forecasting is the pollen count. The count is made by health officials and is issued to give hay fever sufferers an indication of the amount of airborne pollen, which can aggravate their condition.

Folklore and the Weather

Folklore and legends have been associated with the weather since the beginning of humanity. People in early civilizations worshipped deities whose actions were manifested by weather phenomena. Myths were created to account for those occurrences that could not be otherwise explained. In Norse mythology, for example, thunder and lightning indicated the presence of the violent god Thor. Clouds were the cattle of the Greek sun god Apollo, grazing in the meadows of heaven.

> Men judge by the complexion of the sky
> The state and inclination of the day.
>
> —*Shakespeare*, Richard II

As knowledge progressed and people gave up the mythological interpretations of weather, they began associating its behavior with observed phenomena. In this manner a similar observation might allow prediction of future weather conditions. It is these observations that have come down to us as folklore. Usually in the forms of sayings or verse, they have been handed down by word of mouth from generation to generation and often appear in literature.

Some of these sayings are well founded and can be explained scientifically. Others, seemingly without any valid explanation, live on, much the same as superstitions. A few of these well-known sayings are examined in this section. Those related to meteorological explanations will be pointed out. The others are left to the reader's imagination.

Many amateur weather forecasters closely observe the activities of birds and animals. The antics and instincts of these creatures often seem without explanation. However, they form an essential part of folklore. Ducks flapping their wings, the braying of donkeys, and the bolting of horses, for example, are thought by some to be indicative of stormy weather. Loggers in the Pacific Northwest are said to predict snow two or three days before a blizzard by watching elk gather in the shelter of trees. Fiddler crabs have been observed to retreat to inland burrows days before a hurricane's arrival.

Other observations are of a seasonal nature. Marks on a caterpillar and the amount of food stored by squirrels are used to predict the severity of the coming winter. The southward flight of birds may indicate an early winter, whereas wild geese flying north is taken as a sure sign that warm weather is coming soon. In California, the swallows come back to Capistrano on the same day each year.

Probably the most celebrated weather-predicting animal is the groundhog. Legend has it that the groundhog emerges from his winter hibernation each year on February 2 to check on the approach of spring. If he sees his shadow, he returns to his burrow, indicating that six more weeks of winter can be expected. This bit of folklore is greatly publicized each year by the town of Punxsutawney, Pennsylvania, where the local groundhog, "Punxsutawney Phil," is said to be the superior forecaster. It is somewhat surprising that his shadow, which occurs when the Sun is shining, should warn the groundhog of continuing winter, but that's the legend.

More dependable observations result from the sun and its effects.

Above the rest, the sun who never lies
Foretells the change of weather in the skies.

—Virgil

There are several sayings about the sun and the weather indications it gives. Among them are the following:

The weary sun hath made a golden set
And by the bright tracks of his fiery car
Gives token of a goodly tomorrow.

—Shakespeare, Richard II

If the red sun begins his race
Be sure the rain will fall apace.

The Pharisees also with the Sadducees came, and tempting desired him that he would shew them a sign from heaven. He answered and said unto them, When it is evening, ye say, It will be fair weather: for the sky is red. And in the morning, It will be foul weather today: for the sky is red and lowring. Oh ye hypocrites, ye can discern the face of the sky; but can ye not discern the signs of the times?

—Matthew 16:1–4

The weather predictions alluded to in the Bible are more commonly stated:

Red sky at night, sailors delight;
Red sky in the morning, sailors take warning.

"Rainbow" is often substituted for "red sky" in the above saying. All these sayings involve the red sky, which we often see at sunrise and sunset. What then causes the sun and sky to appear red? When the sun is on the horizon, the sunlight travels farther through the atmosphere to reach us than when it is over-head. The blue portion of the sunlight is normally scattered. However, if the air contains impurities such as dust, more of the longer wavelengths are scattered as the sunlight travels near the surface of Earth, with the result that only the red portion of the spectrum may reach an observer. This, of course, makes the sky and sun appear red.

The condition is enhanced if a stable high-pressure region is between the observer and the Sun, as the high pressure holds air contaminants near Earth and scattering is increased. Highs are generally associated with good weather, so if one sees a red sky in the evening, it is quite probable that there is a high-pressure area to the west, and good weather will accompany it as it moves eastward, delighting sailors in the westerly wind zone where this weather movement applies. Should the red sky occur at sunrise in the east, the high has probably passed and will usually be followed by a low-pressure system, which is generally associated with poor weather.

Another belief describing an observed phenomenon of sunlight is as follows:

When the sun draws water, rain will follow.

The sun's rays are often blocked by dense clouds. Occasionally, a cloud may be thin enough in a small area to show sunlight, or a small break in the clouds may allow the sunlight to shine through. In the humid air associated with the clouds, sunlight may be scattered by fine water droplets or other particles, giving rise to diffuse reflection and creating the effect of a fanlike ray of sunlight extending from Earth to the cloud.

This effect also may be observed when sunlight shines through dense leaf coverage in a thickly wooded area or in a flashlight or searchlight beam at night. No drawing up of water occurs, but clouds and particles *are* available for the production of rain.

Mackerel sky and mare's tails
Make lofty ships carry low sails.

Trace in the sky the painter's brush
The winds around you soon will rush.

The cirrus and cirrocumulus clouds referred to usually precede the approach of a warm front. As the front approaches, the warm air rising over the cold air mass is likely to produce the winds predicted by these verses.

The wind in the West
Suits everyone best.

In general, our good weather comes from the west, as opposed to north and east, so the saying is to some degree valid. Remember, however, that some locations on Earth receive very poor weather from the west. Hence the saying is not universal.

When the morn is dry
The rain is nigh
When the morn is wet
No rain you get.

Or in different form and meter:

When the grass is dry at morning light
Look for rain before the night;
When the dew is on the grass
Rain will never come to pass.

The reasoning behind these rhymes is obvious. If condensation in the form of dew has occurred, the air will have a lower relative humidity, and rain will be unlikely. However, a better last line to the second poem might read "Rain will *seldom* come to pass," as the air at higher elevations may have sufficient moisture to produce rain. Also, the lack of dew in the morning is not a positive indication of rain. The general validity of these sayings is therefore questionable.

The moon also shares considerable prominence in weather folklore. Many sayings related to it are unfounded; among these, the indication of rain when "the new moon holds the old moon in its arms." This refers to the time when the crescent new moon is near the lower portion of the moon and appears to hold the upper darkened portion. The rain supposedly results from water being spilled from the saucer-shaped new moon. Such sayings are best answered by this countersaying:

Moon and weather may change together
But a change of the moon does not change the weather.

More reasonable predictions are given by the following:

Clear moon, frost soon.

A ring around the moon is a sure sign of rain.

When the stars begin to huddle
The Earth will soon become a puddle.

The first of these sayings refers to the lack of cloud cover that acts like an insulation to keep Earth warm. In the absence of clouds, the moon is clearly seen and the land masses cool quickly, making frost likely. The last two sayings refer to the appearance of the moon and stars as viewed through cirrostratus clouds. The moon appears with a diffuse halo, whereas the indistinct stars appear to be closer together. Cirrostratus clouds normally precede an approaching warm front, which is accompanied by turbulent weather, usually in the form of rain.

Although not directly related to meteorology, the moon and its phases are often referred to for planting crops. Many gardeners follow the *Farmer's Almanac,* which gives the periods of the proper phases of the moon for planting particular crops. In general, crops that produce above ground are to be planted in the "light of the moon," or in the waxing phase. Those that produce below the surface are to be planted in the "dark of the moon," or in the waning phase.

For example, it was reported that a certain gardener had difficulty in keeping dirt on potatoes that were planted in the light of the moon.

Wood is also said to be affected by the phases of the moon. A board lying on the ground will supposedly curl up at the ends in the light of the moon and stick firmly to the ground in the dark of the moon. Whether this is true is subject to doubt, but some builders will put on wooden shingles only during the waning phase or dark of the moon.

Other weather sayings include the following:

Sound travelling far and wide
A stormy day will betide.

Sound waves may be reflected by air layers of different temperatures in the atmosphere. As a result, the sound is heard at a considerable distance, where it is reflected back to Earth. A reflecting cold air layer may also be the source of precipitation, accounting for the stormy day.

Rain before seven stops before eleven.

This is a reasonably safe prediction for convectional precipitation. If it were raining prior to 7 A.M., little moisture would probably be left in the precipitating cloud by 11 A.M. Moreover, the sun would be rising high in the sky and cause the temperature to rise above the dew point temperature. The clouds would then dissipate and the rain cease, which would bear out the prediction. However, for frontal precipitation, which is controlled by huge air masses, the prediction may not prove to be so accurate.

Leaves turn silver before a rain.

When the wind blows the leaves so that the shiny underside is exposed, they take on a silvery appearance. This turning up of the leaves may result from vertical air motion, which may cause cloud formation. If a nimbus cloud develops, the leaves' prediction of rain will be fulfilled.

It smells like rain.

Before a rain there may be a musty, or earthy, smell in the air. Because convectional precipitation is associated with low pressure and rising air, air and gases in the ground may diffuse out, giving rise to the "smell of rain."

Snow on the ground for three days is waiting for another.

If snow remains on the ground for three days, it is obviously quite cold and additional precipitation is likely to be in the form of snow.

Several common sayings that are without scientific foundation are:

Rain on the first Sunday,
rain every Sunday [of the month].

Rain on Easter Sunday,
rain for seven straight Sundays.

Rain on Good Friday,
the Saint is pouring water on a flat rock.

The last demonstrates how the meanings of folklore sayings may be disguised. Its interpretation is that if it rains on Good Friday, the following summer will be dry, such that the rains will run off the hard, dry ground as though it were a rock.

Another special day for rain is St. Swithin's Day, July 15. If it rains on St. Swithin's Day, the ancient legend says, 40 days of rain will follow. St. Swithin was an English bishop whose wish it was to be buried in the open churchyard. When sainted and moved into the church, his spirit protested with 40 days of rain. A rain occurring on the anniversary of this event will supposedly arouse St. Swithin's spirit for a repeat performance.

Certain weather occurrences are given special names. A period of warm weather in October or November is sometimes referred to as **Indian Summer.** The seasonal cooling at this time of year gives rise to low-lying fogs. It is said that thin fogs lying near the tops of corn shocks reminded the early settlers of smoke coming from Indian teepees, hence the name Indian Summer. There is nothing uncommon about a brief warm "spell" this late in the year, as the season changes from autumn to winter.

The special significance of this period of warm weather is no doubt largely psychological. People are aware of the coming harsh winter and are sentimental toward this last warm reminder of the pleasant summer. The fondness for summer prompts a special name for this last trace. A wintry period in April is not so honored as Indian Winter but is deplored and quickly forgotten. More significance is given to the break in winter called the January thaw, which often occurs in February. A cold snap during the first few days of spring, when blackberries usually bloom, is sometimes called Blackberry Winter.

Some people are able to forecast a change in the weather or rain by an ache in the knee or some other joint. This ability was thought to be a joke for some time; however, it is now believed that changes in the pressure and humidity affect the aches and pains of rheumatic joints. Others, who are not afflicted, may rely on folklore to help predict weather behavior. The date of the first snow is sometimes taken as the number of snows that will occur during the winter. As the number of snows approaches the predicted number, those who believe in this prediction become very discriminating between an actual snow and a noncountable flurry.

Folklore, whether true or unfounded, will exist as long as people talk about the weather, and weather is one of our most talked-about subjects. When we are without anything to say or at a loss for words, it is a favorite topic that comes to our aid. Everyone comments on the weather, and an old English proverb observes:

Weather is the discourse of fools.

Learning Objectives

After studying this chapter, you should be able to do the following without referring to the text:

1. Describe the organization and functions of the National Weather Service.
2. Explain how weather data are processed and how forecasts are distributed.
3. State the instruments, their operation, and the data collected in a typical weather station.
4. Describe the operation and data collected by radar, radiosondes, and weather satellites.
5. Distinguish between folklore sayings with scientific merit and those without.
6. Define and explain the important terms listed in the next section.

Important Terms

National Weather Service
NOAA
National Meteorological Center
instrument shelter
maximum thermometer
minimum thermometer

rain gauge
radar
Doppler radar
radiosonde
Indian Summer

Questions

The National Weather Service

1. What is NOAA?
2. Has the United States always had a National Weather Service or a similar organization?
3. How are weather data processed and forecasts made? How often are forecasts made?
4. What are the locations of the Forecast Office and the Office of the National Weather Service nearest your hometown? your college or university?

Data Collection and Weather Observation

5. What type of data are taken at a typical weather data station?
6. Explain the operation of a maximum-minimum thermometer.

7. What does the word *radar* mean?

8. What is a radiosonde?

9. How are temperature profiles obtained by satellite?

10. What is a GOES, and why is it "stationary"?

11. What regions of the United States have high air pollution potential?

Folklore and the Weather

12. Are folklore sayings concerning the weather reliable? Do they have any scientific merit?

13. How do folklore sayings originate?

14. What are some of the major elements of observation in folklore sayings?

Thought Questions

1. Discuss how weather maps for the South American countries of (a) Brazil and (b) Argentina would be used to make weather forecasts (i.e., weather movements, and so on).

2. What do you think about folklore weather predictions? For example, do the actions of some animals and birds provide reasonable predictions?

Exercises

Folklore and the Weather

1. Examine the following weather sayings and explain their meteorological merit and meaning, if any.

   (a) A red sun has water in his eye.

   (b) Two full moons in a calendar month bring on a flood.

   (c) Mackerel clouds in the sky, expect more wet than dry.

   (d) February rain is only good to fill ditches.

   (e) Candles burn dim before rain.

   (f) March comes in like a lion and goes out like a lamb.

   (g) A year of snow, a year of plenty.

   (h) Dew long on the ground, Jack Frost will be around.

   (i) It's too cold to snow.

2. Examine the following sayings and discuss if they have scientific merit.

   (a) It will be a bad winter if squirrels' tails grow bushier.

   (b) For every frost or fog in August, there will be a snowy day in winter.

(c) The number of days old the moon is at the first snow tells how many snows there will be that winter.

(d) If it's cloudy and smoke rises, there's a chance of snow.

(e) It will rain if smoke goes to the ground.

(f) A long, hot summer means a long, cold winter—the hotter the summer, the colder the winter.

Vocabulary Exercises

Important Words and Terms

preoccupation   335

empirical   335

National Weather Service   335

impetus   335

echelon   336

teletypewriters   337

precipitation   338

percentage probabilities   338

convectional   338

climatology   338

substations   338

instrument shelter   338

psychrometer   339

thermograph   339

hydrothermograph   339

maximum thermometer   339

minimum thermometer   339

graduation   340

rain gauge   340

radar   340

radiosonde   341

wind profiler   341

panoramic   341

infrared measurements   342

Directions: Find each term and read the sentence or paragraph in which it occurs. If the context makes the definition of the word clear, check Yes, and write a definition from the context. If the meaning is not clear from the context, check No, and use a dictionary to find a definition that matches the one the author uses. Some of the words are also followed by a line labeled "Structure." For these terms, describe how the structure of each term relates to its meaning. Use the dictionary to describe the word parts and their meanings if you don't already know them.

1. preoccupation

____Yes   ____ No _____

_____

Structure: _____

2. empirical

____Yes   ____ No _____

_____

3. National Weather Service

    ____Yes   ____ No _____

_____

4. impetus

    ____Yes   ____ No _____

_____

5. echelon

    ____Yes   ____ No _____

_____

6. teletypewriters

    ____Yes   ____ No _____

_____

Structure: _____

7. precipitation

    ____Yes   ____ No _____

_____

8. percentage probabilities

    ____Yes   ____ No _____

_____

9. convectional

    ____Yes   ____ No _____

_____

Structure: _____

10. climatology

    ____Yes   ____ No _____

_____

11. substations

    ____Yes   ____ No _____

_____

Structure: _____

12. instrument shelter

    ____Yes   ____ No _____

_____

13. psychrometer

____Yes   ____ No _____

_____

Structure: _____

14. thermograph

____Yes   ____ No _____

_____

Structure: _____

15. hydrothermograph

____Yes   ____ No _____

_____

Structure: _____

16. maximum thermometer

____Yes   ____ No _____

_____

17. minimum thermometer

____Yes   ____ No _____

_____

18. graduation

____Yes   ____ No _____

_____

19. rain gauge

____Yes   ____ No _____

_____

20. radar

____Yes   ____ No _____

_____

21. radiosonde

____Yes   ____ No _____

_____

22. wind profiler

____Yes   ____ No _____

_____

23. panoramic

   ____Yes   ____ No _____

   _____

   Structure: _____

24. infrared measurements

   ____Yes   ____ No _____

   _____

Abbreviations

This selection uses several abbreviations for agencies or for equipment. It is likely you will see these abbreviations on tests or hear them in lectures, so it is important that you know what they stand for.

Directions: For each abbreviation, first tell what the letters stand for (e.g., "NWS" stands for "National Weather Service.") Then describe the agency or equipment.

1. NOAA (335)

   NOAA stands for: _____

   Describe NOAA: _____

   _____

2. NMC (336)

   NMC stands for: _____

   Describe NMC: _____

   _____

3. VHF-FM (337)

   VHF-FM stands for: _____

   Describe VHF-FM: _____

   _____

4. AFOS (337)

   AFOS stands for: _____

   Describe AFOS: _____

   _____

5. TIROS (341)

   TIROS stands for: _____

   Describe TIROS: _____

   _____

6. GOES (341)

GOES stands for: _____

Describe GOES: _____

_____

7. RASS (342)

RASS stands for: _____

Describe RASS: _____

_____

Application Exercises

1. Engage in Before Reading Activities. First, activate your prior knowledge about the weather and weather forecasting. Then, preview the selection. What are the key concepts? How is the information organized? How does the first half of the selection (about the National Weather Service and data collection) differ from the second half (about folklore)? Will you use different reading and studying strategies for the two parts? Make a reading/studying schedule for this chapter, taking into account the differences in the two parts of the chapter. Decide how much you will read at one time and what rehearsal strategies you will use to learn and remember the material.

2. From your preview, make a skeletal map of the key concepts in the first half of the chapter (including the sections on the National Weather Service and Data Collection and Weather Observation). Your map should show the relationships among the major ideas.

3. Study Figure 23.1 on page 336. This is a map, like ones we discussed in Chapter 10, of the many organizations that help to forecast the weather. As you read about these organizations, use this map to help understand and remember the organizations.

4. Identify at least fifteen terms that are related to the key information in the chapter and that you need to learn (you can refer to the list in the Vocabulary Exercise). Put these terms on concept cards using the format outlined in Chapter 10.

5. Construct at least twenty questions and answers. Use the format discussed in Chapter 8, and make sure that some of your questions are of a higher-level nature and require critical thinking.

6. Using PLAE, devise a study plan that you could use to study for a test on this selection.

Human Diversity

The first time I heard the song was at the 1964 World's Fair in Queens, New York. I was eleven years old at the time, and the exhibit was called "It's a Small World." After waiting in line, my family and I were seated in a boat that transported us from one room of the exhibit to another and treated us to a fantasy-like display that left a lasting imprint in my memory. There were hundreds of animated dolls colorfully dressed as children from all the continents of the world. As the dolls circled and moved about on mechanical platforms, you could hear children's voices all singing in their native languages. The message of this exhibit was that despite differences in language, customs, and geography, the peoples of the world share a common bond.

It's now more than thirty years later, and millions of people continue to tour this exhibit in the Disney parks of Florida, California, Paris, and Tokyo. And the message—that it's a small world—rings truer today than ever before. As many as a billion people have watched the Olympics on TV. Via satellite, the outbreak of war, floods, earthquakes, volcanic eruptions, and royal weddings are broadcast live to all corners of the globe. In Moscow, you can wear Levi jeans, watch MTV, drink Coke, and eat burgers and fries at McDonald's. And in the United States, you can drive a Japanese car, wear clothes made in Taiwan, and eat in restaurants that serve enchiladas, lasagna, won ton soup, pita bread, sushi, sausages, curried lamb, and other international delights.

Computers, high-speed jumbo jets, satellite communications, international trade agreements, educational exchanges, and the like invite an important question: What challenges lie ahead as we approach the twenty-first century, when East meets West and North meets South in the global village? Does the smallness of our world homogenize different cultures and other groups, or does it sharpen our awareness of human diversity? And what about migration patterns within countries? Consider the rapid changes in the American landscape caused by recent influxes of immigrants. Over the next few years, ethnic minority groups will constitute a majority of the population in a number of U.S. cities. Will this increased heterogeneity breed tolerance of others who are different, or will it fuel prejudice? What about recent changes in the social roles played by men and women? As more and more women enter professional schools, join the work force, and seek positions of leadership, new questions are raised about the nature of men and women and the extent to which sex differences are rooted in biological or social factors. Finally, what do psychologists know about sexual orientation? How prevalent is homosexuality, and to what extent is it rooted in biological or social factors?

Over the years, social psychologists have found that people are profoundly affected by the situations they are in (Milgram's obedience experiments illustrate this point in a dramatic way). In this regard, we'll see that cultural factors—such as childrearing practices, social norms, and stereotypes—play a particularly prominent role. The various issues addressed in this chapter converge on another important point: For people to get along with their neighbors, coworkers, fellow citizens, members of the opposite sex, and others with whom we share this planet, there need to be mutual tolerance, understanding, and an appreciation for the diversity of human life. If I had to sum up all of psychology—and the theme of this selection—in just one sentence, it would be this: Everyone is basically the same, yet no two people are alike.

The similarities among us are so self-evident that they are invisible, taken for granted. Regardless of whether you are male or female; regardless of whether the color of your skin is black, white, brown, red, yellow, or olive-toned; regardless of whether you are gay or straight; and regardless of where in the world you live—you squint your eyes in bright sunlight, prefer sweet foods to bitter, get light-headed when you drink too much, smile when you're happy, speak in "baby talk" to infants, have the capacity to hold seven or so items in short-term memory, forget events that took place when you were two years old, repeat behaviors that produce reinforcement, seek the company of others who are similar, respond to social pressure from peers, and react to trauma with anxiety or depression. Similarly, babies all over the world babble before uttering a word, fear strangers in the first year of life, think concretely before using abstract logic, and start thinking about sex during adolescence.

Despite the "universals" of human behavior, there are some differences—(1) between cultures, (2) between racial and ethnic groups within a culture, (3) between men and women, and (4) between gays and straights. We'll see that some of these differences are rooted in biology, while others result from the various physical, economic, and social environments in which people live. Either way, it is clear that there's a good deal of diversity among us.

Cross-Cultural Perspectives

For every two ticks of the second hand on your watch, nine new babies are born, and three people die. The net increase of three human lives per second means that the world's population grows by 10,600 per hour, 254,000 per day, 1.8 million per week, 7.7 million per month, and 93 million per year. According to the United Nations, there are now 5.5 billion people in the world's population, a number that is projected to reach 6 billion by 1998 and 10 billion before the year 2050.

Immersed in our own ways of life, it is all too easy to overlook an important fact: There is no dominant world culture. Look at Table 14.1, for example, and you'll see that of every 100 people in the two hundred or so nations of the world, only 5 live in the United States. We humans are a heterogeneous lot. As a matter of *geography*, some of us live in large, heavily populated cities, while others live in small towns, affluent suburbs, rural farming communities, hot and humid jungles, expansive deserts, high-altitude mountains, tropical islands, and icy arctic plains. Excluding the dialects, more than 6,000 different *languages* are spoken—the most common being Chinese, English, Hindi, Arabic, Russian, Malay, Bengali, Spanish, French, Japanese, Portuguese, and German, in that order. There are also hundreds of *religions* that people identify with—the most popular being Christianity (32 percent), Islam (17 percent),

21	China
16	India
5	United States
5	former Soviet Union
4	Indonesia
3	Brazil
2	Bangladesh
2	Japan
2	Mexico
2	Nigeria
2	Pakistan
1	Egypt
1	Ethiopia
1	France
1	Germany
1	Iran
1	Italy
1	Philippines
1	Thailand
1	Turkey
1	United Kingdom
1	Vietnam
25	all remaining countries

Table 14.1 Where in the World People Live

In 1991, the U.S. Census Bureau estimated that of every 100 people in the world, 21 live in China, 16 live in India, 5 live in the United States, and so on.

Hinduism (14 percent), Buddhism (6 percent), Chinese folk religions (4 percent), New Asian religions (2 percent), various African tribal religions (2 percent), and Judaism (.4 percent). The remaining 20 percent of the world's population are atheists or are simply unaffiliated with a religion.

Cultural Diversity: A Fact of Life

Linked together by space, language, religion, and historical bonds, each cultural group has its own ideology, folklore, music, forms of artistic expression, political system, family structure, sexual mores, fashions, and foods. In China, food is flavored primarily with soy sauce, rice wine, and ginger root; in Greece, olive oil, lemon, and oregano are often used; in Morocco, the food is seasoned with coriander, cumin, cinnamon, onion, and fruit; and in Mexico, tomatoes and hot chile pepper are used (Rozin, 1983).

As world travelers well know, the variations in food are matched by variations in local customs. Visit an outdoor market in Iraq, and you should expect to barter or negotiate the price of everything you purchase. Dine in an Indian home, and you should leave some food on the plate to show the host that the portions were generous and you had enough to eat. Plan a meeting with a native of Brazil, and don't be surprised if he or she is late. Nothing personal. In North America, it is common to sit casually opposite someone with your legs outstretched. Yet in Nepal, it is considered an insult to point the bottom of your feet at a person. In Turkey, it is okay for heterosexual men to embrace, kiss on the cheek, and walk together hand in hand. Yet in North America, such public displays between men are considered unmanly. In Iran, Islamic women wear veils over the face; in many other countries, women paint their lips, shadow their eyes, and powder their faces with makeup. People in some parts of the world eat with forks and knives; others use chopsticks, bread, or their bare hands. Some people exchange greetings by shaking hands or waving; others lower the head and bow. Even the way we space ourselves from each other is culturally determined. Americans, Germans, the British, and Northern Europeans maintain a polite distance between themselves and others—and feel "crowded" by the more intimate, touchier, nose-to-nose style of the French, Greeks, Arabs, Mexicans, and people of South America. In the affairs of day-to-day living, each culture operates according to its own implicit rules of conduct, or **social norms** (see Table 14.2).

Just as cultures differ in their social norms, so too they differ in the extent to which people adhere to those norms. As an example, compare the United States and Japan. In the United States, it is said that "the squeaky wheel gets the grease"—so parents teach their children to be independent, self-reliant, and unique. In Japan, however, it is said that "the nail that stands out gets pounded down"—so children are taught the values of conformity, loyalty, and harmony

---

social norms Implicit rules of conduct according to which each culture operates.

- *Greetings.* Waving and shaking hands may seem universal, but there are different rules for greeting. In Finland you should give a firm handshake, in France you should loosen the grip, in Zambia you should use your left hand to support the right, and in Bolivia you should extend your arm if your hand is dirty. In Japan people bow, in Thailand they put both hands together in a praying position on the chest, and in Fiji they smile and raise their eyebrows. In Venezuela, Paraguay, and certain other parts of Latin America, it is common for people to hug, embrace, and kiss upon meeting. In most Arab countries, men greet one another by saying *salaam alaykum,* then shaking hands, saying *kaif halak,* and kissing each other on the cheek.

- *Nonverbal Communication.* When you don't speak the native language, it's natural to use gestures. Watch out. In Bulgaria, nodding your head means "no" and shaking your head sideways means "yes." In Germany and Brazil, the American "okay" sign (forming a circle with your thumb and forefinger) is an obscene gesture. Personal space habits also vary across cultures. Japanese people prefer to keep a comfortable distance while interacting. But in Puerto Rico and much of Latin America, people stand very close—and backing off is considered an insult. Also beware of what you do with your eyes. In Latin America locking eyes is a must, yet in Japan too much eye contact shows a lack of respect. If you're in the habit of stroking your cheek, you should know that in Italy, Greece, and Spain it means you find the person you're talking to attractive. And whatever you do, don't ever touch someone's head while in Buddhist countries, especially Thailand. The head is sacred.

- *Table Manners.* So much human social activity revolves around eating that acceptance of local foods and table manners is important. First, be prepared for foods you may consider "exotic." For example, you may be served sheep's eyes in Saudi Arabia, raw fish in Japan, bear's paw soup in China . . . and lobster in the United States. Be mindful of strict religious prohibitions, and don't ask for beef in India or pork in Islamic countries. Table etiquette is also tricky. In Zambia, the guest should ask to be served because it's impolite for the host to offer food first. In Saudi Arabia, you show your appreciation of a meal by stuffing yourself. As a dinner guest in Bolivia, you should clean your plate to prove you enjoyed the meal, but in India you should leave some food to signal to the host that you've had enough to eat. In parts of Pakistan, India, Malaysia, and Indonesia, you should never pass, accept, or touch food with your left hand.

- *Gifts.* Giving and accepting gifts is a customary part of social interaction. It also presents an opportunity for misunderstanding. In Japan, gift giving is used to express friendship, gratitude, and respect. But beware: If you receive a gift, you should reciprocate—so don't get caught empty-handed. When you give a gift in Japan, however, make sure that it is not wrapped in white paper (white is associated with death). In China, avoid using red ink (messages written in red imply the severing of a relationship). Of course, what you give is as important as how you present it. Never present a bottle of wine to a Muslim because the Islamic faith prohibits alcohol. In Hong Kong, avoid clocks (which symbolize death) and sharp objects (which signify the breakup of a relationship). Flowers are nice, but in Guatemala white flowers are reserved for funerals, and in Chile yellow flowers signify contempt. If you visit someone in Greece, Morocco, and many Arab countries, be careful not to admire or praise any possession too much or your host will feel obligated to give it to you.

Table 14.2 Helpful Tips for the World Traveler

Social norms from one country to the next are so different that people who travel on business or for pleasure should know the local customs. Here are a few tips from the 1993 edition of Roger Axtell's best-seller, *Do's and Taboos Around the World.*

within the community. As we'll see, this comparison indicates that there are two very different cultural orientations toward persons and the groups to which they belong. One orientation centers on the individual, the other on the group.

Individualism and Collectivism: A Tale of Two Cultures

In the movie *Mr. Baseball,* actor Tom Selleck plays an aging American baseball star who signs a contract with a team in Japan. Selleck plays a brash and colorful character who always swings for the home run, loafs at practice, defies his manager, argues with umpires, and throws his bat when he is frustrated—a personal style that offends the Japanese sense of decorum. Eventually, Selleck's antics become so publicly humiliating to the team that he is suspended. American and Japanese values were caricatured in this film for the sake of art. But there is an underlying truth to the distinction. Baseball is popular in both countries and is played by the same set of rules. But while American players seek personal glory as all-stars and national heroes, Japanese coaches caution their players that "lone wolves are the cancer of the team."

This comparison reveals just the tip of an iceberg. Over the years, social scientists have observed that cultures differ in the extent to which they value **individualism** and the virtues of independence, autonomy, and self-reliance, or **collectivism** and the virtues of interdependence, cooperation, and social harmony. Under the banner of individualism, personal goals take priority over group allegiances. In collectivist cultures, however, the person is, first and foremost, a loyal member of a family, team, company, church, state, and other groups (see Table 14.3). In what countries are these differing orientations most extreme? In a worldwide study of 116,000 employees of IBM, Geert Hofstede (1980) found that the most fiercely individualistic people are from the United States, Australia, Great Britain, Canada, and the Netherlands, in that order. The most collectivistic people are from Venezuela, Colombia, Pakistan, Peru, Taiwan, and China.

What determines whether a culture becomes individualistic or collectivist? Speculating on the origins of the two orientations, Harry Triandis (1989) suggests that there are three key factors. The first is the *complexity* of a society. As people live in increasingly complex industrialized societies—compared, for example, to a life of food gathering among desert nomads—there are more groups to identify with (family, hometown, alma mater, place of employment, church, political party, sports teams, social clubs, and so on), which means less loyalty to any one group and more of a focus on personal rather than collective goals. Second is the *affluence* of a society. As people prosper, they gain financial independence from one another, a condition that promotes social independence, mobility, and, again, a focus on personal rather than collective goals. The third factor is *heterogeneity.* Societies that are homogeneous or "tight" (where members share the same language, religion, and social customs) tend to be rigid and intolerant of those who veer from the norm. In contrast, societies

individualism A cultural orientation in which independence, autonomy, and self-reliance take priority over group allegiances.

collectivism A cultural orientation in which interdependence, cooperation, and group harmony take priority over purely personal goals.

1. If the group is slowing me down, it is better to leave it and work alone. (*I*)
2. To be superior, a person must stand alone. (*I*)
3. I can count on my relatives for help if I find myself in any kind of trouble. (*C*)
4. If you want something done right, you've got to do it yourself. (*I*)
5. It is reasonable for a son to continue his father's business. (*C*)
6. In the long run, the only person you can count on is yourself. (*I*)
7. I enjoy meeting and talking to my neighbors every day. (*C*)
8. I like to live close to my good friends. (*C*)
9. The bigger the family, the more family problems there are. (*I*)
10. There is everything to gain and nothing to lose for classmates to group themselves for study and discussion. (*C*)

Table 14.3 Individualistic and Collectivist Orientations

Read these statements and note whether you agree or disagree with each one. People from collectivist cultures tend to agree with the *C* statements, while those from individualistic cultures tend to agree with the *I* statements. Where do you stand in your cultural orientation? (Hui, 1988; Triandis et al., 1988)

that are culturally diverse or "loose" (where two or more cultures coexist) are more permissive of dissent—thus allowing for greater individual expression.

It is interesting that individualistic values in the United States are even greater today than in the past. Consider this question: If you were a parent, what traits would you like your child to develop? When this question was asked of American mothers in 1924, many chose "strict obedience," "loyalty," and "good manners"—key characteristics of collectivism. But when American mothers were asked the same question fifty-four years later, in 1978, they cited "independence" and "tolerance of others"—important aspects of individualism. Due perhaps to the greater complexity, affluence, and diversity of Western life in general, similar trends were also found in surveys conducted in Germany, Italy, and England (Remley, 1988).

Conceptions of the Self Individualism and collectivism are so deeply ingrained in a culture that they mold our very self-conceptions and identities. According to Hazel Markus and Shinobu Kitayama (1991), people who grow up in individualistic countries see themselves as entities that are *independent*—distinct, autonomous, self-contained, and endowed with unique dispositions. By contrast, people from collectivist countries hold an *interdependent* view of the self as part of a larger social network that includes family, coworkers, friends, and others with whom they are socially connected. In one study, David Trafimow and his colleagues (1991) had American and Chinese college students complete twenty sentences beginning with "I am . . ." The Americans were more likely to fill in the blank with trait descriptions ("I am shy"), while the Chinese were more likely to identify themselves by their group affiliations

("I am a college student"). It's no wonder that in China, the family name comes *before* one's personal name. These conceptions are illustrated in Figure 14.1.

Do these conceptions of the self influence the way people perceive themselves in relation to others? Markus and Kitayama (1991) found three interesting differences between East and West. First, American college students see themselves as less similar to others than do Asian-Indian students. This finding reinforces the idea that people with independent conceptions of the self believe they are unique. Second, while North Americans are quick to express envy, anger, pride, and other "ego-focused" emotions that affirm the self as distinct, many nonwesterners feel "other-focused" emotions that promote interpersonal harmony rather than conflict. For example, people in Japan describe the emotions of *oime* (indebtedness), *fureai* (connection with others), and *sitasimi* (familiarity to others). Third, people in individualistic cultures strive for personal achievement, but those in collectivist cultures derive more self-esteem through the status and accomplishments of a valued group. Thus, whereas North Americans tend to overestimate their own contribution to a team effort, take credit for success, and blame others for failure, Japanese people tend to underestimate their own role and present themselves in more modest, humble terms.

Developmental Influences The culturally prescribed socialization practices that breed independence or interdependence begin soon after a baby is born. In the United States, a vast majority of middle-class parents who can afford it put their babies to bed in a separate room. Indeed, pediatrician Benjamin Spock (1945), author of the best-selling child-care book, advised that it is better "not to take the child into the parents' bed for any reason." When my children were younger, my wife and I never even thought twice about it. Separate sleeping arrangements were just a part of independence training. Yet in most other countries of the world, it is common for young children to sleep in the same room,

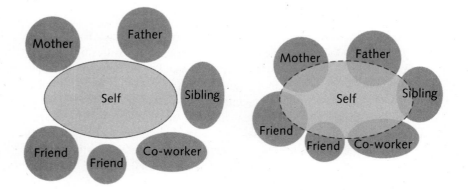

Figure 14.1 Self-Conceptions
Markus and Kitayama (1991) find that people from individualistic cultures see themselves as independent and distinct from others. In contrast, people in collectivist cultures see themselves as interdependent, as part of a larger social network.

even in the same bed, with their parents (Whiting & Edwards, 1988). Perhaps that is all part of *inter*dependence training. To many non-Americans, it is merciless to force helpless babies to lie alone in a dark room. Thus, when Mayan mothers from Guatemala were told of this practice, they reacted with shock, disapproval, and pity. As one disbelieving mother asked, "But there's someone else with them there, isn't there?" (Morelli et al., 1992).

Socialization fosters different cultural orientations in other ways, too. In individualistic cultures, parents are quick to wean infants from the breast and toilet-train their toddlers out of diapers. Teenagers fight to separate from parents, and adults struggle to resolve the "identity crisis" that seems to plague us all. With all the focus on "me," the individual, it's no wonder that bookstore shelves are lined with paperbacks on how to "get in touch with your feelings," "speak your mind," "fulfill your potential," and become "self-actualized." In many ways, we take our cultural orientations for granted. In cultures that value freedom and individual rights, for example, we assume that people should marry for love and romance. Not so in all corners of the world. In parts of India, even today, families make arrangements at birth for the future marriage of their children.

Social Consequences Try as they do to be objective, cross-cultural researchers cannot help but make value judgments about the individualist and collectivist orientations. Is one orientation better or more adaptive or more productive or more humane? There is no quick and simple answer. Predictably, individualists are less likely than collectivists to follow social norms. For example, when American subjects are confronted with confederates who make incorrect perceptual judgments, they conform to this incorrect majority 37 percent of the time. When similar tasks are given to subjects from collectivist cultures, conformity rates are even higher. Among the Bantu of Zimbabwe, an African tribe in which deviance is punished, 51 percent conformed. In fact, John Berry (1979) compared subjects from seventeen cultures and found that conformity rates ranged from a low of 18 percent among Eskimo hunters of Baffin Island to a high of 60 percent among village-living Temne farmers of West Africa. Is conformity a desirable or undesirable characteristic? Cast in a positive light, it promotes harmony and group solidarity—qualities that keep societies from being torn apart by dissension. Cast in a negative light, however, a lack of independence may lend itself to narrow-mindedness, cowardice, and blind obedience.

There is a drawback to individualism. If everyone focuses on personal goals, then the group as a whole may suffer. The baseball player who worries more about his batting average than the team's winning percentage is a case in point (there's a scene in *Mr. Baseball* in which Tom Selleck defies his manager's call for a sacrifice bunt and strikes out swinging for a home run). People often exert less effort, or "loaf" on the job, when they work as part of a group than when they work alone (Latané et al., 1979). To many of us, it seems natural to slack off somewhat when others are there to pick up the slack. But social loafing is not equally strong all over the world. In fact, research shows that

Chinese subjects in Taiwan work harder in a group than they do for themselves alone (Gabrenya et al., 1983). In collectivist cultures, what's good for the group is good for the self.

Ironically, the benefit of collectivism may also be its main flaw. Intimately connected to groups, collectivists are loyal and team-spirited, willing to sacrifice personal gain for their group's long-term well-being, and sometimes even willing to fight and die for their group. But how do collectivists behave toward members of other groups? Because they identify so strongly with their own, collectivists may be more likely to see their own norms as universal and exploit outsiders for competitive gain. In a study of interpersonal conflict, Kwok Leung (1988) found that Chinese subjects were less likely than Americans to pursue a conflict with a friend, but they were more likely to confront a stranger. As Harry Triandis put it, "While collectivists are very nice to those who are members of their own groups, they can be very nasty, competitive, and uncooperative toward those who belong to other groups" (quoted in Goleman, 1990, p. 41). The result: The collective "we" may fuel intergroup tensions and promote ethnic, regional, national, and religious fighting against the collective "them."

Multicultural Perspectives

In June 1993, three hundred Chinese men, women, and children left their families, crowded into a creaky, rusted freighter called the *Golden Venture*, traveled for four months over 17,000 miles, endured a ferocious Atlantic storm, and landed at 2 A.M. in Rockaway Beach, New York. Two hundred yards from the shore, the passengers clambered down the side of the vessel and swam to the beach, where they were met by authorities. Most appeared dazed, disoriented, shivering cold, hungry, and in poor health. Why did these people pay thousands of dollars to illegal alien smugglers and risk their lives on this dangerous and uncertain journey? Upset by the political and economic climate back home, they desperately wanted to start a new life.

Ethnic Diversity: A Fact of Life

The names, dates, and places may change, but this script is replayed over and over again. In 1991, thousands of Albanians seeking political freedom stole into the night and sailed across the Adriatic Sea to Italy. Most but not all were sent back. In just the past few years, thousands of Haitian refugees received political asylum in neighboring countries, Mexicans crossed the border into the United States, Afghans escaped war to Pakistan, Pakistanis moved into Great Britain, Turks sought employment in Germany, and Russian Jews moved from the defunct Soviet Union to Israel. Immigration is not the only source of ethnic diversity within a culture. In some cases, ethnic groups inhabit a country because they do not have their own homeland. Thus many Sikhs live in India and

Pakistan; Kurds inhabit Turkey and Iraq; the Basques live in Spain; the Tamils live in Sri Lanka; Palestinians are scattered throughout the Middle East; and the Navajo, Sioux, and other Native Americans are all citizens of the United States (Demko, 1992). In short, many countries are ethnically diverse.

Like most countries, the United States has a culturally mixed population—which is becoming even more so with time. According to the 1990 census, there are 248 million U.S. citizens, 22 million of whom were born in another country. As categorized by the Census Bureau, 80 percent of the population are white; 12 percent are black; 3 percent are Asians or Pacific Islanders; one percent are Native Americans, Eskimos, and Aleuts; 4 percent are of "other races." Overall, 9 percent of the people in these racial groups are of Hispanic origin and trace their roots to Mexico, Puerto Rico, Central America, Cuba, and other Spanish-speaking countries.

Growing racial and ethnic diversity within many countries around the world presents us all with new challenges and an uncertain future. How do the different groups within a culture coexist? Why so often is there animosity and conflict? More specifically, what are the causes and effects of prejudice, and how can this chronic social disease be treated? These and other questions have triggered an examination of **multiculturalism,** the study of racial and ethnic groups within a culture.

Acculturation and Ethnic Identity

When people migrate from one country to another, they bring with them a cultural heritage and lifestyle that reaches deep into the past. The result is that each racial or ethnic group is unique—similar to the dominant culture in some ways, different in others. For example, black psychologist James Jones (1991) argues that compared to white American culture, black Americans tend to be more present-oriented, improvisational, expressive, spiritual, and emotional. Originating in Africa or among slaves of the American South, many blacks have adopted a colorful and conspicuous behavior style—as seen in a certain slow, casual, rhythmic walk; in handshakes such as the "high five" and "thumb grasp"; and in sports, where athletes "spike" footballs into the endzone and "slam dunk" basketballs through the hoop (Majors, 1991).

Regardless of where racial or ethnic groups come from, how they get there, or why they leave their land of origin, all face the same core dilemma: whether to blend in and "assimilate" into the new culture or retain a separate identity, language and all. There are two radically different historical perspectives on how this conflict between old and new should be managed. One is the romantic American ideal that all immigrant groups discard their heritage culture and blend into the American way of life. This assimilationist view is captured by

Americans use 68 percent more spices today than a decade ago. The use of red pepper rose by 105 percent, basil by 190 percent (American Spice Trade Association).

In 1976 there were 67 Spanish-speaking radio stations in the United States. Now there are 311 (Market Segment Research, Inc.).

multiculturalism The study of diverse racial and ethnic groups within a culture.

the image of a *melting pot* in which different ethnic groups are mixed together to produce one harmonious mainstream culture. In the United States, this ideal is formalized in laws that require immigrants to renounce other citizenships, pass a test of American history, and take an oath of loyalty. The second approach encourages immigrants to retain their ancestral heritage, producing a culture that is ethnically diverse. In 1971, Canada adopted a policy of multiculturalism, in which the melting pot image was replaced by one of a colorful *mosaic* whereby each cultural group takes pride in its own unique identity and tolerates the differences between groups. Research shows, for example, that many recent Greek, Arab, and Italian immigrants to North America want their children to retain their own cultural identity (Moghaddam et al., 1993).

Torn between the need to fit in and a desire to retain their own heritage, ethnic-group members differ in the way they manage **acculturation**—the process by which persons are changed by their immersion in a new culture. According to John Berry and his colleagues (1989), there are four types of coping strategies. At one extreme is *assimilation,* in which the person abandons the old for the new and completely embraces his or her host culture—its language, customs, identity, and ways of life. At the opposite extreme is *separation,* a pattern characterized by a desire to maintain one's ethnic traditions and not become part of the host culture. Native Americans who live on Indian reservations and the Amish who live in Lancaster, Pennsylvania, are good examples. A third strategy is *integration,* a bicultural pattern in which the person tries to make the best of both worlds by retaining old traditions while, at the same time, adapting to the new way of life. The fourth strategy is *marginalization,* in which the person has no desire to maintain traditional ties or adopt the new culture, perhaps due to discrimination.

As a result of acculturation pressures, people who are caught between cultures come to identify with one or both of these cultures in the formation of an **ethnic identity.** Thus French-speaking residents of Quebec may think of themselves as French, Canadian, French-Canadian, or neither; Irish-Americans may identify themselves as Irish, American, or Irish-American. Jean Phinney (1990) notes that our ethnic identities are revealed in the way we label ourselves, our sense of belonging to a group, our pride in that group, and the extent to which we speak the language, study the history, follow the customs, and enjoy the food, music, dance, literature, holidays, and traditions. Phinney also notes that ethnic-identity formation typically begins in adolescence with a passive acceptance of the dominant culture, is followed in early adulthood by an awakening of interest in one's roots, and culminates later on in an ethnic identification. As you might expect, ethnic-group identification is stronger among immigrants

acculturation The process by which persons are changed by their immersion in a new culture.
ethnic identity The part of a person's identity that is defined by an ethnic heritage, language, history, customs, and so on.

who enter the host country as adults than it is among those who arrive at a younger, more formative age.

Regardless of *how* immigrants, refugees, displaced natives, and other ethnic minorities adapt to their cultural environment, some individuals have a more difficult time than others in making the adjustment. The problem used to be called "culture shock." Now the term **acculturative stress** is used. Either way, studies show that entering a new culture may be accompanied by anxiety, depression, and other mental health problems—and that these problems are linked to language barriers, a lack of familiarity with the host culture, a lack of education, rejection of one's group, prejudice, the absence of social support services, and other factors (Berry et al., 1992). For example, Hispanic newcomers to the United States who were interviewed said they felt pressured to learn English, found it difficult to find suitable work, felt guilty about leaving their family and friends behind, did not make use of social services for fear of being deported, and felt that they were rejected because they were Latinos. Needless to say, these immigrants were under more stress at home and in the workplace than were Hispanics born in the United States (Cervantes et al., 1991).

Is there a healthy, optimum way for Hispanic-Americans and others to cope with being strangers in a strange land, fish swimming outside of the mainstream? Consider the acculturation strategies described earlier. Is it better to become "integrated" and bicultural, or should immigrants shed their native past in an effort to become fully "assimilated" into the host culture?

At this point, there is no clear answer. However, a study by Juan Sanchez and Diana Fernandez (1993) provides an important starting point. In Miami, these investigators administered questionnaires to 164 Hispanic college students who were born in Cuba, Puerto Rico, South America, Central America, or the United States. One questionnaire measured the extent to which subjects identified with their ethnic group ("I have a sense of belonging to Hispanic heritage"), a second measured the extent to which they identified with American culture ("I consider myself an American"), and the third assessed feelings of acculturative stress ("People look down on me if I practice customs of my culture," "It is difficult to show off my family"). Students who were integrated— that is, those who had a strong ethnic identification *and* embraced American culture—reported less acculturative stress than students who did not identify with one or both cultures. This correlation should be interpreted with caution, however. It may mean that identification with one's host culture reduces stress, or that a lack of acculturative stress promotes identification. Either way, it is consistent with the increasingly popular notion that bicultural competence is psychologically adaptive, as it enables a person to alternate, without tension, between the two cultures (LaFromboise et al., 1993). As multiculturalist trends

acculturative stress The stress and mental health problems often found in immigrants trying to adjust to a new culture.

continue throughout the world, additional research should help provide some answers.

Discrimination

Of the many obstacles that confront ethnic minorities in any culture, the most vicious is **discrimination**—behavior directed against persons because of their affiliation with a social group. It is tempting to think of discrimination as a sin of the past. Unfortunately, recent incidents suggest that it still exists, and that its victims are avoided, excluded, rejected, belittled, and attacked, often because of their skin color or ethnic background. Discrimination has both cognitive and emotional roots. From a cognitive standpoint, it can often be traced to *stereotypes*—simplistic beliefs that associate whole groups of people with certain, sometimes unflattering, traits.

Stereotypes have a depersonalizing effect on the way people perceive ethnic minorities. In addition, discrimination is often motivated by deep-seated *prejudice*—feelings of hatred toward others based on their membership in a particular group. Whether the targets are blacks, whites, men, women, immigrants, or older people, prejudice is pervasive—and always has been.

Racism in America

Slave trading. The Deep South. Abolitionists. The Civil War. Lynch mobs. Separate but equal. The Ku Klux Klan. Jackie Robinson. The NAACP. Sitting in the back of the bus. Martin Luther King, Jr. Civil rights. Malcolm X. School busing. *Roots.* Affirmative action. Rodney King. Race relations in the United States have had a checkered, troubled, and emotional history—a history marked by both hatred and guilt, violent riots and peaceful marches, tolerance and intolerance, advances and setbacks. At the heart of it all, **racism:** a deep-seated form of prejudice that is based on the color of a person's skin. In the United States, this conflict is multidirectional, as all groups exhibit prejudice in one form or another.

The Problem I have been told, and I believe it, that because I am white I'll never really understand what it feels like to be black and living in the United States. In a poignant, very personal book titled *Race,* Studs Terkel (1992) interviewed ordinary Americans, black and white, about what he calls "the American obsession." Terkel tells penetrating real-life stories that reveal the depth and scope of the problem.

discrimination Behavior directed against persons because of their affiliation with a social group.

racism A deep-seated form of prejudice that is based on the color of a person's skin.

In some cases, he observes overt, old-fashioned prejudice—for example, the new construction worker who complained bitterly about affirmative action because, as he said of all blacks, "they live like low lifes. Don't like to work. Let their homes run down." In other cases, the prejudice is more subtle—as when Terkel's friend's wife, who is white and who thinks of herself as color-blind, drove through a black neighborhood in Chicago: "The people at the corners were all gesticulating at her. She was very frightened, turned up the windows, and drove determinedly. She discovered after several blocks, she was going the wrong way on a one-way street and they were trying to help her. Her assumption was they were blacks and were out to get her."

Another instance involved Terkel himself. He boarded a bus one morning and deposited his fare, only to have the driver, a young black man, say he was a dime short. Terkel was sure he had paid the right amount and was upset. But he fished into his pocket and dropped another dime into the box. "Oh, I understood the man," he thought. "I know the history of his people's bondage. It was his turn—a show of power, if only in a small way. If that's how it is, that's how it is. Oh, well." Then it happened. "As I was about to disembark, I saw a dime on the floor. My dime. I held it up to him. 'You were right.' He was too busy driving to respond. I waved: 'Take it easy.' 'You, too,' he replied. I've a hunch he'd been through something like this before."

This very subtle form of racism may seem invisible, but it is painful and humiliating to its victims. Terkel interviewed a young black woman who said, "It infuriates me to think that some little white woman would get on the elevator with my father and assume, just by the color of his skin, that he's going to harm her, and clutch her purse tighter. To think that my father, who's worked hard all his life, put us through school, loves us, took care of us—to think that she would clutch her purse because he's there. The thought of it makes me so angry." Similarly, a professor talked about the time a black professional he knows, a college graduate who lived in the suburbs, visited a nearby country club. "Someone handed him a bag of golf clubs," he said. "They thought he was a caddy."

The Symptoms Racism in the 1990s is a two-way problem that poisons social relations between blacks and whites. Detecting racism is not as easy as it may seem. In 1933, Daniel Katz and Kenneth Braly found that many white college students believed that black Americans were lazy, happy-go-lucky, aggressive, and ignorant. Thankfully, follow-up surveys taken in 1951, 1967, and 1982 showed that these bigoted images had faded (Dovidio & Gaertner, 1986). Or had they? These days, very few white Americans openly express racist sentiments. But can public opinion polls be trusted, or has racism simply gone underground? And what about the distrust of whites that many black Americans harbor? If people who are prejudiced will not admit it to pollsters, or even to themselves, how can we know that this chronic social disease still exists? What are the symptoms? Better yet, what is the cure?

People may not openly express their prejudices, but racism can be subtle, coloring our perceptions and our behavior. In an old and classic demonstration of this point, Gordon Allport and Leo Postman (1947) showed subjects a picture of a subway train filled with passengers. In the picture were a black man dressed in a suit and a white man holding a razor. One subject viewed the scene briefly and described it to a second subject who had not seen it. The second subject communicated the description to a third subject and so on, through six rounds of communication. The result: The final subject's report often indicated that the black man, not the white man, was holding the razor. Some subjects even reported that he was waving the weapon in a threatening manner.

The way people *interpret* an event may also be influenced by race, even today. In one study, white subjects watched on a TV monitor an interaction involving two men. A discussion developed into a heated argument, and one man seemed to shove the other. When the antagonist was white and the victim was black, only 17 percent of the subjects saw the shove as an act of violence. Most said it was just "horseplay." Yet when the antagonist was black and the victim white, the number of "violence" interpretations rose to 75 percent (Duncan, 1976). Similar results were found among children (Lawrence, 1991; Sagar & Schofield, 1980).

Racist beliefs can also be detected without asking direct questions. Researchers have found that *reaction time*—the speed it takes to answer a question—can be used to uncover hidden prejudices. In one study, for example, white subjects read word pairs and pressed a button whenever they thought the words fit together. In each case, the word *blacks* or *whites* was paired with either a positive trait (*clean, smart,* etc.) or a negative trait (*stupid, lazy,* etc.). The results were revealing. Subjects did not openly associate blacks with negative terms or whites with positive terms. And they were equally quick to reject the negative terms in both cases. However, subjects were quicker to respond to the positive words when they were paired with *whites* than with *blacks.* Since it takes less time to react to information that fits existing attitudes, this finding suggests that subjects were unconsciously predisposed to associate positive traits with whites more than with blacks (Gaertner & McLaughlin, 1983).

This result may seem subtle, but it suggests that racial prejudice may be so deeply ingrained in our culture that the negative images are as difficult to break as a bad habit (Devine, 1989). That's why the wife of Studs Terkel's friend was quick to assume that the black pedestrians who were gesturing at her posed a threat when, in fact, they were trying to let her know she was driving the wrong way on a one-way street. And that is why Terkel himself jumped to the conclusion that the black bus driver who said he was a dime short was being difficult when, in fact, the dime had fallen on the floor. The problem may be more common than we realize. Indeed, many nonprejudiced white Americans admit that they are not always fair to blacks—an insight that causes them to feel embarrassed, guilty, and ashamed of themselves (Devine et al., 1991).

The Treatment Racism is a social disease that gets transmitted from one generation to the next and afflicts millions. Can it be treated? Can stereotypes and prejudice be wiped out by a mass-media blitz designed to inform people that their expectations and fears are unfounded? Social psychologists used to think that such efforts at persuasive communication would prove effective, but they do not. Indeed, when you consider the many sources of stereotypes and prejudice, the prospects seem dim. There is, however, reason for hope. The key is to expose children to diversity, and the ideal setting is the school.

Summary and Key Terms

As the world becomes a global village, it's important to understand both the diversity among human groups and the fact that people around the world are remarkably similar.

Cross-Cultural Perspectives

Cultural Diversity: A Fact of Life   People vary not only in their language, religion, and the geography of their surroundings but also in their *social norms*—a culture's implicit rules of conduct—and in the degree to which they follow these norms.

Individualism and Collectivism: A Tale of Two Cultures   Cultures differ in their orientation toward *individualism* and *collectivism.* Individualistic cultures value independence, autonomy, and self-reliance, while collectivist cultures stress interdependence, cooperation, and group harmony. The United States, traditionally individualistic, is even more so today than in the past. According to Triandis, societies that are complex, affluent, and heterogeneous are the most likely to be individualistic.

Individualism and collectivism mold our self-conceptions. Cultural orientation also influences socialization practices throughout a person's life. The age of weaning, the choice of where a baby sleeps, decisions about whether to marry for love and other considerations relate to society's individualism or collectivism.

Each cultural orientation has advantages and disadvantages. In collectivist societies, people are more likely to follow social norms, which promotes harmony and loyalty and discourages social loafing. But collectivism can also produce narrow-mindedness and a confrontational attitude toward outsiders.

Multicultural Perspectives

Ethnic Diversity: A Fact of Life   As ethnic diversity increases in the United States and elsewhere, more attention is being paid to *multiculturalism,* the study of diverse racial and ethnic groups within a culture.

Acculturation and Ethnic Identity   All ethnic groups face the dilemma of how to adapt to the larger society. Should they blend into a single "melting pot" or retain their heritage as part of a cultural "mosaic"? *Acculturation,* the process of change that occurs when people are immersed in a new culture, entails one of four basic coping strategies: assimilation (abandoning the old culture for the new), separation (maintaining one's heritage and keeping apart from the host culture), integration (retaining the old *and* adapting to the new), or marginalization (identifying with neither culture).

Through acculturation, each person establishes an *ethnic identity,* which is revealed in language, customs, and the individual's sense of belonging. But immigrants may also experience *acculturative stress,* resulting in anxiety, depression, and other mental health problems. The strategy of integration seems to correlate with less acculturative stress than the other three strategies.

Discrimination   The most vicious obstacle for ethnic minorities is *discrimination,* behavior directed against people because of their affiliation with a social group. It stems from stereotypes and feelings of prejudice.

Racism in America   *Racism,* a deep-seated form of prejudice based on the color of a person's skin, is not as overt in the United States as it used to be, but studies still find evidence of it in the workplace and in other settings. It influences both our perceptions and our interpretations of events.

Vocabulary Exercises

Part I

Directions: The list that follows contains the content-specific words used in the "Human Diversity" chapter. For some of these terms, you may think you already know the meaning, but remember that content-specific terms have specialized meanings. Make a concept card for each of the terms listed as outlined in Chapters 6 and 10, writing down the meaning of the word as it is used in this selection. As much as possible, try to put these definitions in your own words. These cards will be very helpful as you study for the exam on this selection.

social norms 359	separation 367
individualism 361	integration 367
collectivism 361	marginalization 367
complexity 361	ethnic identity 367
affluence 361	acculturative stress 368
heterogeneity 361	discrimination 369
independent 362	stereotypes 369
interdependent 362	prejudice 369
multiculturalism 366	racism 369
acculturation 367	reaction time 371
assimilation 367	

Part II

After you have completed your cards, use an organizational activity to group similar words together. For example, you could start by grouping all terms that are associated with cross-cultural perspectives together and all terms that have to do with multicultural perspectives together. Once you group the terms together, they will be much easier to learn.

Part III

After you have rehearsed the terms using the methods outlined in Chapters 6 and 10, do the following application exercise. If you do well on this activity, you should have learned many of the key concepts presented in "Human Diversity."

1. Someone might have a problem determining their *ethnic identity* if _____ _____.

2. I have observed *racism* when _____ _____.

3. If you violate *social norms* _____ _____.

4. When people see themselves as *independent,* they see themselves as _____.

5. When people see themselves as *interdependent,* they see themselves as _____.

6. The factors of *complexity, affluence,* and *homogeneity* determine if _____ _____.

7. When immigrants experience *acculturative stress* they _____ _____.

8. Three characteristics of *individualism* would be _____ _____.

9. Three characteristics of *collectivism* are _____ _____.

10. *Acculturation* occurs when _____

    _____.

11. The difference between *assimilation* and *integration* is _____

    _____

    _____.

12. The difference between *separation* and *marginalization* is _____

    _____.

13. Someone who is *prejudiced* might _____

    _____.

14. An example of a *stereotype* is _____

    _____.

15. When we say that *discrimination* has cognitive roots, we mean _____

    _____.

16. *Reaction time* refers to _____

    _____.

17. *Multiculturalism* is _____

    _____.

Application Activities

1. Be sure to engage in **Before** reading activities. First activate your knowledge about this selection by asking yourself what you know about human diversity. Then preview the selection and think about the two major headings: Cross-Cultural Perspectives and Multicultural Perspectives. Think about which terms go with each of the major headings.

2. Read and annotate the selection to help you stay **Connected** during reading. Be sure that you annotate key examples, not simply definitions. Also, be sure that you can explain the major concepts.

3. Construct and answer a minimum of 20 questions using the question/answer format that was outlined in Chapter 9. Self-test or study with a partner as a way of preparing for your test on this selection.

4. Use the concept cards that you created in the vocabulary exercises earlier to learn the key terms. If you haven't put examples on your cards, you might want to do that. Also, be sure to group terms together as a way to help you to learn to remember them.

5. Create a mnemonic device to help you to remember the four ways that acculturation can occur.

6. Make a study plan using the PLAE model.

7. Construct a talk-through card on which you list, in an organized fashion, the key concepts that you want to learn for the test.

Selection from a Biological Science Text

Genetics: The Science of Inheritance

For thousands of years people have selectively bred plants and animals. The idea of selective breeding is simple. One chooses a few organisms with desirable characteristics to be the parents of a new generation. When that generation is grown, the hardiest plants, the fastest racehorses, or the most obedient dogs are selected for the next round of breeding. It's simple in practice and simple in theory. Offspring tend to resemble their parents, so by patiently choosing parents with the proper characteristics, the breeder can accentuate those characteristics.

Is inheritance really that simple? For hundreds of years, people regarded inheritance as a *blending*—the characteristics of both parents were thought to blend to produce offspring. In most cases, the blending explanation seems to make sense. Most of us look a little like our mothers and a little like our fathers. A cross between a large dog and a small dog usually produces medium-sized dogs. Everything seems to make sense. Well, almost everything.

Inheritance: A Problem

Many people enjoy the common parakeet (*Melopsittacus undulatus*), an attractive bird native to Australia. Because you have a preference for birds with green wings, you select a matched pair of such birds and place them in a breeding cage at home. The birds get along, conditions are right, and before long they are the parents of five little parakeets. But something is wrong. The new generation is not a simple blend of the two green parents. In fact, some of the birds don't look anything like their parents at all.

Two of the new birds are green, one is blue, one is bright yellow, and one is completely white! Where did the new colors come from? And why don't all of the new birds look like their parents? More to the point, what should you do now? You might rush back to the pet store, complaining that the green parakeets do not "breed true." Or you could wonder whether another parakeet had slipped into the cage while you were away.

However, there is something else that you could do. Puzzled by the results of this cross, you might *experiment*. You could conduct more breedings and try to learn the rules by which parakeets inherit their color. You would need more cages, some extra time, and a lot of birdseed. But if you had done this 150 years ago with patience and care and insight, you just might have founded **genetics,** the science of inheritance. As luck would have it, someone else got there first.

Source: From *Biology: Discovering Life,* Second Edition, by Levine and Miller. Copyright © 1994 by D. C. Heath and Company. Used by permission of Houghton Mifflin Company.

Mendel and the Birth of Genetics

Charles Darwin realized that the blending theory of inheritance presented special problems for evolution. Specifically, he wondered whether favorable characteristics might be "blended away" before natural selection had a chance to increase their frequency in a population. Ironically, and unknown to Darwin, this problem was being solved just as *On the Origin of Species* was being published. This ground-breaking work, performed by an Austrian priest named Gregor Mendel, set the stage for a radically new way of thinking about heredity. But because Mendel's work did not receive widespread recognition until the early twentieth century, Darwin probably was unaware of it.

Gregor Mendel was born in 1822 in the town of Heinzendorf. A bright student, he entered the Augustinian monastery at Brno, which, like his birthplace, is now part of the Czech Republic. Mendel became a priest when he was 25. He had a special interest in natural science and took an exam to qualify for a science teaching certificate. Although he failed that exam, his superiors at the monastery thought enough of the young priest to send him to the University of Vienna for two years to study science and mathematics. When he returned to the monastery he was given two assignments: to teach physics and biology in a local high school and to supervise the monastery's gardens. We do not know how well he fulfilled the first assignment. But we know a great deal about his work in the garden.

Mendel took a special interest in the garden's peas. The other gardeners helped Mendel isolate several strains of plants with distinct characteristics: One always produced tall plants, another only short plants; one always produced purple flowers, another only white flowers. Mendel selected plants that bred true—that is, each variety produced seeds that grew into plants identical to the parent.

Mendel knew that peas are self-fertilizing. Because of the structure of the pea flower, the pollen that produces the male reproductive cells usually fertilizes female reproductive cells in the very same flower. To cross one plant with another, Mendel opened the pea flowers and removed the male pollen-producing anthers. He then dusted the female portions of the flower with pollen from another plant (Figure 10.3). In this way, he could carry out controlled pollination from one plant to another—a process known as *crossing*. Because each plant produced many seeds, Mendel could obtain reliable statistics on the offspring of each cross.

Mendel's First Experiments

In one experiment, Mendel fertilized the flowers of a strain that produced purple flowers with pollen from plants that produced white flowers. He also reversed the process by using pollen from purple-flowered plants to fertilize the white-flowered strain. One of his first observations was that it did not matter which plant contributed the pollen and which received it.

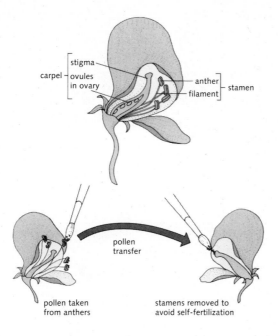

carpel — stigma
ovules in ovary
anther
filament
stamen

pollen transfer

pollen taken from anthers

stamens removed to avoid self-fertilization

Figure 10.3 Although pea plants are normally self-fertilizing, Mendel carried out crossbreeding by brushing the pollen of one plant on the stigma of another.

The original plants involved in the cross are known as the **parental,** or P, generation. The seeds produced from this first cross Mendel called the **first filial,** or F_1, generation (*filial* comes from the Latin root for "son"). All of these seeds produced plants that bore purple flowers, so it seemed that the white-flower trait had disappeared. Mendel took the seeds from this cross, planted them, and allowed the resulting plants to self-fertilize. This $F_1 \times F_1$ cross produced the **second filial,** or F_2, generation. Mendel collected the seeds and planted 929 of them. To Mendel's surprise, the white flowers reappeared in some of these plants; 224 plants bore white flowers and 705 had purple flowers, a ratio of purple to white flowers of 3.1 to 1 (Figure 10.4).

A Theory of Particulate Inheritance

At first, these results must have seemed every bit as confusing as the blue and yellow parakeets mentioned in the opening pages of this chapter. But Mendel was able to explain them. He proposed a system of **particulate inheritance** in which heritable characteristics were controlled by individual "units." Mendel assumed (correctly, as it turned out) that each plant had two such units for each trait. Mendel called each unit a "Merkmal," the German word for "character." Today we call these units **genes,** and we know that the cells of the pea plant

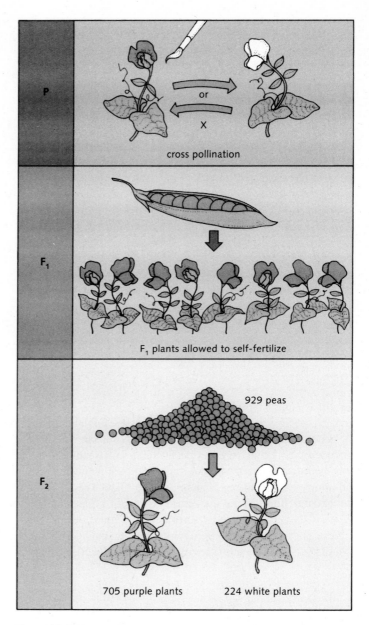

Figure 10.4 Mendel's first experiments involved the crossing of parental (P generation) plants with white flowers and plants with purple flowers. The seeds produced by this cross (F₁ generation) grew into plants which produced purple flowers. When these plants were allowed to cross naturally, both white and purple flowers were produced in the F₂ generation.

carry two genes for most characteristics. If we represent the units with symbols, we might use *P* for Mendel's purple-flower character and *p* for the white-flower character.

P and *p* are known as **alleles,** which are alternative forms of a single gene, in this case the gene for flower color. In Mendel's first cross, the original, true-breeding purple-flowered parent would have been *PP,* and the original white-flowered parent would have been *pp.*

One of Mendel's most extraordinary insights was the realization that when organisms produce their reproductive cells, or **gametes,** each gamete carries only one allele for each gene. Therefore, the two alleles for each gene are **segregated** from each other when gametes are formed. In Mendel's experiment, for example, the F_1 generation received an allele for purple flowers from one parent and an allele for white flowers from the other parent. In this way, each parent makes an individual genetic contribution to its offspring.

The Punnett Square We can visualize the alleles involved in each cross by making a diagram known as a **Punnett square** (Fig. 10.5). On one side of the square we write down all the *gametes* that can be formed by one parent, and on the other side all the gametes that can be formed by the other parent. Then we use the blocks within the square to represent all the possible *combinations* of alleles that may occur in the offspring. When two plants in the F_1 generation are crossed, as shown, the result is that, on average, ¼ of the F_2 offspring have *PP* alleles for flower color, ¼ are *pp,* and ½ are *Pp.* The Punnett square is a powerful predictive tool. In this case, the square predicts that ¾ of the offspring from the $F_1 \times F_1$ cross will be either *PP* or *Pp.*

Dominance

One of the remarkable results of the crosses shown in Figures 10.4 and 10.5 is the fact that plants with contrasting alleles (*P* and *p*) produce purple flowers. The purple allele of the flower-color gene is **dominant** over the white allele. (That is why purple is represented by the capital letter *P.*) Mendel carried out crosses with six other characteristics, including plant size, seed color, and seed shape (Figure 10.6). In each case, one characteristic was "dominant" in the F_1 generation. The characteristic that seemed to disappear in the F_1 generation and to reappear in the F_2 generation he called a **recessive** trait. Mendel explained this phenomenon by proposing that whenever a dominant allele and a recessive allele were found in the same organism, the dominant allele alone controlled the appearance of the plant. Only when two recessive alleles occurred together did the recessive characteristic, or "character," emerge.

Now we can look at the results of the crosses in Figure 10.4 and appreciate the value of Mendel's data. Because both *PP* and *Pp* plants produce purple flowers, the Punnett square predicts a 3:1 ratio of purple to white flowers in the F_2 generation. Mendel's 3.1:1 ratio was a close match.

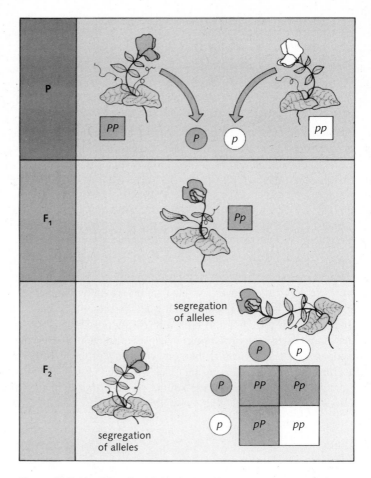

Figure 10.5 Mendel explained the results of his experiment by assuming that each pea plant carried two "characters," or alleles, for flower color. In the F_1 generation, each plant inherits an allele for purple (P) and an allele for white (p). When the F_2 generation is formed, these alleles are segregated as gametes are produced. By analyzing the possible combinations of these gametes using a Punnett square, we can predict the allele combinations that the F_2 generation will inherit.

The same 3:1 ratio held for crosses involving the six other traits. For example, when Mendel crossed plants producing round seeds (alleles: *RR*) with those producing wrinkled seeds (alleles: *rr*), all the F_1 plants produced round seeds, showing that the *R* allele is dominant over the *r* allele. When the *Rr* F_1 plants were crossed with themselves, the F_2 generation included 5474 plants that bore round seeds and 1850 plants with wrinkled seeds, a ratio of 2.96:1. Obviously, Mendel's patience in counting seeds knew no bounds!

Trait	Dominant	Recessive
seed color	yellow	green
seed shape	round	wrinkled
flower color	purple	white
pod color	green	yellow
pod shape	inflated	constricted
flower position	axial	terminal
stem height	tall	short

Figure 10.6 The seven contrasting traits investigated by Mendel

Mendel's First Principles

It is hard for us today to realize just how revolutionary Mendel's theory of particulate inheritance was. With only the evidence of his garden pea crosses, he established the first two of three important principles on which the science of genetics is founded:

- The characteristics of an organism are determined by individual units of heredity called genes. Each adult organism has two alleles for each gene, one from each parent. These alleles are *segregated* (separated) from each other when reproductive cells are formed. This is known as the **principle of segregation.**

- In an organism with contrasting alleles for the same gene, one allele may be *dominant* over another (as round is dominant over wrinkled for seed shape in the garden pea). This is known as the **principle of dominance.**

Although Darwin could not take Mendel's principles into account, it is clear they solved the problems presented by the previously held blending theory of inheritance. When a new and beneficial allele appears in a population, the characteristic that allele produces won't disappear by repeated "blending." Instead, the allele is preserved from one generation to the next. Even a recessive characteristic can appear in a later generation through the changing gene combinations generated by sexual reproduction.

Genotype and Phenotype

A second major contribution of Mendel's experiments was the idea that every organism has a *genetic* makeup called its **genotype.** The actual characteristics an organism exhibits are called its **phenotype.** The genotype is inherited, whereas the phenotype is produced under the influences of the environment and the genotype. Plants may have the same phenotype and different genotypes. For example, about ⅔ of the 705 purple-flowered plants of the F_2 generation in Figure 10.4 have the *Pp* genotype, and ⅓ have the *PP* genotype.

Plants with two identical alleles for the same gene (*PP* or *pp*) are said to be **homozygous** for that gene. Plants with two contrasting alleles for a gene (*Pp*) are **heterozygous** for that gene. How can we determine which of the 705 purple-flowered plants are homozygous for the purple allele of the flower-color gene and which are heterozygous? Mendel developed a simple technique known as a **test cross** that enabled him to determine the genotype of any plant. The plant in question is crossed with another plant that is homozygous for the recessive version of the gene in question. The phenotypes of the offspring from the test cross then reveal the genotypes of the parents.

Figure 10.7 shows how this works in the case of plants with purple flowers. One test cross produces only plants with purple flowers, proving that the plant used for that cross had the *PP* genotype. The second test cross produces 9 plants with purple flowers and 11 with white flowers (roughly a 1:1 ratio), proving that the original genotype was *Pp*. The test cross is a powerful technique that can be used to determine genotype in animals as well as plants. Can you imagine a test cross that might be useful in the case of our parakeets? We'll come back to this problem later.

Independent Assortment

Knowing that Mendel had seven different traits available for study, each of which had two contrasting alleles, what do you think his next experiment might have been? If you guessed that he might have tried to follow the alleles for two different genes at the same time, then you guessed right.

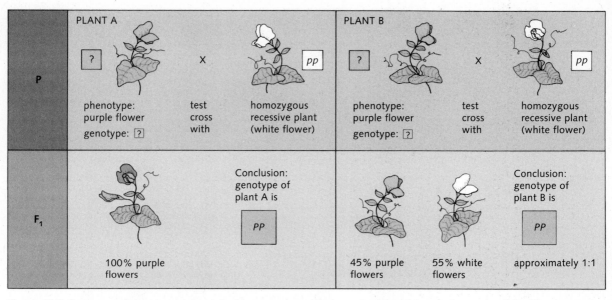

Figure 10.7 Genotypes of plants can be determined in a test cross with plants containing homozygous recessive alleles. The characteristics of the offspring of a test cross reveal the genotypes of the parents.

Mendel wondered whether the alleles for different genes would segregate in the same pattern as alleles of a single gene did. He carried out a series of experiments like those shown in Figure 10.8. A parental line of plants with yellow-colored, round seeds was crossed with a line that produced green, wrinkled seeds. The seeds in the F_1 generation were all round and yellow, showing that those two alleles are dominant over the alleles for wrinkled and for green seeds.

If the alleles for the seed coat and seed color genes were able to assort independently during gamete formation, then plants grown from the F_1 generation seeds could produce four different kinds of gametes:

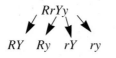

But these four types of gametes could be produced only if the alleles for the two genes were free to segregate and to assort independently of each other. **Independent assortment** means that the allele a gamete receives for the seed coat (R or r) has no effect on which allele it receives for the seed color gene (Y or y). The Punnett square for this cross shows that the 16 possible offspring of an F_1 cross display four different phenotypes and that these plants are present in a 9:3:3:1 ratio. Mendel's breeding experiments produced 556 seeds whose phenotypes matched these ratios almost exactly. These results show that the R and Y genes assort independently.

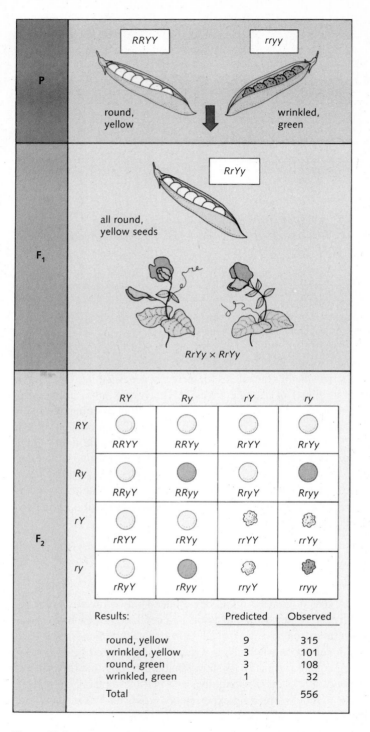

Figure 10.8 A two-factor cross carried out by Mendel
The dominant characteristics of the parents appear in the F$_1$ generation.
When the F$_1$ plants are crossed among themselves, independent assortment
of the alleles for both characteristics produces four distinct phenotypes in
the F$_2$ generation with a 9:3:3:1 ration.

- Each of the seven genes that Mendel investigated obeys the third of Mendel's three important principles, the concept of independent assortment.

  It's interesting to note that Mendel confirmed the genotypes of each of his F$_2$ plants by conducting test crosses. A round, yellow pea from the F$_2$ generation might have any of four possible genotypes: *RRYY, RRYy, RrYY,* or *RrYy.* By growing a plant from each pea and then crossing that plant with a double-recessive (genotype: *rryy*) plant, Mendel determined the genotypes of the offspring (Figure 10.9).

Problem Solving with Mendelian Genetics

We are now in a position to think about parakeets. Feather color in these birds is controlled by two genes. The "B" gene controls black and blue color in the feathers. The dominant allele (*B*) produces blue and black pigmentation, whereas the recessive allele (*b*) does not produce any color. The "C" gene controls yellow color. The dominant allele (*C*) produces yellow feathers, whereas the recessive allele (*c*) produces no color.

  Can we use this information to explain the surprising results of our attempts to breed the two green parakeets we introduced at the beginning of this chapter? As shown in Figure 10.10, we could begin by assuming that our mating pair had the genotype ***BbCc.*** Such birds would contain a combination of blue and yellow pigments that would appear green. By using a Punnett square to analyze the gametes that such birds would produce, we can predict the outcome of a cross between our two parents. As you can see, we would expect about ¹⁄₁₆

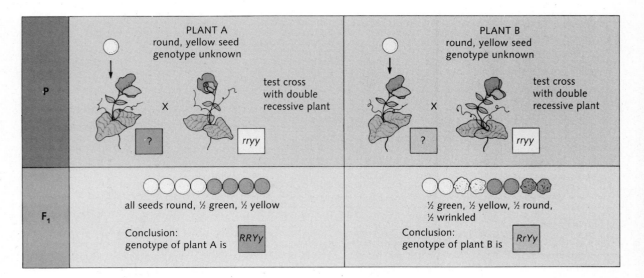

Figure 10.9 Test crosses with plants homozygous recessive for two characteristics reveal the genotypes of the parent plants.

of the offspring to be white (genotype: **bbcc**), so the single white bird in our cross can be explained as a result of Mendelian genetics. We would also expect green, yellow, and blue birds in the offspring, and that prediction came true. Just for fun, you might plan a way to test our explanation of the parental genotypes with a test cross. One of the five parakeets that resulted from crossing the two parental green parakeets is the ideal bird to use for such a test. Can you identify it?

Genetics and the Cell

Mendel's three important principles, the principles of *dominance, segregation,* and *independent assortment,* place certain restrictions on the way genes and their alleles behave. For example, the fact that individuals inherit one allele for each gene from each parent implies that the cells of an adult organism contain two sets of alleles. Similarly, because segregation requires that the two alleles

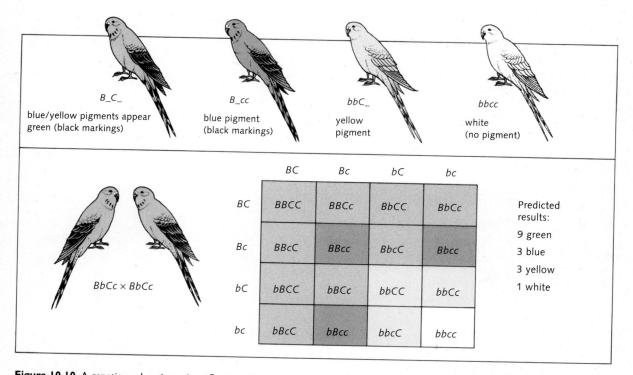

Figure 10.10 A genetic explanation using a Punnett square of how two green-colored parakeets could produce offspring with four different color patterns. Each of the green parents is heterozygous for the two genes that control feather color. The Punnett square shows how birds with four different colorations may be produced by the cross.

for each gene be separated when gametes are formed, there must be a mechanism that accomplishes this separation. What an opportunity! To Mendel, the "gene" was a purely hypothetical factor that controlled heredity. But if genes were real, then we should be able to find physical structures within the cell that behave in accordance with Mendel's three principles.

Unfortunately, no one was ready to seize upon Mendel's work when it was published. It was, after all, just one of hundreds of papers on plant breeding experiments. Mendel's work was generally ignored for more than 30 years after it was published. By the turn of the century, though, other scientists began to take an interest. Mendel's work with peas was confirmed by two other scientists (Erich von Tschermak and Carl Correns), and similar results were found for more than a dozen different plants and for many animals as well. There was no doubt that an important principle had been discovered.

However, as striking as Mendel's work was, it was just one of a number of competing theories of inheritance, and it was destined to remain so as long as his units of inheritance were strictly hypothetical. The ability of theory to explain events is powerful evidence, but biology is never content with theoretical units. It was necessary to actually *find* the units Mendel had postulated. Finding those units was the first step toward making genetics a modern experimental science.

Meiosis: Forming a New Organism

During mitosis each chromosome of the cell appears as a pair of *chromatids*. As mitosis proceeds, the chromatids of each chromosome separate and two daughter cells are formed, each containing the same number of chromosomes as the original cell. To many biologists, the fact that chromosomes were duplicated just prior to mitosis and then carefully separated into the two daughter cells suggested that chromosomes were important structures. Some even suggested that they contained hereditary information.

The critical evidence, however, came from studies of what happened to chromosomes during the formation of reproductive cells, or *gametes*. In sexually reproducing organisms, a new individual is formed by the fusion of male and female gametes to form a single cell known as a **zygote.** The zygote then goes through a process of development and growth to become an independent organism.

Gametes contain only *half* the number of chromosomes found in the cells of the body. The sperm and egg cells of cats, for example, contain 19 chromosomes each. A fertilized zygote, about to develop into a kitten, contains a total of 38 (19 + 19) chromosomes. How does this work? Does the sperm contribute chromosomes *A, B, C,* and *D* while the egg contains *E, F, G,* and *H?* No. In fact, with one exception that we will encounter shortly, the two sets of chromosomes are very similar to each other. A better way to describe it would be to say that the egg contributes *A, B, C,* and *D* while the sperm donates *A', B', C',* and *D'.* For each chromosome contributed by one parent, a corresponding chromosome, or **homologous chromosome,** is contributed by the other parent. Each cell of an adult cat contains two sets of homologous chromosomes; one set is derived from the male parent and one from the female.

Biologists use the term **diploid** to describe a cell that contains two sets of homologous chromosomes. The *somatic* (body) cells of peas, cats, and humans are diploid. Their gametes, however, which contain only a single set of chromosomes, are **haploid** (Figure 10.11). We use the symbol *n* to represent a single set of chromosomes. Diploid cells, therefore, are *2n,* and haploid cells are *n.* (The term *haploid* does not mean that such cells have *half* a set of chromosomes. In fact, haploid cells have a full, single set. A better term for *n* might be *monoploid,* but *haploid* and *diploid* are now firmly entrenched in the scientific vocabulary.)

Reduction Division

Haploid gamete cells are formed by a special process that is often called *reduction division* because it reduces the chromosome number of cells that are

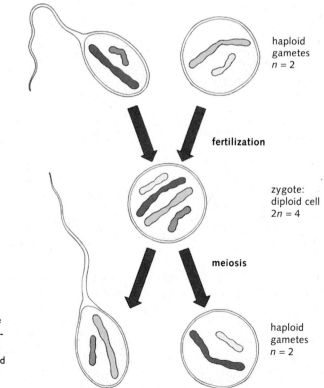

haploid
gametes
n = 2

fertilization

zygote:
diploid cell
2n = 4

meiosis

haploid
gametes
n = 2

Figure 10.11 A diploid organism contains two complete sets of chromosomes, one from each parent. The contributions of each parent are illustrated in the formation of a fertilized zygote in this figure. When the diploid organism reproduces, it too will produce haploid gametes.

developing into sperm or eggs. Reduction division is commonly known as **meiosis,** and it occurs in all organisms that reproduce sexually. Meiosis generally takes place over the course of two rounds of cell division. It may superficially resemble mitosis, but there are big differences in how chromosomes behave in the two processes.

Meiosis is a two-stage process that produces four haploid cells from a single diploid cell. Homologous chromosomes are segregated from each other in the **first meiotic division.** The **second meiotic division** is not preceded by an *S* phase of the cell cycle, so DNA and chromosome duplication do not occur between the two divisions. This results in a reduction of chromosome number. Figure 10.12 illustrates the features of meiosis.

One of the first organisms in which meiosis was intensively studied was the ordinary fruit fly, *Drosophilia melanogaster* (*Drosophila* means "dew lover" and *melanogaster* means "dark belly"). Diploid *Drosophila* cells have eight chromosomes ($2n = 8$). Four of these chromosomes were originally provided by the fly's mother and four by its father. We shall use a female *Drosophila* to trace the details of meiosis (Figure 10.13).

The first meiotic division Prior to meiosis, each of the eight chromosomes is duplicated, so we now have eight chromatids. This duplication is no different from that which occurs before an ordinary cell division. However as the process continues, something interesting happens: the chromosomes *pair* to form bundles known as **tetrads** (the same structure is sometimes referred to as a *bivalent*) composed of four chromatids each. The pairing of homologous chromosomes, also known as **synapsis,** produces an appearance at metaphase that is very different from a mitotic metaphase. As shown in Figure 10.13 a *Drosophila* cell at metaphase I of meiosis has four tetrads.

Which chromosomes pair to form the tetrads? The *homologous* chromosomes derived from both parents. Chromosome *A* from the mother pairs with *A'* from the father, *B* with *B'*, and so on. At metaphase, all four tetrads are aligned across the center of the cell.

Anaphase begins as the tetrads draw apart and the homologous chromosomes are separated. Each daughter cell receives one chromosome from each pair. The alignment of each chromosome pair is random with respect to the others. In other words, the fact that the maternal copy of one chromosome pair moves to a particular cell does not affect the way the maternal copy of a different chromosome pair goes. The chromosomes exhibit *independent assortment!*

The first meiotic division (meiosis I) produces a random shuffling of the genetic deck: each cell has an equal chance of getting either the maternal or the paternal copy of any individual chromosome. As you know, Mendel's principle of *segregation* states that the maternal and paternal alleles of a gene are segregated during gamete formation. The pairing of homologous chromosomes during the first meiotic division makes that possible. As we observe anaphase of the first meiotic division, we are watching the microscopic events that underlie the segregation of alleles. Mendel never worked with a microscope, but micro-

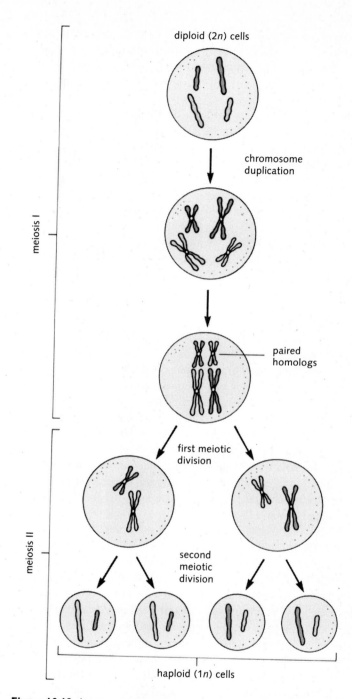

Figure 10.12 An overview of meiosis in an organism with a diploid chromosome number of 4

INTERPHASE
Cell prior to
chromosome
duplication.

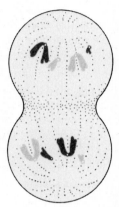

maternal
chromosomes

paternal
chromosomes

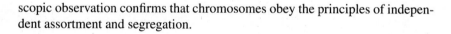

PROPHASE I
Each chromosome
is composed of two
identical chromatids
attached at a
centromere

METAPHASE I
Tetrads of
homologous
chromosomes
align on the
metaphase plate

ANAPHASE I
Tetrads separate
and homologous
chromosomes are
separated.

TELOPHASE I
Cytokinesis occurs,
forming two
daughter cells.

Figure 10.13 Meiosis in *Drosophila*

scopic observation confirms that chromosomes obey the principles of independent assortment and segregation.

The second meiotic division Each of the two cells produced by the first meiotic division now enters a second meiotic division (meiosis II). The cell cycle that occurs between the first and second meiotic divisions is exceptional, because the chromosomes are *not* duplicated during it. Each of our two *Drosophila* cells received four chromosomes (with two chromatids each) from the first division, and these two cells now enter another round of division with exactly the same number of chromatids. In metaphase, four chromosomes are visible in each cell, and anaphase separates these four chromosomes into two new cells, each of which now receives four single chromatids. The four cells formed by the second meiotic division are true haploid cells, each containing

Genes That Cheat at Meiosis

As we have seen, during meiosis the homologous chromosomes of an organism pair to form tetrads. The alignment of chromosomes during metaphase is random, which gives each cell roughly a 50–50 chance of getting either the maternal or the paternal homologue when the first meiotic division occurs. Each gamete, therefore, has a gene composition decided by the chance mechanisms of meiosis. All of this is true—*assuming* that the gene-sorting mechanism plays fair. But what would happen if a gene "cheated" during meiosis?

A gene could cheat by making certain that it was *always* included in reproductive cells, ensuring that it, and not its homologue, was passed along to succeeding generations. How could it do this? James F. Crow and his associates at the University of Wisconsin have discovered exactly such a system in *Drosophila*.

The genetic system is known as **segregation distorter,** or **sd** for short. The genes that produce *sd* carry on a kind of genetic warfare during meiosis— one that ensures that chromosomes carrying the *sd* genes, and *only* the *sd* genes, are passed on to the next generation. When *sd* is present in the heterozygous form, it actually sabotages the homologous chromosome, the one that doesn't have *sd*. The sabotage occurs at the beginning of meiosis, and the results are evident a few days later when sperm cells begin to develop. *Drosophila* sperm are normally produced in packets of 64 cells each. [An] electron micrograph shows *sd* "cheating" in action: 32 of the cells have begun normal development, but 32 are failing to develop. Which 32? The ones that lack *sd*. Somehow, the *sd* gene has destroyed every cell containing its competition in the next generation. It actually breaks the rules of meiosis: It cheats!

How does the rest of the genetic system respond to this outlandish behavior? The surprising answer may be that the entire system is organized to keep the cheaters under control. Several biologists have suggested that genetic recombination (crossing over) is actually a defense mechanism against *sd* and other cheating genes. By reshuffling the combinations of genes on chromosomes, recombination occasionally separates cheating genes from the closely linked marker genes that usually protect the chromosome containing *sd* from its own deadly effects. This prevents *sd* and other cheaters from spreading throughout the population and gives "honest" genes a chance to compete fairly.

four distinct chromosomes ($n = 4$). Although the cellular details of meiosis differ in male and female animals (a sperm cell is produced quite differently from an egg cell), the nuclear details of meiosis are similar in both sexes and in plants as well as animals.

Vocabulary Exercises

Part 1: Using the Context

Directions: Some of the terms that you have to understand in this chapter are familiar words with specialized meanings. Find the following words, read the context in which they occur, and write a definition that shows the specialized meaning.

blending   (377) _____

crossing   (378)_____

parental   (379) _____

segregated   (381) _____

dominant   (381) _____

recessive   (381) _____

independent   assortment   (385) _____

Directions: Other terms are not familiar, but the author provides context clues to help you with the meaning. Find the following words, read the context in which they occur, and write a definition based on the context clues the author provides.

first filial   (379) _____

particulate   inheritance   (379)_____

alleles   (381)_____

gametes   (381) _____

phenotype   (384) _____

zygote   (390) _____

diploid   (390) _____

haploid   (390) _____

tetrads   (391) _____

synapsis   (391) _____

Part II: Using the Structure

Many of the new terms in this selection were invented by scientists—using prefixes, roots, and suffixes—to describe the genetic process. Analyzing the structure of these words helps in understanding and remembering them. In this exercise, use the chart that follows and:

1) Identify one key term from the reading selection that uses this prefix or root.

2) Read the context in which the word is introduced, then write a definition of the term.

3) Look up the prefix or root in the dictionary, and decide which definition was used to help form the word. Write down this definition.

Parts of the chart are done for you.

Prefix/Root	Key Word	Definition from Context	Prefix/Root Definition
chromo-	chromosome		color (because it determines coloring in next generations)
soma-		body (defined through a context clue, p. 390)	
homo-			
hetero-			
diplo-	diploid		
haplo-			
geno-			from *genos*—"race"
pheno-			from *phaino*—"to show"

The five stages of meiosis all end in "-phase". The prefixes relate to what happens to the chromosomes. Answer the following questions (Figure 10.13 on page 393 may help you).

1. inter = with each other; together

    In interphase, the chromosomes are _____
    _____.

2. pro = forward in time or direction

    Why is the second phase called "prophase"? _____
    _____.

3. meta = changed in place or form

    Why is the third phase called "metaphase"? _____
    _____.

4. ana = up; upward

    Why is the fourth phase called "anaphase"? _____
    _____.

5. telo = final, complete

    Why is the fifth phase called "telophase"? _____
    _____.

Devise a mnemonic device to help you remember the proper order of these five stages. (Mnemonic, or memory, devices are described in Chapter 11.)

Application Exercises

1. Preview the selection on genetics. Try to determine from the headings and subheadings how the chapter will tell you about the solution to the first heading—"Inheritance: A Problem." There are several figures interspersed in the text. Look these over before reading. What information do they convey? How can you use them to improve your understanding of the chapter?

2. Formulate What, Where, Why, and How questions for each heading in the selection. For example, a subheading under "Mendel and the Birth of Genetics" is "A Theory of Particulate Inheritance." You might ask:

   What is the theory of particulate inheritance?
   Why did Mendel develop this theory?
   How is it different from other theories of inheritance?

3. Annotate the selection as you read. Make your annotations flow like a topical outline, so that you can see how the concepts tie together.

4. Make two maps from this selection to see how the concepts fit together. One map should include concepts from "A Theory of Particulate Inheritance" through "Genetics and the Cell." The second map would include concepts from "Meiosis: Forming a New Organism" to the end of the selection.

5. Make concept cards for the key terms (most of which are highlighted in the text).

6. Using PLAE, devise a study plan that you could use to study for a test on this selection.

Information Systems
and Marketing Research

Objectives

- To be able to describe the nature and importance of information systems in marketing decision making
- To explore how tools such as databases, electronic bulletin boards, online information services, and the Internet facilitate marketing research
- To learn the five basic steps for conducting a marketing research project
- To become familiar with the fundamental methods of gathering data for marketing research

Betcha can't eat just one. At least that's what Frito-Lay hopes is true of its new Baked Lay's Potato Crisps. The new chips have 1.5 grams of fat per serving, compared with 10 grams for a serving of the firm's all-American favorite Lay's Potato Chips. In 1994, 1,439 low-fat products hit the marketplace, up from 626 in 1989, and there are certainly plenty of low-fat corn chips, pretzels, and other snacks on the market, but until January 1996, there was no low-fat potato chip.

In the early 1990s, marketing researchers at Frito-Lay found that most consumers disliked low-fat chips because, frankly, they tasted like cardboard. Karen Snepp, Frito-Lay's vice president of customer and consumer insights says, "Yet even as our focus groups told us they hated low-fat chips, they also kept saying that they would do anything for a low-fat potato chip with a decent taste."

Thus was born Project Liberty, a play on Frito's goal of liberating potato chips from the deep-fat fryer. After three years of extensive research into different types of potatoes, oils, slicing and baking methods, and taste tests, a potato chip worthy of the name Lay's emerged from test ovens. But the research wasn't over. The new Baked Lay's Potato Crisps next went to test marketing in Midland, Texas, and Cedar Rapids, Iowa, because the incomes, ethnic mix, and average number of kids per family in those communities represent what Frito-Lay considers mainstream America. When executives saw sales in the two cities jump by 15 to 20 percent, they knew they had a hit.

Frito-Lay projected national sales of Baked Lay's to reach $200 million by the end of 1996, which would set a record for a first-year product in the snack-food business. The company is also researching other low-fat temptations, including low-fat granola bars, and it has already introduced a Ruffles Reduced Fat Chip. In fact, expecting that low-fat snacks will comprise a third of its business by 1998 (up from 10 to 15 percent today), Frito-Lay is investing $225 million to build factories and add fifteen manufacturing lines to existing plants to handle the new products. Their optimism is reflected in the new dare: "Betcha can't eat just one . . . bag."[1] The marketing research conducted by Frito-Lay demonstrates that in order to implement the marketing concept, marketers require information about the characteristics, needs, and wants of their target markets. Such information, well used, fosters relationship marketing by helping marketers fashion their efforts toward meeting and even anticipating the needs of their customers. In fact, "Know thy customer" may well be "the first commandment of successful marketing in the 1990s."[2] Marketing research and information systems that can provide practical and objective information to help firms develop and implement marketing strategies are therefore essential to effective marketing.

In this selection, we focus on how marketers gather information needed to make marketing decisions. We first define marketing research and marketing information systems and distinguish between them. Next we look at how technology, particularly the evolution of the Internet, is facilitating marketing research and marketing information systems. Then we examine the individual steps of the marketing research process, including various methods of collecting data.

Marketing Research and Marketing Information Systems

Marketing research is the systematic design, collection, interpretation, and reporting of information to help marketers solve specific marketing problems or take advantage of marketing opportunities. As the word *research* implies, it is a process for gathering information not currently available to decision makers. Marketing research is conducted on a special-project basis, with the research methods adapted to the problems being studied and to changes in the environment. The American Marketing Association defines marketing research as follows:

> Marketing research is the function which links the consumer, customer, and public to the marketer through information—information used to identify and define marketing opportunities and problems; generate, refine, and evaluate marketing actions; monitor marketing performance; and improve understanding of marketing as a process. Marketing research specifies the information required to address these issues; designs the method for collecting information; manages and implements the data collection process; analyzes the results; and communicates the findings and their implications.[3]

A **marketing information system (MIS)** is a framework for the day-to-day management and structuring of information gathered regularly from sources both inside and outside an organization. As such, an MIS provides a continuous flow of information about prices, advertising expenditures, sales, competition, and distribution expenses. Kraft General Foods, Inc., for example, operates one of the largest marketing information systems in the food industry, maintaining, using, and sharing information with others in ways that increase the value of what the company offers consumers. Kraft seeks to develop a dialogue with consumers by providing toll-free numbers. It receives about half a million calls a year from consumers who ask questions and express concerns about products.[4]

The main focus of the marketing information system is on data storage and retrieval, as well as on computer capabilities and management's information requirements. Regular reports of sales by product or market categories, data on inventory levels, and records of salespersons' activities are all examples of information that is useful in making decisions. In the MIS, the means of *gathering* data receives less attention than do the procedures for expediting the *flow* of information.

An effective marketing information system starts by determining the objective of the information—that is, by identifying decision needs that require certain information. Then the firm can specify an information system for continuous monitoring to provide regular, pertinent information on both the external and internal environment. FedEx, for example, has developed interactive marketing systems to provide instantaneous communication between the company and its customers. Through the telephone and computer information services, customers can track their packages and receive immediate feedback concerning delivery. Online services provide information to FedEx about customer usage, and FedEx can find out directly what consumers think about company services. The evolving development of telecommunications and computer technology is allowing marketing information systems to cultivate one-to-one relationships with customers.

The main difference between marketing research and marketing information systems is that marketing research is an information-gathering process for specific situations, whereas an MIS is a system that provides continuous data input for an organization. Nonrecurring decisions that deal with the dynamics of the marketing environment often call for a data search structured according to a specific problem and decision. Marketing research is usually characterized by in-depth analyses of a major problem or issue. Often the information needed is available only from sources outside an organization's formal channels of information. For instance, an organization may want to know something about its competitors or may need to gain an unbiased understanding of its own customers. Such information objectives may require an independent investigation by a marketing research firm.

The real value of marketing research and marketing information systems is measured by improvements in a marketer's ability to make decisions. Marketers should treat information in the same manner as other resources utilized by the firm, and they must weigh the costs of obtaining information against the benefits derived. Information is judged worthwhile if it results in marketing activities that better satisfy the needs of the firm's target markets, that lead to increased sales and profits, or that help the firm achieve some other goal.

Capitalizing on New Technologies for Marketing Research

Technology is making information for marketing decisions ever more accessible. The ability of firms to track customer buying behavior and better discern what customers want is changing the nature of marketing. For example, the airlines have discovered that many of their most desirable customers have computers and can communicate with the carriers online. Frequent flyers—people who fly ten or more times a year—account for just 8 percent of all airline customers but book 44 percent of all trips. With interactive communication through devices such as fax, telephone, and computer online access, Northwest Airlines invited customers to take part in survey research. From this research, Northwest learned that its affluent frequent flyers travel at Christmas, like beach vacations, and most important, want flights to be on time.[5]

The integration of various types of telecommunications and computing technologies is allowing marketers to access a growing array of valuable information sources related to industry forecasts, business trends, and customer buying behavior. Electronic communication tools can be effectively utilized to gain accurate information with minimal customer interaction. Most marketing researchers have e-mail, voice mail, teleconferencing, video conferences, and faxes at their disposal.[6] Because some of these communications tools—particularly databases, electronic bulletin boards, online services, and the Internet—are radically changing the way marketers conduct research, we'll take a closer look at them now.

Databases

A **database** is a collection of information arranged for easy access and retrieval. Databases allow marketers to tap into an abundance of information useful in making marketing decisions: internal sales reports, newspaper articles, company news releases, government economic reports, bibliographies, and more, often accessed through a computer system.

Many marketing researchers use commercial databases developed by information research firms to obtain useful information for marketing decisions. These commercial online databases are accessible via a telephone hookup for a fee. They can also be obtained in printed form or on computer compact discs (CD-ROMs). In most commercial databases, the user typically does a computer search on a key word, topic, or company, and the database service generates abstracts, articles, or reports that can then be printed out. Accessing multiple reports or a complete article may cost extra.

CompuServe, for example, has a special neighborhood report option that provides summaries of demographics for any ZIP code in the United States. In addition, a menu allows the researcher to select demographic, sales potential, or neighborhood reports, but these carry a surcharge. For example, two sales potential reports for the automotive parts market cost approximately $100. Medical/health insurance data for a ZIP code in Ohio costs $25. CENDATA, another database available through CompuServe, allows marketers to access 1990 U.S. Census Bureau data in both tabular and report form. It also lists names, addresses, and phone numbers for local, regional, and national census offices. CENDATA supplies statewide population and housing characteristics for variables such as income, education, and language spoken, as well as others.[7]

Information provided by a single firm on household demographics, purchases, television viewing behavior, and responses to promotions such as coupons and free samples is called **single-source data.**[8] For example, Behavior Scan, offered by Information Resources, Inc., screens about 60,000 households in twenty-six U.S. markets. This single-source information service monitors consumer household televisions and records the programs and commercials watched. When consumers from these households shop in stores equipped with scanning registers, they present Hotline cards (similar to credit cards) to cashiers. This enables each customer's identification to be electronically coded so that the firm can track each product they purchase.

Many marketers also develop their own databases. An example is NSS, a firm that markets software to banks. Facing a challenge of qualifying thousands of new sales leads, NSS developed a database program to track customers and prospects according to specified criteria. NSS's database provides detailed data that ranks prospects in terms of those who can make a buying decision within a year and those who can make one within two years or more. Such information gives NSS greater control in managing its sales force.[9]

Finally, firms can also sell their databases to other firms. *Reader's Digest,* for example, markets a database that includes 100 million households. One of the best databases available to assess potential markets for consumer products, it lets *Reader's Digest* management know the likes and dislikes of many of its readers. It also permits a linkup to test products, assess retailers, examine media alternatives, and evaluate the effectiveness of promotions. In fact, the *Reader's Digest* database is possibly as valuable to the company as the magazine itself.[10]

Electronic Bulletin Boards

Computer networks (systems that link multiple computers through phone lines or satellite) allow marketers to interface with data sources and customers with almost instantaneous information about products and sales performance. Through such networks, firms can exchange electronic mail (e-mail) internally, among their employees, and externally, with suppliers and customers. *Electronic bulletin boards (BBSs)* are another method of communicating through computers. BBSs enable users to post a message for any participant to read and discuss, just as if they had tacked a handwritten notice to an actual bulletin board in an office hallway for all to see. Many business computer networks include a BBS for employees to pose questions, discuss work (and sometimes nonwork) issues, and air grievances. For example, Texas Instruments Incorporated maintains a bulletin board on which employees can anonymously express concerns and complaints. Their messages can be routed to executives who coordinate and integrate the firm's efforts to develop positive customer relations. One frequent reader of the Texas Instruments bulletin board is Jerry Junkins, the company's chief executive.[11]

More firms are also installing BBSs that can be accessed by customers to develop information for the marketing information system, which assists in developing marketing strategies. Some companies even use bulletin boards to answer customer questions. Pharmaceutical companies have long relied on them to monitor patients' reactions to new drugs. Most large computer software and hardware companies operate bulletin boards to help their customers solve problems. Compaq Computer Corporation's bulletin board receives about 500 messages a week, which Compaq then compiles and evaluates as a way to monitor product quality, company productivity, and service needs.[12] Currently, 13.5 million people use electronic bulletin boards, and the number rises 70 percent a year.[13] Some firms' bulletin boards allow customers to exchange ideas for creative problem solving related to products. Customers learn from one another, and the firm gains new insights into the marketing of its products.

Online Information Services

A technological step above electronic bulletin boards is online information services, such as CompuServe, Delphi, Prodigy, GEIS, DIALOG, and NEXIS. These services typically offer their subscribers access to e-mail, discussion groups (depending on the service, these may be called bulletin boards, forums, or newsgroups), files for downloading, chat rooms (where users can converse with each other in "real time" like a telephone call, except the conversation is typed instead of spoken), news, databases and related research materials, and other services, such as airline reservations. Accessing online services is as simple as calling in, hitting the return key, and typing in a password (once the user has arranged payment). Marketers can subscribe to "mailing lists" that periodically deliver electronic newsletters to their computer screens, and they can participate in on-screen discussions with thousands of network users. This enhanced communication with a firm's customers, suppliers, and employees provides a high-speed link that boosts the capabilities of a firm's marketing information system.

The Internet

Previously, we defined the Internet as a network of business, university, government, and other networks. In essence, the Internet is a collection of computers hooked together with telephone lines that enables users to communicate and share information around the globe. Whereas the online information services (such as CompuServe and America Online) limit their services to subscribers, the Internet permits the exchange of e-mail, global discussion through public forums called newsgroups on everything ranging from *Star Trek* (the original cybertopic) to presidential elections and just about everything in between with participants around the world, as well as files for downloading, chat rooms, and more.

Although the Internet has been in existence for several decades, it was not until 1992, with the development of the World Wide Web (WWW, or "the

Web"), that the Internet became significant as a medium for obtaining marketing information. The WWW organizes much of the vast array of information available on the Internet into a series of interconnected "pages" that may include text, graphics, sound, and video. The introduction in 1994 of Mosaic, a popular software program for navigating the Web, has turned WWW into a true multimedia communication tool. Today, some 37 million North Americans have access to the Internet, and that number will have grown considerably by the time you read this.[14] Experts believe there will be more than 100 million users around the world on the Internet by the year 2000. Based on the developments of the last few years, the pace of Internet growth will only accelerate.

The Internet has evolved as the most powerful communication medium, linking customers and companies around the world via computer networks. An entire industry is emerging to make marketing information easily accessible to both marketing firms and customers.[15] Nordstrom's, a large department store, has set up an interactive shopping effort through e-mail that links frequent customers with a personal shopper. Nordstrom's keeps personal information such as shirt and shoe size on file for easy reordering. In addition, Nordstrom's marketing information system tracks the changing desires and buying habits of its most valued customers.[16]

While most WWW home pages are open to anyone with Internet access, big companies like U.S. West are creating internal Web pages, called "intranets," that allow employees to access internal data such as customer profiles and product inventory—information once hidden in databases only technicians could unlock. Such sensitive corporate information can be protected from outside users of the World Wide Web by special security software called "firewalls." Turner Broadcasting System uses intranets to test products during the development phase. Marketing department employees can view animated clips and listen to sound bites from popular cartoon talk shows. Employees can then express their opinions by e-mailing the animators directly. The animators use this feedback to revise the cartoon before moving onto the firm's public cartoon site on America Online. Most marketers who get in the habit of accessing their companies' internal Web pages often move on to seek information externally via the rest of the WWW as well.[17]

Perhaps the ultimate in relationship marketing is giving customers access to nonproprietary internal information. FedEx, for example, allows customers to track their packages by logging onto FedEx's Web home page, which is linked to the company's internal database. Netscape, which markets a World Wide Web navigator, or browser, offers rewards as incentives for users of its software to report product deficiencies.[18]

The U.S. Census Bureau also employs WWW pages to disseminate information that may be useful to marketing researchers. Data can be accessed by Data Map and 1990 Census Lookup. Data Map enables users to view profiles of states and counties in both tabular and graphic form. Researchers can select which state to display simply by clicking on a map. The Census Lookup option allows marketing researchers to create their own customized information. With this online tool, researchers can select tables by clicking boxes to select the state and then within the state, the county, place, and urbanized area or metropolitan statistical area to be examined.

The Marketing Research Process

Marketing research, as described earlier, is the systematic design, collection, interpretation, and reporting of information to help marketers solve specific marketing problems or take advantage of marketing opportunities. The difference between good and bad research is the quality of the input, which includes effective control over the entire marketing research process. To maintain the control needed for obtaining accurate information, marketers approach marketing research in logical steps. Figure 5.1 presents the five steps of the marketing process: (1) defining and locating problems, (2) designing the research project, (3) collecting data, (4) interpreting research findings, and (5) reporting research findings. These five steps should be viewed as an overall approach to conducting research rather than as a rigid set of rules to be followed in each project. In planning research projects, marketers must consider each of the steps carefully and determine how they can best be adjusted to resolve the particular problems at hand.

Defining and Locating Problems

Problem definition, the first step toward finding a solution or launching a research study, focuses on uncovering the nature and boundaries of a negative, or positive, situation or question. The first sign of a problem is usually a departure from some normal function, such as conflicts between or failures in attaining objectives. If a corporation's objective is a 12 percent sales increase and the result is 6 percent, this discrepancy should be analyzed. It is a symptom that something inside or outside the organization has blocked the attainment of the desired goal or that the goal is unrealistic. Declining sales, increasing expenses, or decreasing profits also signal problems. Conversely, when an organization experiences a dramatic rise in sales, or some other positive event, it may conduct marketing research to discover the reasons and maximize the opportunities stemming from them.

To pin down the specific causes of the problem through research, marketers must define the problem and its scope in a way that requires probing beneath

Figure 5.1 The Five Steps of the Marketing Research Process

the superficial symptoms. The interaction between the marketing manager and the marketing researcher should yield a clear definition of the problem. Researchers and decision makers should remain in the problem definition stage until they have determined precisely what they want from the research and how they will use it.

The research objective specifies what information is needed to solve the problem. Deciding how to refine a broad, indefinite problem into a precise, researchable statement is a prerequisite for the next step in planning the research: designing the research project.

Designing the Research Project

Once the problem has been defined, an overall plan for obtaining the information needed to address it must be formulated. In designing research, marketing researchers must ensure that research techniques are both reliable and valid. A research technique has **reliability** if it produces almost identical results in successive repeated trials. But a reliable technique is not necessarily valid. To have **validity,** the method must measure what it is supposed to measure, not something else. A study to measure the effectiveness of advertising would be valid if advertising could be isolated from other factors or variables that affect sales. It would be reliable if the study or experiment on the effectiveness of advertising could be repeated in successive trials.

The objective statement of a marketing research project should include hypotheses drawn from both previous research and expected research findings. A **hypothesis** is an informed guess or assumption about a certain problem or set of circumstances. It is based on all the insight and knowledge available about the problem or circumstances from previous research studies and other sources. As information is gathered, a researcher can test the hypothesis. For example, a consumer food products manufacturer such as H. J. Heinz might propose the hypothesis that children today have more influence on their families' buying decisions for ketchup and other grocery products. A marketing researcher would then gather data, perhaps through surveys of children and their parents, and draw conclusions as to whether the hypothesis is correct. Sometimes several hypotheses are developed during the actual study; the hypotheses that are accepted or rejected become the study's chief conclusions.

The kind of hypothesis being tested determines which approach will be used for gathering general data: exploratory, descriptive, or causal. When marketers need more information about a problem or want to make a tentative hypothesis more specific, they may conduct **exploratory studies.** For instance, they may review the information in the firm's database or examine publicly available data. Questioning knowledgeable people inside and outside the organization may also yield new insights into the problem. An advantage of the exploratory approach is that it permits marketers to conduct ministudies with a very restricted database.

If marketers need to understand the characteristics of certain phenomena to solve a particular problem, **descriptive studies** can aid them. Such studies may range from general surveys of consumers' education, occupation, or age to specifics on how many consumers purchased Ford Explorers last month or how many adults between the ages of 18 and 30 eat a microwaved meal at least three times a week. Some descriptive studies require statistical analysis and predictive tools. For example, a researcher trying to find out how many people will vote for a certain political candidate may have to survey registered voters to predict the results. Descriptive studies generally demand much prior knowledge and assume that the problem is clearly defined. The marketers' major task is to choose adequate methods for collecting and measuring data.

Hypotheses about causal relationships call for a more complex approach than a descriptive study. In **causal studies,** it is assumed that a particular variable X causes a variable Y. Marketers must plan the research so that the data collected prove or disprove that X causes Y. To do so, marketers must try to hold constant all variables except X and Y. For example, to find out whether new carpeting, miniblinds, and ceiling fans increase the number of rentals in an apartment complex, marketers need to keep all variables constant except the new furnishings.

Collecting Data

Marketing researchers have two types of data at their disposal. **Primary data** are observed and recorded or collected directly from respondents. This type of data must be gathered by observing phenomena or surveying respondents. **Secondary data** are compiled inside or outside the organization for some purpose other than the current investigation. Secondary data include general reports supplied to an enterprise by various data services and internal and online databases. Such reports might concern market share, retail inventory levels, and consumers' buying behavior. Commonly, secondary data are already available in private or public reports or have been collected and stored by the organization itself. In the next section we discuss the methods of gathering both secondary and primary data. In the early 1990s, about 70 percent of marketing information was based on primary research. By the year 2000, however, it is estimated that the scales will be reversed: 60 percent or more of all marketing research data is expected to come from secondary sources.[19]

Secondary Data Collection

Marketers often begin the marketing research process by gathering secondary data. They may use available reports and other information from both internal and external sources to study a marketing problem.

Internal sources of secondary data can contribute tremendously to research. An organization's marketing database may contain information about past marketing activities, such as sales records and research reports, which can be used to test hypotheses and pinpoint problems. Accounting records are also an excellent source of data but, strangely enough, are often overlooked. The large volume of data an accounting department collects does not automatically flow to the marketing area. As a result, detailed information about costs, sales, customer accounts, or profits by product category may not be part of the MIS. This condition develops particularly in organizations that do not store marketing information on a systematic basis.

Secondary data can also be gleaned from periodicals, government publications, unpublished sources, and online databases. Periodicals such as *Business Week, The Wall Street Journal, Sales & Marketing Management, American Demographics, Marketing Research,* and *Industrial Marketing* print general information that helps in defining problems and developing hypotheses. *Survey of Buying Power,* an annual supplement to *Sales & Marketing Management,* contains sales data for major industries on a county-by-county basis. Many marketers consult federal government publications such as the *Statistical Abstract of the United States,* the *Census of Business,* the *Census of Agriculture,* and the *Census of Population,* available from the Superintendent of Documents in Washington, D.C.; some of these government resources are available through online information services or the Internet World Wide Web. Table 5.1 summarizes the major external sources of secondary data, excluding syndicated services.

Primary Data Collection

The collection of primary data is a more lengthy and complex process than the collection of secondary data. The acquisition of primary data utilizes survey methods, sampling procedures, and observation methods.

Survey Methods **Survey methods** include interviews by mail, telephone, e-mail, and personal interviews. Survey results are used to describe and analyze consumer behavior. Selection of a survey method depends on the nature of the problem, the data needed to test the hypothesis, and the resources, such as funding and personnel, available to the researcher. Table 5.2 summarizes and compares the advantages of the various survey methods.

Gathering information through surveys is becoming more difficult because response rates are declining. Many researchers believe that nonresponse is the single biggest problem facing the research industry.[20] Some causes of nonresponse are fear of invasion of privacy, overly long questionnaires, dull topics, time pressures, and general skepticism regarding the personal benefits of participating in a research study.[21] Moreover, fear of crime makes respondents unwilling to trust personal interviewers. The use of sales techniques disguised as market surveys has also contributed to decreased respondent cooperation.

Table 5.1 Guide to External Sources of Secondary Data

Databases	Many databases are a collection of information arranged for easy access and retrieval through online information services or the Internet. Users select key words (such as the name of a subject) to search a database and generate references.
Government	The federal government, through its various departments and agencies, collects, analyzes, and publishes statistics on practically everything. Many government agencies have data available online.
Periodical Indexes	The library's reference section contains indexes on virtually every discipline. *The Business Periodicals Index,* for example, indexes each article in all major business publications.
Trade Journals	Virtually every industry or type of business is covered by a trade journal. These journals give a feel for the industry—its size, degree of competition, range of companies involved, and problems. To find trade journals in the field of interest, check *Ulrich's,* a reference book that lists U.S. and foreign periodicals by subject.
Trade Associations	Almost every industry, product category, and profession has organized its own association. These often conduct research, publish journals, provide training sessions, and hold conventions. To find out which associations serve which industries, check the *Encyclopedia of Associations.*
WWW Pages	Many companies have established "home pages" on the Internet's World Wide Web for disseminating information on their products and activities.

In *mail surveys,* questionnaires are sent to respondents, who are encouraged to complete and return them. Mail surveys are used most often when the individuals chosen for questioning are spread over a wide area and funds for the survey are limited. A mail survey is the least expensive survey method as long as the response rate is high enough to produce reliable results. The main disadvantages of this method are the possibility of a low response rate or misleading results if respondents are significantly different from the population being sampled.

Premiums or incentives encouraging respondents to return questionnaires have been effective in developing panels of respondents who are regularly interviewed by mail. Mail panels, which are selected to represent a market or market segment, are especially useful for evaluating new products, providing general information about consumers, and providing records of consumers' purchases. Consumer mail panels and consumer purchase diaries are much more widely used than custom mail surveys, but both have shortcomings. Research indicates that the people who take the time to fill out a consumer diary have higher income and are more educated than the general population. If researchers include less educated consumers in the panel, they must risk poorer response rates.[22]

Table 5.2 Comparison of the Three Basic Survey Methods

	Mail and E-Mail Surveys	Telephone Surveys	Personal Interview Surveys
Economy	Potentially the lowest cost per interview if there is an adequate return rate.	Avoids interviewers' travel expenses; less expensive than in-home interviews.	In-home interviewing is the most expensive interviewing method; shopping mall, focus-group interviewing lower costs.
Flexibility	Inflexible; questionnaire must be short, easy for respondents to complete.	Flexible because interviewers can ask probing questions, but observations are impossible.	Most flexible method; respondents can react to visual materials, demographic data are more accurate; in-depth probes are possible.
Interviewer Bias	Interviewer bias eliminated; questionnaires can be returned anonymously.	Some anonymity; may be hard to develop trust in respondents.	Refusals may be decreased by interviewers' rapport-building efforts.
Sampling and Respondents' Cooperation	Obtaining a complete mailing list is difficult; nonresponse is a major disadvantage; e-mail surveys require computer and online access.	Sample must be limited to respondents with telephones; telephone answering machines used to screen calls, busy signals, and refusals are problems.	Not-at-homes are more difficult to deal with; focus-group, shopping mall interviewing may overcome these problems.

In *telephone surveys,* respondents' answers to a questionnaire are recorded by interviewers on the phone. A telephone survey has some advantages over a mail survey. The rate of response is higher because it takes less effort to answer the telephone and talk than to fill out a questionnaire and return it. If there are enough interviewers, telephone surveys can be conducted very quickly. Thus they can be used by political candidates or organizations seeking an immediate reaction to an event. In addition, this survey technique permits interviewers to gain rapport with respondents and ask probing questions. According to a survey by the Council of American Survey Research Organizations (CASRO), telephone interviewing is the preferred survey method in more than 40 percent of the projects conducted by commercial survey research firms.[23]

However, only a small proportion of the population likes to participate in telephone surveys. By contrast, over three-fourths of us feel indifferent toward telephone surveys or don't like them at all.[24] This poor image can significantly limit participation and distort representation in a telephone survey. Moreover, telephone surveys are limited to oral communication; visual aids or observation cannot be included. Interpreters of results must make adjustments for subjects who are not at home or who do not have telephones. Many households are excluded from telephone directories by choice (unlisted numbers) or because the residents moved after the directory was published. Telephone answering machines are often used to screen calls and prevent access to potential respondents.

These findings have serious implications for the use of telephone samples in conducting surveys. Some adjustment must be made for groups of respondents that may be undersampled because of a smaller-than-average incidence of telephone listings. Nondirectory telephone samples can overcome such bias. Various methods are available, including random-digit dialing (adding random numbers to the telephone prefix) and plus-one telephone sampling (adding one to the last digit of a number in the directory). These methods make it feasible to dial any working number, whether or not it is listed in a directory.

Voice mail has much potential for asking simple questions and obtaining quick responses. Questions can be communicated by voice mail, and voice mail messages may be saved, passed along, or returned. Voice mail thus permits efficient survey participation without wasting respondents' time.[25]

Telephone surveys, like mail and personal interview surveys, are sometimes used to develop panels of respondents who can be interviewed repeatedly to measure changes in attitudes or behavior. Reliance on such panels is increasing.

E-mail surveys are evolving as an alternative to telephone surveys. Questionnaires can be transmitted to respondents who have provided their e-mail addresses and agree to be contacted individually. Moreover, because e-mail is semi-interactive, recipients can ask for clarification of specific questions or pose questions of their own.[26] The potential advantages of e-mail interviewing are quick response and lower cost than traditional mail and telephone surveys, but these advantages have not yet been realized because of limited access to respondents and unreliable response rates.[27]

Given the growing number of households owning PCs and connected to on-line information services or the Internet, marketing research is likely to rely heavily on e-mail surveys in the future. And, as negative attitudes toward telephone surveys render that technique less representative and more expensive, the integration of e-mail, fax, and voice mail functions into one PC-based system provides a promising opportunity for survey research. E-mail surveys have especially strong potential within organizations whose employees are networked and for associations that publish members' e-mail addresses. However, there are some ethical issues to consider when using e-mail for marketing research.

Marketing researchers have traditionally favored the *personal interview survey,* chiefly because of its flexibility. Various audiovisual aids—pictures, products, diagrams, or prerecorded advertising copy—can be incorporated into a personal interview. Rapport gained through direct interaction usually permits more in-depth interviewing, including probes, follow-up questions, or psychological tests. In addition, because personal interviews can be longer, they can yield more information. Finally, respondents can be selected more carefully, and reasons for nonresponse can be explored. In one study, it was found that respondents questioned by personal contact methods had the most favorable attitudes toward survey research in general. The respondent liked seeing the person who was asking the questions and having the personal contact that is part of the interview.[28]

One such research technique is the *in-home (door-to-door) interview.* The in-home interview offers a clear advantage when thoroughness of self-disclosure and the elimination of group influence are important. In an in-depth interview of forty-five to ninety minutes, respondents can be probed to reveal their real motivations, feelings, behaviors, and aspirations.

The object of a *focus-group interview* is to observe group interaction when members are exposed to an idea or concept. Often these interviews are conducted informally, without a structured questionnaire. Consumer attitudes, behavior, lifestyles, needs, and desires can be explored in a flexible and creative manner through focus-group interviews. Questions are open-ended and stimulate consumers to answer in their own words. Researchers can ask probing questions to clarify something they do not fully understand or something unexpected and interesting that may help explain consumer behavior. Cadillac used information obtained from focus groups to change its advertising to emphasize the luxury car's safety features. The new advertisements increased Cadillac sales by 36 percent in test markets.[29] JRP Marketing Services, Inc. and QCS (Quality Controlled Services) are two marketing research firms that arrange for and conduct focus-group interviews.

The nature of personal interviews has changed. In the past, most personal interviews, which were based on random sampling or prearranged appointments, were conducted in the respondent's home. Today most personal interviews are conducted in shopping malls. *Shopping mall intercept interviews* involve interviewing a percentage of persons passing by certain "intercept" points in a mall. Although there are many variations of this technique, the reaction toward mall intercept research is mixed, nearly equally split among positive, negative, and neutral. Almost half of major consumer goods and services companies use this technique and report shopping mall intercept interviewing as their major expenditure on survey research.[30]

Like any face-to-face interviewing method, mall intercept interviewing has many advantages. The interviewer is in a position to recognize and react to respondents' nonverbal indications of confusion. Respondents can be shown product prototypes, videotapes of commercials, and the like, and reactions can be sought. The mall environment lets the researcher deal with complex situations. For example, in taste tests, researchers know that all the respondents are reacting to the same product, which can be prepared and monitored from the mall test kitchen or some other facility. In addition, lower cost, greater control, and the ability to conduct tests requiring bulky equipment make shopping mall intercept interviews popular.

On-site computer interviewing, a variation of the mall intercept interview, consists of respondents completing a self-administered questionnaire displayed on a computer monitor. A computer software package can be used to conduct such interviews in shopping malls. After a brief lesson on how to operate the software, respondents can proceed through the survey at their own pace. Adaptive design questionnaires may be developed so that the respondent sees only those questionnaire items (usually a subset of an entire scale) that provide useful information about the respondent's attitude.[31]

Questionnaire Construction A carefully constructed questionnaire is essential to the success of any survey. Questions must be designed to elicit information that meets the study's data requirements. These questions must be clear, easy to understand, and directed toward a specific objective. Researchers need to define the objective before trying to develop a questionnaire because the objective determines the substance of the questions and the amount of detail. A common mistake in constructing questionnaires is to ask questions that interest the researchers but do not yield information useful in deciding whether to accept or reject a hypothesis. Finally, the most important rule in composing questions is to maintain impartiality.

The questions are usually of three kinds: open-ended, dichotomous, and multiple-choice.

Open-Ended Question

What is your general opinion of the American Express Optima Card?

_____

_____

_____

Dichotomous Question

Do you presently have an American Express Optima Card?
Yes ____   No ____

Multiple-Choice Question

What age group are you in?
Under 20 _____   40–49 _____
20–29 _____   50–59 _____
30–39 _____   60 and over _____

Researchers must be very careful about questions that a respondent might consider too personal or that might require him or her to admit activities that other people are likely to condemn. Questions of this type should be worded in such a way as to make them less offensive.

Sampling Because the time and the resources available for research are limited, it is almost impossible to investigate all the members of a population.

A **population,** or "universe," includes all the elements, units, or individuals that are of interest to researchers for a specific study. For example, for a Gallup poll designed to predict the results of a presidential election, all registered voters in the United States would comprise the population. By systematically choosing a limited number of units—a **sample**—to represent the characteristics of a total population, marketers can project the reactions of a total market or market segment. In the case of the Gallup presidential poll, for example, a representative national sample of several thousand registered voters would be selected and surveyed to project the probable voting outcome. (Of course, the projection would be based on the assumption that no major political events would occur between survey time and the election.) The objective of **sampling** in marketing research, therefore, is to select representative units from a total population. Sampling procedures are used in studying the likelihood of events based on assumptions about the future. Sampling techniques allow marketers to predict buying behavior fairly accurately on the basis of the responses from a representative portion of the population of interest.

When marketers employ **random sampling,** all the units in a population have an equal chance of appearing in the sample. Random sampling is basic probability sampling. The various events that can occur have an equal or known chance of taking place. For example, a specific card in a regulation deck should have a 1/52 probability of being drawn at any one time. Similarly, if each student at a university or college has a unique identification number and these numbers are mixed up in a large basket, each student's number would have a known probability of being selected. Sample units are ordinarily chosen by selecting from a table of random numbers statistically generated so that each digit, zero through nine, will have an equal probability of occurring in each position in the sequence. The sequentially numbered elements of a population are sampled randomly by selecting the units whose numbers appear in the table of random numbers.

In **stratified sampling,** the population of interest is divided into groups according to a common characteristic or attribute, and then a probability sample is conducted within each group. The stratified sample may reduce some of the error that could occur in a simple random sample. By ensuring that each major group or segment of the population receives its proportionate share of sample units, investigators avoid including too many or too few sample units from each group. Usually, samples are stratified when researchers believe that there may be variations among different types of respondents. For example, many political opinion surveys are stratified by sex, race, and age.

Area sampling involves two stages: (1) selecting a probability sample of geographic areas, such as blocks, census tracts, or census enumeration districts, and (2) selecting units or individuals within the selected geographic areas for the sample. This approach is a variation of stratified sampling, with the geographic areas serving as the segments, or primary units, used in sampling. To select the units of individuals within the geographic areas, researchers may choose every nth house or unit, or random selection procedures may be used to pick out a given number of units or individuals from a total listing within the selected geographic areas. Area sampling may be used when a complete list of the population is not available.

Quota sampling differs from other forms of sampling in that it is judgmental—that is, the final choice of respondents is left to the interviewers. A study of consumers who wear eyeglasses, for example, may be conducted by interviewing any person who wears eyeglasses. In quota sampling, there are some controls—usually limited to two or three variables, such as age, sex, and education—over the selection of respondents. The controls attempt to ensure that representative categories of respondents are interviewed.

Quota samples are unique because they are not probability samples; not everyone has an equal chance of being selected. Therefore, sampling error cannot be measured statistically. Quota samples are used most often in exploratory studies, when hypotheses are being developed. Often a small quota sample will not be projected to the total population, although the findings may provide valuable insights into a problem. Quota samples are useful when people with some common characteristic are found and questioned about the topic of interest. A probability sample used to study people allergic to cats would be highly inefficient.

Observation Methods In using **observation methods,** researchers record respondents' overt behavior, taking note of physical conditions and events. Direct contact with respondents is avoided; instead, their actions are examined and noted systematically. For example, researchers might use observation methods to answer the question "How long does the average McDonald's restaurant customer have to wait in line before being served?"

Observation may also be combined with interviews. For example, during personal interviews, the condition of a respondent's home or other possessions may be observed and recorded, and demographic information such as race, approximate age, and sex can be confirmed by direct observation.

Data gathered through observation can sometimes be biased if the respondent is aware of the observation process. An observer can be placed in a natural market environment, such as a grocery store, without biasing or influencing shoppers' actions. However, if the presence of a human observer is likely to bias the outcome or if human sensory abilities are inadequate, mechanical means may be used to record behavior. Mechanical observation devices include cameras, recorders, counting machines, and equipment to record physiological changes in individuals. For instance, a special camera can be used to record eye movements of respondents looking at an advertisement; the sequence of reading and the parts of the advertisement that receive greatest attention can be detected. Electronic scanners in supermarkets are mechanical observation devices that offer an exciting opportunity for marketing research. Scanner technology can provide accurate data on sales and consumers' purchase patterns, and marketing researchers may buy such data from the supermarket.

Observation is straightforward and avoids a central problem of survey methods: motivating respondents to state their true feelings or opinions. However, observation tends to be descriptive. When it is the only method of data collection, it may not provide insights into causal relationships. Another drawback is that analyses based on observation are subject to the biases of the observer or the limitations of the mechanical device.

Summary

When implementing the marketing concept, marketers need information about the characteristics, needs, and wants of their target markets. Marketing research and information systems that furnish practical, unbiased information help firms avoid the assumptions and misunderstandings that could lead to poor marketing performance. Indeed, information is often the key to a successful marketing strategy.

Marketing research is the systematic design, collection, interpretation, and reporting of information to help marketers solve specific marketing problems or take advantage of marketing opportunities. It is a process for gathering information that decision makers do not have. A marketing information system (MIS) is the framework for gathering and managing information from sources both inside and outside an organization. An MIS provides a continuous flow of information about prices, advertising expenditures, sales, competition, consumer behavior, and distribution expenses. The main difference between marketing research and marketing information systems is that marketing research is an information gathering process for specific situations, whereas an MIS provides continuous data input. The real value of marketing research information is measured by improvements in a marketer's ability to make decisions. Marketers treat information like other resources utilized by the firm and weigh the costs of obtaining information against the benefits derived.

Technology and databases allow marketers to retrieve a variety of information that is useful in making marketing decisions. Databases may include newspaper articles, company news releases, government reports, economic data, or bibliographies and are typically accessed electronically, through computer systems. Many firms install electronic bulletin boards to communicate with employees and customers and to develop information for the marketing information system. Online information services and the Internet also enable marketers to communicate with customers and obtain information.

The five steps of the marketing research process are (1) defining and locating problems, (2) designing the research project, (3) collecting data, (4) interpreting research findings, and (5) reporting the findings.

Defining and locating the problem, the first step toward finding a solution or launching a research study, focuses on uncovering the nature and boundaries of a negative, or positive, situation or question. After defining the problem, marketing researchers must formulate an overall plan for obtaining needed information—that is, design the project. They must also ensure that the research techniques are both reliable and valid. A technique is reliable if it produces almost identical results in successive repeated trials; it is valid if it measures what it is supposed to measure and not something else. The objective statement of a marketing project should include hypotheses. A hypothesis is an informed guess or assumption about a problem or set of circumstances. It is based on insight and knowledge gleaned from earlier research studies and other sources. The type of hypothesis being tested dictates which of three approaches will be used for gathering general data: exploratory, descriptive, or causal studies.

For the third step, collecting data, two types of data are available: primary and secondary. Primary data are observed and recorded or collected directly from respondents. Secondary data may be collected from an organization's database and other internal sources; from periodicals, government publications, and unpublished sources. Methods for collecting primary data include surveys, sampling, and observation. Survey methods range from mail surveys, telephone surveys, e-mail surveys, personal interview surveys, and shopping mall intercept interviews to on-site computer interviews, focus-group interviews, and in-home interviews. Questionnaires are instruments used to obtain information that meets the study's data requirements. A carefully constructed questionnaire is essential to the success of any survey. Sampling involves selecting representative units from a total population. Four sampling techniques are random sampling, stratified sampling, area sampling, and quota sampling. In using observation methods, researchers record respondents' overt behavior and take note of physical conditions and events but avoid direct contact with respondents. They may use mechanical observation devices, such as cameras, recorders, and other equipment.

Important Terms

Marketing research
Marketing information system
  (MIS)
Database
Single-source data
Problem definition
Reliability
Validity
Hypothesis
Exploratory studies
Descriptive studies
Causal studies

Primary data
Secondary data
Survey methods
Population
Sample
Sampling
Random sampling
Stratified sampling
Area sampling
Quota sampling
Observation methods
Statistical interpretation

Notes

1. Based on information from Laurie Freeman, "Brands in Demand," *Advertising Age,* Feb. 27, 1995, pp. 21–22; Skip Hollandsworth, "Hot Potatoes," *Texas Monthly,* Jan. 1996, pp. 104–108, 112–114; and "Taking the Low-Fat Route to Fat City," *Fortune,* Feb. 20, 1995, pp. 18–19.

2. Robert P. Bush, "Up Close and Personal," *Business Perspectives,* Spring 1995, p. 2.

3. Reprinted from *Dictionary of Marketing Terms,* Peter D. Bennett, ed., 1988, pp. 117–118, published by the American Marketing Association. Used by permission.

4. Jim Masterson, "Research Adds Value to Products," *Marketing News,* Aug. 16, 1993, p. A6.

5. Keith L. Alexander, "For Fliers, First Class No Longer Means Prestige," *USA Today,* Nov. 24, 1995, p. 1B.

6. R. Douglas Shute, "Connecting to the Source," *Inc.,* Nov. 14, 1995, p. 27.

7. Christel Beard and Betsy Wiesendanger, "The Marketers' Guide to Online Databases," *Sales & Marketing Management,* Jan. 1993, p. 49.

8. Laurence N. Goal, "High Technology Data Collection for Measurement and Testing," *Marketing Research,* Mar. 1992, pp. 29–38.

9. "Sales Automation: Tracking Sales Leads Online," *Inc.,* Jan. 1993, p. 31.

10. Richard S. Teilelbaum, *"Reader's Digest:* Are Times Tough?: Here's an Answer," *Fortune,* Dec. 2, 1991, pp. 101–102.

11. Kyle Pope, "To Whom It May Concern: Electronic Bulletin Boards Are Helping Firms Swap Information and More with Customers and Staff," *Wall Street Journal,* Nov. 15, 1993, p. R22.

12. Pope, "To Whom It May Concern."

13. Ibid.

14. Commercenet Consortium/Nielsen Media Research, in "Who's on the Web?" *Newsweek,* Nov. 13, 1995, p. 14.

15. James Kim, "Businesses Bet on the Future," *USA Today,* Nov. 13, 1995, p. 1E.

16. Ellen Neuborne, "Shoppers Can Get Holiday Jollies on the 'Net," *USA Today,* Nov. 13, 1995, p. 4E.

17. Alison L. Sprout, "The Internet Inside Your Company," *Fortune,* Nov. 27, 1995, pp. 161–168.

18. Sprout, "The Internet Inside Your Company."

19. Bush, "Up Close and Personal," p. 3.

20. Lynne G. Coleman, "Researchers Say Non-Response Is the Single Biggest Problem," *Marketing News,* Jan. 7, 1991, p. 32.

21. Ibid.

22. Martha Farnsworth Riche, "Who Says Yes?" *American Demographics,* Feb. 1987, p. 8.

23. Diane K. Bowers, "Telephone Legislation," *Marketing Research,* Mar. 1989, p. 47.

24. Peter S. Tuckel and Harry W. O'Neill, "Call Waiting," *Marketing Research,* Spring 1995, p. 8.

25. Shute, "Connecting to the Source."

26. Martin Oppermann, "E-mail Surveys—Potentials and Pitfalls," *Marketing Research,* Summer 1995, p. 32.

27. Oppermann, "E-mail Surveys," p. 29.

28. Cynthia Webster, "Consumers' Attitudes Toward Data Collection Methods," Robert L. King, ed., *Marketing: Toward the 21st Century,* Proceedings of the Southern Marketing Association, Atlanta, Ga. Nov., 1991, p. 221.

29. James B. Treece and Wendy Zellner, with Walecia Konrad, "Detroit Tries to Rev Up," *Business Week,* June 12, 1989, p. 82.

30. *Practices, Trends and Expectations for the Market Research Industry 1987,* Market Facts, Inc., Apr. 29, 1987.

31. Jagdip Singh, Roy D. Howell, and Gary K. Rhoads, "Adaptive Designs for Likert-Type Data: An Approach for Implementing Marketing Surveys," *Journal of Marketing Research,* Aug. 1990, pp. 304–321.

Discussion and Review Questions

1. What is a marketing information system and what should it provide? How is the value of a marketing information system measured?

2. Where are data for a marketing information system obtained? Give examples of internal and external data.

3. Define database. What is its purpose and what does it include?

4. How can marketers use online services and the Internet to obtain information for decision making?

5. What is the difference between defining a research problem and developing a hypothesis?

6. Describe the different types of studies in marketing research and indicate when they should be used.

7. What are the major limitations of using secondary data to solve marketing problems?

8. In what situation would it be best to use random sampling? quota sampling? stratified or area sampling?

9. Make some suggestions for ways to encourage respondents to cooperate in mail surveys.

10. If a survey of all homes with listed telephone numbers is conducted, what sampling design should be used?

Application Questions

1. After observing traffic patterns, Bashas' Markets repositioned the greeting card section in its stores, and card sales increased substantially. When considering marketing research, what information from consumers might be useful in increasing sales for the following types of companies?

   a) furniture stores

   b) gasoline outlets/service stations

   c) investment companies

   d) medical clinics

2. When a company wants to conduct research, a problem or potential problem must be recognized or possible opportunities must exist to market its goods or services. Choose a company in your city that you think might benefit from a research project. Develop a research question and outline a method to approach this inquiry. Explain why you think the research question is relevant to the organization and why the particular methodology is suited to the question and the company.

3. Input for marketing information systems can come from internal or external sources. Nielsen Marketing Research is the largest provider of single-

source marketing research in the world. Indicate two firms or companies in your city that might utilize internal sources and two that would benefit from external sources and explain why they would benefit. Suggest the type of information each should gather.

4. Texas Instruments utilizes an internal computer network bulletin board on which employees can make suggestions or air complaints. Choose a company with which you are familiar, and write a memo to the president that would persuade him or her to install a similar system in that company.

5. Suppose that you were opening a health insurance brokerage firm and wanted it to market your services to small businesses with under fifty employees. Determine which database for marketing information you would use in your marketing efforts, and tell why you would use it.

Vocabulary Exercises

For this chapter, it may be wise to spend a little time thinking about its organization as you preview and begin to examine the vocabulary. Answer the following questions about the vocabulary in the selection before you proceed:

1. Do there appear to be many general words that might give you trouble understanding the selection? Remember that general words are those that either cut across any content area or those that you might be just as likely to see in a novel or magazine article as in a textbook. _____

   _____

   _____

2. Do there appear to be many content-specific words that might give you problems understanding the selection? Remember that content-specific words are those that you would be most likely to encounter in a specific content area, in this case, marketing or computer science. _____

   _____

   _____

If you can tell from your previewing that you have a pretty good grasp of the general vocabulary, you might want to examine the content-specific terms in a little different way for this selection. Remember that it is important to be flexible in your approaches to vocabulary, just as you are flexible in the strategies you select. One way to approach the vocabulary for this and similar selections might be to see how the terms are related. Examining the vocabulary in this manner would also take care of a large portion of the previewing, so, in effect, you would be killing two birds with one stone. In order to see how the terms were related, you could use one of two approaches—a brief modified outline, as we have started for you below, or a skeletal map (see Chapter 10 for a review of both of these strategies). Using either technique, you will organize your new terms under the headings and subheadings in the selection so that you can see how the ideas are connected.

We have filled in sections of an outline for you below and have provided some cues as to how many terms might go with each appropriate heading. Each term has an asterisk (*). Try to complete the outline by putting a new term in each of the blanks that is preceded by an asterisk. If it is too difficult for you to do this in outline form, try to create a skeletal map. The map will give you a better visual representation of how the ideas fit together.

Marketing research and marketing information systems
    *marketing research
        *

Capitalizing on new technologies for marketing research
    *databases
        *single-source data
        *
        *
        *

The marketing research process
Defining and locating problems
Designing the research project
    *reliability
*
*
        *exploration studies
        *
        *

Collecting data
    *primary data
        *survey methods
            *mail surveys
            *
            *
            *
            *
            *
            *
            *on-site computer interviews
        *questionnaire construction
*
        *random
        *
        *
        *
        *observation methods
    *secondary data

Application Exercises

1. We have already dealt with most of the previewing, the BEFORE, portion of the BCA system. What else might you do to preview? In selections such as this one, and in similar texts such as those used in economics and business courses, examining text organization is a crucial part of previewing. And as we have seen, it can also help with beginning to see how the new terms are related.

2. Read and annotate the selection, paying close attention to the organization. Would you have to modify your regular annotating procedures for this selection? Why or why not? What kinds of information would you want to be sure to target during annotation?

3. Construct a map that depicts the marketing research process by using an example. Pretend that you want to market a new product called LACE SE-CURE, which are athletic shoe laces guaranteed not to come untied. No double knotting needed with these laces! Be sure that you include enough information so that it is clear to anyone looking at your map how you went about doing marketing research for this product.

4. Construct a chart that compares and contrasts the different types of sampling that you might use in doing marketing research.

5. Make concept cards for the terms that are problematic for you.

6. Use the outline you completed as a talk-through card for part of the earlier vocabulary exercise. Be sure to be precise and include enough detail as you talk through the important concepts.

7. Predict and write out the answer to one essay question using the PORPE procedure outlined in Chapter 12.

8. Use PLAE, as outlined in Chapter 11, to construct a study plan for this selection. What do you think would be the best strategies to use if you were to have an objective test (multiple-choice, true/false items)? What would the best strategies be if you were to have a short answer/essay exam?

Index

Reviewing, 4, 219–242
    after reading, 35
    after studying, 154
    annotations used for, 183
    chapter, 232
    daily, 78–79
    for discussion classes, 74
    frequency of, 116
    goals for, 221, 230–231
    group, 247
    imagery and, 227–228
    for lab classes, 74
    learning principles, 219, 220–221
    lecture notes, 36, 67, 75, 79
    mnemonic devices for, 224–227
    notes from previous lectures, 36
    organizing and reducing information while, 33, 34
    PLAE model for, 229–242
    planning systematically and consistently, 246–247
    question/answer technique for, 204
    rehearsal and, 34
    retention and, 12
    for small lecture, 73
    strategies, 219, 221–239
    talk-throughs and, 222–224
    for weekly quizzes, 245–246
Robinson, Kim Stanley, 111–113
Robinson, T. L., 138–141
Rogers, Adam, 56–58
Role models, motivation and, 45
Roots of words, 100

Savage, Brian, 5
Saying information out loud, 33, 35, 126, 153
Schedule/scheduling, 63–68
    class, 64
    essay test preparation, 254–255
    overloading, 48
    rest and relaxation, 48, 246
    term, 2, 64–66
    test preparation, 231–232, 246
    underloading, 48
    weekly, 2, 26, 66–68
Sciences
    labs, 74
    multiple-choice tests, 248
    textbooks, 118, 119, 120, 121
    word structure and, 84
Seat, for lecture, 36, 75

Selectivity
    outlining and, 213
    in reading, 158, 179
Self
    psyching up, 31
    responsibility for, 46
Self-awareness
    assessing strengths and weaknesses, 4–14
    breaking bad habits and, 7
    improvement and, 1
    reading journals for, 14–16
Self-awareness journal, 14–16
Self-discipline, 26, 60
Self-evaluation, 1
Self-image, 43
Self-monitoring, see Monitoring
Self-questioning, 32
Self-recitation, 197
Self-regulated learner, 4
Self-testing, 36
    rehearsal strategy, 197
    summary notes for, 247
    vocabulary, 110
Seligmann, J., 138–141
Sentence, example, dictionary definition and, 97
Sharing journal entries, 18–19
Short-answer questions, 121
Short-term memory, 179–180, 195
Signals, key word, 130
Similarities, charting, 207–210
Similes, 121
Skeletal annotations, 186
Skeletal map, 17, 18
Skimming chapter, 160
Smart students, unmotivated, 2
Smith, Vern E., 149
Social sciences
    tests, 121, 248
    textbooks, 118, 119, 120, 121
Speech
    part of, 96
    word as more than one part of, 97
Speed reading, 132
Spellings, lecture notes, 76
Spencer, Herbert, 82
Split-page method for lecture notes, 72–80
Standardized assessment, 5–6
Standardized tests, 46, 56–58
"State," key word used in essays and papers, 259

Staying connected during lecture, 2, 36
    listening and, 75–78
    note taking and, 78
Staying connected during note taking, 32–33
Staying connected during reading, 2, 153, 178–193
    annotation and, 34–35, 178, 180–193
    learning principles, 178–180
    reflecting on reading and, 35
Staying connected while studying, 32–33
Stem, in objective test question, 248
Strengths
    assessing, 4–14
    awareness of, 1
Structure, of words, 84, 100–106
Students
    e-mail with other, 27
    older, 46
Study group, 247
    location for, 29
    maintaining positive attitude and, 47
    motivation and, 48
    summarizing information, 28
Study guide, 216–217
Studying
    active approach to, 156
    adjusting to task, 116
    after reading, 35, 153–154, 194–218
    amount of time spent, 67, 230, 245
    assessment, 9–13
    background knowledge and interest and, 115, 116, 117, 120–121
    before, 25, 26–32
    daily, 44
    demands, 1–2, 10–13
    distributed practice and, 230
    distributing time, 221, 231
    efficiency in, 115
    flexibility in, 115
    goals, 34, 153
    location for, 26–27
    making decisions while, 32–33
    monitoring effectiveness of strategies, 115
    organization and, 32
    previewing and, 31
    principles guiding, 1
    question/answer technique for, 204
    range of strategies, 115, 116
    rate of, 132–133
    scheduling time for, 26, 65, 67
    staying active while, 32